Tom Pe...

Reminiscences of Early Queensland

Constance Campbell Petrie, the granddaughter of
Brisbane's pioneer settlers Andrew and Mary Petrie, was
born in 1872. She was Tom's daughter, and was probably
in her early thirties when she began recording her father's
stories. Constance herself remains something of an
enigma. *Tom Petrie's Reminiscences of Early Queensland*
is her only known major publication. She died in July
1926 aged fifty-four.

Mark Cryle was born in 1956 and graduated with honours
in History from the University of Queensland. He is a
qualified librarian and works at the University of
Queensland's Central Library.

Tom Petrie's Reminiscences of Early Queensland

Constance Campbell Petrie

With an Introduction by Mark Cryle

University of Queensland Press

First published 1904 by Watson, Ferguson & Co.
Second edition 1932
Third edition 1983
This edition published 1992 by University of Queensland Press
Box 42, St Lucia, Queensland 4067 Australia

Introduction © Mark Cryle 1992

Printed in Australia by The Book Printer, Victoria

Distributed in the USA and Canada by
International Specialized Book Services, Inc.,
5602 N.E. Hassalo Street, Portland, Oregon 97213-3640

Cataloguing in Publication Data
National Library of Australia

Petrie, Tom, 1831-1910.
    Tom Petrie's reminiscences of early Queensland.

    [1.] Aborigines, Australian — Queensland — Social life and
    customs. 2. Queensland — History — 1824-1900. 3. Queensland —
    Social life and customs — 1824-1900. I. Petrie, Constance
    Campbell. II. Cryle, Mark. III. Title.

994.302092

ISBN 0 7022 2383 2

TO
MY FATHER
TOM PETRIE
WHOSE FAITHFUL MEMORY
HAS SUPPLIED
THE MATERIAL FOR
THIS BOOK

NOTE

THE greater portion of the contents of this book first appeared in the *Queenslander* in the form of articles, and when those referring to the aborigines were published, Dr Roth, author of *Ethnological Studies*, etc., wrote the following letter to that paper:—

TOM PETRIE'S REMINISCENCES

(By C.C.P.)

To THE EDITOR.

SIR,—It is with extreme interest that I have perused the remarkable series of articles appearing in the *Queenslander* under the above heading, and sincerely trust that they will be subsequently reprinted. . . . The aborigines of Australia are fast dying out, and with them one of the most interesting phases in the history and development of man. Articles such as these, referring to the old Brisbane blacks, of whom I believe but one old warrior still remains, are well worth permanently recording in convenient book form— they are, all of them, clear, straight-forward statements of facts— many of which by analogy, and from early records, I have been able to confirm and verify—they show an intimate and profound knowledge of the aboriginals with whom they deal, and if only to show with what diligence they have been written, the native names are correctly, *i.e.*, rationally spelt. Indeed, I know of no other author whose writings on the autochthonous Brisbaneites can compare with those under the initials of C.C.P. If these reminiscences are to be reprinted, I will be glad of your kindly bearing me in mind as a subscriber to the volume.

I am, Sir, etc.,

WALTER E. ROTH.

COOKTOWN, *23rd August.*

PREFACE

MY father's name is so well known in Queensland that no explanation of the title of this book is necessary. Its contents are simply what they profess to be—*Tom Petrie's Reminiscences*; no history of Queensland being attempted, though a sketch of life in the early convict days is included in its pages. My father's association with the Queensland aborigines from early boyhood, was so intimate, and extended over so many years, that his experiences of their manners, their habits, their customs, their traditions, myths, and folklore, have an undoubted ethnological value. Realizing this, I determined as far as lay in my power to save from oblivion, by presenting in book form, the vast body of information garnered in the perishable storehouse of one man's—my father's—memory.

To my friend, Dr Roth, Chief Protector of Aboriginals, Queensland, I am indebted for the proper spelling of aboriginal words, and I wish to thank him for all his kindly interest and help. The spelling thus referred to is that adopted by the Royal Geographical Society of London, and followed in other continental countries. In this connection, I may mention that the Brisbane or Turrbal tribe is identical with the Turrubul tribe of Rev. W. Ridley. It was my father who gave this gentleman the original information concerning these particular blacks.

Scientific names of trees and plants have been obtained through the courtesy of Mr F. M. Bailey, F.L.S., Government Botanist, Brisbane.

CONSTANCE CAMPBELL PETRIE.

"Murrumba," North Pine,
     October, 1904.

PREFACE TO SECOND EDITION

A FEW years ago, when living on Queensland's north coast not far from Brisbane, I was delighted to come across a copy of this book, published nearly thirty years before. Why was it that these Reminiscences of Early Queensland should be so welcome and satisfying? It was because the mind, quickened by that strangely beautiful region, was hungry for some knowledge of its human past. What had those shining bays, fantastic Glasshouses, and rich valleys meant to the white settlers who had first come upon them? What to the tribes whose vast home they had been before? Through the memories of Tom Petrie these questions seemed to find their answer.

We need such interpretations. It might seem likely for Australians, of all people, to be aware of their early days, which are still so near. In the case of a Frenchman or a German, for instance, the matter is far more difficult: he has much overlapping and conflicting history to survey, and long before his eye travels back to his earliest times, it encounters something like an impenetrable fog. Yet he lives like one at home in his inheritance. Australian experience began recently in a period that was articulate, a period when people wrote letters and ran newspapers and produced books, maps, records. How easy it must be, then, for any Australian to become acquainted with his origins! Yet we find that most Australians are aware of nothing in their country before their own generation, their own life with its personal impressions. It is as if, not content with belonging to the newest of nations, they desired to be new every minute, to know nothing but the present. Yet we know the present has no existence: as when Yates sings:

Of what is past, and passing, and to come.

The present is merely what is passing. What of the past?
Can a man in any country afford to ignore what came
before him and still live fully? In Australia such a man
lives in a poverty of spirit that is hard to describe but easy
to recognize. If he believes that the life led in his country
by his forefathers in the three generations previous to his
own was totally without interest and unworthy to be remembered or recorded, what is he likely to think of the
time and place in which he himself lives?

Will he not regard them as a mere continuance of the
same banality? A life that for any interest must ever draw
on the world outside, a life, in a word, "colonial" and
derivative.

The only means of realizing some of our past rests in
the hands of the families with old homesteads or diaries or
letters. What is there in our general way of living to let
people value their memories, preserve family diaries, sift
old letters and papers? *Tom Petrie's Reminiscences*
stands as the result of such an impulse toward civilized
behaviour. The book exists as a result of respect for old
landmarks, a homestead long-established and deeply-loved,
family diaries and papers reverently preserved. If the social
history of Brisbane and the Brisbane Valley generally is
to-day a matter of common knowledge, this state of affairs
is largely due to the existence of such a book as this; more-
over, its existence has made it possible for other books like
it to appear. We may indeed count among its kin a very
recent book, simple and charming, *Memories of Pioneer
Days in Queensland*, by Mary McLeod Banks. In more
than one place this record, based on a homestead in the
Esk Valley, cuts across Tom Petrie's tracks.

Petrie fills up the landscape for us in two ways. Through
him we come to know what it meant to the blacks and then
what it meant to the early settlers for whom he personally opened up so many possibilities. His knowledge of the
blacks and their ways is readily acknowledged on all sides
to be unique. When the chapters of this book first appeared
in the *Queenslander*, ethnologists like Dr Roth hastened
to assure Constance Campbell Petrie of the importance

of her work in transcribing her father's memories. Praising the "gentle compulsion" that she used in drawing him out, they showed what had been lost by the lack of such records in earlier times. It is indeed curious to notice how the great scientist Leichhardt, exploring in the forties, and even at some point being shown the way by Tom Petrie, then still a boy, had no scientific nor human curiosity about the blacks. After his first great journey across North Australia, he glories in bringing home his pockets full of new mountains, metals, and rivers: the blacks when he encountered them were mere obstacles of no interest.

While we are appalled in reading in this book of the atrocities committed against the blacks, we are, at the same time, astounded to see how small an understanding of the blacks' ways and needs would probably have sufficed to alter the whole treatment they received. A persistent belief of the white settler was, of course, that any blacks they drove off from a certain spot desired for a homestead would have no difficulty in finding other regions for their nomadic lives. The new homestead needed permanent water and good soil: the blacks could use the rest of Australia! Of course the case was far otherwise, in two ways. The first was that once beyond his tribal area a black was an outlaw if he hunted the game or gathered nuts or roots. In desperation he might turn on the white man's sheep or sweet potatoes, which grew on the soil that had been his own: an attack which would be regarded as totally unprovoked. Tom Petrie knew better, and up and down this book will be found instances in which blacks who have attacked white settlers or their possessions have, in his mind, been exonerated and have become his friends and helpers. This series of interpretations may be said to culminate in Petrie's long conversation with the aged Dalaipi, former native owner of North Pine, where the Petrie homestead was established.

The second misunderstanding by the white settlers was in regard to the area of land required by the blacks. Planting no seed and with no conception of agriculture, they needed "the kindly fruits of the earth" as they grew over

great tracts of land. This involved the right to gather
bunya nuts in the ranges, roots on the plains, fish on the
coast. All this becomes clear from the simple account of
Petrie's own experiences as a boy, when for a fortnight
at a time he roamed with the blacks on one of their bunya
feasts in the ranges.

Every day was spent in hunting for the food shared at
the appointed stage in the journey reached by the evening.
As we read these astonishing pages, with their intimate
knowledge of the blacks' ways in feasting, in sport, in jest
and mimicking, in taboos and loyalties, we gradually realize
that the book as a whole embodies a boy's memories written
down by a sympathetic woman. That is its weakness and
its strength. The book is unpretentious in its range; exact,
with a boy's powerful memory, in its detail. In so far as
it is scientific, it has the science of a field naturalist, not
at all of a laboratory worker. Open-hearted in his boyish
courage, Tom Petrie forms an immense contrast with certain other pioneers in their timid and uninformed accounts
of the blacks in different parts of Australia.

If Petrie knew his district as it seemed to the blacks, he
knew it also as a developing home for the white man. His
topography gives depth to every study of the past. Constance Petrie's own handling of native names has been
much commended, and one could wish that it had been
reflected in the maps and railway charts of the government.
Dr Roth says that her system of spelling is rational, which,
within the limitations of our appallingly irrational alphabet,
it surely is. The general result of her method of spelling
is that native names and words in this book—as in how
few others!—can be pronounced and used. Dalaipi, Murrumba, Yibri, Durramboi (this last written down by H. S.
Russell, by the law of Hobson-Jobson, as Durham Boy!).
It is easy to believe that historical novelists in the future
will thank Constance Petrie for their liberty to move among
these names that somehow accord with the outlines of the
country to which they belong.

But these names were only a means to the end: sign-
posts, so to speak, on the roads laid out before our eyes.

We see first of all, and repeatedly, early Brisbane itself. We follow certain figures as they move across this background in the forties. There are squads of leg-ironed convicts marching up to the round, stone windmill, which was the treadmill, serviceable sometimes for the grinding of corn, sometimes for sheer punishment, but always with appalling fatigue and pain. We follow the rascal "Millbong Jemmy" on one of his most adventurous days, as he zigzags through the town, pilfering and bartering right and left. Or we see the big wicker fish-traps, the work of Bribie the basket-maker, set "at the mouth of the creek which formerly ran up Creek Street"—a street now near the centre of the city. Or there is the impressive figure of Andrew Petrie himself, Tom Petrie's father, blinded in middle age but still scrupulously and responsibly inspecting every building as it was done in early Brisbane.

We come to realize that this early town with its great curving river and central hill with the remarkable windmill on its brow is the visible basis of the present-day city that has climbed all the surrounding hills and streamed along the river flats. Tom Petrie leads us further out, along the coastal valley of the Brisbane. We go up past North Pine, a gathering place of the blacks, with its two kippa rings, and a starting-place for many a roving party. We break inland toward the Archer station of Durandur, and seaward towards the long stretch of Bribie Passage, with its islands and its countless legends. Following (or indeed leading) the modern methods of geographical study, the place-list in the back of the book opens with what was nearest to the author. First comes "Murrumba," the homestead established so long ago at North Pine on land willingly surrendered to Tom Petrie because no one else would dare to live among the wild blacks whose gathering-place it was. "Murrumba," he called it, "the good place." In his old age, as he leaned back in his verandah chair, he would recall the blacks who had been friends of his youth, and let his daughter Constance question him in detail about corroborees and customs. Neither he nor she ever pretended to know more than they did. If some of the stories are incomplete, some of the corroboree themes apparently pointless, some of the place-names missing or uncertain— well, it must be so: they had set down what they could, and a large part of their virtue, as recorders, is their close adherence to the truth of memory.

Murrumba stood, as it does to-day, on a slight rise in the North Pine settlement, which for twenty years has rightly borne the name of Petrie. Native names of the places near have been faithfully recorded. From this district the place-list branches out to include and explain whatever names are important to the book. We are given the blacks' names for those astonishing Glasshouse Mountains; while in the course of the book we have met with the legends that would inevitably haunt such a great group of pyramids and domes rising sheer from a plain.

Enough has been said, I think, to show how important this book is as a record of one corner of our country. One corner? Yes, but by its light one may also glimpse the past of the whole continent. And books like this serve a deeper purpose than the mere spread of information. They humanize a landscape that otherwise might be alien, enrich it with memories and overtones, preserve the legends and associations that are the springs of natural poetry. In this way, they make for a culture as valid as any other. We should be proud of the pioneer whose character shines forth in these pages, and grateful to the woman whose "gentle compulsion" unlocked his stored mind.

NETTIE PALMER.

Melbourne, 1932.

INTRODUCTION*

Since its first publication in serial form in *The Queenslander* in 1902, *Tom Petrie's Reminiscences of Early Queensland* has attracted considerable attention and favourable comment. Enthusiastically received by critics at the time of its publication in book form,[1] it remains an authoritative and oft-quoted source on early Queensland history, particularly that of the Aborigines of the Moreton Bay area. For A.G. Stephens, writing in *The Bulletin* in 1905, it was "one of the most interesting and valuable books yet printed in Australia".[2] Likewise, in 1905, *The Telegraph* correctly foretold that "future historians will be glad of the assistance of such a book".[3] In the same year, Thomas Hardcastle used the Petrie account as a benchmark against which to check the information gleaned from his own fieldwork with the Yuggarabul people of the Boonah district.[4] More recently, John Steele has urged readers to view *Reminiscences* as an "indispensable source of information on the Aboriginals [sic] of the Brisbane area".[5]

Reminiscences is doubtless a remarkable document, yet an accurate assessment of its value can only be made in the knowledge that the book was not written by Tom Petrie, but by his daughter, Constance. Unlike many other so-called "primary sources", *Reminiscences* is not a diary, nor a collection of official or personal correspondence. It is, in fact, a blend of autobiography, biography, ethnology and anecdote, based — as are many sources in social history — on oral evidence. Indeed, *Reminiscences* often unfolds in much the same way as an oral history transcript — anecdotal and disconnected, moving back and forth between stories and characters. This element of chaos was relatively common to popular memoir writing of the period. Indeed, it is more

* I would particularly like to thank Raymond Evans for his assistance with this Introduction.

prevalent in many other works than it is in *Reminiscences*. Here it is tempered, especially in the first half of the book, by Constance's attempt to present the material in some sort of "scientific", ordered way.

Historians have debated at length the respective strengths and weaknesses of oral sources.[6] Vicki Cowden has argued incisively that a verdict on the issue should be suspended in favour of a simple appreciation that oral testimony poses different problems from those presented by other source material.[7] Certain criteria must be applied to the oral source and, when applied to *Reminiscences*, they pose problems in one important respect: the significant gap in time between some of the events taking place and when they were actually recorded.

Many of the events discussed took place before Tom Petrie left the Moreton Bay colony for the Turon gold diggings in 1851. The available evidence indicates that Constance had not begun recording her father's memoirs before late 1901 or early 1902. Tom himself was contributing comments on local ethnology to *The Queenslander* in August and September 1901, without mention of a forthcoming publication from his daughter.[8] In a letter dated November 1902, Constance implied that she was currently working on *Reminiscences*,[9] the first instalment of which appeared in *The Queenslander* on 26 April 1902 (the final one was on 7 November 1903). The irregularity of appearances, sometimes weekly, others with gaps of over one month separating them,[10] suggests that some sections were still being written in 1903. Not all of the published version actually appeared in *The Queenslander*.[11] Indeed, at one point in the text, Constance specifically refers to "the present time (October 1904)".[12] Consequently, a significant portion of *Reminiscences* was probably written fifty years or more after the events which it describes had taken place.

Contemporary reviews of Constance Petrie's book stressed its reliance on her father's memory, for which they showed profound respect. "He was a boy of keen observation, almost everything he saw or heard he remembered. His book of reminiscences exhibits that rare combination of a child's memory, minute and sure, interpreted with a woman's sympathy."[13] *The Sydney Morning Herald* admired too the "marvellous memory of the man",[14] as did Nettie Palmer in the preface to the second edition.[15] In the preface to the first edition, Constance wrote: "I determined as far as lay in my power to save from oblivion, by presenting in book form, the vast body of information garnered in the perishable storehouse of one man's — my father's — memory."[16]

With due respect to A.G. Stephens, what we have here is not a "child's memory, minute and sure", but the memory of a 70-year-old man (Petrie was born in 1831). It is reasonable to suggest that the "perishable storehouse" may have fallen into disrepair over the years. At one point Constance acknowledges her father's failing memory powers,[17] yet attempts to reassure us that he "can remember events of those days better than he can happenings of twelve months ago".[18] Notwithstanding the claims of the book's reviewers, judgment of Tom Petrie's memory by his contemporaries was not unanimously favourable. In 1901, prior to the book's publication, Archibald Meston had challenged Petrie's opinion on certain ethnological details, suggesting that: "Mr Petrie's memory is misleading him, as well it may do after so long a time . . . I am not surprised at his memory failing under the strain of fifty years."[19] He subsequently reiterated this claim in 1906.[20]

There is a popular view espoused that old age brings with it a renewed clarity of early memory,[21] yet there is no reassuring body of scientific evidence to support this premise.[22] Indeed, one authority states that: "The empirical record of psychology suggests that most people's ability to remember declines as they grow older. The ways in which this happens vary from one person to another but it is fair to say that the long term memories of the elderly are likely to be less retentive, less accurate, and less able to be mobilised quickly than those of their juniors."[23]

Despite Meston's carping and the theoretical evidence, other factors lend conviction to Petrie's recollections. As Nettie Palmer points out, there is no obvious attempt by Constance or Tom to pretend to know any more than they did, to fabricate evidence, or to round off stories for the sake of completeness. "If some of the stories are incomplete, some of the corroboree themes apparently pointless, some of the place names missing or uncertain — well it must be so: they had set down what they could."[24] Furthermore, there is consensus that repeated patterns of people's lives, their normal routines, are better remembered than single events.[25] The detailed description of Aboriginal culture, a feature which might justifiably be considered the essence of the book, is likely to be more accurate than the retelling of historical incidents. As Tom Petrie himself said in reply to Meston's challenge, "I find that one does not easily forget what at one time formed part of one's whole life . . . I repeat again that the 'Turrbal' tribe extended from the Pine to the Logan, and in some old notes of mine, taken before my memory failed me, I find I have said the same thing."[26] Petrie's sarcastic response is quite revealing. Constance was not reliant simply on the "perishable storehouse" of her father's memory. There was also the rather more durable record of his written notes. While the full extent of Petrie's note-taking is difficult to gauge, sufficient material existed for an associate of Tom's to suggest to Constance in 1914, after Tom's death, that she might "add, by a new edition, to the valuable information you have already published".[27]

Constance does not rely solely on evidence from her father. She also records the memories of others. She acknowledges oral sources, other than Tom, for anecdotes and descriptions[28] and frequently recounts events in detail — for example, the Petries' arrival at Moreton Bay in 1837,[29] and the aftermath of the drowning of Walter Petrie, of which Tom could have had no personal recollection.[30] This adds another factor for consideration. Constance recounts stories told to her father from a wide range of sources, including Aborigines, convicts and other members of her family.

There is no justification for doubting the authenticity of Aboriginal sources of stories told to Constance Petrie by her father, any more than that of any other sources. Indeed, some studies suggest that orally communicated history thrives best in non-literate cultures.[31] Constance claims that the "Blacks" had "excellent memories",[32] yet elsewhere notes that propensity for exaggeration and the tendency for stories, after constant retelling, to be corrupted to a state bearing slim relation to their earliest form.[33] Other evidence suggests that Tom Petrie himself had rather less respect for the testimony of Aborigines than did his daughter. During the 1861 Select Committee on the Native Police Force, St George Gore asked Tom a question about reports of shootings by Native Police Officers:

Gore: Do you think the blacks are likely to have exaggerated a good

deal?
Petrie: Yes they do generally.
Gore: Then you do not place implicit reliance in their statement
Petrie: No.[34]

John Steele has warned that the convict stories told to Petrie should be treated with "special caution, if not scepticism".[35] Yet Petrie's eyewitness account of the Moreton Bay settlement offers something special, beyond mere "officialese". Our principal sources for understanding and evaluating convict Brisbane are official records housed in state archives in Queensland and New South Wales. Our view of this community, with its extremes of social control, is filtered and tempered through the process of official reporting. Petrie offers a rare glimpse — a "non-official" perspective with no vested interest in reporting what ought to have happened. Rather it relates what did happen. Petrie supplements what Raymond Evans has called "sketchy official accounts which tend to fall curiously silent at crucial moments".[36]

An example is found in the official account of the capture of Yilbong of the Ningy Ningy people after his attempt to steal goods from the windmill in July 1839. The prisoner acknowledged his guilt and was sentenced to twenty-eight days in the house of correction, later reduced to seven days at the recommendation of Dr Ballow.[37] This version suggests that the perpetrator's crime was considered relatively minor and, perhaps in a bid to maintain equitable relations with the blacks, Yilbong's sentence was commuted. *Reminiscences* fills in the gaps when it describes Yilbong's flogging in Queen Street, the day after his arrest.[38] This fact is ignored in the official report, probably because it would not have been sanctioned by superiors in Sydney.

Petrie offers additional insights into the other side of the penal frontier. Constance comments on the murder of Captain Logan, notorious commandant of the penal colony: 'the blacks . . . got the credit of [sic] the murder, but they themselves [the convicts] knew who did it, and it was alright for he deserved his death.''[39] William Coote likewise records these rumours.[40] To date the empirical evidence has not supported this view. Historical consensus supports Charles Bateson's conclusion that Logan was murdered by Aborigines.[41] The fact remains that Logan's death occurred in 1830, before Tom Petrie was born, and seven years before he ar-

rived at Moreton Bay. If the story is being related to him as seems
likely in the mid-1840s, it is conceivable that the sources of Petrie's
story had heard it second or third hand themselves, thus shedding
greater doubt on its authenticity. Raymond Evans, however, has
recently uncovered a deposition by a convict, Thomas Jones,
dated 22 September 1831, in which Jones claims that John Burn, a
convict associate, confessed to Logan's murder.[42] While this evidence is, by itself, inconclusive, it suggests that the rumour reported by both Petrie and Coote may have more substance to it
than was originally thought. At the very least, the issue warrants
further investigation.

Petrie's bid to shift the blame for Logan's murder from the
blacks, or to mitigate on their behalf, is consistent with the book's
overall response to black/white conflict in the colony. *Reminiscences* goes to some lengths to present Aborigines as compassion-
ate, humane and honourable — to rewrite popular notions of their
treachery and barbarity. "And those who know no better say the
aborigines are treacherous and untrustworthy! Father says he
could always trust them; his experience has been that if you treated
them kindly they would do anything for you."[43] On numerous occasions the book justifies violent Aboriginal actions in terms of
the cruelty and injustice they received at the hands of white settlers.[44] "Can one wonder that the blacks committed murder? . . .
To him they were always kind and thoughtful and he wishes this to
be clearly understood, for sometimes the blacks are very much
blamed for deeds they were driven to."[45]

Reminiscences was published in an age when violent struggle
was still prevalent in the far north and west of Australia and a very
recent phenomenon in the more settled areas. Intolerance and bru-
tality underwrote the white response to Australia's indigenous
population during the nineteenth century. In the light of
Reminiscences' seeming iconoclasm, how then do we account for
the highly favourable response it received in the press? Most of the
early reviews, in fact, failed to elaborate on this theme. *The Bulletin* states Petrie's position clearly without editorial judgment.[46]
The Sydney Morning Herald voiced scepticism — in somewhat
convoluted terms: "It is however, obvious that this cruelty cannot
have been so general as it pleases some writers to imagine or else

the young observer [Petrie] would have passed instances by as unworthy of notice."[47]

This broad tacit approval, the very lack of outrage at Petrie's accusations, suggests that changes may possibly have occurred in perceptions of the Aborigines and indeed in the perception of white behaviour towards them. There are clear signs of shifts in the white discourse on Aborigines, at least in Queensland, from the late 1890s. Most important, perhaps, is the simple reappearance of the issue on the popular agenda at the close of the century, in contrast to the "almost total silence" that one researcher has observed in the journalism of the 1890s.[48] Whether this modulation in popular discourse actually signals fundamental changes in attitude is doubtful. In no sense did it betoken the disappearance of intolerance, oppression and exploitation. Rather, these responses were framed in the light of the apparent imminence of Aboriginal extinction and the reality of the Aborigines' depressed social condition on the fringes of white settlement.

It was this redrafting of perceptions, rather than their renunciation, which became enshrined in the *Aborigines Protection and Restriction of the Sale of Opium Act* (1897). In turn, this Queensland act became the model for subsequent legislation in Western Australia (1905), the Northern Territory (1910) and South Australia (1911).[49] Between 1899 and 1901, the Queensland parliament debated the Aboriginal issue at length. While opinion was far from unanimous, there was significant acknowledgment of past injustices — "parading their guilt" one researcher has called it.[50] The tone of these debates was informed, in the main, by the myth of the doomed Aboriginal race. Though this notion had been voiced as early as the 1820s,[51] it gained a new momentum in the closing years of the nineteenth century.

Outside the political arena, the painter Oscar Fristrom captured on canvas the images of "the last surviving man of Moreton Island" and the "last" Brisbane Aboriginal female.[52] The Brisbane historical authority Thomas Welsby expressed regret that the blacks were "disappearing slowly but surely from our midst".[53] This supposition sets the tone for *Reminiscences* too — from its very first page.[54] It is reflected further in the reviews of the book. *The Australian Christian World* noted, with "a touch of sadness", the fate of "this vanishing race". *The Daily Telegraph* also passed comment on "the pathos of the life history of the doomed race . . . condemned by the inexorable law of survival of the fittest to certain extinction".[55]

This sense of the imminence of Aboriginal extinction spawned a flurry of Darwinist-inspired anthropological field activity in Australia from the late nineteenth century. Driven by a sense of urgency, scientists devoted enormous energy to collecting ethnological data on what they perceived to be a living relic of "primitive man".[56] Dr Walter Roth, a prolific ethnologist and the designated "Northern Protector of Aborigines",[57] endorsed *Reminiscences* in the following terms: "The Aborigines of Australia are fast dying out, and with them one of the most interesting phases in the history of the development of man."[58]

Tom Petrie completed questionnaires sent to him by A.W. Howitt, the Victorian Anthropologist. Petrie's observations were specifically acknowledged in Howitt's *Native Tribes of South-East Australia*.[59] Prior to the publication of *Reminiscences*, Petrie contributed, from his own pen, to the journal of the then-recently formed Anthropological Society of Australasia, *Science of Man*.[60] Unlike their academic associates whose findings they informed, the Petries carried no theoretical brief for their work. *Reminiscences* does not seek to postulate a theory and support it with evidence. Nonetheless, in important ways it is influenced by "scientific" writing, periodically adopting the conventions of that genre to assert its authority. For example, Chapters IX to XIV are itemised with subheadings and descriptive notes. Along with the popular names of plants, Constance frequently provides Latin botanical names[61] which doubtless would have needed researching.

It is no coincidence that Petrie's *Reminiscences* appeared in the wake of this renewed interest — lay, scientific and political — in the Aborigines. The principle architect of the 1897 legislation, Archibald Meston, had published his *Geographic History of Queensland* (1895) in which he gave laudatory accounts of Aboriginal civilisation pre-contact.[62] Meston had first met Petrie in 1870,[63] and in subsequent years had numerous lengthy conversations with him about the blacks in the Moreton Bay area.[64] During 1901, Meston was making contributions to *The Queenslander*'s "Ethnology" column. A statement he had made about the local Aboriginal name for the Brisbane River solicited a polite corrective from Tom Petrie — who had been "asked several times for my opinion on the subject".[65] Meston replied at length, suggesting that Petrie's grasp of local indigenous languages was less than complete and making the disparaging comments about Petrie's memory noted above.[66] Petrie replied in turn: "After Mr Meston's long outpour no doubt I shall be expected to 'lie low' or acknowledge my shortcomings on bended knee; but — let me whisper it — strange as it may seem, Mr Meston is able to make mistakes, and possibly there are a few among my friends who will not think me absurd when I actually stand by all I said in my former letter."[67]

In the wake of this initial fracas, the first instalment of *Reminiscences* penned by Constance appeared in *The Queenslander* on 26 April 1902, more than likely in a bid to reassert Petrie's authority regarding the local blacks and to act as an antidote to flaws Petrie perceived in Meston's writings. The publication of *Reminiscences* did not prove to be the final word on the matter, however. Meston's and Petrie's mutual antagonism subsequently spilled over on to the pages of *The Brisbane Courier* in April 1906. In response to a Meston article, "The Last Brisbane Aboriginal", Petrie wrote:

> I hope you will give space to a few remarks from a man who knew the Brisbane blacks before Archie Meston was born. (How the world got on without him I do not know and neither does he!) Re his letter in Saturday's "Courier" it so often seems [a] waste of time contradicting but I wish he would leave my name out in the misstatements he makes.[68]

Predictably, Meston replied. "Petrie", he claimed, "had acquired a reputation quite unjustified by his knowledge or experience".[69] This in turn solicited a response from Constance in defence of her father.[70] Meston did not even have the good grace to quit his carping after Tom's death in 1910.[71]

The Petrie-Meston squabble continued to linger on into the second generation. In 1931, Meston's son, Leon, gave an account in *The Brisbane Courier* of the origin of the word *Wooloowin*, the current name of a Brisbane suburb, in which he echoed, relatively innocuously, his father's belief that Tom Petrie may have confused some of the local dialects.[72] Tom's youngest son, Walter, took up the pen in defence of his father's authority:

> Mr L.A. Meston hopes that his opinion concerning the old Brisbane blackfellows will be accepted in preference to that of the late Tom Petrie! What next? And what induces Mr Meston to make such wrong statements about Tom Petrie's knowledge of the blacks? Even his father (the late Mr Archie Meston) was a neophyte compared to Tom Petrie in Aboriginal lore.[73]

While it was clearly important for the two chief protagonists in this debate, Petrie and Meston, to respectively establish their credentials, in hindsight their duel appears inconsequential. It seems irreverent that, in the face of the potential genocide of Queensland's indigenous population, both men devoted their energies to point-scoring on ethnographic detail. It is ironic, but indicative of the times, that the momentous issue of Aboriginal rights and welfare could become diverted and bogged down in a debate on the pronunciation of certain words.

For the record, Petrie's ethnological observations have generally assumed prominence over Meston's. The former's description of the male initiation process — "kippa making" — has since been described as the "exemplar"[74] by contemporary anthropologists. Petrie also left an account of the total lifestyle of the Turrbal people whom he knew, with detail on the activities of women, food-gathering, child care, tool-making and daily camp activities.[75] These features so often escaped the attention of other male ethnologists with their bias for warfare, hunting and arcane rituals — though these too are dealt with in Petrie's account.

On the negative side, Petrie's experience was — unlike that of some other observers — limited geographically. According to Constance,

> Father was very familiar with the Brisbane tribe (Turrbal) and several other tribes all belonging to Southern Queensland who had different languages. My father could also speak to and understand any black from Ipswich, as far north as Mount Perry, or from Frazer, Bribie, Stradbroke, and Moreton Islands.[76]

Meston's claim that Petrie's knowledge of the language was relatively confined[77] are supported in other sources. On comparing words from Petrie's vocabulary with those spoken by the

Yuggarabul people of the Boonah district in 1905, Thomas
Hardcastle was told by users of that dialect: "Petrie − him salt
water fella."[78] Likewise, Gaiarbu of the Jinibara people told the
anthropologist L.P. Winterbotham in 1950 that Petrie's knowledge of languages other than those of the Turrbal people was less
than complete. He also said the same of Meston.[79]

Petrie had argued that the information collected by Meston and
other late arrivals could well be corrupted by long years of contact.[80] Meston later made the charge, after Petrie's death, that
Petrie's knowledge too was thus affected.[81] Meston was right on
this, of course. Both men were salvaging pieces of information
from a society already in the process of breaking down. Petrie arrived at the wreckage earlier than Meston, but there can be little
doubt that his observations do not reflect a culture in totally
traditional mode.[82]

Apart from their polemical value, there were other ways in
which Meston's activities had effectively helped solicit Petrie's
Reminiscences and indeed primed a market for them. Constance
wrote in 1902 that "nowadays it is seldom one sees an aboriginal
[sic]". True enough, but this had as much to do with their enforced removal to reserves under Meston's authority as it had to
do with their biological extinction. In May 1897, Meston oversaw
the relocation of Brisbane-based Aborigines to reserves at Deeb-
ing Creek and Fraser Island.[83] By 1900 Brisbane was virtually free
of fringe-dwellers.[84] Meston sought to supplant the reality of the
Aboriginal fringe-dweller, with its implicit offence to Victorian
sensibilities, with the image of the noble savage warrior. He or-
ganised parades and exhibitions of Aborigines in simulated com-
bat which, by all accounts, created great interest.[85] Constance
actually refers to them in the text of *Reminiscences*.[86] This element
of voyeurism, with Aborigines as an exotic antiquarian curiosity,
also helps account for the appeal of *Reminiscences*. The Petries,
like Meston, replaced the familiar image with a romanticised version from some remote past, leaving no doubt who was responsible for the Aborigines' fall from grace: "They used to be fine,
athletic men [sic], remarkably free from disease, tall well-made
and graceful, with wonderful powers of enjoyment; now they are
often miserable diseased and degraded creatures. The whites have
contaminated them."[87] The long oration by Tom's associate

Dalaipi, which Constance presents in parentheses, has all the elements of the noble savage myth — the plea from the aggrieved tribal elder who cannot account for the injustices committed against his people.[88]

This nostalgia for a utopian past was not confined to renewed interest in the Aborigines. Some Australians perceived the closing of the century as the end of a chapter in Australia's vibrant colonial past. *Reminiscences'* reviewer in *Figaro* drew our attention to the "tragedies and comedies" associated with Brisbane landmarks "where humdrum lines of warehouses or other business premises stand today".[89] This was a period of considerable activity for local historians. J.J. Knight, who possibly had a hand in the publication of *Reminiscences*, had produced his own work — *In the Early Days* — in 1895.[90] He also promoted the writings of Nehemiah Bartley, whose posthumous *Australia Pioneers and Reminiscences* (1896) Knight edited. It was a period, too, when Thomas Welsby was active in collecting and preparing material for publications which appeared in the years subsequent to the release of the Petrie book. There prevailed a sense that vital elements of our past were disappearing with the first generation of pioneers. The review in the *Daily Mirror* summed up *Reminiscences'* appeal:

> It is interesting to those whose lives were cast in the same stirring times, and who can themselves remember similar incidents of early days, and interesting also to a younger generation who only hears of the early days from the lips of those who are gradually passing to the great beyond.[91]

Thus there were broad factors at play in Queensland society which helped induce the appearance of *Reminiscences* and create a market for its reception: political debate on the fate of the Aborigines, the sense of their imminent extinction, Meston's activities and writings, an upsurge in anthropological activity and a prevailing sense that the thrill of frontier life was a thing of the past. One historian has suggested that the humbling effects of the depression in Queensland from the mid-1890s, the bursting of the bubble of enterprise, development and growth, may have been a contributing factor to this period of reflection and contemplation of Queensland's past.[92] One can say with much greater certainty that economic factors had a significant part to play in the decision to

produce *Reminiscences*. In 1862 Tom Petrie had sufficient capital
resources to repurchase from the Queensland government 90 per
cent of the land he had originally squatted upon at the North Pine
in 1859.[93] The late 1890s depression and the severe drought of
1901-1902[94] meant that by 1902 Petrie had lost all of his stock and
part of his run to the private banks.[95] In a letter to the anthropologist A.W. Howitt, dated November 1902, during the period of
Reminiscences' serialisation in *The Queenslander*, Constance
wrote:

> You think me a bad correspondent, the fact is I am trying just now in
> these terrible drought-stricken times to earn a little with my pen. As I
> have a busy life otherwise, it is not so easy to find time in which to an-
> swer letters which bring in nothing. Please don't think me mercenary.
> I don't suppose you know what it is to feel obliged to consider every
> sixpence before spending it. It is said that people who become rich
> grow spoilt, but it should not be — I should like to have the chance to
> try.[96]

Thus when Constance records her father's attempts to encourage the runaway convict James Davis to publish for profit the account of his life,[97] it may have been with an irony which was
intentional rather than unwitting.

No attempt to evaluate *Reminiscences* would be complete
without the realisation that we are not dealing with Tom Petrie's
memoirs *per se*, but with Constance's rendition of her father's
past. The relationship between informant (father) and chronicler
(daughter) bears critically on the prose we read. It was not condu-
cive to presenting a balanced objective account of Tom Petrie's
achievements. Constance's work is very much a product of the literary age, echoing the markedly hagiographic trend of Victorian
biography.[98] As she herself wrote elsewhere, "a daughter can en-
large on a man's good qualities when he cannot do so for
himself".[99] While Constance resists the excesses of hero worship
indulged in by some family biographers,[100] there are nonetheless
significant traces of this in the text:

> At last in desperation my father got up, and said he would show he
> wasn't afraid, and off he went into camp among them all, where he
> picked up a waddie and a shield, and declared in the blacks' language

that he would fight everyone of them, one at a time if only they came to him face to face, and not behind his back.[101]

Earlier she had justified her father's need for an Aboriginal guide: "One could never lose him in the bush, but, of course, over the mountains the blacks had tracks cut, and it saved time to be shown these."[102] It seems that the "trusty chronicler"[103] referred to in the *Sydney Morning Herald* review of 1905 had been motivated by more than a simple desire to preserve for posterity a personal history of the Moreton Bay district.

Indeed, Constance's role in the production of *Reminiscences* warrants further investigation. It has, to say the least, been understated. Tom Petrie, through Constance's efforts as much as anyone else's, has taken centre stage. On the rare occasion that Constance does mention herself, it is in a self-deprecating fashion. She is chastised, for example, at a meeting with one of her father's Aboriginal acquaintances for her lack of knowledge of the language.[104] Constance is not even mentioned by name on the title pages of the 1904 or 1932 editions. When she does receive praise in the reviews, it is as a "sympathetic listener".[105] "Miss Constance Petrie deserves infinite praise for the gentle compulsion she must have put upon her father, Mr Tom Petrie, to tell the things he has seen and the things he knows about."[106] In Constance's own obituary in *The Brisbane Courier*, she merely bathed in the reflected glory of her father. "It was," *The Courier* claimed, "the very fine mind and very fine character of her father . . . [which were] faithfully reflected in the reminiscences."[107]

Yet a careful reading of *Reminiscences* belies the notion that Constance did no more than record her father's anecdotes and reflections. As well as recording the oral accounts of others, as described above, Constance cites or refers to the published writings of J.J. Knight, Thomas Archer, Nehemiah Bartley, H.S. Russell, J.D. Lang, Walter Roth, John Campbell and Ludwig Leichhardt.[108] Furthermore, she cites newspaper accounts from *The Brisbane Courier*, an unnamed South Brisbane newspaper and the *Town and Country Journal*.[109] Constance also solicits information from other sources,[110] as well as quoting at length from Andrew Petrie's diary.[111] Thus the "capable amanuensis" complimented in a *Figaro* review of 1905,[112] was in fact actively researching and absorbing much of the conventional wisdom on Queensland's past.

One might be suspicious, therefore, of the extent to which Petrie's "reminiscences" may have been affected by those other sources. For example, the book gives an account of the hanging of the "aboriginal murderer" Dundalli (5 January 1855).[113] Tom Petrie was doubtless in the crowd at the time, as Constance states, yet the rendition of the story, the details of the narrative and the order in which they are related bear sufficient resemblance to J.J. Knight's version of the same event[114] to suggest that a reading of Knight's work may have "reminded" Tom of what happened, or that Constance may have simply "borrowed" the Knight account, confident that it presented the details as her father had witnessed them. For his part, Knight had already "borrowed" his version from the contemporary account in *The Moreton Bay Courier*.[115]

Constance's introduction of other sources into the text was not done merely to fill gaps in the narrative. They are used in three important ways. Firstly, the "misinformation" of earlier sources is corrected. J.D. Lang's sensational account of the sacrifice of young Aboriginal girls is quoted and then duly dismissed.[116] Secondly, outside evidence is used to validate the Petrie version. Thomas Archer's *Recollections of a Rambling Life* and H.S. Russell's *Genesis of Queensland* attest to the precedence of Andrew Petrie's explorations.[117] Likewise Roth's, Leichhardt's, Archer's, Campbell's and Russell's ethnological observations confirm those of Tom Petrie.[118] Thirdly, Constance cites other accounts of her family's, especially her grandfather's, achievements and character, thus honouring and enhancing their reputation as important pioneers.[119] It was a reputation for enterprise, practicality and efficiency, blended with humanity and compassion in the face of frontier hardship, personal trauma, bureaucratic incompetence and intolerance.

These elements are nowhere better illustrated than in the *Reminiscences'* account of Andrew's repair of the windmill. On his arrival in the colony in 1837 as Superintendent of Works, Andrew repaired the mill used for grinding corn. Since its construction eight years earlier, it had never functioned properly, and had been driven as a treadmill by the labour of convicts. Thus, according to the account, Andrew humanely saved the convicts from this

strenuous labour and simultaneously illustrated the benefits of
Scottish practicality and ingenuity over bureaucratic bungling.[120]
This version of events actually predates *Reminiscences*. It appears
in Andrew Petrie's obituary in *The Brisbane Courier* (1872) and is
recounted by J.J. Knight (1895).[121] In the wake of *Reminiscences*,
it is retold in Tom Petrie's obituary (1910), in W.W. Craig's account of the Moreton Bay Settlement (1925), in school textbooks
in the 1930s, and is now emphatically inscribed on the mill itself.[122] Grenfell Heap has since shown that the windmill was in
fact operational throughout the 1830s, as a windmill, and that a
lightning strike in 1836 had disabled it.[123]

Whatever their origins, the episodes and themes taken up and
retold in the "official" history of the Petrie family have become
inextricably interwoven into the "official" history of Queensland.
The ascendancy of individual enterprise over government incompetence remains a powerful element in our mythology. So too does
the emphasis placed on the Petrie's pragmatism. Tom Petrie's
credibility as an observer of ethnographic detail stems from his
practical everyday contact with the blacks. As A.G. Stephens put
it in *The Bulletin*, "Baldwin and Spencer and Howitt and Roth,
have studied the life of the blacks; Tom Petrie has lived it."[124] "In
so far as it is scientific," wrote Nettie Palmer in her 1932 preface
to *Reminiscences*, "it has the science of a field naturalist, not at all
of a laboratory worker."[125] It was these credentials which Petrie
was able to mobilise to such effect in his duels with Archibald
Meston.[126] Similarly, this home-grown practicality meant that
Tom's critique of the actions of white settlers and his advocacy of
the rights of Aborigines were viewed with rather more respect than
they might be in other writers.

The precise nature of this advocacy bears further investigation.
Despite the patronising attitude adopted by *Reminiscences* — the
references to "faithful blackfellows" and the specific analogies
drawn between Aborigines and children[127] — compassion prevails
in the book's recounting of the injustices perpetrated. This con-
trasts markedly with some other contemporaneous published accounts. Rosa Praed, for example, describes with amused
detachment the cruelties practised against Aborigines which she
witnessed in her youth.[128] In his memoirs, published a decade and
a half earlier, Harold Finch-Hatton had noted callously, "when

the blacks are troublesome, it is generally considered sufficient punishment to go out and shoot one or two''.[129]

This was only one of a range of views, as Henry Reynolds has illustrated.[130] Just as attitudes to blacks varied, so too did frontier relations themselves, ranging from violent confrontation to degrees of accommodation and protection.[131] Petrie's protection of the Aborigines functioned along the lines of a personal patronage. Petrie himself explains it best in his evidence to the 1861 Select Committee:

> *Gore:* Then they [the Aborigines] have a sort of private friendship for you?
> *Petrie:* Yes.
> *Gore:* But do you not think, if a stranger were to settle in the district, they might not be so well behaved towards him?
> *Petrie:* Perhaps not.
> *Gore:* You mean to say that, from your long acquaintance with the blacks, you have a certain control over them, which another person would not possess?
> *Petrie:* Yes.[132]

A review of the 1932 edition of *Reminiscences* expresses the opinion that Petrie's benevolence on a violent frontier was something unique.[133] In fact, similar relationships between individual pastoralists and local Aborigines were, if not the norm, nonetheless known. Anne Allingham describes three such arrangements in the Kennedy district alone.[134] The pervading notion is one of "my blacks", with the whites showing a preparedness to protect, quite actively in the case of Robert Christison of Lammermoor,[135] their charges against the activities of such as the Native Police. Petrie's sympathy, like that of other pastoralists, had a pragmatic underpinning. As well as removing the threat of stock and other capital loss from Aboriginal depredations, Petrie also had a skilled and plentiful labour supply on a frontier where such a resource was lacking.[136] There can be no doubt that Tom Petrie took advantage of his intimacy with the blacks to pursue his own economic ends. He utilised their help in searching for gold as well as in other commercial activities.[137]

The other side of this coin is that Petrie also gave of his own time voluntarily in efforts to improve the Aborigines' condition. He had an active role in the establishment of a reserve at Bribie, as

Reminiscences reminds us. The book's interpretation of the demise of that enterprise, however, leaves some interesting gaps:

> . . . everything went well, and the settlement bid fair to become self-supporting, when in 1879 the Palmer government did away with the whole thing . . . 'I cannot help it,' father had to tell them; 'I have got orders from the government to break up the settlement, and so it has to be.' "[138]

Yet in Petrie's own report on the reserve, written in 1878, he states:

> I visited Bribie Island on the third of this month and found very little work done since I was there on November 15 . . . The man in charge tells me they will do nothing for him. They act with him as if they had a right to rations, any work they do they expect money for it . . . all they think of is money to buy rum . . . they will steal or starve to get drunk and when drunk brutally ill-treat each other.[139]

No one can blame Tom Petrie for reporting what he had seen, yet such a report from a noted expert would have done little to convince an administration already vacillating on this issue[140] of the virtue of the Bribie Reserve. Meston later challenged Petrie over this report, suggesting that it proved that Petrie had "no control over the blacks".[141] Constance in turn defended her father's actions, claiming that: "A well-known Church of England Bishop [Mathew Hale] and others did all they could to change the views of a government which had no sympathy for the blacks."[142] The issue here is not whether Tom Petrie's actions were moral or not, but the disparity between Tom's version and Constance's rendition more than twenty years later.

Despite his benevolence and his co-operation in the Bribie scheme, Tom Petrie does not emerge through his own actions as a great champion of Aboriginal rights. It was a platform he generally shunned. At the 1861 Select Committee on the Native Police, Tom's testament eschewed censure of the actions of that organisation. Indeed, others were considerably more vocal in their condemnation than Petrie:[143]

> *Robert Ramsay MacKenzie:* Do you think, on account of that danger, it is necessary that a detachment of Police should be stationed at Sandgate, where they can be sent for if required?

Petrie: Oh, yes.

MacKenzie: You are of the opinion that the presence of the Force there is likely to have a beneficial effect, although it may not be necessary to send for them?

Petrie: Yes.

MacKenzie: Are you in favour of disbanding the Native Police Force?

Petrie: No.[144]

The stenographer's recording of Petrie's replies to the obviously leading questions allows no scope for interpretation. Subtle nuances of speech which may have accompanied the replies have been rendered mute and monosyllabic. Indeed, Petrie may have made statements which were simply edited from the official version of the transcript. This inquest was, in fact, a pro-squatter sham, a whitewash. That judgment was conferred by *The Brisbane Courier* at the time,[145] and has been echoed since by contemporary historians.[146] The fact that Tom Petrie's title to the Murrumba property was still dubious at the time[147] may have been pertinent here in his choosing to avoid controversy.

Petrie was never likely to launch into an invective against the Native Police or against the squatter ascendancy which supported it, because he was a part of that ascendancy *Reminiscences* presents the squatters in these terms: "my father says he does not remember the squatters doing anything really wrong or unmanly. Indeed, he maintains at bottom they were kind-hearted, and he wishes there were more of their stamp nowadays."[148] Yet it was those who Petrie described as men "of the good old sort" who, more than any other single group, were responsible for the near-genocide practised on the Moreton Bay frontier and many others. Petrie could not have been ignorant of these proceedings. Indeed, the book exposes them. What we have, then, is a kind of selective amnesia on this issue. Petrie throws his lot in with both sets of protagonists in the frontier conflict.

There are few signs that Petrie suffered the ridicule and ostracism which so often went with sympathy for the Aboriginal cause.[149] One colonial campaigner for Aboriginal rights wrote: "I have found too generally a certain disposition to regard and treat as fanatic, anyone who shows an inclination to advocate the cause of the Aborigines or to benefit them".[150] The very author of these words, Duncan McNab, is made an object of ridicule in *Reminis-*

cences,[151] though he wrote sympathetically of Petrie.[152] McNab was a Scottish Catholic priest whose zeal and dedication to the task of improving the material and spiritual welfare of the Aborigines was unequalled.[153] He is sold short in the Petrie narrative with the comment "the priest having found he could do no good, gave up the attempt altogether".[154]

While McNab is singled out for special treatment, missionaries on the whole received very short shrift in *Reminiscences*.[155] The Petries were no doubt cynical about their desire to transform Aboriginal culture into a poor replica of that of the whites. They echoed, too, a scepticism expressed elsewhere in colonial Queensland about the role of missionaries,[156] or for that matter any "outsider" who levelled criticism at the treatment of Queensland Aborigines. Petrie's own critique had credibility by virtue of its being home grown. It was the opinion of a local, practical man and not some evangelical theorist.

There still remains something of a disparity between the values espoused in *Reminiscences*, written in the early years of the twentieth century, and Tom Petrie's behaviour in the fifty years previous. A number of oral history researchers have commented on the tendency for the informants' recall of past experiences to be shaped by present values. Memory is inclined to normalise past events in terms of current ideology.[157] Thus the values we encounter in *Reminiscences* are informed by the shift in opinion concerning the Aborigines which dated from the mid-1890s. Doubtless reflected, too, are the sensibilities of Constance Petrie, whose response to the issue was not forged in the flame of violent frontier confrontation.

Reminiscences is also influenced by the decline in fortunes of Tom's branch of the family. There prevails a sense that they, much like the Aborigines, have been unjustly treated. Recognition of the family's contribution to the colony's expansion had not been forthcoming. Credit for the discovery of the Bunya Pine had been usurped by another.[158] Place names given by Andrew during his explorations had subsequently been changed.[159] Constance at one point states baldly: "My father deserves some recognition for all he has done for his country gratuitously."[160] These sentiments were taken up in Tom's obituary in *The Brisbane Courier* in 1910:

Much that he has done has been appropriated by others; like his father his modesty made it comparatively easy for others to claim credit for much that he found and work that he did . . . So far there has been no official recognition of the great work of the Petries; the laying to rest of the last of the original members of the family may perhaps suggest how great a debt Queensland owes to them, and indicate a way of doing something which ought to have been done years ago.[161]

Constance's plea, and that of Tom's obituarist, both seem to have struck a responsive chord in some influential quarters. A year after his death, a monument was erected at North Pine to honour Tom Petrie's efforts. It was unveiled by the governor, Sir William MacGregor, a personal friend of the family. Representation by some "leading men on behalf of the Petrie family" to obtain a "grant of public money or public land" for the embattled family led the Premier to suggest to the Railway Commissioner that the name of North Pine station be changed to Petrie to coincide with the unveiling of the monument.[162] The decision to change the station name was gazetted in June of 1911[163] and the name board duly changed. As the post office was attached to the station, this spelt, in effect, a change of name for the whole locality from North Pine to Petrie. This decision proved highly controversial and divisive in the North Pine/Petrie community. The storm of protest and the enmity which ensued had not abated eighteen years after the decision was made.[164] While some of the resentment can be attributed to the mere decision to change names, the use of the name Petrie was bitterly resented by a number of key protestors who obviously had personal gripes with the family.[165] Constance and her sister Ida led the resistance to these protests — organising petitions to retain the new name in the face of similar bids to discard it; writing lengthy letters to government ministers which paid tribute to their father's memory; and ensuring their side was heard in the press.[166] While their resistance was ultimately successful, it was not without emotional cost. These Petries emerge in the first decades of the twentieth century as a family besieged by economic misfortunes and local indignation. Even the petty criticism from Meston and his son for one of their lasting contributions to Queensland's history — Tom's knowledge of the Aborigines — plagued the family.

During the controversy which surrounded the name change,

one contributor to the debate suggested that Constance Petric's name, along with that of her father, would be perpetuated.[167] Despite the importance of Constance's efforts and the significance of her influence over the writing of Brisbane's history, she herself remains something of an enigma. The sources tend to be mute on the details of her life. There is no entry for her in the *Australian Dictionary of Biography*, nor does she rate more than a passing mention in histories of the Petrie family.[168] Details of her life remain sketchy. She was born on 16 December 1872[169] and thus was in her early thirties when writing *Reminiscences*. As far as can be ascertained, she lived on the family property, *Murrumba*, until she married George Philip Stuart of the Union Bank in the grounds of that property in July 1918.[170] She appears not to have left any other extant writings than *Reminiscences*, apart from some letters referred to herein, though her obituary claims that she did "considerable literary work".[171] She acted, she tells us, as her father's secretary[172] and was, it seems, content to avoid the limelight. In her surviving letters written to politicians and bureaucrats, she adopts a very deferential tone. Similarly, in a letter to A.G. Stephens of *The Bulletin*, thanking him for his glowing review, she appears underconfident and anxious about the book's reception. "Do you know I was strongly advised not to send a book for review to the 'Bulletin', as it was sure to be 'cut up' very much . . . you would have smiled had you seen me watching every issue with fear and trembling."[173]

Yet the life of this woman, described by a contemporary as "bright, affectionate and industrious" and ready to help anybody",[174] assumed a tragedy of its own in its final years. On 3 September 1924, Constance was admitted to Goodna Asylum, as it was then known, with what was described then as "resistive melancholia".[175] The symptoms might be rendered in contemporary psychiatric parlance as acute depression. Whatever the nomenclature, her doctors remarked that the opposition shown by the residents of North Pine throughout the name change controversy, "seemed to affect her mentally".[176] Similarly, her sister Ida later wrote: "My dear sister Constance (the late Mrs G.P. Stuart) and our grand old mother suffered so much from the agitations here, that we feel the name of North Pine on Petrie Station would be showing a want of reverence to their memories."[177] Ironically for Constance, the book which had contributed so much to the making of her family's reputation may have contributed to her own undoing. It was a reputation she was to spend much of the rest of her life defending — at tragic cost, it seems, to her own emotional welfare.

Recent studies have added considerably to our understanding of the patriarchal values which have traditionally underwritten the process of confining "mad women". One might speculate that Constance's illness was, like many others, a form of protest — a desperate attempt to communicate frustrated literary ambition, perhaps, or an expression of her own powerlessness.[178] The case notes themselves give few clues. They simply tell a tale, in cold, clinical fashion, of tragedy, neglect and decline. Constance languished in Goodna for nearly two years, haunted by — amongst other delusions — the belief that a black man stood at her window threatening her.[179] She died there, on 4 July 1926, of complications resulting from a duodenal ulcer. She was 54 years of age. The funeral procession, two days later, left from her home, *Dundalli*, in Old Sandgate Road (now Bonney Avenue), Clayfield — the house named, perhaps in another gesture of protest, after the Bribie renegade whose death her father had witnessed.[180]

In A.J.P. Taylor's view, "written memoirs are a form of oral history set down to mislead historians" and are "useless except for atmosphere".[181] That view must be seriously challenged, and *Reminiscences* is strong evidence to support its denunciation. What we need in the place of such dismissals is the kind of "source criticism" called for by Isabel McBryde over a decade ago,[182] but which has not, by and large, been forthcoming. It is hoped that this introductory essay has helped to fill this gap in some small way by examining the background to the publication of Tom Petrie's Reminiscences. Such sources need only "mislead" historians when the historical and personal context from which they have emerged is ignored.

NOTES

1. See *Tom Petrie's Reminiscences of Early Queensland, Extracts From Reviews* (Brisbane: Watson and Ferguson, 1907). This seven-page booklet collates extracts from contemporary reviews of *Reminiscences*.
2. A.G. Stephens, *"[Review of Reminiscences]", The Bulletin*, 30 March 1905, "Red Page".
3. *Extracts From Reviews*.
4. Thomas Hardcastle, "A Vocabulary of the Yuggarabul Language", *Queensland Geographical Journal* 51, 1946-47: 21.
5. J.G. Steele, *Aboriginal Pathways* (St Lucia: University of Queensland Press, 1983), p.124.
6. For example, the *Oral History Association of Australia Journal* 5, 1982-83, presents a range of perspectives on this issue.
7. Vicki Cowden, "Historiography and Oral History: a Plea for Reconciliation", *Oral History Association of Australia Journal* 5, 1982-83: 40.
8. Tom Petrie, "Native Name of the Brisbane River", *The Queenslander*, 31 August 1901.
9. C.C. Petrie to A.W. Howitt, 23 November 1902, Box 1 Folder 6, Howitt papers, La Trobe Library, Melbourne.
10. For example, one instalment appeared on 18 July 1903, the next not until 22 August of that year.
11. See the note on the page preceding the preface of Constance Campbell Petrie, *Tom Petrie's Reminiscences of Early Queensland* (Brisbane: Queensland Book Depot; Sydney: Angus & Robertson, 1932). All future references will be to this edition (unless otherwise noted), hereafter abbreviated to *Reminiscences*.
12. *Reminiscences*, p. 189.
13. A.G. Stephens, *The Bulletin*, 30 March 1905, "Red Page".
14. *Sydney Morning Herald*, 28 June 1905, p. 4.
15. *Reminiscences*, p. xiv.
16. ibid., p. [ix].
17. ibid., p. 239.
18. ibid., p. 231.
19. A. Meston, "The Old Brisbane Blacks", *The Queenslander*, 21 September 1901, p. 547.
20. A. Meston, "Reply to Tom Petrie", *Brisbane Courier*, 19 April 1906.
21. Paul Thompson, "Oral History and the Historian", *History Today* 33, June 1983: 26.

22. Louise Douglas, Alan Roberts and Ruth Thompson, *Oral History: A Handbook* (Sydney: Allen & Unwin, 1988), p. 22.
23. David P. Henige, *Oral Historiography* (London: Longman, 1982), p. 112.
24. *Reminiscences*, pp. xv-xvi.
25. Thompson, "Oral History and the Historian": 26, 28.
26. T. Petrie, "The Old Brisbane Blacks", *The Queenslander*, 28 September 1901, p. 624.
27. William MacGregor to C.C. Petrie, 22 June 1914, A/12611. Q.S.A.
28. *Reminiscences*, pp. 149, 207, 208, 232, 234, 250, 254, 282.
29. ibid. p. 1.
30. Tom was away on a trip when Walter's body was discovered: ibid., p. 301.
31. Barbara Allen and William Lynwood Montell, *From Memory to History: Using Oral Sources in Local Historical Research* (Nashville: American Association for State and Local History, 1981), p. 69.
32. *Reminiscences*, p. 119.
33. ibid., p. 116.
34. "Minutes of Evidence" in "Select Committee on the Native Police Force and the Conditions of the Aborigines Generally", p. 112, *Votes and Proceedings of the Legislative Assembly (Queensland)*, 1861.
35. J.G. Steele, *Brisbane Town in Convict Days, 1824-1842* (St Lucia: University of Queensland Press, 1975), p. 172.
36. Raymond Evans, "The Mogwi Take Me-an-jin", *Brisbane History Group Papers*, forthcoming.
37. "Deposition regarding an Aborigine called Ilboo [sic], 8 July 1839" *Moreton Bay Book of Trails, 1835-1842*, film 0114/C1, John Oxley Library.
38. *Reminiscences*, p. 168.
39. ibid., p. 233.
40. William Coote, *History of the Colony of Queensland, 1770-1859* (Brisbane: William Thorne, 1882), p. 23.
41. Charles Bateson, *Patrick Logan: Tyrant of Brisbane Town* (Sydney: Ure Smith, 1966), p. 170; Ross Fitzgerald, *A History of Queensland: From the Dreaming to 1915* (St Lucia: University of Queensland Press, 1986), p. 83.
42. Thomas Jones, "Deposition to Police Office Commandant", 22 September 1831, NSW Colonial Secretary, Letters relating to Moreton Bay, Reel 6, John Oxley Library.
43. *Reminiscences*, p. 5.
44. ibid. pp. 6, 9, 148, 171, 174.
45. ibid., pp. 6, 149.
46. *The Bulletin*, 30 March 1905, "Red Page".
47. *Sydney Morning Herald*, 28 June 1905, p. 4.
48. Susan Sheridan, " 'Wives and Mothers Like Ourselves, Poor Remnants of a Dying Race': Aborigines in Colonial Women's Writing" in *Aboriginal Culture Today*, ed. Anna Rutherford (Sydney: Dangaroo Press, 1988), p. 77.
49. William Thorpe, "Archibald Meston and Aboriginal Legislation in Colonial Queensland", *Historical Studies* 21, 2, April 1984: 52.

50. Suzanne Welborn, "Politicians and Aborigines in Queensland and Western Australia, 1897-1907", *Studies in Western Australian History* 2, March 1978: 22; Tom Petrie's nephew Andrew Lang Petrie featured in some of these debates, e.g. *Queensland Parliamentary Debates* 78: 1544.

51. Raymond Evans, *'A Permanent Precedent': Dispossession, Social Control and the Fraser Island Reserve and Mission, 1897-1904* (St Lucia: Aboriginal and Torres Strait Islander Studies Unit, 1991), p. 27.

52. Thomas Welsby, "Recollections of the Natives of Moreton Bay: Together with Some of Their Names and Customs of Living", *Historical Society of Queensland Journal*, 3, August 1917: 118; Raymond Evans, "Aborigines of the Brisbane Area" in *Moreton Bay Sesqui-Centenary* (Brisbane: Library Board of Queensland, 1974), no pagination.

53. Quoted in A.K. Thomson, "Introduction" to *The Collected Works of Thomas Welsby* (Brisbane: Jacaranda Press, 1967), v. 1, p. 17.

54. *Reminiscences*, p. 1.

55. *Extracts From Reviews*.

56. D.J. Mulvaney, "The Australian Aborigines: Opinion and Fieldwork, Part 2, 1859-1929", *Historical Studies Australia and New Zealand* 8, 3, November 1958: 307.

57. *Australian Dictionary of Biography* (Melbourne: Melbourne University Press, 1988), v. 11, pp. 463-64.

58. Walter Roth, "Note", *Reminiscences*, p. [vii].

59. A.W. Howitt, *The Native Tribes of South-East Australia* (London: MacMillan, 1904); noted on seventeen occasions — see Howitt's index for page numbers.

60. T. Petrie, "Native Name of the Brisbane River", *Science of Man* 4, 22 January 1902: 203.

61. *Reminiscences*, pp. 62, 74, 76, 78-80, 92-93.

62. Archibald Meston, *Geographic History of Queensland* (Brisbane: Government Printer, 1895), pp. 77, 88; on Meston see William Thorpe, "Archibald Meston and Aboriginal Legislation . . .": 52-67.

63. A. Meston, "Lost Tribes of Moreton Bay", *Brisbane Courier*, 14 July 1923.

64. W.R. Petrie, "Native Names" [Letter to the Editor], *Brisbane Courier*, 22 June 1931.

65. T. Petrie, "Native Name of the Brisbane River", *The Queenslander*, 31 August 1901. It was this item which was later reprinted in *Science of Man*.

66. A. Meston, "The Old Brisbane Blacks", *The Queenslander*, 21 September 1901.

67. T. Petrie, "The Old Brisbane Blacks", *The Queenslander*, 28 September 1901.

68. T. Petrie, "Correcting Mr Meston", *Brisbane Courier*, 19 April 1906.

69. A. Meston, "Reply to Tom Petrie", *Brisbane Courier*, 19 April 1906.

70. C.C. Petrie, "Tom Petrie's Statements Defended", *Brisbane Courier*, 20 April 1906.

71. A. Meston, "Lost Tribes of Moreton Bay", *Brisbane Courier*, 14 July 1923.

72. L. Meston, "Wooloowin and Wonga" [Letter to the Editor], *Brisbane Courier*, 5 June 1931.

73. W.R. Petrie, "Native Names", *Brisbane Courier*, 22 June 1931.

74. Leonn Satterthwait and Heather Andrew, "Determinants of Earth Circle Location in the Moreton Region, Southeast Queensland", *Queensland Archaeological Research* 4, 1987: 14.

75. *Reminiscences*, pp. 20, 87, 92-96, 106-7, 117.

76. ibid., pp. 4-5.

77. A. Meston, *The Queenslander*, 21 September 1901.

78. Hardcastle, "A Vocabulary of the Yuggarabul language": 21.

79. L.P. Winterbotham, "Some Native Customs and Beliefs of the Jinibara Tribe as Well as Those of Some of Their Neighbours in South-East Queensland: the Gaiarbu story", *Queensland Ethnohistory Transcripts* 1, 1: 28.

80. T. Petrie, *The Queenslander*, 31 August 1901.

81. A. Meston, *Brisbane Courier*, 14 July 1923.

82. Satterthwait and Andrew, "Determinants of Earth Circle Location . . .": 12.

83. Raymond Evans, European-Aboriginal Relations in Queensland, 1880-1910: a Chapter of Contact, BA(Hons) Thesis, Department of History, University of Queensland, 1965, p. 44.

84. Thom Blake, "Excluded, Exploited, Exhibited: Aborigines in Brisbane, 1897-1910" in *Brisbane, Aboriginal, Alien, Ethnic* (Brisbane: Brisbane History Group, 1987), p. 50.

85. ibid., pp. 56-57.

86. *Reminiscences*, p. 210.

87. ibid., pp. 14-15.

88. ibid., pp. 14-15.

89. *Extracts from Reviews*.

90. Knight's book was dedicated to Tom's brother, John Petrie.

91. *Extracts from Reviews*.

92. Welborn, "Politicians and Aborigines in Queensland . . .": 22.

93. N.C. Stewart, The History of the Pine Rivers Shire, BA(Hons) Thesis, Department of History, University of Queensland, 1970, p. 73.

94. Lawrence S. Smith (ed.), *Tracks and Times: a History of the Pine Rivers District* (Pine Rivers: Pine Rivers Shire Council, 1988), p. 237.

95. Rollo Petrie, "The Petrie Family", Mss. OM79-2/26 John Oxley Library.

96. C.C. Petrie to A.W. Howitt, 23 November 1902, in Howitt papers, Box 1, Folder 6, La Trobe University. A photocopy is held in the Australian Institute of Aboriginal and Islander Studies Library, Canberra.

97. *Reminiscences*, p. 139.

98. Robert Skidelsky, "Only Connect: Biography and Truth" in *The Troubled Face of Biography* eds Eric Homberger and John Charmley (London: MacMillan, 1988), pp. 4-10; Harold Nicolson, *The Development of English Biography* (London: Howarth, 1928), p. 126.

99. C.C. Petrie [Letter to the Editor], *Brisbane Courier*, 20 April 1906.

100. For example, M.M. Bennett's biography of her father, *Christison of Lammermoor* (London: Alston Rivers, 1928). The parallels between this work and *Reminiscences* are interesting. Here is another daughter's account of her father's sympathetic dealing with Queensland Aborigines. Bennett actually quotes Petrie at some length in the text (pp. 88-89).

101. *Reminiscences*, p. 193.

102. ibid., p. 157.

103. *Sydney Morning Herald*, 28 January 1905.

104. *Reminiscences*, p. 119.

105. *Brisbane Courier* in *Extracts from Reviews*.

106. *Figaro* in *Extracts from Reviews*.

107. *Brisbane Courier*, 6 July 1926.

108. *Reminiscences*, pp. 143, 144, 234, 242, 253, 259, 270 (Knight); 77, 254, 257 (Archer); 287 (Bartley); 71, 257, 270-73 (Russell); 18, 251-52 (Lang); 29, 99, 101, 106, 110 (Roth); 71, 276 (Campbell); 76 (Leichhardt).

109. ibid., pp. 221, 250 (*Courier*); 230 (unnamed); 259 (*Town and Country Journal*).

110. ibid., pp. 251 (W. Lees); 285 (J.T. Bell); 230 ("a reliable correspondent"); 189 (William Pettigrew).

111. ibid., pp. 258, 260, 269.

112. *Figaro* in *Extracts from Reviews*.

113. *Reminiscences*, p. 175.

114. Knight, *In the Early Days*, pp. 336-37.

115. *Moreton Bay Courier*, 6 January 1855.

116. *Reminiscences*, p. 118.

117. ibid., pp. 254, 270-73.

118. ibid., pp. 99, 101, 106, 110 (Roth); 76 (Leichhardt); 77 (Archer); 71 (Campbell); 71-72 (Russell).

119. ibid., pp. 253, 259, 270 (Knight); 221, 250 (*Brisbane Courier*); 259 (*Town and Country Journal*); 230 ("South Brisbane paper").

120. ibid., p. 242.

121. *The Brisbane Courier*, 21 February 1872; J.J. Knight, *In the Early Days*, p. 52.

122. *Brisbane Courier*, 29 August 1910; W.W. Craig, *Moreton Bay Settlement or Queensland Before Separation* (Brisbane: Watson Ferguson, 1928), p. 52; Grenfell Heap, *The Old Windmill at Brisbane Town* (Brisbane: Boolarong, 1983), p. 3.

123. Heap, *The Old Windmill*, pp. 3-7.

124. *The Bulletin*, 30 March 1905, "Red page".

125. *Reminiscences*, p. xiv.

126. T. Petrie, *Brisbane Courier*, 18 April 1906.

127. *Reminiscences*, pp. 199, 195.

128. Rosa Praed, *My Australian Girlhood: Sketches and Impressions of Bush Life* (London: T. Fisher Unwin, 1902), pp. 18-35.

129. Harold Finch-Hatton, *Advance Australia: an Account of Eight Years' Work, Wandering and Amusement in Queensland, New South Wales and Victoria* (London: Allen, 1885), p. 149.

130. Henry Reynolds, *Frontier: Aborigines, Settlers and Land* (Sydney: Allen & Unwin, 1987), pp. 83ff.
131. ibid., p. 90.
132. "Minutes of Evidence", p. 112.
133. [Review] Newspaper cutting, source unknown in James Porter papers, OM68-18, John Oxley Library.
134. Anne Allingham, " 'Taming the Wilderness': the First Decade of Pastoral Settlement in the Kennedy District (Townsville: History Department, James Cook University of North Queensland, 1988), pp. 166-67.
135. Bennett, *Christison of Lammermoor*, p. 84.
136. William Thorpe, A Social History of Colonial Queensland: Towards a Marxist Analysis, PhD Thesis, University of Queensland, Department of History, 1985, p. 21.
137. *Reminiscences*, pp. 5, 62, 155-56, 204, 181-82, 192.
138. ibid., pp. 214-15.
139. T. Petrie, "Report to the Commissioners for the Amelioration of the Aborigines", 12 January 1878, Col/A 252, Letter no. 459 of 1878, Q.S.A.
140. Raymond Evans, "Queensland's First Aboriginal Reserve: Part 2 — the Failure of Reform" *Queensland Heritage* 2, 5, November 1971: 8.
141. A. Meston, "Reply to Tom Petrie", *Brisbane Courier*, 19 April 1906.
142. C.C. Petrie, "Tom Petrie's Statements Defended", *Brisbane Courier*, 20 April 1906.
143. Compare Petrie's testimony with that of Henry Challinor or John Mortimer; "Minutes of Evidence", pp. 2-6, 12-16, 101-7.
144. "Minutes of Evidence", p. 112.
145. *Brisbane Courier*, 30 May 1861, 27 July 1861.
146. Denis Cryle, *The Press in Colonial Queensland: A Social and Political History, 1845-1875* (St Lucia: University of Queensland Press, 1989), pp. 68-69; Bill Rosser, *Up Rode the Troopers: The Black Police of Queensland* (St Lucia: University of Queensland Press, 1990), pp. 10-13.
147. L.S. Smith (ed.), *Tracks and Times*, pp. 60, 76.
148. *Reminiscences*, p. 284.
149. See, for example, the activities of Frederick Bode in Allingham, *'Taming the Wilderness'*, p. 167; or James Dawson, *Australian Dictionary of Biography* v. 4, pp. 35-36.
150. D. McNab to J. Douglas reprinted in *Votes and Proceedings of the Queensland Legislative Assembly*, 1876 v. 3: 166.
151. *Reminiscences*, p. 216.
152. McNab to Douglas, 16 October 1877, reprinted in *Votes and Proceedings of the Queensland Legislative Assembly* 1878, v. 2: 66.
153. Mark Cryle, Duncan McNab's Mission to the Queensland Aborigines, 1875-1880, BA(Hons) Thesis, Department of History, University of Queensland, 1989.
154. *Reminiscences*, p. 216.
155. ibid., pp. 16, 141-43, 178, 183-84.
156. Finch-Hatton, *Advance Australia*, p. 144; "Editorial", *The Queenslander*, 26 November 1876.

157. Cowden, "Historiography and Oral History . . .": 38; Anon, "Editorial", *History Workshop* (UK) 8, Autumn 1979: iii.

158. *Reminiscences*, p. 243.

159. ibid., p. 270.

160. ibid., p. 212.

161. *Brisbane Courier*, 29 August 1910.

162. D.F. Denham to Commissioner for Railways, 16 June 1911, A/12611, Q.S.A.

163. L.S. Smith (ed.), *Tracks and Times*, p. 123.

164. Ida M. Petrie to Commissioner for Railways, 14 September 1929, A/12611, Q.S.A. Discussion with Mr M. Ewart of Petrie, whose assistance in researching the controversy was crucial, suggests that enmity may have lingered much longer.

165. "Report of John Greer, Constable North Pine Station, to Senior Inspector of Police", 20 August 1915, A/12611, Q.S.A.

166. A/12611, Q.S.A.

167. P.W.L. Raymont [Letter to the Editor], *Brisbane Courier*, 26 July 1911.

168. Jacqueline Whitely, Two Families of Early Brisbane: a Study of the Families of Andrew Petrie and James Campbell Throughout Three Generations, 1831-1910, BA(Hons) Thesis, Department of History, University of Queensland, 1963; D. Dornan and D. Cryle, *Building Colonial Brisbane: the Petrie Family* (St Lucia: University of Queensland Press, forthcoming).

169. Copy of her death certificate in possession of the author.

170. ibid.

171. *Brisbane Courier*, 6 July 1926.

172. *Brisbane Courier*, 20 April 1906.

173. C.C. Petrie to A.G. Stephens, 10 May 1905, Ms. no. 2/2020, Fryer Library, University of Queensland.

174. Casebook 68, Female Admissions, p. 84, A/45680, Q.S.A.

175. ibid.

176. ibid.

177. I.M. Petrie to Commissioner for Railways, 14 September 1929.

178. Phyllis Chesler, *Woman and Madness* (London: Allen Lane, 1974); Jill Julius Matthews, *'Good and Mad Women': The Historical Construction of Femininity in Twentieth Century Australia* (Sydney: George Allen and Unwin, 1984); Elaine Showalter, *The Female Malady: Women, Madness and English Culture, 1830-1980* (New York: Pantheon Books, 1985).

179. Casebook 68, Female Admissions, A/45680, Q.S.A.

180. *Brisbane Courier*, 7 July 1926.

181. Quoted in Paul Thompson, *The Voice of the Past*, p. 94.

182. I. McBryde, "Ethnohistory in an Australian Context: Independent Discipline or Convenient Data Quarry" *Aboriginal History* 3, Part 2 (1979): 140.

CONTENTS

PART I

CHAPTER I

CHAPTER II

CHAPTER III

CHAPTER IV

CHAPTER V

CHAPTER VI

CHAPTER VII

CHAPTER VIII

CHAPTER IX

CHAPTER X

CHAPTER XI

CHAPTER XII

CHAPTER XIII

CHAPTER XXI

CHAPTER XXII

CHAPTER XXIII

CHAPTER XXIV

PART II

CHAPTER I

CHAPTER II

CHAPTER IX

CHAPTER X

CHAPTER XI

CHAPTER XII

PART I

CHAPTER I

PERHAPS no one now living knows more from personal experience of the ways and habits of the Queensland aborigines than does my father—Tom Petrie. His experiences amongst these fast-dying-out people are unique, and the reminiscences of his early life in this colony should be recorded; therefore, I take up my pen with the wish to do the little I can in that way. My father has spent his life in Queensland, being but three months old when leaving his native land. He was born at Edinburgh, and came out here with his parents in the *Stirling Castle* in 1831. He is now the only surviving son of the late Andrew Petrie, a civil engineer, who, as every one interested knows, had much to do with Queensland's young days.

The Petrie family landed first in New South Wales, but in 1837 (about twelve years after foundation of Brisbane) came on to Queensland in the *James Watt*, "the first steamer which ever entered what are now Queensland waters." The late John Petrie, the eldest son, was a boy at the time, and "Tom," of course, but a child. Their father, the founder of the family, was attached to the Royal Engineers in Sydney, and was chosen to fill the position of superintendent or engineer of works in Brisbane. The Commandant in the latter place had been driven to petition for the services of a competent official, as there seemed no end to the blunders and mistakes always being made. The family came as far as Dunwich in the *James Watt*, then finished the journey in the

pilot boat, manned by convicts, and landed at the King's
Jetty—the present Queen's Wharf—the only landing place
then existing.

Although my father cannot look back to this day of arrival
he remembers Brisbane town as a city of about ten buildings. Roughly speaking it was like this: At the present
Trouton's corner stood a building used as the post office,
and joined to it was the watchhouse; then further down the
prisoners' barracks extended from above Chapman's to the
corner (Grimes & Petty). Where the Treasury stands stood
the soldiers' barracks, and the Government hospitals and
doctors' quarters took up the land the Supreme Court now
occupies. The Commandant's house stood where the new
Lands Office is being built (his garden extending along the
river bank), and not far away was the chaplain's quarters.
The Commissariat Stores were afterwards called the Colonial Stores, and the block of land from the Longreach Hotel
to Gray's corner was occupied by the "lumber yard" (where
the prisoners made their own clothes, etc.). The windmill
was what is now the Observatory, and, lastly, a place formerly used as a female factory was the building Mr Andrew
Petrie lived in for several months till his own house was
built. The factory stood on the ground now occupied by
the post office, and later on the Petrie's house was built at
the present corner of Wharf and Queen Streets, going towards the Bight (hence the name Petrie's Bight). Their
garden stretched all along the river bank where Thomas
Brown and Sons' warehouse now stands, being bounded at
the far end by the salt-water creek which ran up Creek
Street.

Kangaroo Point, New Farm, South Brisbane, and a lot
of North Brisbane, were then under cultivation, but the rest
was all bush, which at that time swarmed with aborigines.
So thick was the bush round Petrie's Bight that one of the
workmen (a prisoner) engaged in building the house there
was speared; he wasn't much hurt, however, and recovered.

While living at the Bight when a boy my father remembers watching the first steamer which ever came up the river

(the *James Watt* stayed in the bay). When she rounded Kangaroo Point, with her paddles going, the blacks, who were collected together watching, could not make it out, and took fright, running as though for their lives. They were easily frightened in those days. Father remembers another occasion on which they were terrified. His father one night got hold of a pumpkin, and, hollowing it out, formed on one side a face, which he lit up by placing a candle inside, the light shining through the openings of the eyes and mouth. This head he put on a pole, and then wrapping himself in a sheet with the pole, he looked to the frightened blacks' imagination for all the world like a ghost, and they could hardly get away fast enough.

From early childhood, "Tom" was often with the blacks, and since there was no school to go to, and hardly a white child to play with, he naturally chummed in with all the little dark children, and learned their language, which to this day he can speak fluently. A pretty, soft-sounding language it is on his lips, but rather the opposite when spoken by later comers; indeed, I do not think that any white man unaccustomed to it from childhood can ever successfully master the pronunciation.

"Tom," and his only sister, when children used to hide out among the bushes, in order to watch the blacks during a fight; and once when the boy had been severely punished by his father for smoking, he ran away from home, and after his people had looked everywhere, they found him at length in the blacks' camp out Bowen Hills way. There was one blackfellow at that time these children used to torment rather unmercifully: a very fierce old man, feared even by the blacks, who believed he could do anything he choose in the way of causing death, etc. He was called "Mindi-Mindi" (or "Kabon-Tom" by the whites), was the head of a small fishing tribe who generally camped at the mouth of the South Pine River, and was a great warrior. One day the children found him outside their home. They teased and called him names in his own tongue till the man grew so fierce that he chased the youngsters right inside.

The girl got under a bed, and "Tom" up on a chair, where the blackfellow caught him, and taking his head in his hands started to screw his neck. One hand held the boy's chin and the other the top of his head, and in a few minutes more his life would have ended, but the screams brought the mother just in time. Father's neck was stiff for some time after this, and the children never tormented old "Kabon-Tom" again. They declared always that this man had a perfectly blue tongue, and the palms of his hands were quite white. It was said that he screwed his own little daughter's neck, and thought nothing of such things. However, he and "Tom" were generally friends; indeed, this is about the only occasion on which the boy fell out with a blackfellow. "Kabon-Tom" must have been about ninety when he died, and was a very white-haired old man. He was found lying dead one day in the mud in the Brisbane River.

Later on in life, when my father employed the blacks, they were always kind and considerate about him. They are naturally an affectionate people, and he with his good and kindly disposition, and his fun—for the blacks do so enjoy a joke—was very popular with them all. Nowadays it is seldom one sees an aboriginal, but some years ago, when they would come at times and camp round about here (North Pine), it was amusing to see the excitement when they found their old friend in the mood for a yarn. To watch their faces was as good as a play, and to hear father talk with them!—it seemed all such nonsense, and many a time has someone looking on been convulsed with laughter. A good-natured people they surely are, for amusement at their expense does not call forth resentment; rather would they join in the laugh.

Queensland is a large country, and the tribes in the north differ in their languages, habits, and beliefs from the blacks about Brisbane. Father was very familiar with the Brisbane tribe (Turrbal), and several other tribes all belonging to southern Queensland who had different languages, but the same habits, etc. The Turrbal language was spoken as far inland as Gold Creek or Moggill, as far north as North

Pine, and south to the Logan, but my father could also speak to and understand any black from Ipswich, as far north as Mount Perry, or from Frazer, Bribie, Stradbroke, and Moreton Islands. Of all the blackfellows who were boys when he was a boy there is only one survivor; most of them died off prematurely through drink, introduced by the white man.

On first coming, nearly forty-five years ago, to North Pine, which is sixteen miles by road from Brisbane, the country round about was all wild bush, and the land my father took up was a portion of the Whiteside run. The blacks were very good and helpful, lending a hand to split and fence, and put up stockyards, and they would help look after the cattle and yard them at night. For the young fellow was all alone, no white man would come near him, being in dread of the blacks. Here he was among two hundred of them, and came to no harm.

When with their help he had got a yard made, and a hut erected, he obtained flour, tea, sugar, and tobacco from Brisbane, and leaving these rations in the hut, in charge of an old aboriginal, went again to Brisbane, and was away this time a fortnight. Fifty head of cattle he also left in the charge of two young blacks, trusting them to yard these at night, etc.; and to enable the young darkies to do this, he allowed them each the use of a horse and saddle. On his return all was as it should be, not even a bit of tobacco missing! And those who know no better say the aborigines are treacherous and untrustworthy! Father says he could always trust them; and his experience has been that if you treated them kindly they would do anything for you.

On the occasion just mentioned, during his absence, a station about nine miles away ran short of rations, and the stockman was sent armed with a carbine and a pair of pistols to see if he could borrow from father. Arrived at his destination, the man found but blacks, and they simply would give him nothing until the master's return. The hut had no doors at the time, and yet they hunted for their own food, touching nothing.

A further refutation of the treachery and untrustworthiness of the blacks is the following:—One young fellow, learning to ride in those days, was thrown several times. My father, vexed with the mare ridden, mounted her himself, and giving the animal a sharp cut with his riding whip, sent her off at full gallop. He carried a revolver in his belt, which he always had handy, as often the blacks would get him to shoot kangaroos they had surrounded and hunted into a water-hole. The mare galloped on, then, stopping suddenly, somehow threw her rider in spite of his good seat. The first thing he remembered afterwards was seeing a company of blacks collected round him, crying, and one old man on his knees sucking his back, where the hammer of the revolver had struck. They then carried him to his hut, and in the morning he was nothing but stiff after his adventure. And there was no white man about!

Many a time when the blacks wished to gather their tribes together for a corrobboree (dance and song), or fight, they would send on two men to inquire of father which way to come so as not to disturb his cattle. This was more than many a white man would do, he says. To him they were always kind and thoughtful, and he wishes this to be clearly understood, for sometimes the blacks are very much blamed for deeds they were really driven to; and of course they resented unkindness. For instance, the owner of a station some distance away used to have his cattle speared and killed. Father would remonstrate and ask the why, and the blacks would answer: It was because if that man caught any of them he would shoot them down like dogs! Then they told this tale: A number of blacks were on the man's run, scattered here and there, looking for wild honey and opossums, when the owner came upon them and, shooting one young fellow, first broke his leg, then another shot in the head killed him. The superior white man then hid himself to watch what would happen. Presently the father came looking for his son, and he was shot; the mother coming after met the same fate.

My father knew the blacks well who told him this, and was satisfied they spoke truthfully. It may strike the reader why did he not make use of his information and bring punishment to the offender? Well, because in those days a blackfellow's evidence counted as nothing, and no good would therefore be gained, but rather the opposite, as the bitterness would be increased, and the blacks get the worst of it. You see, the white men had so many opportunities for working harm; at that time several aboriginals were poisoned through eating stolen flour, it having been carefully left in a hut with arsenic in it.

To show that the aborigines were not unforgiving, here is an example: The squatter before mentioned, who shot the blacks, went once to father to see if he would use his influence with the aborigines and get them to go to his station and drive wild cattle from the mountain scrub—a difficult undertaking. He agreed to see what could be done, on condition that the blacks were considerately treated, and advised the man to leave all firearms behind, and accompany him to their camp, where he would do his best. "Oh, no! I can't do that," was the reply. "If you won't come to the camp," replied father, "they will not understand, and won't go; you need fear nothing; they will not touch you while I'm there."

After some discussion, the man was persuaded, though he evidently was in fear and trembling during the whole interview. The blacks agreed to go next day, which they did, leaving their gins and pickaninnies under father's care till their return. In three days they were back, and reported they had got a number of cattle from the scrub, and that the man—"John Master" they called him—had killed a bull for them to eat, and was all right now, not "saucy" any more. They added that they had agreed to go back again and strip bark for him.

This second time the blacks took their women folk and children, and were away for two or three weeks working for the squatter, cutting bark, etc., and were evidently quite contented and happy. However, in the meantime, a report was got up on the station to the effect that the blacks were killing some of the cattle; so a man was sent to where Sandgate now is to ask assistance from the black police, who were stationed there.

These black police were aborigines from New South Wales and distant places, and they, with their white leader, came and shot several blacks, the remaining poor things returning at once to their friend in a great state, protesting they had not touched a beast. Father met the squatter soon after, and said to him: "You're a nice sort of fellow; how could you cause those poor blacks to be shot like that? You know perfectly well they did not kill your cattle." The man excused himself by saying that it was done without his knowledge, that he had a young fellow learning station work who got frightened over the blacks, and went for the police on his own account.

Another time, while out riding in the bush, my father heard a great row, and a voice calling, "Round them up, boys!" And on galloping up he came upon a number of poor blacks—men, women, and children—all in a mob like so many wild cattle, surrounded by the mounted black police. The poor creatures tried to run to their friend for protection, and he inquired of the officer in charge what was the meaning of it all. The officer—a white man, and one, by the way, who was noted for his inhuman cruelty—replied that they merely wished to see who was who. But father knew that if he hadn't turned up, a number of the poor things would have been shot. Can one wonder there were murders committed by the blacks, seeing how they were sometimes treated? This same police officer (Wheeler, by name), later on was to have been hanged for whipping a poor creature to death, but he escaped and fled from the country. It is possible he is still alive. His victim was a young blackfellow, whom he had tied to a verandah post, and then brutally flogged till he died.

Three men were once murdered at St Helena Island by aboriginals, and this is the side of the question given by "Billy Dingy" (so called by the whites), one of the blacks concerned. Billy said that he and two other young men, each with his young wife, were taken in a boat by three white men, who promised to land them at Bribie Island, as it was then the great "bunya season," and the aborigines always met there before travelling to the Bunya Mountains (or, to be correct, Bon-yi Mountains—the natives always pronounced it so). Of the "bon-yi season" I will speak later on.

Well, these men, instead of doing as they had promised, landed at St Helena and there set nets for catching dugong, acting as though they had not the slightest intention of going near Bribie. They also took possession of the young gins, paying no heed to Billy, who pleaded for their wives and to be taken to Bribie as promised. So Billy, poor soul, didn't know what to do, and at last bethought him to kill the men. He did it in this way: Some distance from where they were camped a cask was sunk in the sand for fresh water, and Billy, in broken English, called to one of the men, Bob Hunter by name: "Bob, Bob, come quick, bring gun, plenty duck sit down longa here." Bob went to Billy all unthinking, and, passing the cask in the sand, knelt to drink. There was Billy's chance, and he took it, striking the man from behind with a tomahawk on the back of the head. Bob threw up his arm to save himself, only to be cut on the arm, and then again on the head, and was killed. Billy then dragged him down to the water, and that was the end of that man.

On returning to the camp after this "deed of darkness," Billy told the gins in his own language what had happened, and that he meant to finish by killing the other two, and they then could all get away together. The gins begged of him not to kill the others, but his mind was fixed, and remained unmoved. Fortune favoured him surely, for he found one man alone sitting by a camp-fire smoking, and, creeping up stealthily behind him, cut open his head with the tomahawk; and this man's body was in turn dragged to the water.

There now remained but one other, and he at that time away in the scrub shooting pigeons. Billy followed, and, watching his opportunity, struck the white man as he stooped to go under a vine. This last body was also dragged to the water, and that was the end of the three; and who can say the blacks were wholly to blame?

After the white men were thus disposed of, the natives all got into the boat and came to the mouth of the Pine River, where they left the boat, and walking round on the mainland opposite Bribie, swam across to the island. Bob Hunter's body was afterwards recovered, and it had a cut on the arm even as Billy described it to my father. The other bodies were never found, and it was thought they were eaten by sharks.

My father had these three men—Billy and the others—working for him afterwards till their death, and found them all right. He was also alone for days with Billy in the forest looking for cedar timber.

An old man called Gray was killed at Bribie Island (July 1849). This is the blacks' version as told to their friend: Gray used to go to Bribie with a cutter for oysters; he had a blackboy as a help when gathering the oysters on the bank, and he imagined this boy wasn't fast enough in his work, so beat him rather unmercifully, being blest with a bad temper. The boy escaped and ran away from the oyster bank, swimming to the island, and he told the blacks of his ill-treatment. They were worked up to resentment, and went across and killed Gray. Father says of the latter: "I knew poor old Gray well; he was a very cross old man, and many a slap on the side of the head I got from him when a boy."

CHAPTER II

HAVING given some instances as proof of the statement that
the blacks were murderers or quite otherwise, according to
the white man's treatment of them, I will pass now to their
native customs, and tell you of the "Bon-yi season."
"Bon-yi," the native name for the pine, *Araucaria Bidwilli,*
has been wrongly accepted and pronounced bunya. To the
blacks it was bon-yi, the "i" being sounded as an "e" in
English, "bon-ye." Grandfather (Andrew Petrie) discovered this tree; but he gave some specimens to a Mr
Bidwill, who forwarded them to the old country, and hence
the tree was named after him, not after the true discoverer.
Of this more anon.

The bon-yi tree bears huge cones, full of nuts, which the
natives are very fond of. Each year the trees will bear a
few cones, but it was only in every third year that the great
gatherings of the natives took place, for then it was that
the trees bore a heavy crop, and the blacks never failed
to know the season.

These gatherings were really like huge picnics, the aborigines belonging to the district sending messengers out to
invite members from other tribes to come and have a feast.
Perhaps fifteen would be asked here, and thirty there, and
they were mostly young people, who were able and fit to
travel. Then these tribes would in turn ask others. For
instance, the Bribie blacks (Ngunda tribe) on receiving
their invitation would perchance invite the Turrbal people
to join them, and the latter would then ask the Logan, or

Yaggapal tribe, and other island blacks, and so on from tribe to tribe all over the country, for the different tribes were generally connected by marriage, and the relatives thus invited each other. Those near at hand would all turn up, old and young, but the tribes from afar would leave the aged and the sick behind.

My father was present at one of these feasts when a boy for over a fortnight. He is the only free white man who has ever been present at a bon-yi feast. Two or three convicts in the old days, who escaped and lived afterwards with the blacks—James Davis ("Duramboi"), Bracefield ("Wandi"), and Fahey ("Gilbury"), of course, knew all about it, but they are dead now. Father met the two former after their return to civilization, and he has often had a yarn with the old blacks who belonged to the tribes they had lived with.

In those early days the Blackall Range was spoken of as the Bon-yi Mountains, and it was there that Duramboi and Bracefield joined in the feasts, and there also that father saw it all. He was only fourteen or fifteen years old at the time, and travelled from Brisbane with a party of about one hundred, counting the women and children. They camped the first night at Bu-yu—ba (shin of leg), the native name for the creek crossing at what is now known as Enoggera.

After the camp-fires were made and breakwinds of bushes put up as a protection from the night, the party all had something to eat, then gathered comfortably round the fires, and settled themselves ready for some good old yarns, till sleep would claim them for his own. Tales were told of what forefathers did, how wonderful some of them were in hunting and killing game, also in fighting. The blacks have lively imaginations of what happened years ago, and some of the incidents they remembered of their big fights, etc., were truly marvellous! They are also born mimics, and my father has often felt sore with laughing at the way they would take off people, and strut about, and imitate all sorts of animals.

When aborigines are collected anywhere together, each morning at daylight a great cry arises, breaking through the silence: this is the "cry for the dead." Imagine it, falling on the stillness after the night! It comes with the dawn and the first call of the birds; as the Australian bush awakens and stirs, so do Australia's dark children—or, rather they used to, for all is changed now. It must have been weird, that wailing noise and crying; but one could imagine the birds and animals expecting it and listening for it; and the sun in those days would surely have thought something had gone wrong, had there been no great cry to accompany his arising. Whether the dead were the better for the mourning who can say? But they were always faithfully mourned for, each morning, and at dusk each night. It was crying and wailing and cursing all mixed up together, and was kept going for from ten to twenty minutes, such a noise being made that it was scarcely possible to hear oneself speak. Each person vowed vengeance on their relative's murderer, swearing all the time. To them it was an oath when they called a man "big head," "swelled body," "crooked leg," etc.; and so they cursed and howled away, using all the "oaths" they could think of. There was never a lack of someone to mourn for; so this cry was never omitted, night or morning.

After the dying down of the cry at daybreak, the blacks would have their morning meal, and then, as in the case of this journey to the Bon-yi Mountains, when my father accompanied them, they made ready to move forward on their way. A blackfellow would shout out the name of the place at which they were to meet again that night—this time it happened to be the Pine—and off they all went, hunting here and there, catching all sorts of animals, getting wild honey, too, and coming into the appointed place that night laden with spoil. This same thing went on day by day, and father was treated like a prince among them all. They never failed to make him a humpy for the night, roofed with bark or perhaps grass; while for themselves they didn't trouble, unless it rained. The third night they camped at Caboolture (Kabul-tur, "place of carpet snakes"), and next day started for the Glasshouse Mountains.

During this journey my father noticed some superstitions

of the blacks. For instance, going up the spur of a hill a dog ran through between the legs of a blackfellow, and the man stood stock still and called the dog back, making it return through his legs. When asked why, he said they would both die otherwise. Then, again, they travelled along a footpath, which ran up a ridge, where there was but room to walk one by one, and the white boy noticed a half-fallen tree leaning across the way. Coming to the tree, the first blackfellow paused and pulled a bush from the road-side, and, throwing it down on the path, quietly walked round the tree, the rest following him. Father asked the reason, and the man said that if anyone walked under that tree his body would swell, and he would die; he also said that he threw the bush down as a warning to the others. My father, of course, boy-like, wished to show there was nothing in all this, and walked assuredly under the tree, drawing attention to the fact that he didn't die. "Oh, but you are white," they said.

It was the same thing always with regard to a fence; the aboriginals would never climb through or under a fence, but always over, thinking here, too, that their body would swell and they would die. In the same way a blackfellow would rather you knocked him down than have you step over him or any of his belongings, because to him it meant death. Supposing a gin stepped over one of them—naughty woman!—she would be killed instantly. Father has lain on the ground, and offered to let men, women, and children all step over his body, and if he died they were right in their belief; but, if not, they were wrong. He offered blankets, flour, a tomahawk; but no, nothing would induce them, for they said they did not wish to see him die. As he survived the great ordeal of walking under a tree, because of being a white man, one would think they would risk the other, especially with a promised reward in view. But not they.

Of course, we are speaking of the past; the blacks one sees of late years will go through a fence or under a tree, or anything; just as they will smoke, and drink spirits. They used to be fine, athletic men, remarkably free from disease, tall, well-made and graceful, with wonderful powers of enjoyment; now they are often miserable, diseased, degraded creatures. The whites have contaminated them.

On the fourth day of this journey, about 4 o'clock, the party arrived near Mooloolah, at a creek with a scrub on it, and all hands fell to making fires for cooking purposes, etc., and they stripped some bark to make a hut ("ngudur") for their white friend to sleep in, some placing a "pikki" (vessel made from bark) of water ready to his hand, others bringing him yams and honey or anything he fancied to eat. He had a little flour and tea and sugar with him, which the blacks carried, but never touched, leaving them for him. They did not think it worth while making huts for themselves for one night, but just camped alongside the fire with opossum rug coverings.

Arriving at the Blackall Range, the party made a halt at the first bon-yi tree they came to, and a blackfellow accompanying them, who belonged to the district, climbed up the tree by means of a vine. When a native wishes to climb a tree that has no lower branches he cuts notches or steps in the trunk as he goes up, ascending with the help of a vine held round the stem. But my father's experience has been that the blacks would never by any chance cut a bon-yi, affirming that to do so would injure the tree, and they climbed with the vine alone, the rough surface of the tree helping them.

This tree they came first upon was a good specimen, 100 feet high before a branch, and when the native climbing could reach a cone he pulled one and opened it with a tomahawk to see if it was all right. (The others said if he did not do this the nuts would be empty and worthless, and father noticed afterwards that the first cone was always examined before being thrown to the ground.) Then the man called out that all was well, and, throwing down the cone, he broke a branch, and with it poked and knocked off other cones. As they fell to the ground, the blacks assembled below would break them up, and, taking out the nuts, put them in their dilly-bags. Afterwards they went further on, and, camping, made fires to roast the nuts, of which they had a great feed—roasted they were very nice.

Next day they travelled on again, till they came to where the tribes were all assembling from every part of the country, some hailing from the Burnett, Wide Bay, Bundaberg, Mount Perry, Gympie, Bribie and Frazer Islands, Gayndah, Kilcoy, Mount Brisbane, and Brisbane. When all turned up there numbered between 600 and 700 blacks. According to some people, the numbers would run to thousands at these feasts. That may have been so in other parts of the country, but not there on the Blackall Ranges. Each blackfellow belonging to the district had two or three trees which he considered his own property, and no one else was allowed to climb these trees and gather the cones, though all the guests would be invited to share equally in the eating of the nuts. The trees were handed down from father to son, as it were, and every one, of course, knew who were the owners.

Great times those were, and what lots of fun these children of the woods had in catching paddymelons in the scrub with their nets, also in obtaining other food, of which there was plenty, such as opossums, snakes, and other animals, turkey eggs, wild yams, native figs, and a large white grub, which was found in dead trees. These latter are as thick as one's finger and about three inches long. They were very plentiful in the scrubs, and the natives knew at a glance where to look for them. They would eat these raw with great relish, as we do an oyster, or they would roast them. Then the young tops of the cabbage-tree palm, and other palms which grew there, served as a sort of vegetable, and were not bad, according to my father. The bon-yi nuts were generally roasted, the blacks preferring them so, but they were also eaten raw.

It will be seen that there was no lack of food of different kinds during a bon-yi feast; the natives did not only live on nuts as some suppose. To them it was a real pleasure getting their food; they were so light-hearted and gay, nothing troubled them; they had no bills to meet or wages to pay. And there were no missionaries in those days to make them think how bad they were. Whatever their faults father could not have been treated better, and when they came into camp of an afternoon about four o'clock, from all directions, laden with good things—opossums, carpet snakes, wild turkey eggs, and yams—he would get his share of the best—as much as he could eat. The turkey eggs were about the size of a goose egg, and the fresh ones were taken to the white boy, while addled eggs, or those (let me whisper it) with chickens in them, were eaten and relished by the blacks, after being roasted in the hot ashes.

My father always noticed how open-handed and generous the aborigines were. Some of us would do well to learn from them in that respect. If there were unfortunates who had been unlucky in the hunt for food, it made no difference; they did not go without, but shared equally with the others.

CHAPTER III

Sacrifice—Cannibalism—Small Number killed in Fights—Corrob-
borees — "Full Dress" — Women's Ornaments — Painted Bodies —
Burying the Nuts — Change of Food — Teaching Corrobborees —
Making new ones—How Brown's Creek got its Name—Kulkarawa—
"Mi-na" (Mee-na).

It has often been given out as a fact that the blacks grew so
tired of nuts and vegetable foods during a bon-yi feast
that, to satisfy the craving that grew upon them for animal
food, they terminated the meeting by the sacrifice of one
gin or more. This is quite untrue, according to my father.
As I have shown, the blacks had plenty of variety in the
way of food during these gatherings, and, besides, on their
way to the Bon-yi Mountains they travelled along the coast
as much as was possible, and got fish and oysters as they
went along. Then, after the feast was all over, they repaired
again to the coast, where they lived for some time on the
change of food.

The following passage from Dr Lang's "Queensland,"
issued in 1864, was quoted once by a gentleman (Mr A. W.
Howitt), who doubted its accuracy and wished my father's
opinion on the subject:—"At certain gatherings of some
tribes of Queensland young girls are slain in sacrifice to
propitiate some evil divinity, and their bodies likewise are
subjected to the horrid rite of cannibalism. The young girls
are marked out for sacrifice months before the event by the
old men of the tribe." Dr Lang, says Mr Howitt, gave this
on the authority of his son, Mr G. D. Lang, who, as the
good doctor puts it, "happened to reside for a few months in
the Wide Bay district."

My father says there is no truth in this statement; it is
just hearsay, as there was no such thing as sacrifice among
the Queensland aborigines, neither did they ever kill any-

one for the purpose of eating them. They were most certainly cannibals, however, as they never failed to eat anyone killed in fight, and always ate a man noted for his fighting qualities, or a "turrwan" (great man), no matter how old he was, or even if he died from consumption! It was very peculiar, but they said they did it out of pity and consideration for the body—they knew where he was then—"he won't stink!" The old tough gins had the best of it; no one troubled to eat them; their bodies weren't of any importance, and had no pity or consideration shown them! On the other hand, for the consumer's own benefit this time, a young, plump gin would always be eaten, or anyone dying in good condition.

I do not mean to infer that the aborigines ate no human flesh during a bon-yi feast, for someone might die and be eaten at any time, and then, too, they always ended up with a big fight, and at least one combatant was sure to be killed. People speak of the great numbers killed in fight, but after all they were but few, though wounds, and big ones, too, were plentiful enough.

At night during the bon-yi season, the blacks would have great corrobborees, the different tribes showing their special corrobboree (song and dance) to each other, so that they might all learn something fresh in that way. For instance, a northern tribe would show theirs to a southern one, and so on each night, till at last when they left to journey away again, they each had a fresh corrobboree to take with them, and this they passed on in turn to a distant tribe. So from tribe to tribe a corrobboree would go travelling for hundreds of miles both north and south, and this explains, I suppose, how it was that the aborigines would often sing songs the words of which they did not understand in the least, neither could they tell you where they had first come from.

When about to have a corrobboree, the women always got the fires ready, and the tribe wishing to show or teach their special corrobboree to the others, would rig themselves out in full dress. This meant they had their bodies painted in different ways, and they wore various adornments, which

were not used every day.   Men always had their noses
pierced (women never had), and it was considered a great
thing to have a bone through one's nose! This bone was
generally taken from a swan's wing, but it might be from
a hawk's wing, or a small bone from the kangaroo's leg;
and was supposed to be about four inches long.   It was only
worn during corrobborees or fights, and was called the
"buluwalam."

In every-day life a man always wore a belt or "makamba,"
in which he carried his boomerang.   This belt measured
from six feet to eight feet in length, and was worn twisted
round and round the waist.   It was netted either from
'possum or human hair—but only the great men of the tribe
wore human hair belts.   A man could also wear "grass-
bugle" necklaces ("kulgaripin") at any time; these being
made from reeds cut into little pieces and strung together
on a string of fibre.   But in addition to his everyday dress,
during a corrobboree a blackfellow would wear round his
forehead a band made from root fibre, very nicely plaited,
and painted white with clay; also the skin of a native dog's
tail (cured with charcoal and dried in the sun), or, rather,
a part of one, for one tail made three headdresses when cut
up the middle.   This piece of tail stuck round the head like
a beautiful yellow brush—the natives called it "gilla," and
the forehead band "tinggil."   Then on his arm kangaroo-
skin bands were worn, and these had to be made from the
underbody part of the skin, which was of a much lighter
colour than the back.   Lastly, a man was ornamented with
swan's down stuck in his hair and beard, and in strips up
and down his body and legs, back and front; or, if he was an
inland black, parrot feathers took the place of the down.

Women wore practically no ornaments except necklaces,
and feathers stuck in their short hair in bunches, with beeswax. (The feathers and beeswax were always ready in their
dillies.)   Their hair was always kept short, as they were apt
to tear at each other when fighting.   Men's hair grew long,
and some of the great men had theirs tied up in a knob on
the top of the head, and when such was the case they wore
in this knob little sticks ornamented with yellow feathers

from the cockatoo's topknot. The feathers were fastened to
the ends of the sticks with beeswax, and these sticks were
stuck here and there in the knob of hair, as Japanese place
little fans; and they looked quite nice.

When a good fire was raging the gins all sat in rows of
three or four deep behind the fire. The old and married gins
would have an opossum rug folded up between their thighs,
which they beat with the palms of their hands, and so kept
time with the song they sang. The young women beat
time on their naked thighs. They held the left wrist with
the right hand, and then, with the free hand open, slapped
their thighs, making a wonderful noise and keeping excellent time. A pair of blackfellows standing up in front of the
gins between them and the fire, would beat two boomerangs
together, and these men were in "full dress," as were those
who danced on the other side of the fire. First these latter
stood some distance off in the dark, but so soon as the singing and beating of time began they would dance up to the
others.

The men and women learning the corrobboree stood behind the rows of gins seated on the ground, and two extra
men, other than those with boomerangs, stood placed
like sentinels before the women, with torches in their hands,
and they were generally also strangers learning. The
torches were fashioned from tea-tree bark, and made a
splendid blaze, aiding the fire in its work of lighting up the
dancers for the benefit of those concerned. Some few women
would dance, but they kept rather apart in front of the
others, and their movements were different to those of the
men—somewhat stiffer. Always there were two or three
funny men among the dancers, men who caused mirth and
amusement by their antics—even the blacks had members
who could "act the goat."

The aborigines painted their bodies according to the tribe
to which they belonged, so in a corrobboree or fight they
were recognised at once by one another. In the former there
would perhaps be ever so many different tribes mixed up,
for they might all know the same dance. Father says it
was a grand sight to see about 300 men at a time dancing

in and out, painted all colours. There they would be, men white and black, men white and red, men white and yellow, and yet others a shiny black with just white spots all over them, or, in place of the spots, rings of white round legs and body, or white strips up and down. Yet again there were those who would have strange figures painted on their dark skins, and no matter which it was, one or the other, they were all neatly, and even beautifully, got up. There they would dance with their head-dress waving in the air—the swan's down, the parrot feathers, or the little sticks with the yellow cockatoo feathers. And, of course, the rest of the dress added to the spectacle—the native dogs' tails round their heads, the bones in their noses, and the various belts and other arrangements.

The dancers would keep up these gaieties for a couple of hours and then all would return to camp, where they settled down to a sort of meeting somewhat after the style of a Salvation Army gathering. One man would stand up and start a story or lecture of what had happened in his part of the country, speaking in a loud tone of voice, so that all could hear. When he had finished, another man from a different tribe stood forth and gave his descriptions, and so on till all the tribes had been represented. Then perhaps a man of one tribe would accuse one from another of being the cause of the death of a friend, and this would lead to a challenge and a fight.

Things would be kept going sometimes up to midnight, when quiet reigned supreme again till the daybreak cry for the dead. And if this was a strange sound when two or three tribes were gathered together, what must it have been coming from all these many peoples assembled for a bon-yi feast. It would start perhaps by one old man wailing out, and then in another direction someone would answer, then another would take up the cry, and so on, till the different crying and chanting of all the different tribes rose on the air, with the loud "swears" and threats of what they would do when the enemy was caught, relieving the wailing, monotony.

So the days went on for a month or more, and the blacks employed their time in various ways; some would hunt,

while others made weapons preparing for the great fight
which always came off at the finish. When a time for this
was fixed, all would repair to an open piece of country and
there would keep the fight going for a week or so. Of the
way this was managed, I will speak another time.

At the finish of the great fight the tribes would start off
homewards, parting the very best of friends with each other,
and carrying large supplies of bon-yi nuts with them. The
blacks of the district sought out a damp and boggy place—
soft mud and water, with perhaps a spring—and buried
their nuts there, placed in dilly-bags. Then off they went
to the coast, living there on fish and crabs for the space
of a month, when they returned, and, digging up the nuts,
had another feast, relishing them all the more no doubt because of the change to the seaside! The nuts when
unearthed would have a disagreeable, musty smell, and
would be all sprouting, but when roasted were improved
greatly. The blacks from afar would also go to the coast
if they had friends there who invited them, and they would
be glad of a corrobboree that took them seawards, if only
for the one reason that they might have a change of food.

I omitted to mention that on the way to these feasts
the blacks in those days would often catch emus in the
vicinity of the Glass House Mountains, and also get their
eggs. This my father knew from what was told him, though
none were found when he accompanied them. The feathers
the gins used to stick in their hair on state occasions.

At any time when a certain tribe had learnt a new corrobboree they would take the trouble to go even a long distance
in order to pass it on. They first sent messengers—two
men and their gins—to say they had learnt, or perhaps
made, a fresh song and dance, and were coming to teach it.
They would very likely stay a week and then go home
again, or perhaps a number of tribes would all congregate.
Father has seen about five hundred aborigines at a corrobboree on Petrie's Creek, and they came from all parts—
some from the far interior. Some of them there had never
seen a boat before, and made a great wonder of it, looking
it over and examining it everywhere.

Father knew an old Moreton Island man, a great character, head of that tribe, who was a good hand at making corrobborees. He would disappear at times to a quiet part of the island (the others saying he had gone into the ground), and when he reappeared he had a fresh song and dance to impart. The blacks would sing sometimes of an incident which had happened, and in the dance make movements to carry out the song; for instance, if they sang of rowing, they moved in the dance like an oarsman. At times if the words were decided upon, the whole tribe would suggest movements which best carried them out. One of the songs my father can sing was composed by a man at the Pine, and was based upon an incident which really happened. Father heard of the happening at the time, and afterwards learnt the corrobboree. Here is the whole story:

Three boats went out in winter time turtling from Coochimudlo Island ("Kutchi-mudlo"—red stone). It was after the advent of the whites, and the natives wanted the turtles for sale, not for their own use. In one of the boats was a man called Bobbiwinta, who was always successful in his ventures after turtles, being very good at diving, and clever in handling the creatures. Presently this boatload espied a turtle, and gave chase, and whenever Bobbiwinta got a chance he jumped overboard, diving after it. However, it was an extra big one, and he could not manage to bring it up. Those watching above saw bubbles rise to the surface, and knew he was blowing beneath the water to cause the bubbles, so that someone would come down to his assistance. Two more men jumped in at this, and catching the turtle, they managed to turn him over and bring him alongside the boat. Others in the boat got hold of the creature, and between them all it was hauled on board. Then the men in the water got in.

It was not till now, when the excitement was passed, that they found a man was missing—Bobbiwinta. All looked and could see him nowhere; men jumped overboard and searched, and the other boats coming up helped, but to no avail, he was gone. A great wailing and crying arose then, and by-and-bye a shark was seen floating quietly about, and all remaining hope went.

What seemed to strike the blacks was that they had seen
no sign of the man, not even a particle of anything—it was
such a complete disappearance. Natives are exceedingly
tender-hearted in anything like this, and they were dread-
fully cut up. Bobbiwinta's wife was in one of the boats.
All camped that night at Kanaipa (towards the south end of
Stradbroke), and next morning the beach was searched and
searched, but nothing, not even a bone, was found.

The story of Bobbiwinta's mysterious disappearance was
told from tribe to tribe; the natives seemed as though they
could never get over the sadness of it. One night the man
already mentioned belonging to the Pine was supposed to
have had a dream, in which a corrobboree came to him
descriptive of the event. The song ran as though the man
from under the water, appealed for help—pitifully, plead-
ingly, all in vain. This corrobboree was sung and danced
everywhere, and years afterwards the mere mention of it
was enough to cause tears and wailings. The words had
this meaning: "My oar is bad, my oar is bad; send me my
boat, I'm sitting here waiting," and so on, sung slowly.
Then quickly, "dulpai-i-la ngari kimmo-man" (jump over
for me friends), and so to the finish. The following is the
first portion of the song.[1]

Another good corrobboree was based on an incident
which happened when my father was a boy. This time it had

[1] Music arranged by W. A. Ogg.

reference to a young gin—Kulkarawà—who belonged to the
Brisbane or Turrbal tribe. A prisoner, a coloured man (an
Indian), Shake Brown by name, stole a boat, and making
off down the bay, took with him this Kulkarawa, without
her people's immediate knowledge or consent. The boat
was blown out to sea, and eventually the pair were washed
ashore at Noosa Head—or as the blacks called it then,
"Wantima," which meant "rising up," or "climbing up."
They got ashore all right with just a few bruises, though
the boat was broken to pieces. After rambling about for a
couple of days, they came across a camp of blacks, and these
latter took Kulkarawa from Shake Brown, saying that he
must give her up, as she was a relative of theirs; but he
might stop with them and they would feed him. So he
stayed with them a long time, and the bon-yi season coming
round, he accompanied them to the Blackall Range, joining
in the feast there.

Before the bon-yi gathering had broken up, Shake Brown,
grown tired of living the life of the blacks, left them to
make his way to Brisbane. He got on to the old Northern
Road going to Durundur, and followed it towards Brisbane.
Coming at length to a creek which runs into the North
Pine River, there, at the crossing, were a number of Turrbal
blacks, who, recognising him, knew that he was the man
who had stolen Kulkarawa. They asked what he had done
with her, and he replied that the tribe of blacks he had
fallen in with had taken her from him, and that she was
now at the bon-yi gathering with them. But this, of course,
did not satisfy the feeling for revenge that Shake Brown
had roused when he took off the young gin from her
people, and they turned on him and killed him, throwing
his body into the bed of the creek at the crossing. A day
or two later, men with a bullock dray going up to Durundur
with rations, passing that way, came across Brown's body
lying there, and they sent word to Brisbane, also christening the creek Brown's Creek, by which name it is known
to this day.

Kulkarawa, living with the Noosa blacks, fretted for her
people, and she made a song which ran as follows: "Oh,

flour, where oh where are you now that I used to eat? Oh, oh, take me back to my mother, there to be happy, and roam no more." She evidently missed the flour which her own tribe got from the white people. The Noosa blacks made a dance to suit the song, and the corrobboree was considered a grand one.

Kulkarawa, after living with the Noosa blacks for about two years, was at length brought back to her own people. Father happened to be out at the Bowen Hills, or "Barrambin" camp, with two or three black boys, looking for some cows, at the time she arrived. The strange blacks bringing her, both went and sat down at the mother's hut without speaking, and the parents of the young gin, and all her friends, started crying for joy when they saw her, keeping the cry going for some ten minutes in a chanting sort of fashion, even as they do when mourning for the dead. Then a regular talking match ensued, and Kulkarawa was told all that had happened during her absence, including the finding and murder of Shake Brown (or "Marri-dai-o" the blacks called him), on his way to Brisbane. Then she told her news, and father heard afterwards again from her own lips of her experiences.

The Noosa blacks introduced the corrobboree at the "Barrambin" camp, and so it was sung and danced all round about, spreading both near and far.

In the song of a corrobboree there were not generally many words, but these were repeated over and over again with different shades of expression. Once my father had the honour of being the subject of a corrobboree; they sang of him as he was seen sailing with a native crew through the breakers over Maroochy Bar. The incident and its danger I will mention later. The song described the way he threw the surf from his face, etc. Who knows but what it lives somewhere yet, for it was possible for a corrobboree to travel to the other end of the continent.

A Manilla man (who afterwards died at Miora, Dunwich, and whose daughter lives there now) once taught a song he knew to the Turrbal blacks. They did not understand its meaning in the least, but learnt the words and the tune, and it became a great favourite with all. My father also picked it up when a boy, and it has since soothed to sleep in turn all his children and two grandchildren. Indeed Baby Armour (the youngest of the tribe) at one time refused to hear anything else when his mother sang to him. "Sing Mi-na" (Mee-na), he would say, if she dared try to vary the monotony. Here is the song:—[2]

In learning a fresh corrobboree some of the young fellows were very smart, and, as to going to a dance, they were just as keen about it as many white boys are.

---

[2] Music arranged by W. A. Ogg.

CHAPTER IV

BEFORE going further, it is necessary for me to tell you something of a "turrwan" or "great man." Well, a "turr-wan" was one who was supposed to be able to do anything. He could fly, kill, cure, or dive into the ground, and come out again where and when he liked; he could bring or stop rain, and so on—all by means of the "kundri," a small crystal stone, which he made the gins and others believe he carried about inside him, being able to bring it up at will by a string and swallow again! But my father has seen these stones, and they were really carried in small grass "dillys," under the arm, and were attached with beeswax to a string made from opossum hair. These stones were generally obtained from deep pools, where they were dived for. The natives believed in a personality they called "Taggan" (inadvertently spelt "Targan" in Dr Roth's Bulletin, No. 5), who seemed be the spirit of the rainbow, and he it was who was respo͞sible for these stones or crystals. Wherever the end of the rainbow touched the water, there they said crystals would be found—they knew where to dive for them.

Several men possessing these stones belonged to every tribe; they were never young men, but those who had been through many fights, and had had experience. Each one was noted for something special. For instance, one was a man who could bring thunder, another could cure, and so on. Whenever there was a storm or a flood, the aborigines always blamed a "turrwan" of another tribe for sending it. Supposing the storm came from the north, it was a turrwan from a tribe in the north who was responsible, or if from the south they blamed a southern tribe.

When anyone was ill, he was taken to a "turrwan" to be cured, and the latter would make believe that he sucked a stone from the sick person's body, saying that was the cause of the mischief, another "turrwan" of another tribe having put it into him. For whenever anyone was ill, no matter under what circumstances, a stranger "turrwan" (or rather his spirit) had most surely seen the afflicted one, and thrown the "kundri" at him. And a spirit could fly, and thus do damage on a man miles away. If found out too late nothing could save him.

Aborigines do not believe they ever die a natural death; death is always caused through a "turrwan" of another tribe. When a man dies, they think that at some previous time he has been killed before without its being known to anyone even himself. Verily a strange belief. They think he was killed with the "kundri" and cut up into pieces, then put together again; afterwards dying by catching a cold, or perhaps, being killed in a fight. The man who killed him then is never blamed for the deed; "he had to die, you see!" But they blame a man from another tribe for the real cause of death, and do their best to be revenged; this causes all their big fights. They manage to decide on the murderer—how I will tell you again.

If anyone was ill in camp, and a falling star was seen, there would be a great crying and lamenting. To the natives it was a sign that the sick one was "doomed." The star was the fire-stick of the turrwan, which he dropped as he flew away after doing the mischief.

Talking of how the aborigines regard death, brings us to their burial customs. Whenever the death of an aboriginal took place, all friends and relatives would gather together and cry, each man cutting his head with a toma-hawk, or jobbing it with a spear, till the blood ran freely down his body, and the old women did the same thing with yamsticks, while the young gins cut their thighs with sharp pieces of flint stone till their legs were covered with blood. In the meantime a couple of men would get some sheets of tea-tree bark on which to place the body, and if the corpse was not to be eaten, it would be wrapped up in this bark and tied round and round with string made from the inside of wattle bark. The feet were always left exposed. Then two old men would carry the body, those mourning following behind continually crying all the time. You could hear their cry a long way off. They would go some distance till they came to a tree (generally in a gully out of sight) with a fork in the stem, six or eight feet from the ground. Here they would pause and seek about for two suitable forked sticks to match this tree, and these they fixed in the ground at a little distance from it, making the forks correspond in height with that of the tree. Next two sticks cut about seven feet long would be placed from the forked sticks to the tree fork, and from this three-cornered foundation a platform would be made with sticks put across and bound with the wattle-bark string. All being ready, the body would be lifted up on to this platform, which, without fail, would be made so that when the head was placed next the tree the feet would point always towards the west.

After this, a space in the ground underneath the body about four feet square would be cleared bare of grass, and at one side of it a small fire would be built. This was that the spirit of the dead man might come down in the night and warm himself at the fire, or cook his food. If the body was that of a man, a spear or waddy would be placed ready, so that the spirit might go hunting in the night; if a woman then a yamstick took the place of the other weapon, and her spirit could also hunt, or dig for roots. These weapons were left that the spirits might obtain food; it was not supposed that they would ever fight.

After finishing these preparations, the blacks would go away lamenting, and the body was left in peace. Then the day after burial—if it could be called burial—an old "turr-wan" would go without the knowledge of the others, back to where this platform stood erect with its burden, and stealthily he would print on the cleared ground beneath a mark like a footprint with the palm of his hand. After

his departure, two women—old women (near relatives of
the deceased, a mother and her sister if alive)—would
appear on the scene. They, of course, would see this mark,
and at once would imagine that the murderer had been
there and left his footprint behind him. Strange to say, too,
they would recognise to whom the footprint belonged!
So back they went to the others, and told them all who was
the murderer—it was generally someone they had a spite
against in another tribe—and there would be no question
or doubt.

After that no one went near the body till the flesh had
dropped off, when two old women, relatives, again went,
and, taking it down they would proceed to separate the
bones from each other. Certain of these were always reli-
giously put aside and kept—they were the skull, leg, arm,
and hip bones—while those of the ribs and back, etc., were
burnt. The bones kept were put in a dilly, and so carried
to the camp, and this dilly, with its sacred contents, accompanied the old woman relative on all her wanderings for
months afterwards. In the meantime, however, the following happened:—

At the camp a fire would be made some fifty or one
hundred yards from the huts, and all hands were called to
come and witness the performance. The bones were cleaned
and rubbed with charcoal, and one of the old gins who
discovered the murderer's footmark would sit in the middle,
the rest surrounding her, and she would take the hip bones,
and, with a stone tomahawk, would chop them, accompanying each chop with the name of some black of another tribe
sung in a chanting fashion. Now and again the bone would
crack, and each time it did this the woman happened to call
the name of the man she had told them of, who had left
his footprint behind on the cleared ground, and the rest
would exchange glances, saying he must be the guilty party.

Father has been present on these occasions, and the blacks
would always draw his attention to the unquestionableness
of the conclusion arrived at. Nothing could persuade them
that it was not fair, and should they come across the poor
unfortunate singled out his death was a certainty. Perhaps
some night he would be curled up asleep in the dark, when

suddenly he was pounced upon and put out of existence; or perhaps he would be innocently engaged at some occupation when a dark form, sneaking up behind him, would send a spear through his skull, or otherwise do the deed. A death always roused great desire for revenge, and the friends of the deceased would watch and plan in every way till at last their end was accomplished. And even when revenged like this, many a big fight took place over a death. For the tribe to which the dead man had belonged would send a challenge to the tribe of the man held responsible for the deed, by two messengers, carrying a stick marked with notches cut in it. This stick served to show that there were a great number of blacks, and that they were in earnest. The messengers suggested a place of meeting for the fight, and after staying perhaps a week would return to their friends, who would look forward to the affray.

I have spoken of the blacks as cannibals, mentioning that it was only ordinary men and women of no condition who were buried. Here is how a cannibal feast would be proceeded with: First, the body was carried about a mile away from the camp, and there placed on sheets of tea-tree bark near a fire. I may mention that it was a practice with the aboriginal to keep his body (minus the head) free from hair, by singeing himself with a torch. It was similar to the habit of shaving. Should an aboriginal be unsinged he was unkempt, as a white man is who has not shaved. He could do his own arms and hands, etc., but would ask the assistance of others for the back. The singeing over, he rubbed his body with charcoal and grease, feeling then beautifully clean and nice. So perhaps it was this habit which made the aborigines singe their dead for the last time before devouring them.

A "turrwan" would take a piece of dry sapwood from an old tree, and lighting it well by the fire would keep knocking off the red ashes till it burnt with a flame like a candle. With this he would give the body an extra good singeing all over, excepting the head, until the skin turned from black to a light brown colour. Then the body would be rubbed free of any singed particles, and turned face downwards, and three or four men, who had been solemnly standing at some distance from the others, would slowly advance, one by one, singing a certain tune, to the body. Each of these men held a shell or stone knife in his hand, and the first would start by slitting the skin open from the head down the neck, then retiring; his place would be taken by the second man, who would carry the opening on down the body, the third man down the legs, and so on till the skin was opened right to the heels, and would peel off in one whole piece.

During all this performance never a joke nor a laugh was heard, but everything was carried out with the utmost quietude and solemnity. The body would be cut up when skinned, and the whole tribe, sitting round in groups in a circle, each group possessing a fire, would watch expectantly for their share of the dainty. One can imagine how they would look forward to a feast as time advanced, and doubt- less they watched with hungry eyes as the old men divided out the flesh in pieces to each lot. Immediately on grabbing their portion, each group would roast and devour it, and in no time "all was over and done." The heart and waste parts would be buried in a hole dug alongside the fire, and this interesting hole was marked by three sticks driven into the ground, standing about a foot high, and bound round with grass rope. The hair, ears, nose, and the toes and fingers, without the bones, would be left on the skin, which was hung on two spears before a fire to dry. Sometimes it would take some time to dry, and would have to be spread out each day; then, when ready, it would be blackened with charcoal and grease. After that the skin was folded up and put into a "dilly," and so carried everywhere by a relative with the certain bones that were kept.

These remains were always carried by a woman relative, who kept them for six months or so, when she tired of the burden, or there was a fresh one ready to carry; and so a hollow tree or a cave in a rock was used as a depository. When my father came to North Pine there was a hollow gum tree near where he settled, full of skins and bones of the dead. This tree was burnt by bush fires, so, though part of it may still be seen, there is, of course, no trace of anything exciting in the way of remains. A tree used in this

way was considered sacred, or "dimmanggali," and no one
dare trifle with its contents. The remains were not just
thrown into the hollow, but must be carefully left in dillies,
and thus hung on forked sticks in the tree. A hollow tree
was looked for with a hole in the trunk several feet from
the ground (it must not open right down), or else a hollow
one with no opening would be cut out as desired. The
idea was to place the forked sticks in the earth, so that
they stood upright, with the bags hanging on them.

When my father was quite a boy he was sent once to
look for some strayed cows to York's Hollow (the present
Brisbane Exhibition Ground), which was all wild bush, and
was a great fighting ground for the blacks. At the time of
which I speak, the blacks were all camped there, and when
young "Tom" arrived on the scene he came across an old
gin crying, and going up to her asked what was the matter.
The woman replied that her "narring" (son) had been
killed and pulling an opossum-skin covering from her dilly,
displayed his skin. It made the boy start to see the hair of
the head and beard, the fingers, etc., all on the skin, and
going home he told grandfather about it. The latter offered
flour, tea, sugar, tobacco, a tomahawk, anything for the
skin; but the old woman would not part with it. Her
husband, man-like, was more willing, however, and after
some weeks turned up with a nice little new "dilly," containing four pieces of his son's skin, two from the breast
and two from the back, and this he presented to "Tom"
for his father. The scars or markings could be seen on these
pieces, which were as thick almost as a bullock's hide.

The old blackfellow took pride in giving this present,
and after so honouring "Tom," called him his son, and all
the tribe looked upon the boy as such, and from that time
forth he was considered a great man or "turrwan," no one
saying him nay, but doing anything for him and letting
him know all their secrets. It got to be known all over
the place from tribe to tribe that he had been presented
with portions of Yabba's son's skin, and so he was received
everywhere with open arms as it were, for Yabba was well
known and respected.

Women relatives of a dead person, possessing a skin, might give small portions from the back or breast to their friends of other tribes, when meeting them. The receivers would lament again over the skin when in their own camp, but having been given this, they felt quite safe about their men relations visiting the tribe of the deceased, for this giving of skin meant that the recipient was not connected in any way with suspicion.

The bodies of children were never skinned; they were placed up on trees unless in extra good condition, when they would be eaten. Very young children or babies were roasted whole, and women generally ate them. In some instances babies were killed at birth, and then eaten by the old women—for instance, if the mother died, for they blamed the child.

Cripples or deformed people were met with often enough among the aborigines, some with withered limbs, and these were invariably treated kindly, as indeed were also all old people. Aborigines would live to be seventy or eighty years of age, and if at any time they were unable to fend for themselves, their relatives took them in hand, treating them with great respect and veneration. However, at death the bodies of cripples were just shoved anyhow into hollow logs.

An aboriginal camp was always shifted immediately whenever a death took place, and the trees round about where a native had died, or where he had been eaten, would be nicked as a sign of what had taken place.

CHAPTER V

How Names were given — "Kippa"-making — Two Ceremonies — Charcoal and Grease Rubbed on Body—Feathers and Paint—Exchanging News—Huts for the Boys—Instructions given them— "Bugaram" — "Wobbalkan" — Trial of the Boys — Red Noses — "Kippa's Dress."

ABORIGINES seldom had names alike, indeed they never had in the same camp. In that respect, they surely were more original than we are with our "Tom, Dick, and Harry," handed down from father to son. When an aboriginal child was about a week old, the mother would, after consulting with her friends, give it some pet name. The child would be called by the name of some animal, fish, or bird, or perhaps by that of a hollow log, or Daylight, Sundown, Wind, Flood, Come-quick, Fetch-it, Go-away, Left-it, and so on. The name, if the child was a girl, would remain with her her life through, but a boy's name was afterwards changed.

During a man's life he would possess three different names—the first as a child, the second when he was transformed into a "kippa" (young man), and again the final when he became a grown man ("mallara") with a beard. This latter name was decided by men of his own tribe, and no special ceremony was held, but friends would consult about it during some corrobboree. No man was allowed to marry until he had come to possess his last name.

Aboriginal boys were transformed into "kippas" in this wise:—When they were a certain age, say, from twelve to fifteen years, they went through a long ceremony, at the end of which they were looked on as young men. There were two different ways in which this ceremony might be carried out; the simple or "Kurbingai" was resorted to when there were not so many boys to be put through, and these "kippas" did not take as high a rank as those who had gone through the greater ceremony, in the same way as a boy nowadays, who has been to an inferior school cannot be expected to be as capable as another who has gone to a superior one. And often a boy would go through the greater ceremony when he had already been initiated at the "Kúrbíngai."

The simpler ceremony was carried out as follows:— When a certain tribe wished to convert their boys into kippas, they first picked two men and sent them as messengers to a neighbouring tribe to see how many boys there were in that tribe ready to be initiated. Arriving in the near neighbourhood of the camp, these men paused and decorated themselves. First a mixture of charcoal and grease was rubbed all over the body from head to foot, and this produced an extra glossy blackness. The aboriginals obtained plenty of grease from iguanas, snakes, fish, dugong, etc., and it was carried about with them in their "dillies" always, rolled up in nice soft pieces of grass. They ate this grease at times, but apart from that must have used a great deal of it, for, whenever they wanted to "spruce up," they always rubbed themselves with grease and charcoal. It was evidently to them what our bath is to us— they felt nice and fresh, and dressed, as it were. The charcoal was the same as that used dry to rub on wounds, and will be referred to again. It was a very fine and soft powder, and mixed up well with the grease. When children were born, they were rubbed almost immediately with this mixture—it made them blacker than they would otherwise have been.

To return to the two messengers. After anointing themselves in this fashion they would stick either feathers or swan's down in their hair with more grease, and then, according to the tribe to which they belonged, they decorated their bodies either in red, yellow, or white designs or patterns. After that, loitering till the sun went down, and darkness was upon them, they made towards the camp, each beating two boomerangs together, and singing as they went the recognised "kippa" song; till from the camp came an answering cry, the blacks there taking up the song and beating their boomerangs, giving thus an invitation to enter. The messengers would do so, and the song was continued, and sung to a finish by the whole of the blacks assembled.

One can imagine how, after this, all would cluster round the visitors, hearing and telling the news, talking over affairs, and making arrangements for the journey to the scene of action, where the first tribe were camped. The journey was probably undertaken next day, and the messengers were accompanied by the whole tribe, with the exception of two men, who in turn went to their next neighbours; and so in the same way the news was carried from tribe to tribe, till all the people round about—men, women, and children—were finally gathered together for the ceremony.

In the meantime, the blacks at the appointed place were not idle; they would build a large bush fence or shade (some distance away from the main camp), formed in a half-circle, to be used in the daytime as a protection from the sun for the boys, and also partly to hide them. Two or three huts nicely fashioned from tea-tree bark were also put up about one hundred yards from the bush shade, and these last were the sleeping abodes for the youngsters. Though each fresh tribe as it arrived would camp just as it was for the first night—men, women, and children together —the women had afterwards to build their own huts some good distance from the boys' quarters.

The morning after the arrival of each tribe, the youngsters who were to go through the ceremony would all be taken away from the camp, so that they could not hear what their parents and others were talking about there, and when they were out of sight the fathers, mothers, and the rest would get together and suggest names for the boys. When agreed as to each name, the men would proceed to where the boys were, leaving the gins behind, and when there a "turrwan," going up to a boy, would whisper in his ear a name, then turning round, would call it out in a loud voice, the result being a regular roar and howl as the others present took up the name. After each boy had

had his turn, the men would start singing the "kippa" song;
then all proceeded back to the camp, the boys returning to
their parents.

This little preliminary over, the men of one tribe would
go to another tribe and demand the lads from their mothers,
who, of course, had to submit. These men must be of no
relation to the boys. They would take them again into
the bush, far enough away so that the gins could not see
nor hear them, and there they gave the boys their instructions. The youngsters were told that they must not, on
pain of death, ask for anything, in fact speak at all; neither
must they eat eggs, roes of fish, nor any female animal,
and they must not look up to the sky. If they desired even
to scratch themselves, they must do it, not with their hands,
but with a stick. The men maintained that if the boys
looked up the sky would fall and smother them, and the
youngsters were made to believe this. Some, I suppose,
were more credulous than others. As for the non-eating
of eggs, roes, etc., that was kept up after the ceremony—
in fact, the boys were not allowed to eat these things till
they had become grown or full-bearded men. My father
used to think the idea a good excuse for the old people to
claim the best and daintiest food.

An instrument called the "bugaram" was now brought
into use; it was a thin piece of wood a quarter of an inch
thick, cut in the shape of a paper knife, and was about
seven inches long and two inches wide; it was attached
by means of a hole at the end, to a string eight or nine feet
long, and when swung round the head would make a roaring
noise like a bull. The gins, who were never allowed to see a
"bugaram," and to whom the actual ceremony of kippa-
making was never revealed—for if they were discovered
seeking out the secrets of the mystery they would certainly
be killed—were persuaded that the "great men" actually
swallowed the boys, afterwards vomiting them up again
on the day of the "great fight," which ended the ceremonies. The unearthly roaring sounds made with the
"bugaram" were supposed by the gins to be the noise the
"great men" made in swallowing.

After sounding these instruments and displaying them for some time before the boys (of whom there might be some fifteen or twenty), the men took their charges to the bush shade prepared for their use, and here they were placed lying down on the ground in the half-circle, each boy's head on another's hip. In this position they stayed till they tired, when they might sit up with their legs crossed tailor fashion, but only provided their heads were covered with an opossum rug. For sitting up, they were out a little from the shelter of the bushes, and could otherwise see the sky. Sentries (old men) armed, of course, were posted over the boys, prepared to spear any youngster who might be tempted to look up or laugh, or otherwise break through the rules, and the rest of the men went out hunting, generally returning before sunset, when they gave the boys something to eat and drink. Father, who saw all these ceremonies when a boy, would sometimes plague the lads when the old warriors had their backs turned, tempting them to look up, etc.; the boys would grin and perhaps do so, though they dare not before the men. Children, black and white, are much the same the world over, I suppose, and of course these boys would speak if they got the chance.

When dusk came on the men would assemble in a crowd before the boys, and go through all sorts of antics—jumping, and dancing, and laughing, and mimicking everything they could think of. With their fun they tried to tempt the boys to laugh and speak or look up; and they chaffed the lads considerably, shouting that their mothers were calling and appealing to their superstitious notions. The capers some of these men would cut, and the way they walked and talked and strutted about, must indeed have been laughable. They would get hold of firesticks, and two or three would perhaps hold a poor, unfortunate companion by the shoulders and legs in mid-air, while yet another would poke a firestick at him from below, making him squirm and jump. Even that would not bring a laugh from the boys, who knew better, having been warned beforehand.

In addition to all this, the men went through with a half

song, half dance, which was kept sacred for these occasions, and was a secret from all the womenfolk. They also played with the "wobbalkan," an instrument like a "bugaram," only smaller, being a flat piece of wood one inch wide, and four inches long, which was tied fast to three feet of string, ending, unlike the "bugaram," in a handle similar to that of a stockwhip; and like a whip it was used, making a humming noise when whirled round; then, as it was cracked, the noise resembled the bark of a dog. The boys beheld these for the first time; they were too precious for everyday use; women never saw them.

With regard to the "bugaram" and "wobbalkan," the writer can say from experience that there is no exaggeration in the description of the noises made, the bark, for instance, being remarkably like that of a dog. No wonder the gins were afraid and crouched back into their huts, not knowing what the sound came from. Thirty or so of these going all at once would make a frightful row, and in the dark it would be most uncanny. The peculiar sound struck a chord of doubtful sympathy in our dog's nature one day evidently, when father twirled and cracked a "wobbalkan" to show us its nature, for the animal ran as though he never meant to come back again.

To return to the kippa-making. This trial of the boys, as it were, was kept up for a couple of hours or so; then in pairs the lads were marched off with their heads covered, two men leading the way with spears and waddies, the rest walking on either side, until they arrived at their sleeping camp, where they were put into the huts for the night, men camping all round them. Much the same sort of programme was carried out day and night for three or four weeks, at the end of which time (according to this lesser ceremony) the boys had become "kippas."

Always after "kippa-making," the blacks had a great fight. To prepare for this event, each boy was now taken in hand by a blackfellow belonging to a tribe other than his own, who would dress him up. First, it goes almost without saying, that the lads were rubbed over with charcoal and grease from head to foot; they would not be dressed other-wise. Then their noses were painted red with a fine red powder procured by rubbing two stones ("Cinnabar" sulphide of mercury) together (these stones could only be got in certain places), and when rubbed into the skin this powder produced a beautifully glossy colour. On any important occasion, the black men always had their noses red; bodies were painted in different styles, but noses were all the same. So it was with the boys.

I have described how a man in full dress would perhaps be all white down one side, and black the other, and so on, according to his tribe, and these boys were now painted in the same way. Also, like the men, they would have the various bands and belts mentioned. In addition, however, a "kippa" would wear a snake-throttle tied round his forehead, which had previously been cut out, slit open, and wound round a stick to keep it flat. This belonged especially to a "kippa's" dress, as did also a sort of tail which hung from the back of one of the forehead bands, almost to the ground. This tail ("wonggin") was made from opossum hair, twisted up on the thigh into strings. Similar strings were worn crosswise over the chest and back, forming what was called a "barbun." The rest of the dress was similar to a man's—the parrot feathers, or the swan's down, the necklace, etc.

When a boy was ready dressed, he would have a small "dilly" presented to him, which had been made especially by his mother or sister. He never owned such a thing before, though he might often play with one. The string handle would be put over his head, and the bag itself under his arm. He would carry red powder for his nose in this, also a "wobbalkan," which latter was given him that he might play with it when alone in camp. Being now "full dressed," he was allowed to speak.

CHAPTER VI

AFTER this dressing up of the boys a time was arranged for the "great fight." Two men were sent to the gins to order them with a few old men to move the whole camp to a ridge bordering an open piece of country suitable for a fight. The gins, who would start off first, had sometimes to go perhaps miles, though it was generally to a stated place, where fights were often held. There the camps were arranged about one hundred yards from each other, the different tribes having theirs faced north, south, east, or west, according to that part of the country they had come from. On entering a camp, father could tell at a glance to where any of the tribes belonged, by noticing the huts. For the doorways pointed to whence they had come, even in spite of the wind, which could be guarded against by breakwinds of bushes. However, if wet weather set in, and things could be improved by the turning round of a hut, it was done. The boys or "kippas" had their camps made some six hundred yards from the others, and when these were occupied, several old men were left in charge.

The day of the fight would come round, and the women then repaired to the open piece of ground selected, having with them each a yam-stick with a small bunch of bushes tied to the end. A yam-stick ("kalgur") is like a spear, but thicker; it is about six feet long, and tapers to a point; men never used it, but women did as a weapon, and also for digging for wild yams—the roots of a vine, something similar to sweet potatoes, which the natives were fond of.

Sticking these yam-sticks in the ground in front of them, the gins would stand awaiting the arrival of the newly-made "kippas," and the men, seeing they were ready, would start off with their charges down towards the fighting-ground.

Before starting the youngsters would be formed in a line of two deep, with two great men, each a "turrwan," taking the lead, and these men were armed with spears, waddies, and boomerangs, and were dressed as for a fight, with paint and feathers or down on their bodies, like the boys according to their tribe. Like the boys, also, each man's nose was a glossy red, but through it he wore his bone. Then he had the human hair belt—as they were great men. Each boy would be armed with two little spears, a boomerang stuck in his belt, and a small shield, also a waddy. In addition, he now wore a fringe of green bushes stuck in the belt round his waist.

When the youngsters were ready to start with the two men in the lead, the others, also dressed up, would range themselves behind, and on either side of the boys, then before moving they all gave an unearthly yell to let the gins know they were starting. Off they would then go in a half trot, half walk, singing a war song as they proceeded, and beating time with their waddies and boomerangs, keeping good time too, though they made a frightful row. When the gins saw them approaching, they also would start dancing about and singing, apparently rejoiced at the reappearance of the "kippas," who with the men would, when they came up, career gaily round the group of women three times, dancing and yelling their hardest. Then the women would snatch up their yam-sticks and point with the bushy end at whichever boy was their son or relation, and the boys would grasp the bushes, pulling them off and putting them under their arms, and all danced round again thrice as before.

The "kippas" divided into companies then, each to his own tribe, standing in line about thirty yards apart. The old warriors of the tribe stood behind them, and the women in a third rank behind again. The newly-made "kippas" would then fall upon each other, fighting with their little spears and waddies, the rest looking on, no doubt enjoying the fun, which would last some twenty minutes or so.

After that the serious business of the day began, the "kippas" drawing back, and the seasoned warriors taking their place in the play. The young fellows would generally fight in solemn earnest, burning to earn distinction; but the elders had many an ancient feud to satisfy, many a story of murder and abduction they remembered when they saw the grim line of painted warriors before them, and the fight was sure to be a fierce one, the excitement growing as the blows increased. What a gruesome sight it must have been! Spears would fly fast, waddies sound with a crash against thick skulls, and blood would flow freely. Also the women from outside, and the men who were too old to join in, would hurl sticks, stones, and curses in amongst the fighters, who chased and fought each other, keeping on the go for about an hour. All the time the young fellows looked on and learnt, probably thinking of the time when they would be able to do as well or better, as is the way with young people. Becoming exhausted at the end of a certain time, the warriors would take a well-earned rest, each side squatting down on the ground some two hundred yards apart.

It was remarkable to notice what little real harm was done after all this fierce excitement, though the wounds in some cases seemed ghastly enough. Should any one be killed, that ended hostilities for the time. Otherwise, it would not be long before two men of one side would jump up, and frantically running half-way across to the others, they would brandish and wave their spears in a most threatening manner, as though to say, "Come along, you black-hearted villains, and just see what you will get!" The "black-hearted villains" weren't to be frightened, however, and to show their contempt for any such threat, and that they would not be behind-hand in any fight, they were soon on their feet going through exactly the same sort of antics themselves, as the others retreated. Back would come the other two to threaten again, and so on turn about, till at last all these threats ended in a challenge from four or five of one side to the same number on the other side for a single-handed fight, man to man. The challenge was, of course, accepted, and the men then got into position twenty or thirty yards apart, and began to throw spears and waddies at each other. Father says it was just wonderful to see how the weapons were dodged; there perhaps would scarcely be a wound inflicted, even though things would be kept going for half-an-hour or so.

When this handful of blacks had played out their little part of the play, a "turrwan" of one tribe would rise up majestically and challenge a man of another tribe at whose door he laid the blame of the death of a relative. These two would then go at it, swearing at one another, fighting, too, at close quarters, which the others had not done. They would both hold a stone knife in their teeth, not using it at first, but doing their best to strike each other with waddies, protecting themselves with shields. The shields used when waddies were the weapons in use were stouter and thicker than those used as a protection from spears.

Sometimes one man would receive a blow on the head, sometimes on the leg, and the moment a blow found its way home thus shields and waddies were dropped at once, and the two men would close in, using the left arm and hand to clutch the enemy, while with the stone knife, now in the right hand, they would stab and hack at each other, cutting great gashes in the shoulders and back or thighs of the opponent. They dared not cut the breast, nor indeed any front part of the body; if those looking on saw this done they would interfere immediately and kill the offender. The onlookers also took upon themselves to separate the two if they thought one was receiving more than his due share, and the friends of the most severely wounded promptly gave the other a few more gashes to make things equal!— the victor being bound to stand quietly and submit to this being done. They fought very fiercely, these men; some of the gashes were terrible. Father has seen dozens on their backs, and sometimes extra deep ones on their thighs. To heal the wounds, they used charcoal powder, and sometimes just wood ashes pounded down.

The aborigines never laid up with their wounds, though one wonders at it. Father has seen in a fight the skin of the head cut right through to the skull with a waddy. These deep cuts on the head were treated in the same way as those on the body—just charcoal put in them, and the wounds seemed to recover in a few weeks' time. It would without doubt kill a white man to be treated in the same way.

This fighting was kept up on the whole for about five hours in the fore part of the day. After these champions had had their "go," other fighting men would follow, and so on. When all was ended, everybody would retire to camp, the "kippas" who were thus being initiated into the art of warfare, being escorted to their quarters by a dozen men. The rest of the day was employed in hunting for food, and at night the boys would play with the "wob-balkan" and watch the men dance, etc. This was not for one day only, but for about a week the fight went on, at the end of which time the "kippas" were supposed to be fighting men, able to fight their own battles. All through, though, they were kept away from their mothers, and for three months or so after this they did not return to the women's camp, but would hunt and camp with the elder men, keeping more or less to their dress meanwhile.

After the great fight was over the "kippas" would have their noses pierced, and their bodies ornamented with scars, the latter being done in different ways, according to the tribe to which they belonged. The natives here did not tattoo, but marked their bodies. The nose-piercing and body-marking was generally done in dull, damp weather, if possible, the idea being that it would not hurt so much then. And when all was over, the visiting tribes would depart to journey homewards, taking each with them their own "kippas," or young men, the latter travelling apart from the others.

The greater ceremony of kippa-making was carried out in the following fashion, and what is known as the "bora" ceremony of other tribes is not unlike it. First a circle—called "bul" by the Brisbane blacks, and "tur" by the Bribie Island tribe—was formed in the ground, very like a

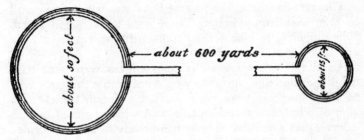

circus ring, the earth being dug from the centre with sharp
sticks and stone tomahawks, and carried to the outside on
small sheets of bark to form a mound or edging round the
ring about two feet high. The circle itself was about forty
or fifty feet across, and was quite round. Then a road five
feet wide was made from the circle, running about six
hundred yards to another smaller circle, just the same, but
half the size. All along both sides of the roadway were
placed peculiar images in clay or grass, two or three feet
high, of kangaroos, opossums, native bears, emus, turtles,
snakes, fish, and nearly all sorts of animals, as well as of
men. Images were also cut in the bark of trees which grew
along the roadway.

Now a straight wattle tree was sought for, measuring
from eight to nine inches through the trunk, and the blacks
would grub all round this tree three feet or so away from
the stem, cutting the roots through, and so falling it. This
was easily done, as the wattle has no tap-root, and the
other roots are all spread out near the surface. They were
nice and flat these roots, and the blacks would trim them
up a little, and also top the tree, leaving the barrel about
eleven feet in length. Then the whole thing would be lifted
and carried to the smaller circle, where in the centre a hole
three feet deep had been dug ready to receive it. The
stem would be well rammed into this hole, and the roots
being uppermost, they would be laced with wattle bark, so
making a sort of network, beautifully done, resembling
somewhat the bottom of a large cane chair; and this formed
a platform six feet across. This stump or platform the
natives called "kakka," meaning "something wonderful."

The remains of a "kippa-ring," as we call it, may still be seen near Humpybong. There used to be one at North Pine, opposite to where the blacksmith's shop now stands, and another at Samford.

As in the lesser ceremony, messengers were sent to a neighbouring tribe, and they would act in just the same way as then, but this time, they carried a notched stick as a sign of what was to take place, and which pointed out, as it were, that a number of boys were ready to be transformed into "kippas." The stick on being presented to a "turrwan," meant an invitation for the tribe to come and bring along their boys.

While this was going on the blacks at the ring were busy fixing it up for the ceremony, and making their camps two hundred yards away. Sometimes two or three weeks would pass before all the different tribes rolled up, and every batch of fresh arrivals fell to like a lot of busy ants or bees, and made their own huts. The time, too, was employed in hunting for food, and so it passed till the tribes had all assembled. Then the boys would be taken away, and in their absence names were suggested for them, also they had to listen to the instructions about speaking and eating, etc.

This finished, the youngsters were packed off to the large ring, and there they were placed inside, lying down all round the ring, each boy's head on another's hip—there would be probably forty or fifty of them. The gins would go into the circle, and dance and sing the "kippa" song for about half-an-hour, the men doing the same on the outside. Then the boys were made to sit up in twos all round on the mound, a space between each pair, their legs inside the ring, and a gin standing outside behind each boy—a mother, sister, or some other relation. The singing would go on all the time, and the boys must never look up at the sky, but simply straight ahead.

Several men carrying boomerangs would now enter the ring, and a man going up to each boy would point at him with the boomerang. The boy was supposed to catch hold of the end, and at the moment that he did so a gin behind clutched him by the hair of the head, and lifted him up.

Then, still holding on, the lads would follow the men across the ring, the gins behind, till they came to where the roadway started out to the smaller circle. Here the women were ordered back by the old warriors, and they remained in the larger ring dancing and singing till the boys returned. They were never allowed to go up this roadway, nor might they see the "kakka" on pain of death.

The boys were shown the images lining both sides of the way, the men drawing their attention to them with the continual cry—"Kor-é, kor-é, kor-é" ("Kor-é," with the e accented and sounded as an a, means "wonder"). Thus they would reach the smaller circle, where in the centre the "kakka" stood supreme, and on this platform five or six blacks would be found standing, freshly blackened and all dressed up. These gentlemen were the great men of the day—they were all "turrwans," and when the boys appeared before them each man would pull a "kundri" stone from his mouth, showing it to the boys as much as to say, "Look at this wonder." They would also point out the "kakka" as something marvellous. The boys from their babyhood had been taught to look on the "kundri" and its possessor with awe, and though they had never seen a "kakka" before, they had heard mysteriously of its wonders.

CHAPTER VII

"Fireworks Display"—Warning the Women—Secret Corrobboree —"Look at this Wonder"—Destroying the "Kakka"—How Noses were Pierced — Site of "Kippa-rings" — Raised Scars — Inter-tribal Exchange of Weapons, etc.—Removing Left Little Finger—Fishing or Coast Women.

WHEN the boys had been shown all there was to be seen in the smaller circle, they were taken again to the larger one, and there placed as before, with the men and women all round outside dancing and singing, some quite close, and others fifty yards or so away from the ring. Then down the roadway would come the warriors from the "kakka" and, going up to each boy, a man would whisper in his ear the name formerly agreed on; then out this name would be shouted, and the roaring and singing and dancing which followed continued for the space of half-an-hour, when it gradually ceased and died down. After that the gins and a few old men were left in charge, while the others went out hunting, to return with food, a supply of which they gave to the boys.

At night, the lads, still in twos round the ring, were treated to a "fireworks" display. "Kundri" men would come running down the roadway to the big ring, with small firesticks in either hand, and these they would shake and brandish in front of the boys as they ran round the ring, making a great noise all the time. The men and women on the outside added to the row by singing and dancing, and they also carried firesticks, twisting them into all shapes and forms with their movements.

It was a sight worth seeing. Let us in fancy look at it in the solitude of the bush. The dark forms ever on the move, the fire-sticks twisted into fantastic shapes and hoops of fire, lighting up the little sober faces of the boys as they sat round the ring watching the performance. And the white boy looking on at it all. What were his thoughts of it? To him it was a common occurrence; but to us, could we but see it now, it would, indeed, be a strange and memorable scene. And as we look the men in the ring, after running till they surely tire, stand and brandish their sticks for the last time, then cast them into the centre of the ring, where they blaze up, illuminating the night. This would end the performance, and the "kippas" were marched to the special camp prepared for them away from the others.

The next morning, after the cry for the dead and the early meal, etc., the "kippas" were once more taken to the ring and placed there in the old position with the men and women singing round them as usual. In the bush, fifty yards away, dark forms were hidden, two on either side of the ring. These were some of the great men, and presently one lot would start whistling as a sort of warning of what they meant to do, and, being answered by their companions of the opposite side, they would all then go forward with a dance and song to where the gins were, and start chasing the latter, calling them to be off and camp by themselves, taking also their belongings. These poor creatures were threatened with instant death if they disobeyed, or came near and dared to look at anything about the ring. If black women are as curious as we are supposed to be, this was hard lines! Let us hope they are not.

After the women had gone out of sight and hearing, the young men, or "kippas," were taken to their quarters, and there fully dressed in the style described before. The men also dressed in their fighting dress, and when ready they marshalled the boys back to the ring. The youngsters then were shown the "bugaram" and the "wobbalkan," the men swinging the former and making it sound, also playing with the latter, and instructing the boys how to use it. In between, too, they would sing and dance the secret corrobboree that the women must never hear nor see.

Each boy would now be presented with his "dilly," and the "wobbalkan" to put in it. Afterwards the men began to pick quarrels with each other, calling names, and wrestling, even throwing one another to the ground; and this was all for the boys' benefit, that they might be tempted to speak. They were tempted in every way, spoken to, laughed at, jeered at—all as in the lesser ceremony.

The second night the boys were taken up the roadway, and shown the wonders there by firelight this time. Their guides would carry lighted torches, and all along on both sides bright fires burned, casting their radiance on the fantastic figures which lined the way, and thus stood out in strange relief. They went on thus to the smaller circle, and there the "kakka" came in for a share of attention.

This sort of thing went on day and night for two or three weeks, sometimes longer; then a time was fixed for the "great fight." But before that event came off, the boys would be one day taken from the big ring along the roadway to the smaller one, where they were made to stand facing the "kakka" with the great men thereon. Hardly would they be so placed when half-a-dozen blacks would come with a roar and a rush, and, grabbing hold of the "kakka," would shake it with a will, the warriors on top pulling the "kundri" from their mouths, and crying, "Look at this wonder." Still the men went on shaking until the "kakka" became quite loose, when they would lift it out of the hole (the warriors still on top), and lay it down on the ground. The boys looking on would now have their heads covered with opossum rugs, so that they could not see what was done, and the "kakka" was chopped into little pieces and scattered here and there.

This over the boys were taken to their camp and allowed to speak. Perchance before the fight they had their noses pierced, or perhaps it was after. Placed again round the large ring, they sat while a "turrwan" went one behind and one in front of each boy. The man in front would have long sharp nails, and with these he pinched through the soft part of the boy's nose; that done, he thrust a small sharp spear through the opening, after which a piece of stick formed for the purpose three inches in length was put in, and this was kept there till the nose healed. Every day during the healing period water was poured on, and the stick was turned round. Then afterwards a round ball of bees' wax was kept in the hole for about a month in order that it might be kept open.

All the time the boring of the nose was going forward, the "turrwan" at the back would keep beating with his open hands the boys' ears, and making a roaring noise. This was supposed to prevent the youngster from feeling pain! The "kippas" would remain in full dress during all this time, and when the nose-piercing was over, all proceeded towards where the gins were camped, but the "kippas" still kept from their women friends, having their camp apart as usual.

Each night now the young fellows would play with the "wobbalkan," making it hum and bark like a dog, and the men made the "bugaram" roar, so that the gins in their camps, hearing these noises, grew afraid, and kept well inside their huts, thinking no doubt that the poor boys were being swallowed.

For "kippa" making the aborigines did not each time make fresh rings, but there were certain ones that different blacks always used, and these they would fix up. For instance, the natives coming from the direction of Ipswich, Cressbrook, Mount Brisbane (inland blacks) would, with the Brisbane tribe, generally use the ring at Samford, while the Logan, Amity Point, North Pine, Moreton and Bribie Islands blacks (coast tribes) had their ring at North Pine. Others again from further north, such as the Maroochy, Noosa, Kilcoy, Durundur, and Barambah blacks would use the Humpybong ring. But it depended on which tribe had the most boys ready for the ceremony, and did the inviting. If a coast tribe invited, then all the others went to the ring that tribe would naturally use, and so on.

In the same way, there was generally a certain picked place for holding the fight after "kippa" making. The inland tribes went from the Samford ring to the site of the Roma Street Railway Station in Brisbane, and the coast tribes went either to Eagle Farm or to what used to be known as York's Hollow, where the Exhibition now is.

The great fight I have already described, and when that was over the "kippas" had their various ornaments taken off and put in a dilly, and these were kept for another occasion for fresh boys. Boys who had gone through the "kippa" ceremony thought a great deal of themselves. Father was often amused at the way in which a small boy —a "kippa" though—would lord it over a much bigger one who was not yet a "kippa." He would tweak the other's ear, pull his hair, and otherwise treat him disrespectfully, and the big chap would be bound to submit as quite an inferior. Or the little fellow would chase the other as hard as he could go, his string tail flying out behind, and it was all quite right! How would white boys like this?

It was the duty of the "kippas" to leave no trace behind of the "bugaram" or the "wobbalkan." They were supposed to burn these instruments when finished with, so that the gins might not see them.

At the end the boys were marked with body scars, on the back, the breast, and on the shoulders and arms, in patterns according to the tribe to which they belonged. These marks were made with sharp flint stones or shells, and had fine charcoal powder rubbed into them. It was remarkable how the scars became raised after a short time; a white man's skin is not the same. Father saw "Duramboi" (Davis, the convict) after he had lived seventeen years with the blacks, and his body was marked, but the scars were flat, not raised as those of the blacks.

When all the ceremonies were over the blacks would still linger, hunting by day and having their corrobborees by night, and then—as always after any gathering, even a fight—they would in the end part well pleased with each other, and excellent friends. But before leaving any common meeting ground, the aborigines always exchanged possessions. For instance, the inland blacks would give weapons, opossum rugs, dogs, etc., to the coast blacks for dillies made of rushes that grew only on the coast, shells for ornaments, and reed necklaces. It was a great practice, this intertribal exchange of various articles, and accounts for the way in which some weapon, for instance, or perhaps a dilly bag, might be found far from its original home, having gradually made its way after many years to scenes and pastures new. So when some instrument was found in the possession of a certain tribe, it did not by any means follow that they had originally made that instrument.

I may mention here that the aborigines, men and women, all had the same body markings—that is, in the same tribe, for all different tribes had different patterns. Each individual received them as children; little boys or girls, when old enough, might be taken at any time and marked, without any ceremony, by old men (never women) of the tribe. However, boys could never receive their shoulder marks till they had come to the "kippa stage."

Another practice was that of removing the left little finger of all young girls. This was to show that they were fishing or coast women. When nine or ten years of age, a little girl would have her finger performed on by her mother, or some old woman, in this way. The gin would hunt round for some strong spider's web, and get the string from this, or, failing that, she obtained some long hair from a man's head (women's hair was always short), and then with this she would bind round and round the little finger on the first joint as tightly as possible. In time the string would cut into the joint and the finger would swell up, the end mortifying. At this stage the child was taken to an ant-bed, and there the woman sat patiently holding the finger for some hours, allowing the ants to get at it (but preventing them from going up the arm), till such time as they had eaten into the joint, and so caused the end to come off easily. Afterwards the skin grew over the bone.

This was a regular practice with the blacks living on the coast; the inland people never did it. It was not done out of any hardness towards the children, but as a matter of course. Indeed, the aborigines were very fond of and kind to their children, and were continually "skylarking" with them. They would dress the little pickaninnies up, even painting them, and then get them to dance and go through with mimic corrobborees, etc., laughing and thinking it a great joke when the children responded. They also took a lot of trouble and interest in the way of teaching them to swim, climb, or use weapons of all sorts.

CHAPTER VIII

Mourning for the Dead—Red, White, and Yellow Colouring—No Marriage Ceremony—Strict Marriage Laws—Exchange of Brides —Mother-in-Law—Three or Four Wives—Blackfellows' Dogs—Bat Made the Men and Night-Hawk the Women—Thrush which Warned the Blacks—Dreams—Moon and Sun—Lightning—Cures for Illness —Pock Marks—Dugong Oil.

In contrast to white people, the aborigines wore red when mourning for their dead. Black being their natural colour, it would not of course express anything as it does with us. Red was put on all over the body, even the face, and then for deep mourning (for instance, if the deceased were a brother or sister) splashes of white clay relieved the monotony here and there. It was only the old people who troubled to mourn thus, however; and the old gins in addition wore feathers coloured red, stuck in little bunches here and there in the hair with bees' wax. (The bees' wax, which was carried about in dillies, would be warmed and put on the feathers, and then quickly, ere it hardened, the little bunches would be stuck in the hair—the women helping one another.) The close friends and relatives would remain so adorned for a month or two, but other old people, putting on mourning, would discard it again in a few days' time.

The red colouring used for mourning was not the same as that used for reddening noses. They were both got from stones, but the latter was more uncommon, and the Turrbal tribe could only obtain it by barter with inland blacks. In both instances, two stones were rubbed together, and the powder coming from them just rubbed into the skin, but the mourning colour was a dull red, while the other was beautifully bright and glossy. Red colouring was called "kutchi," which, however, was the name given to any paint.

When putting on white clay ("banda") the natives would wet a piece well with their tongue, and so plaster it on. The yellow colouring, or "purgunpallam," used at other times (never for mourning) was obtained from a toadstool (*Polysaccum olivaceum*) which grew, strange to say, always beside a big ant's nest. My father says to his knowledge they never grew anywhere else. They were big and round, these toadstools, and were full of a yellow powder which the blacks rubbed dry into their skins. White toadstools of the same shape are common enough.

For a woman about to become a wife, there was no painting up of the body, neither was there any particular ceremony or rejoicing of any kind. The aborigines, however, were most strict and particular with regard to their marriage laws—indeed, they would not dream of allowing things we do; for instance, a man might not even marry any of his former wife's relations, and those we call cousins and second cousins were quite out of the question. Marriages were generally arranged without the contracting parties having any say whatever in the matter, and a man would often so get a wife from a tribe other than his own, though this wasn't necessary.

At corrobborees the different tribes exchanged their goods, such as shields, spears, nets, etc., and often they made use of the same occasion to give and take wives. It was always a correct thing—indeed a general rule—for a "turrwan" of one tribe to give his daughter to the son of a great man of another, and then the son's father gave his daughter back for the other's son. Or else they exchanged sisters. Or perhaps in the corrobboree there would be a man who danced and joked especially well; this man would take the fancy of a "turrwan" in an opposite tribe, and so he would generously present the capable young fellow with his daughter, or if he had none, his sister or next relation. Then the young man who had gained such a prize would give back his sister to the old man's son, and so on, for it was always give and take.

If there was a widower in the camp, and the others thought him deserving of a wife, or if there was a man

unmarried and deserving, the blacks would consult together
to choose a wife for him without his knowledge. Then,
if all relations agreed, the gin would be told by her friends
who was to be her husband, and the man would be told
in the same way whom he had to take for his wife.

In spite of all this arranging, two young people would
sometimes make use of their own fancy, and run away together. There was such a thing as that inconvenient passion
called love amongst the aborigines, I suppose. These two
young unfortunates would be followed and brought back
after a time, and straightway a fight was arranged between
their respective tribes. If his friends should win, he was
allowed to keep her, but, should her party have the better
of it—then, oh, injustice!—she was beaten and cut about
most frightfully, almost killed, and the pair were separated,
she being sent back to her parents. Woman—poor woman
—is there no justice for you anywhere?

Sometimes when these exchanges were being made, a
little girl—a mere baby—of five or six years, might be given
to a man of thirty or forty. However, she would stay with
her parents until she was about fourteen years old. Then
one day a hut would be made and a fire built in it, and
the blackfellow would go alone into the hut, and sit beside
the fire, the mother and father would bring the girl to him,
leave her alongside, and then walk away without speaking
a word. Ever afterwards the mother must shun her son-
in-law, and if she saw him she covered her face. She,
however, might speak to her daughter. A mother-in-law
was called "bugo-i," and she always avoided her son-in-law
thus. Even with the blacks you see a son and mother-in-
law was not supposed to "hit it," indeed with them it was
a law that there should be no communication whatever
between the two. According to some people, this law with
us would save trouble!

Different tribes would be related one to the other all over
the place by these intermarriages, and father always found
some woman from another tribe in every fresh one he came
across. The woman belonged to her husband's tribe then,
and children were always spoken of as their father's son or

daughter, not their mother's. And if a man died and left a wife and family, his brother was supposed to take the widow; if there were no brother, however, then the next male relation of the deceased was responsible. Failing any relation, the widow was given to a man the tribe thought should have a wife, or perhaps if she and some man had a fancy for one another, and the friends did not object, their marriage was allowed.

A great man, or "turrwan," might have two or three, or even four, wives. In such a case he would take one out hunting when he went, leaving perhaps two to seek for roots and prepare them against his return. Then next day a different one would accompany him, and so on. These wives all lived happily enough together—the poor savages knew no greater happiness apparently, than to serve their lord and master. They were useful in carrying the burdens from one place to another. A woman, because she was a woman, always carried the heaviest load. A man took his tomahawk, his spear, and waddy, and that sort of thing; a woman humped along the weighty kangaroo and 'possum skin coverings, the dillies with eatables, and sometimes also a heavy little piece of goods in the form of a child. At times, too, she would carry tea-tree bark on her back for the humpies, while ever and anon as they travelled along the men enjoyed themselves hunting and looking for "sugar-bags" (native bees' nests), etc.

Sometimes old men (never young ones) would carry puppies too young to walk, but it was mostly women who did this also. Aborigines were "awful fond" of their dogs —they were the only pets they had. They would never by any chance kill a puppy, but would keep every one, and this, no doubt, accounted for the poor condition of these followers. Father says that even in old days they were a mangy-looking lot. Probably they did not get sufficient food, but had to live on the scraps and bones thrown to them. However, a gin would nurse a puppy just as care- fully as any baby; all dogs would sleep with their owners, and they would drink from the same vessel. Children—in spite of their parents' fondness for them—if they dared ill-use a dog, would call down torrents of abuse upon their little black selves, and they would be smacked soundly. Dogs would be taught to hunt; they were always native dogs in the old times, but those of the white man soon got amongst them, and my father knew one blackfellow who carried a domestic cat about with him.

The aborigines used always to declare that the "billing" (what we know as the small house bat) made all their menfolk, and the "wamankan" (night-hawk) made the women. They did not eat either of these, but might catch and kill them. If the men got hold of a "wamankan" they would bring it into camp, and holding it up would chaff the women about it. They also chased the "fair sex" all over the place with this hawk, and with it plagued the life out of them in every conceivable way. For instance, they rolled it up in bark as though it were a dead body ready for burial, and putting it over their shoulder strutted about so. But supposing the women got possession of a "billing," then their turn came, and the men were laughed at and taunted and chased. This kind of thing would generally start with jokes and yells and screams of laughter, but sometimes it ended pretty seriously in big fights and squabbles. Great cuts and gashes would then be the result, the women fighting just as viciously as the men.

A bird, the piping shrike-thrush (*Collyricincla Harmonica, Latham*), which the blacks christened "mirram," was always watched when it came near a camp, and it was spoken to and asked questions about certain things. The blacks noticed whether it called out in reply or not, and they took warning and acted accordingly. If the bird were silent all was well. Supposing, however, in spite of its silence something went wrong after all, then instead of losing faith in the bird they blamed themselves for not having asked it the correct question.

On one occasion, when my father returned from the Turon diggings in 1851, he showed the blacks some gold dust, and they informed him they knew where there was lots of it. So they took him to Samford to a creek in the scrub there, and sure enough there was plenty "yellow" showing, but the white boy saw at once it was only mica. However, they camped for the night there in the scrub.

Samford was all wild bush then. As darkness was descending a bird (a "mirram") came and settled on a branch above their heads, and called out. An old blackfellow got up and spoke to it, asking if there were any strange blacks in the neighbourhood. The bird did not answer but flew away, so the natives felt safe. However, later on, a sound like something heavy hitting against a hollow tree broke the stillness. The sound was rather peculiar: to this day my father says he can hear it in fancy in the quietude of the scrub. He suggested that it was a tree falling; but his dark companions would not hear of this, and began to lament and blame themselves that they had not spoken properly to the "mirram." It certainly would have answered if they only had asked the right question! They said the sound was a strange blackfellow knocking, and though it did not occur again, nothing quietened them, and one man sat up all night watching. All to no purpose though, for nothing happened. It was on the way back to Brisbane from this trip next day that the blacks showed father the "kippa" ring at Samford.

If an aboriginal dreamt anything special at any time, he would always repeat the dream to his companions, and they would take it seriously. A dream was called "pai-abun," and during one a man would often see a person who had died, and imagine that he was told to do this or that— probably kill some one. Also, if he saw anything dreadful in his dream he became exceedingly afraid, and would be convinced that the awful things he saw were really to happen. Again, if the moon or sun became eclipsed, it was a sure sign to the natives of the death of some one. Lightning, too, frightened them, and they always hid their spears and tomahawks during a storm. Spears when not in use were left standing upright against the doorway of a hut, and father says that as a storm came up you would see the natives taking these and their tomahawks and laying them down on the ground under tufts of grass. Later on when they had learnt the white man's habit of smoking they always took their pipes from their mouths when a storm was raging.

The aborigines had peculiar habits with regard to illnesses. The "kundri"—the crystal stone before spoken of —was held to be the cause of pretty well everything in that way. A great man possessing one of these stones was always to the fore. At corrobborees he would come forward, and, wetting his breast with his hand, would shake himself and then, with a noise like a frog or a crow, would pull forth the string, with stone attached, from his mouth, amidst a great cry and wonder from the onlookers. Father has seen one of these men kneeling and sucking a sick man's body on the part where the pain was, then, rising after a time, pull the "kundri" from his mouth, saying he had sucked it from the sufferer's body. There is said to be power in belief, and it would seem so, for the sick man believing his enemy's stone was removed would feel better and probably recover. The "turrwan" would be cute enough not to do this if he thought the case hopeless.

Another idea was, when any one was ill, to tie 'possum hair string round the invalid's ankles and wrists. Father has seen a man far gone in consumption, with hair tied on thus, and also round and round his body; an old gin sitting about a yard off had hold of the end of the body string, and with both hands she dipped it into some water she had ready in a "pikki" (pot made from bark, or the flower-leaf of the palm), and from the water to her mouth. Constantly she did this, and so urgently, that her gums bled freely with the rubbing, and the water became thick with blood she expectorated into it. The sick man seeing this believed the woman had taken bad blood from his body. It was a habit to let out blood in cases of swelling and bruises.

The natives cured headaches in the following fashion:— Two big flat stones were procured; these were made very hot, and then one would be placed on the ground with an opossum rug over it. On this the patient would lay his head, and the other stone would be put on top of that again with another piece of rug in between to prevent burning. There the man would lie grinning for some time, until the great heat took the headache away. Two other cures they had for headaches—one was to dive under water, and stop there as long as possible, and the other was a very hard knock on the head with a waddy. The latter my father has given them many a time at their request.

Often for pains such as toothache the blacks would burn with a fire-stick—(for instance, on the cheek)—their idea must have been that one pain would cure another. Flesh wounds would be washed and scraped with a stick till they ceased to bleed, then, as mentioned, fine charcoal powder or ashes would be put on them—sometimes even only ordinary dirt. It was wonderful how splendidly they healed up under this treatment. The blacks were always very good to their sick, but they had their own ideas of kindness. If at any time a man became unconscious, to make him recover, his ears would be banged and shouted into. So long as he could hear he was thought to be better.

When my father first came to North Pine pock marks were very strong on some of the old men; they explained to him how the sickness had come amongst them long before the time of the white people, killing off numbers of their comrades. Pock marks they called "nuram-nuram," the same name as that given to any wart. (From this Neurum Neurum Creek, near Caboolture, gets its name.) The scourge itself was "bugaram," and the latter was what the instrument similar to the "wobbalkan" was called. There was probably some connection, in that they were both awe-inspiring in their way. The "bugaram," which the women never saw, was no common everyday instrument, and was looked on with wonder, while small-pox was something to be spoken of in a whisper and with bated breath. After the advent of the whites, consumption took hold of the race, and where before natives lived to a good old age, one would hardly see any old people—their remarkable freedom from sickness seemed to disappear.

The natives were great believers in the curative properties of the dugong. Father has seen sick blacks, unable to walk, apparently in consumption, carried carefully to the mouth of the Brisbane River, and there put into canoes and taken across to Fisherman's Island, to where dugong were being caught. There they would live for some time on the flesh of the dugong, and the oil would be rubbed all over their bodies, and in the end they would return quite strong and well. In the early days of Brisbane, my father mentioned how he had seen this for himself to Dr Hobbs, who was greatly interested, and afterwards recommended the use of dugong oil as a remedy similar to cod-liver oil, and this is how it came to be first used medicinally in Queensland.

If all the old aboriginals of Brisbane could come to life again they would not recognize their country—the country we have stolen from them. If they went hunting in the forests, where would be their spoil?—where, indeed, would they find the forests to hunt in? Oh! how they must have loved those forests—their forests; and could they return now, their cry would surely be as despairing as that of "Œnone," as Tennyson paints her lamenting the destruction of "my tallest pines, my tall dark pines, that plumed the craggy ledge." Never, never more would she see "the morning mist sweep through them," and never more shall one of Australia's dark children see Brisbane as God made it. "God made the country, man made the town." As the black hunted careless and free in those days long gone, little dreamed he of what his brother-white would do— little dreamed there was a brother-white.

The waters even have changed since those times. Dugong used to be very plentiful then, when there was nothing much in the way of disturbances. The blacks would catch them at Fisherman's Island, at St Helena, at a place near Dunwich they called "Gumpi," at Bribie Passage, and at the mouth of the Pine River.

CHAPTER IX

Food—How It was Obtained—Catching and Cooking Dugong—An Incident at Amity Point—Porpoises Never Killed; but Regarded as Friends—They Helped to Catch Fish—Sea Mullet and Other Fish—Fishing Methods—Eels—Crabs—Oysters and Mussels—Cobra.

DUGONG.—For catching dugong the blacks used strong nets made from the inside bark of a scrub vine (*Malaisia tortuoso*), which they called "nannam." This bark is exceedingly strong; indeed, pulling at it one cannot but be struck with its strength. To get the bark the blacks would cut the vine in lengths, and then beat these well with sticks until it peeled off easily with the teeth. This they would then soak in water for several days, at the end of which time the rough outer bark would be thrown away, while with their thumb nails the men would split the inner bark into fibre. This fibre was dried and then twisted on their thighs into excellent string, which was very useful in many ways. On account of its strength it was suitable for the "bugaram" and the "wobbalkan." These instruments were twirled round with great force, and the string attached would indeed need to be strong. Then, also, nets for large game or dugong needed great strength. Those for the latter were formed of big meshes, and were sewn up in the shape of huge pockets; they were hand nets, and were finished off at the top by two pieces of stick ending in a handle. When making nets the natives used to measure to get the correct size of mesh.

Dugong were only to be caught at certain seasons, and as the time approached the blacks would be on the lookout. Seeing little bits of seaweed floating on the water, they knew it was time to expect what they awaited, for this seaweed spoke to them as it were, with the message that the dugong were coming. (Feeding on seaweed as they came along, they naturally broke off little bits.) Two or three men would, therefore, climb tall trees near at hand, and keep watch, for with the tide the dugong often came in, making towards the banks near the shore, where they got more seaweed. Coming up to make their peculiar blowing sound as they swam in, the creatures would, of course, expose themselves to the gaze of the watchers on the trees, who would at once let their companions know without a word or sound by signalling and pointing out the direction with their hands. Then two blacks would get into a canoe and paddle quietly out, so as to get behind the dugong, other nine or ten would go with their large hand-nets out into the water up to their necks, on the banks, and they would stand there all in line, each holding an end of the other's net, as well as his own, so making a regular wall. Then, when the creatures came up to blow again near this trap, the men in the canoe would hit the water with sticks and make a great noise, so frightening their prey towards the nets. When one got into the pocket of a net, the men would all help and hold on, till the creature rolled itself round and round, and so got drowned. Sometimes they would catch an old and a young dugong in different nets, and sometimes just one huge chap, who would be too strong to hold, and would have to be let go. However, in this case next day they would probably find him floating drowned, rolled up in the net.

When a dugong or "yangon" (yung-un) was pulled ashore it would be rolled up on to dry ground. The aborigines had a peculiar superstition that should the gins see a dugong before it was cut up it would not be fat—would not, in fact, be in good condition. The gins knew to keep out of the way when one was captured. Another idea was that a twig or piece of grass must be put at once in each earhole, or else the creature would be no good. Then a large fire was made, and the dugong rolled into it, and more fire placed on top, till the carcass was half-cooked. Then head and tail were cut off, the back opened down the middle, and the blubber and flesh taken from the ribs in a large flake. The whole carcass would be cut up after that, and divided out, the gins, who were then allowed to come along with their pickaninnies, getting their share, and a rare old feast was indulged in, after the further cooking of the pieces.

Talking of dugong, here is an incident which really happened in after years, when the blacks used the white man's harpoon: The scene was Amity Point, Stradbroke Island. Five blacks went out in a whale boat to catch dugong, and they succeeded in harpooning one off Pelican Bank, but when the creature had taken the whole length of rope, he broke it, and made off. The blacks, who were very excited, pulled after him with all their strength, one man, known as Scroggins, standing up watching. He could see the dugong plainly, as the water was shallow with a white sandy bottom, and at last by diving down he managed to catch the end of the rope, holding to it bravely while the dugong pulled him along. When the creature came up to blow, Scroggins came up also, and when it went down, Scroggins went down, and so on for about eight hundred yards, when the wounded dugong gave in and lay on the top of the water. In the meantime, the four in the boat had done their best to keep up, and they now came upon poor Scroggins lying quite still with the rope in his hands, so lifted him on board, still holding to it. Then they hauled in the rope till able to harpoon the dugong again, and so kill and take him ashore.

Scroggins was none the worse for his jaunt through the water, though he swallowed a lot at each ducking. He said he was determined to hold to his prize or get drowned in the attempt, and when all the blacks were gathered together for the feast, they praised him for his pluck, also laughed till tired at the way he went up and under with the dugong. The incident was told and described always at any corrobboree or meeting afterwards, and was a source of great amusement. One of these five blacks ("Noggi") is alive yet at Stradbroke.

PORPOISES.—The blacks never by any chance killed porpoises, for, they said, they helped to catch fish. When my

father was a boy, his father sent men down to Moreton
Island to work at the pilot station there. Once he accompanied these men to the island, and while there went out
with the blacks to see how they caught tailor fish. These
fish come inland in schools, like sea mullet. The blacks
there called them "punba," and further north "dai-arli."
They came in in great numbers, generally at the time of
westerly winds, when the sea would be calm. From father's
experience at that island, he says it certainly looked as
though the porpoises understood, and were the friends of
the blacks. The following is what he told me:—

"The sea would be calm, and there would be no sign
anywhere of a porpoise ("Talobilla") the blacks would
go along the beach jobbing with their spears into the sand
under the water, making a queer noise, also beating the
water with the spears. By-and-by, as if in response, porpoises would be seen as they rose to the surface making
for the shore and in front of them schools of tailor fish.
It may seem wonderful, but they were apparently driving
the fish towards the land. When they came near, the
blacks would run out into the surf, and with their spears
would job down here and there at the fish, at times even
getting two on one spear, so plentiful were they. As each
fish was speared, it was thrown to shore, and there picked
up by the gins. The porpoises would actually be swimming
in and out amongst all this, apparently quite unafraid of
the darkies. Indeed, they seemed rather to be all on good
terms, and I have with my own eyes more than once seen
a blackfellow hold out a fish on a spear to a porpoise, and
the creature take and eat it. One old porpoise was well
known and spoken of fondly. He had a piece of root, or
stick of some sort, stuck in his back, having evidently at
one time run into something, and by this he was recognised,
for it could be seen plainly. The blacks told me, it had
been in him for years, and they declared that the great
man of the island had put it there, thus making him
the big fellow of the tribe of porpoises. I have seen this
creature take fish from a spear, and the white men working
on the island told me they often saw him knocking about

with the blacks. At all times porpoises would be spoken of with affection by these Moreton Island blacks (the ngugi tribe), who said they never failed when called to drive in fish to them."

Since writing the above, I have come across the written statements of two early authorities on this same subject. Mr John Campbell, after describing the way the blacks signalled to the porpoises, etc., says:—

"Doubtless this statement about the porpoises and blacks fishing together will be pronounced—as I myself did upon hearing it—to be a myth; in fact, all nonsense; but further inquiry and observation has convinced me that it was a fact, and any persons doubting it can convince themselves by going to Amity Point during the fishing season. The blacks even pretend to own particular porpoises, and nothing will offend them more than to attempt to injure one of their porpoises."

Mr Henry Stuart Russell, in "Genesis of Queensland" (page 290), talking of a scene he saw enacted at Amity Point, but no other place, says:—

"It was so curious, that the evidence of my own senses alone permits me to mention it. Cause and effect, however, were, in the matter, quite intelligible.

"We know that porpoises drive the smaller fry into shallows in which they are able more easily to prey upon them. The affrighted shoals leap when so pursued out of the water with loud splashings; these their hidden pursuers follow, as stock-keepers round up and keep their cattle together.

"At Amity Point, if the watchful natives can detect one of the shoals so common in the offing there, a few of the men would at once walk into the water and beat it with their spears. The wary porpoises would be seen presently coming in from seawards, fully alive and accustomed to the summons, driving in the shoal towards the shelving beach. Scores of the tribe would be ready with their scoop nets to rush in and capture all they could, but not before the men who had summoned their ministering servants had speared some good-sized fish, which was held out, and taken off the

end of the weapon by the porpoise nearest at hand. There
was one old fellow, said to be very old; as tame—with those
blacks—as a pussy cat! had a large patch of barnacles or
some fungus on his head, and a name which they believed
he knew and answered to."

MULLET.—In winter sea mullet (although spears were
used more often than nets) were caught on the coast in
somewhat the same way as dugong were captured. A pair of
blacks would climb a tree, and so watch for the schools
of fish as they came in to the shore. The natives had
wonderful eyesight, and nothing would escape them. When
they saw the fish coming, they made signs to their companions as to direction, etc., and a dozen or more men would
go into the water, with hand nets, and when the fish were
about twelve yards or so from the shore, other blacks would
throw stones and sticks in great quantities into the water,
landing them seawards of the shoal. This would frighten the
fish and cause them to shoot in towards the shore, the men
in the water would quickly rush forward, meeting in a circle,
and the fish were thus caught in their nets. Father has
seen the blackfellows hardly able to draw their nets ashore,
they were so full.

Of course, fish was very much more plentiful in those
days, and the natives were also very cunning in the way they
managed things. Great feasts they would have in the mullet
("Andakal") season, catching more than they could eat.
Those over they did not waste, however, but would save
for future use. A soft grass, not unlike kangaroo grass,
grew on the coast, and this they would gather and twist
into fine ropes, which would be wound round and round
each fish very closely, so that the flies could not get at
them. These fish would then be placed in dillies, and hung
up on bushes or trees near the camp, and they would keep
so for a long time. Father has tasted them a fortnight old,
and they were then quite fresh and sweet. Of course, it
was cold weather.

Fish were scaled by the blacks with the "donax" shell,
or "yugari" (the native name), and then put whole on a
nice fire of mostly red-hot coals. When about cooked, a

finger would be shoved in below the head at the fin, and the whole inside drawn off, leaving the fish beautifully clean and nice. Fish were always cooked so.

Fish in creeks were caught in this wise: The narrow and shallow parts of a creek would be blocked by stakes and bushes put across, and in this wall of bushes two or three openings would be left wide enough to permit of a black-fellow standing at each of them with his hand net ready. (Of course, nets for fish were much smaller than those for dugong.) They would not go near, however, until the tide was on the turn, when they went and stood up to their necks in the water, ready to catch the fish. As a net began to fill the owner would close the mouth, and lifting up the pocket part, he would catch hold of each fish in turn, and, putting the head in his mouth, would give it a bite through the net to kill it. All the fish being killed, and so unable to escape, the man placed the net again in the opening, and stood ready for more, and so they went on till the tide had gone down, emptying their nets now and again, if they got too heavy, by throwing the fish to the bank.

With the constant use of their fishing nets, a hard tumour grew on the outer bone of the wrist of each hand of the men. One could always tell an old fisherman by this mark, which was caused by the handle of the net continually rubbing the bone.

Women never fished in the old times. Since, however, the blacks learnt the use of the white man's lines, the gins were great ones for fishing, and my father has often been amused by a sort of clicking noise they made with their mouth, after throwing the line out. Laughed at, and asked why they did this, they replied that it encouraged the fish to bite. For the same reason they also tapped with the end of the rod on the water two or three times immediately the line was thrown out. Men would do this, too, at times.

A fishing net was called "mandin," and the portion of the North Pine River near where the railway bridge now crosses was known by that name, for it was a great place for fish, and the blacks used to have a breakwater of bushes built there.

One way the aboriginals had of capturing fresh-water fish was by poisoning the water with a certain plant (Polygonum hydropiper). This plant—"tanggul"—which is not very large, and grows on the edge of scrubs or in swampy places, was pounded up with sticks, and then thrown into the waterhole, and the water stirred up with the feet. Soon after the fish would seem to be affected, and would rise to the surface wrong side up, when they would be caught with the hands and thrown on to the bank.

Eels.—These were caught by nets, in salt water. Two men would block the mouth of a small creek by holding hand nets on the ground, and other men would go some distance up and return down the creek, muddying the water as they came by moving about their feet. This would drive the eels down to the nets. In fresh water eels were gradually caught in times of drought, when the water was low, by men muddying the water, and feeling for them with their feet. At other times they would dam a small portion of water with mud banks, leaving openings in each wall, and then, when the eels (or fish) went through, the holes would be blocked and small hand nets used to scoop up the fish; or they were speared. Sometimes spears would have three or four prongs, which were all tied firmly to the centre handle. Often a blackfellow, going out alone, would spear fish in clear water.

Crabs.—These were caught by a long-hooked stick. It would be put in a hole in the bank of a creek at low water, and the crab ("yirin") felt for and pulled out. The blacks could easily tell if there was a crab in the hole by the marks it had left in the mud round about the mouth. Crabs were carried in dillies. Always in these dillies a lot of small mangrove twigs were put. This, the blacks said, prevented them fighting, and so breaking their claws. Even of late years, when the natives used bags given them by white people, they always put in these twigs.

I may mention here that the Turrbal tribe called the mangrove "tintchi," and it is interesting to know that quite a different variety grew at Noosa, the blacks there calling it "pirri," the name they gave their fingers. This was because of the peculiar finger-like roots which seemed to clutch the soil.

Women and men both caught crabs, which they ate roasted, as they did fish.

OYSTERS ("KIN-YINGGA"), MUSSELS, ETC.—The blacks would eat oysters raw, but were very fond of them roasted, too, probably because they opened so easily then. In the old days the natives had no idea whatever of boiling. Peri-winkles ("niggar") they would roast, also mussels, such as the "yugari," and a larger fresh-water mussel. The latter they sought for by going into waterholes, and feeling all round the sides among the weeds with their feet.

COBRA.—This was another food the blacks were fond of. The Brisbane tribe called it "kan-yi." It is a long and white grub which grows in old logs the salt water gets at, and was swallowed raw like an oyster. The aborigines got it out with stone tomahawks, by cutting up the wood it was in, and then knocking the pieces against a log, so dislodging the grubs, which fell out. These were gathered up and put into a "pikki," and so carried to camp. Generally gins or old men got this cobra. They all took care to have plenty coming on by cutting swamp oak saplings and carrying these on to a mud bank dry at low water, and piling them up there. These piles were some two feet high and six feet wide. Father has seen them made in the Brisbane River, in Breakfast Creek, in the North and South Pine Rivers, Maroochy, and Mooloolah Rivers, and several creeks. The grubs in the swamp oaks were considered the largest and best, although plenty were got from other trees which fell in the water. The swamp oaks grew near the water, and so were easily got at. These piles would be dry at low water always, and covered at high, and the natives would visit them in about a year's time, making fresh ones then to take their place.

CHAPTER X

Grubs as Food—Dr Leichhardt and Thomas Archer Tasting Them
—Ants—Native Bees—Seeking for Honey—Climbing with a Vine—
A Disgusting Practice—Sweet Concoction—Catching and Eating
Snakes—Iguanas and Lizards—Another Superstition—Hedgehogs—
Tortoises—Turtles.

GRUBS.—It was, of course, the coastal blacks who made
these piles for cobra; the inlanders got grubs in trees. Large
white ones were found principally in dead hickory trees in
the scrubs; they were cut out with stone tomahawks. Then
bluegum saplings often contained grubs. The natives knew
when they did by noticing dust on the ground, so, climbing
the sapling to where the dust came out, they would knock
the bark off at the hole, shove a small hooked twig up
this till the grub was felt, and, with a twist, pull it out.
These grubs were sometimes roasted, sometimes eaten raw.
Other grubs were found in the grass-tree, or *Xanthorrhœa*
("dakkabin"), at its base, and always a native knew of their
presence by the dead leaves in the centre. Kicking the
tree with his foot, it would break off at the bottom and four
or five grubs were sometimes found. These latter were
always eaten raw.

With regard to this practice the blacks had of eating
grubs, Dr Leichhardt says:—

"They seem to have tasted everything, from the highest
top of the bunya tree and the seaforthia and cabbage palm,
to the grub which lies in the rotten tree of the bush, or
feeds on the lower stem or root of the Xanthorrhœa. By
the bye, I tasted this grub, and it tastes very well, particularly in chewing the skin, which contains much fat. It has
a very nutty taste, which is impaired, however, by that of
the rotten wood upon which the animal lives."

My father says he has often eaten this grub in days gone

past, and, what is more, declares he liked it. Once, when a boy, he was out in the scrub where Toowong is now, with a couple of natives, and the latter came across some grubs and took them to where several sawyers were at work, to roast them. A man named Jack was awfully disgusted, and said he felt ill at the mere thought of eating such things! However, when the white boy took one, he followed suit after some persuasion, and liked the morsel so well that he ate more. In the end that man grew so fond of grubs that he would give the blackfellows tobacco to find him some. Of course, there were different varieties—some more eatable than others.

The following is an extract from an interesting book printed in Yokohama—"Recollections of a Rambling Life," by Thomas Archer, whose family and name are well-known in Queensland:—

"Our way lay for several days through the trackless bush; we were sometimes pretty hard up for food, and to Dusky Bob belongs the honour of first initiating me into a proper appreciation of the luscious and delicate tree grub, which he cut with his tomahawk, out of the stems of the forest oaks as we wandered along. When roasted in the ashes these grubs make a dish fit for gods and men, and even when raw they are not to be sneezed at, if one is only hungry enough."

ANTS, ETC.—Father has never seen the blacks about here eat ants of any kind or their larvæ. March flies, however, were eaten (principally by children)—at least, not the flies themselves, but a little bag of honey they contained, and which was pulled out. Blacks were by no means dainty in their tastes! They also ate the contents of wasps' nests, of the large, round, honeycomb kind, when the insects were nearly mature. A nest would be approached quietly, a burning torch of the tea-tree bark held beneath to dislodge the clinging wasps, and then it was pulled, and held over a fire till half roasted, when the contents were knocked out and eaten.

NATIVE BEES.—There were two kinds of native honey. One called "kabbai" was pure white and very sweet, and was found always in small, dead, hollow trees. "Kú-ta" was dark honey, of a somewhat sour taste, and might be found in any kind of tree; it was much more plentiful than the other. My father gave the latter name to the Government for the hill near One-tree Hill, as in the old days that was a great place for native honey, and it has been mispronounced and spelt "Coot-tha." Of course, when the English bees came their honey was taken too, and it was remarkable how, though they were used to their own harmless bees, the natives did not seem to mind being stung, but would unconcernedly pull out the sting. They had then also the Englishman's tomahawks. These saved them trouble, for their own took a long time to prepare.

In seeking for honey, if a dull day, tiny particles of dirt the bees dropped were looked for at the roots of trees. These particles were very minute, and the aborigines would go on their knees looking for them, blowing leaves, etc., gently aside in their search. If found, the tree would be ascended and the honey taken. On a bright summer's day the bees themselves were looked for; the natives would shade their eyes with their hands, and gaze up the tree, and the bees, if there, were seen flying round the hole. If a nest were found too late in the day to admit of its being robbed, the finder would put a cut in the tree with his tomahawk, or print a footmark in the soil at the base, or probably just a stick would be stuck up against the trunk. This showed the nest had been discovered, and no one else would touch it. The man would either send some one next day or come himself.

To climb trees the natives used lengths of a scrub vine (*Flagellaria indica*) they called "yurol." A length was cut about twelve feet long, and after the outer bark was peeled off with the teeth it would become quite supple, and a loop was made at one end. When about to climb, this vine was put round the tree, the loop end would be held in the left hand, and the other in the right, then with his right foot placed against the trunk, and his body thrown backwards, the native would commence to ascend by a succession of springs. At every spring the vine was jerked upwards, and so with wonderful rapidity the ascent was accomplished.

This helper in the way of climbing was called "yurol," after the vine it was principally cut from, and each native was very careful of his after finishing with it for the day; he would soak it in water and so keep it supple and unlikely to break. On some trees notches or steps were cut to assist the climbing, and when this was the case the unlooped end of the vine was twisted round the man's thigh, then round his calf, and from there it went to his foot, where he held it firmly with his big toe, so leaving his right hand free to cut the steps in which to place his feet as he went up. Sometimes a bees' nest was found half way up in the barrel of a hollow tree, and when the man came to this he would pause, and cutting rests for his feet, would proceed with his free hand to cut out the comb. Climbing without using his tomahawk, the man would generally carry it in his belt, but sometimes it was held by the muscles of the neck—head on one side.

With regard to honey, the aborigines had a disgusting practice, which I shall describe. They carried with them a piece of stuff resembling an old rag, which was really chewed bark fibre. Bark for the purpose was generally cut from the stinging tree (*Laportea sp.*), which has since disappeared from these parts—the root bark was used for making string. The natives called this tree "braggain," and, as was the custom, the chewed up pieces of fibre went by the same name. To make the latter, bark cut in lengths was pounded till the rough outer surface came away, then beaten again till it became soft, when the darkies chewed it into the semblance of a rag. This rag a man always carried with him in his dilly when he climbed a tree for honey. Coming to the bees' nest, he would cut the honeycomb out and let it fall to those below, who deftly caught it. If after eating what they wanted there was some over, it was put into a "pikki" ready to carry away. The man on the tree also ate some, then, when all had been taken, he wiped out the hollow limb with the "braggain," which soaked up all the remaining honey, and afterwards this rag was carefully placed back in his dilly ready for future use. It would perhaps be wanted several times again, or they might not find another nest that day. When back in camp the "braggain" was soaked in water in a "pikki," then loosely wrung out, and this made the water quite sweet. The rag would then be passed round to each in the hut, and, disgusting as it may seem, all took a suck or chew in turn till it had become dry. It would then be put in the "pikki" again, and so on till the water was used up. Each group possessing a "braggain" would do the same, but there would be those who had none, and the fortunate ones would remember these, for at all times food was shared. White people blessed with a large supply of this world's goods have not always this savage (?) instinct "to share."

Another sweet concoction was made in summer time, when the grass tree and what we call honeysuckle were in bloom. Early in the morning, when the dew was on the grass, and the air sweet with perfumes, the old men and women would go forth, each carrying a "pikki" full of water, while the younger people went to hunt. Wending their way, some to the ridges where the grass-trees grew, others to the low flats where the small honeysuckle would be found, they went from flower to flower despoiling them all of their sweetness by dipping them up and down in the "pikki" of water till the latter became sweet. Then they turned them campwards, and, arriving there, would gather in groups to enjoy themselves—all, young and old alike, having their turn with the rag. A drink might be taken from the "pikki," but this used the precious fluid up too quickly. It was greatly relished, and was called "minti" after the small species of honeysuckle (*Banksia amula*), whose flower was used in its manufacture. The flower of the larger kind (*Banksia latifolia*), was also used, but not so much. The blacks called this one "bambara," and the wood from it was the special wood used in the making of a "bugaram" or a "wobbalkan."

SNAKES.—A carpet snake was called "Kabul," hence the name Caboolture, which meant to the Brisbane tribe "a place of carpet snakes," for they were plentiful there in the old days. These snakes were found in swamps or anywhere, often up on staghorn ferns in the scrub. The natives were at times helped in their search for game by the cry of birds, as they gathered round a snake, for instance. Carpet snakes were caught by the neck, and father has several times seen a native catch and then feel a carpet snake, and if he were poor let him go. Other snakes were hit on the head with a stick, and then on the back to break it.

A black snake was called "tumgu," brown snake "kuralbang," death-adder "mulunkun," and so on. The natives were more frightened generally of a death-adder than of any of the others, seemingly because of how it could jump, and they would not go near one. Once when my father was a boy in Brisbane, while playing near where the Valley Union Hotel now stands with a number of blackboys, throwing small spears, etc., he almost sat down upon a death-adder. The boys saw it in time to prevent him, and made a great row, calling to him to "Look out." He was so near the reptile, however, that it was a wonder he escaped. He wished to kill it, but the blacks kept him back, saying it would "jump," and they themselves did the deed by throwing waddies at it.

Snakes, iguanas, and lizards were put on hot cinders and roasted whole. The natives never attempted to clean any of their food beforehand, as we do. Roasted thus they were much more easily cleaned when half-cooked. Sometimes when opened a carpet snake would contain as many as twenty-five or twenty-six eggs, and an iguana perhaps a dozen; these would be taken out and probably roasted further. Fat, too, was greatly relished, and some would be saved for the body greasing spoken of.

IGUANAS AND LIZARDS.—The small kind of iguana was called "barra," while the larger one was "gi-wer." They were found at times in hollow logs; the natives would look for them there, feeling with a stick, then when an iguana was felt, his distance up the log was measured and he was cut out. If when chased at any time an iguana ran up a tree before he was captured, a man would climb up after him and either kill him there or send him down to the death awaiting beneath. Dogs would help in the chase after these reptiles. When one was killed, the natives would never by any chance proceed to cook him till they smashed each leg with a waddy, and also beat along his neck and tail. Father's curiosity was raised to know why they should do this when the thing was dead, and he found it was a superstition with them—"He never can run away again," they said. Iguanas' eggs were sought for, and were found generally near ants' nests in soft soil, covered up in the earth; the blacks would find them by the tracks the creature made.

Large lizards of several kinds and their eggs were eaten in the same way, and some of them were considered dainties. A large "water-lizard," which sat on a log in the water, and if any disturbance came along jumped in, was called "magil" (moggill), and here we have the meaning of the name Moggill Creek.

HEDGEHOGS ("KAGGARR").—The natives could tell when these had passed by scratching marks they made, and would track them till discovered. Dogs would help. They would be found on the edge of swamps, or in scrubs, or ferny flats; often under a log, or in a hollow one, when they were cut out. They were roasted, and the prickles knocked off. Sometimes these prickles were kept for piercing 'possum rugs sewn by the women and old men.

TORTOISES.—A tortoise was called "binkin," and "Binkinba" was the native name for New Farm, which meant a place of the land tortoise. Father, as a boy, used to go there with the blacks to catch tortoises in the swamps. Who, seeing New Farm now, would think it possible? What we call Pinkenba the blacks knew as "Dumben." The native name for New Farm has been pronounced incorrectly and given to the wrong place. The land tortoises were caught in fresh waterholes with nets, or in swamps just with the hand. When caught they were roasted whole lying on their backs, and when cooked the shell uppermost was removed, while that of the back served to catch the gravy, which was supped up with great relish.

TURTLES.—These were cooked in the same way, on their backs to save the juices, and the flesh was cut up and divided round. Great quantities of turtle were seen in the old times at Humpybong, and they were also plentiful in

Bribie Passage. There were no steamers or white men to disturb them, and the natives had it all their own way. To catch a turtle they would go out on a calm day, three or four of them in a canoe, stealing along quietly and gently over the water, one man standing up in front on the lookout. As soon as the turtle came to the surface near them, the man standing would dive into the water near where it had appeared, and, if possible, catch and turn it over on its back, so making it quite powerless. Another occupant of the boat would immediately follow this man, taking with him a rope made for the purpose, and he would take his turn under the water in holding the turtle while the first man came up to breathe. And so each man in the boat would have a turn if the water were deep, and in the end the turtle would be got to the surface with rope attached to a flipper. It would then receive a blow on the head, and was towed ashore, where a big fire was made ready to receive it, after its head and flippers were removed. A turtle was called "bo-wai-ya." Its eggs were found in the sand.

CHAPTER XI

Kangaroos—How Caught and Eaten—Their Skins—The Aboriginal's Wonderful Tracking Powers—Wallaby, Kangaroo Rat, Paddymelon, and Bandicoot—'Possum—'Possum Rugs—Native Bear—Squirrel—Hunting on Bowen Terrace—Glass House Mountain—Native Cat and Dog—Flying Fox.

KANGAROOS.—Kangaroos were caught in the forests with two or three inch mesh nets, and these were made from fibre, in the same way as those for dugong; but instead of being sewn up into hand nets they were just made in one long piece, standing some four feet high, and when used were stretched across a pocket, bounded by a creek, in the forest, the ends being tied to trees. In this pocket kangaroos were very likely feeding, and a number of natives, spreading out in the shape of a circle, would hunt them towards the net by beating their waddies and making a great noise. A dozen or two blacks, ready near the net, and armed with spears and waddies, knocked the kangaroos down, or speared them as they became entangled. Blacks' dogs were never much good in catching kangaroos.

Sometimes a couple of men would lie hidden near where they expected these creatures to come for a drink, and spears were then made use of. At other times, kangaroos were driven into waterholes, and there speared. Again, they might be tracked, and sneaked up to in the extreme heat of the day, while they were resting in the shade of trees. Natives always hunted going against the wind, for otherwise their prey would get scent of them. To encourage kangaroos to come about, my father has known the blacks set fire to the grass; the marsupials appreciated the young and tender shoots coming up after a bush fire.

An "old man," or large kangaroo, was always skinned for the sake of his hide, which was taken off with the help of sharp stone knives or shells. When off, the skin was stretched out, and pegged on the ground with small sharpened sticks, then wood ashes were rubbed into it, and it was left to dry in the sun. When cured the bare side was ornamented with a sort of scroll pattern done with pieces of sharp flint stones, then rubbed with charcoal, or coloured red with "kutchi." Kangaroo rugs were used for lying on, not for coverings. Each skin was used singly, they were not sewn together as 'possum skins were.

If kangaroo skins were not worth keeping the animal was first singed in the fire till all hair was off, then roasted, and when nearly cooked opened and cleaned out, and large red-hot stones were shoved into the inside to help the cooking. The carcass was kept on its back to preserve the gravy. An "old man" kangaroo was called "groman," while an ordinary one was "murri."

The aboriginals used to possess really wonderful tracking powers. Some people have the idea that they could track by means of a sense of smell, but that was not so; what really helped them was their marvellous eyesight. Father has been with them while they followed a wounded kangaroo, which had previously got away with a spear in his body. They followed the track for nearly a quarter of a mile, just walking along and pointing out to the white boy as they went a spot of blood on a blade of grass here and there, which he could hardly see, and at other times a track in the grass which he could not see at all. They went on thus till they came to a large flat rock on the side of a ridge, and here they went down on their knees and commenced to blow on the rock. Father asked what they did that for? "We want see which way that fellow go 'cross." At last they called to him to look, and said, "That fellow been go over here." The white boy looked, and saw, when they blew on the rock, tiny loosened particles of moss moving. Evidently as the kangaroo passed that way his feet displaced the minute leaves of the moss. They had not much further to go before they came to the animal, lying dead with the spear through his body.

I have mentioned this habit of stooping and blowing with

regard to the search for a bees' nest, and one can understand how the practice has been mistaken for the "smelling"
of scent. The only animal found by the sense of smell was
the scrub 'possum, which is much larger than the forest
one, and also much darker in colour; it has a very strong
scent of its own. Without seeing these, father has been
aware of their presence often in the scrub when getting
cedar.

WALLABY ("BUG-WAL"), KANGAROO RAT ("BARRUN"),
PADDYMELON ("KU-MANG"), AND BANDICOOT ("YAGGO-I").—
These were all caught, killed, and cooked in much the same
way as the kangaroo. When first coming to North Pine,
father has seen about fifty blacks go into the scrub on the
river just below his home, and there catch over twenty
paddymelons in their nets at one trial. Pockets in the
scrubs were blocked in the same way as those in the forests.

OPOSSUM.—The forest 'possum was called "ku-pi," and
the scrub one "kappolla." As mentioned, the whereabouts
of the latter was often discovered by its scent. 'Possums
were captured during the day, not by moonlight, as they
are by white people. The blacks disliked having their
night's rest disturbed; indeed, they seemed also rather
afraid of the night. The only food they sought at night
was fish—the old fishermen always took advantage of a
good tide then. As for 'possums and native bears, etc., what
jolly nights they must have had, when the blacks allowed
them to skip and caper about unmolested! But they made
up for it, poor things, and paid dearly for their fun when
the day came, and they were dragged forth unmercifully
to their death.

Sometimes the whereabouts of an opossum, or any animal
which slept in a hollow limb, was found by means of the
birds which clustered round the hole proclaiming loudly
their find to the world. At other times the blacks would
look for fresh clawmarks on the base of tree trunks. How
they did so, their white friend often wondered, but they
seemed to be able to tell whether the clawmarks were those
of a cat, a bear, an opossum, a squirrel, or what. Climbing
the tree to where the 'possum was, if by putting their hand

down the hollow limb they could reach him, they did so, and dragging him quickly forth, would give him a blow on the head and send him flying to the ground. If, however, the 'possum was beyond their reach, they would perhaps feel with a stick for his whereabouts, and then cut him out, or by hammering away on the wall of his retreat, they frightened him up to where he was easily got at.

'Possum skins were greatly prized as coverings when the nights were cold. They were sewn together, and so made nice rugs. They were sewn with string, which was really kangaroo-tail sinew. This sinew was kept on purpose for sewing, and when wanted was damped to make it soft. The holes for the string were pierced either with hedgehog quills or sharp bones. It was only in the winter that the natives troubled to preserve the skins, however, for in the summer the hair came out.

These 'possum rugs the gins carried from place to place with them. They were folded in half, and then hung round the neck, kept in place there by a string put through the fold. Over the rug a dilly was always hung, containing fish, birds, or food of any kind, also bones of the dead, etc. This dilly had a long string handle which passed over the shoulders, and so helped to keep the rug firm, in fact when there was a little pickaninny to carry, the string through the fold was done away with, the dilly handle being all that was required. The child was put in between the rug and the woman's back, and the dilly, with its contents, hanging below the infant, though on the outside of the rug, prevented him slipping down. The furry side of the rug was next the child, who only showed his little black head, and when a mother wished to get him out from this snug retreat, she reached over, and taking hold of a little arm, hauled him by it over her shoulder. This was done no matter how young the child, and the treatment seemed to have no ill effects. When children were older, but still too young to walk, they were carried on the shoulders —one leg on each side of the neck. Men sometimes took their share in carrying the children so, and this was how they carried sick people.

NATIVE BEARS.—These were caught as 'possums were. As food they were much appreciated. The Turrbal tribe called them "dumbripi," and the Bribie tribe "kul-la." The latter name evidently accounts for the "koala" of the white man.

SQUIRRELS.—The large black flying squirrel was called "panko," and the small gray one "chibur." Squirrels, the moment they heard any noise, would run out of their hiding place, and fly down in a slanting direction to the butt of another tree, up which they would scamper—they did not wait to be pulled out. Father says it was great sport chasing squirrels. Often as a boy he went hunting with the blacks on what is now Bowen Terrace. He has seen them there get two or three 'possums out of one large turpentine tree, and sometimes a large flying squirrel, and then there would be the "sugar-bags."

The flying squirrel was always the best fun. When a native climbed up the tree, the squirrel would hear him coming, and, running out of his hole, would fly down to the base of another tree. If the blacks on the ground did not succeed in knocking him down before he got beyond their reach they would climb the second tree, and then afterwards perhaps a third, and so on, till in the end the poor thing was captured. Boys always think that sort of thing fun, and my father, as a boy, was no exception. He says that many a happy day has he spent with his dark companions hunting on Bowen Terrace, Teneriffe, Bowen Hills, Spring Hill, Red Hill, and all round where the hospital now stands. What changes can take place in a lifetime! It must surely seem strange to look back on a time when one hunted where now houses crowd and trams run, and to think of the fish and crabs one caught in the quiet creeks and rivers which railways now span. Breakfast Creek, near where the Enoggera Railway crosses (Barrambin) was a great place for fish.

At a certain time of the year, the small flying squirrel ("chibur") had a habit of biting the bark of the trunk of a tree: one would see a tree all marked so. The natives called one of the Glass House Mountains "Chirburkakan."

"Kak-an" meant "biting," hence the mountain was called after a "biting squirrel."

NATIVE CAT AND DOG.—Native cats were caught and eaten. Dingoes, however, so far as my father's experience went, were not eaten: but the natives would capture the pups for taming. Often all round a hollow log tracks would be seen where the youngsters had come out to play, and so the natives knew where to look. A native dog was called "mirri," and native cat "mibur."

FLYING FOX.—Flying foxes were caught always in the daytime at their camping place in the scrub. Two or three blacks would climb trees the foxes were sleeping on, carrying with them about a dozen small waddies made for the purpose. Standing on branches the natives would frighten the foxes, and then as they flew hurl the waddies at them, knocking great numbers easily, for these creatures will not fly far away in the daytime from trees they are camping on, but circle round and round. Men and women standing beneath the trees picked the foxes up as they fell, and all the time the creatures made a frightful row, so that one could hardly hear oneself speak.

A flying fox was singed on the fire, then rubbed all over till free from hair, when it was roasted, and when nearly done a native put his thumb in between the neck and breast-bone, and pulling these apart, took away the waste parts. After that the fox was put again on the fire to cook further. A flying fox was called "gramman." St Helena was a great camping place for them in those days, and the blacks from Wynnum used to go across in their canoes to catch them there, watching for calm weather both to go and return. If the return was not delayed, they would bring back foxes cooked ready for the companions left behind, but they went prepared with fishing nets, etc., as the wind might keep them there some time.

CHAPTER XII

Emus—Scrub Turkeys—Swans—Ducks—Cockatoos and Parrots—
Quail—Root and Other Plant Food—How it was Prepared—Meals
—Water—Fire—How obtained—Signs and Signals.

EMUS.—The blacks used their nets to catch emus at times.
They knew where these birds came for water, and would
set nets accordingly to entangle them, and, if successful,
would despatch them with weapons. At other times, the
natives would lie hidden and spear the birds as they went
by. Emu feathers were much valued; the gins wore them
in their hair on occasions. Eggs were found and eaten.
An emu was called "ngurrun."

SCRUB TURKEYS.—These were hunted, and their nests
were sought. The latter sometimes contained a great number of eggs—several birds evidently laid in the same place.
The eggs were just laid on the ground, and covered over
with a multitude of leaves and small sticks, and left to come
out on their own account. They were never sat upon.
These nests or heaps were easily discovered, as they were
quite big, sometimes two feet high. A scrub turkey was
called "wargun."

SWANS.—The Turrbal or Brisbane tribe (not the natives
of the Maroochy River) called a black swan "marutchi"
(Maroochy). Swans were caught in the moulting season,
they could not fly then; the blacks went after them in their
canoes. Gins kept the small feathers for ornamenting their
hair, and the men always kept the down, carrying it in
dillies. This down was used to dress up the body for
fights or corrobborees. Bribie Passage and South Passage
were favourite resorts of the swan. The natives caught
their young and found their eggs.

DUCKS ("NGAU-U").—Nets were put across one end of a

large lagoon which ducks frequented. The natives hid themselves, and when the ducks came, frightened them up, and then threw two or three boomerangs in among them. The ducks, thinking these were hawks, would shoot downwards, and get stuck in the net. The aborigines used two kinds of boomerangs. One, when thrown, would return to the sender's feet, the other did not return. The latter was used in fighting, while the former was chiefly a plaything. It was, however, the one which returned which was used in this way to frighten birds.

In large swamps in summer time, the natives would go into a waterhole, and standing there with the water up to their necks, they held a little bush in front of them which hid their heads. The ducks, thinking this was just an ordinary bush, swam gaily near and nearer as they fed, and were suddenly grabbed by the legs and pulled under. Ducks were very plentiful then, and sometimes several were caught this way. At other times they took fright and were off. The eggs of a duck were much appreciated, and ducklings were often caught.

Birds were generally singed and rubbed free of feathers, then cooked in the usual way on ashes, but sometimes a duck would be rolled in a big ball of mud—feathers and all —then put right under the ashes. When cooked the mud and feathers would all come off together, and the inside, too, would readily come away, leaving the duck nice and clean. No other bird was cooked in this way. Duck's feathers were kept for the women's hair, as were all small feathers.

PARROTS ("PILLIN"), COCKATOOS ("KAI-YAR").—Towards sundown, from the low-lands, the parrots flew in flocks up the gorges of the mountains to roost for the night, after their feed of the day. The natives set nets across the trees where they knew they would pass, and as the flocks flew along boomerangs were thrown in among them, and the parrots, thinking, like the ducks, that these were hawks, dived down, and were caught in the nets. Great numbers were captured this way. Parrots were also sneaked upon when sitting on nests, and the young birds were likewise caught and eaten. If any bird's nest (on the ground or on a tree) were discovered, it was watched for the sake of the bird that came to it. Many different kinds were caught so. Cockatoos were greatly valued for their yellow top-knots, which were called "billa-billa," and were worn by men as described. They built their nests in hollow limbs.

QUAIL ("DU-WIR").—The natives went out in four or five lots in different directions, and as these birds were frightened up they threw little waddies at them. The different lots worked into each other's hands. New Farm and Eagle Farm were great places for quail; my father has hunted there for them.

PLANTS.—Animals, birds, and fish were all roasted on hot cinders, and so were certain roots and tubers of plants. The natives got the root of a fern (*Blechnum serrulatum*) which grew in the swamps in great quantities. It was mostly the gins who dug this up and put it in their dillies to carry to camp; great loads there would be at times, for the root was highly esteemed. It was called "bangwal," and was first roasted, then scraped and cut up finely with sharp stones on a log, when it was ready to eat. "Bangwal" was generally eaten with fish or flesh, as we use bread, though also eaten separately. In a camp, my father says, one would hear the chop-chop continually all over the place, as this food was prepared. It was very much used.

The root of a fresh-water rush (*Typha augustifolia*) was also eaten. This was something like arrowroot, and was called "yimbun." The outer skin was taken off, and then the roots were chewed raw until nothing was left but fibre, which was thrown away.

A large leaved plant, which grew on the edge of the scrubs (*Alocasia macrorrhiza*), was also sought for its roots. It is well known as "cunjevoi," but the Brisbane blacks called it "bundal." This plant is poisonous, but the blacks prepared the roots by soaking them a long time, and then they were pounded up and made into cakes, and so roasted on the cinders.

The wild yam (*Dioscorea transversa*) was found on the edge of the scrubs. This is a small vine, with a root like a sweet potato. The gins would have to dig three feet some-times for this root ("tarm"), which was very nice roasted.

Different kinds of flowering ground orchids were dug up and the tuberous roots eaten, but these were very small.

The cabbage-tree palm (*Livistonia Australis*) and common palm (*Archontophœnix Cunninghamii*): Young shoots coming out at the top were just pulled and eaten raw as a vegetable. The cabbage-tree was called "binkar," and the common palm "pikki." Of late years the latter name has grown to "pikkibean."

A large bean (*Canavalia Obtusifolia*) ("Yugam") which grew in the scrub on vines was pulled before it was ripe while soft, and the beans taken from the pods and soaked in water. These were then pounded up and made into cakes, and roasted. If not prepared so they were poisonous. The natives declared that the soaking and roasting took all badness away. For soaking beans, roots, or nuts, netted dillies were used. This prevented them getting lost, and yet allowed the water to get at them. After white people came the blacks soaked corn in the same way to soften it.

The Moreton Bay chestnut (*Castanospermum Australe*), or "mai," was also poisonous. The nuts were cracked and soaked, then pounded, and made into cakes, and roasted. The blacks called the white man's bread "mai" after this, when they first got into the habit of using it.

The nut of the zamia (*Cycas media*) was another poison-ous form of food used. It was cracked, then soaked, and afterwards roasted.

Several nuts and different kinds of berries were just eaten raw. The "bon-yi" I have already spoken of.

The fruit of the geebung (*Persoonia*), or "dulandella," as the Brisbane tribe called it, was eaten raw, and greatly relished. The natives got dillies full of these in the right season. They swallowed the pulp and the stone, which they squeezed from the skin with their fingers. It is a small green fruit.

Two kinds of wild fig were also just eaten raw. The larger kind was "ngoa-nga," and the smaller "nyuta."

A white, green-spotted berry, which grew on a small

green bush (*Myrtus tenuifolia*) on sandy islands was very sweet. The natives called it "midyim." Another berry ("dubbul") grew on sandy beaches. Wild strawberries and raspberries were also found.

Dog-wood or "denna" (*Jacksonia scoparia*) gum was much eaten, and different kinds of blossoms were sucked for the honey.

The Pandanus, or bread fruit ("winnam"), was chewed at the end and sucked.

MEALS.—The aborigines had no stated times for meals —they ate whenever they had food, and were hungry. Generally, however, there was a feast in the evening after the day's hunting. In the morning all would start out in different directions for the day, and if travelling, they arranged where to meet for the night, or supposing they were stationary, they all turned up at the same place again. About the middle of the day, while hunting thus, they might rest at some creek or waterhole to cook food, and very likely have a swim. Very happy they were, always laughing and joking, and extra merry after a good meal, when they danced and sang. Father says it was a great sight seeing them come into camp in the evening, a little before sunset. They would come in from all directions, laden with all sorts of things—kangaroos, 'possums, snakes, honey, eggs, birds, fish, crabs, different kinds of roots and fruit, etc. They started cooking these, and as the sun bid his farewell there arose that weird cry for the dead already mentioned. The gins would have wood all ready gathered for the fire, and also a supply of water.

WATER.—When water ("tabbil") was scarce, to get some the blacks dug small wells in swamps. This water would be muddy, and to clear it a lot of fern leaves were put in the hole: this they said made the sediment sink to the bottom. Also, in carrying water in a "pikki" from place to place, fern leaves or grass were always put in with it; as well as clearing the water they said this prevented it spilling. To obtain water the blacks also tapped the tea-tree; they got a little that way, but it had an unpleasant taste.

FIRE.—The natives obtained fire ("darlo") by friction. To do so, they used the dead (stick-like) flower stems of the grass tree in this way: One thick stick was taken, and the surface split off on one side, this was then placed on the ground with the flat side uppermost, and in the centre of the stick a tiny hole was made. All round this hole, on the ground, were placed pieces of dry grass and leaves, also rotten powdered sapwood. Now another stick was got, somewhat thinner than the other, and the native sat down on a log beside the first, and placing the point of the second into the hole, he held the first with both feet firmly to the ground, while with his hands he rolled the second round and round very rapidly, pressing it down all the time in the hole. This continual rubbing and rolling gradually wore through the hole, and in the end the friction caused sparks, which falling on the dry leaves and sapwood, were carefully blown into a blaze.

My father has tried to obtain fire in this way, but never managed it, being unable to roll the stick properly. It was only on rare occasions that the natives needed to do this, for they took care always to carry lighted firesticks with them wherever they went. These were principally of ironbark, as that wood kept lighted longest. Walking along, these sticks were held in front carefully from the wind, and a fire was set going wherever a halt was called. Even crossing to an island in a canoe, the natives did not forget their firesticks. Two or three were always kept burning on some clay at one end of the canoe.

SIGNS, ETC.—When travelling from one place to another the blacks, if they wished to let their friends know of their approach, would set bushfires going. For the same purpose, as they passed along, they pulled up a bunch of grass, and twisting it round another bunch would bend the whole in the direction in which they went, thus giving their friends the idea in which way to follow. In the scrub a twig would be broken or bent here and there. However, after the advent of the whites, they were careful not to make distinct tracks, for fear of being followed by the police. In travelling from one place to another they generally took the same track,

and this was always the shortest way—they never journeyed in a roundabout fashion.

When a young man and woman ran away together, so
that their tracks might not be followed, they would walk
along the beach into the sea, then travelling in the water
for some little distance, they at length walked out backwards, so leaving a misleading track behind them.

Often the natives would signal across the water with their
hands from one point to another—for instance, they were
in the habit of doing this from Kangaroo Point to North
Brisbane. Signs they called "mirrimbul," and they could
understand one another thus. They were in the habit of
signalling from the two points of Moreton and Stradbroke
Islands—in those early times South Passage was very much
narrower than it is now. Father remembers it so, and says
the natives used to cross there in their canoes. The old
natives said that long ago there was no passage at all, but
the two islands were one, and this is possible, even probable.

CHAPTER XIII

Canoe-making—Rafts of Dead Sticks—How Huts were Made—
Weapon Making—Boomerangs—Spears—Waddies—Yam Sticks—
Shields—Stone Implements—Vessels—Dilly-Bags—String.

CANOES.—The aborigines made their canoes from bark in the following fashion:—Bark for the purpose was, if possible, got from the bastard mahogany, a tree the blacks called "bulurtchu," which grows on low ground near a swamp. But if one of these trees was not procurable, then a stringy bark or "diura" was sought. The bark from the former was preferable, because it would not split, while that of the latter could not be depended upon.

The first thing to do was to climb the tree to the height required, which was done in the usual way with a vine. Then all the rough outer scaly bark was picked off with a small pointed stick, those below cleaning the bark within their reach, while the man on the tree did the rest; then the bark was cut right round the tree at the bottom, and also at the top, as far up as they thought it would strip off easily. Springtime was chosen, when the sap was up, because, of course, bark would not come off otherwise—and the natives knew this. Sometimes they would get but a short length, and sometimes a long one—perhaps twenty feet.

When the bark was cut right through in these circles, the man on the tree cut downwards in a straight line, so dividing the bark, which they wished to peel off in one whole piece. Then a stick about four feet long, flattened at the end, was used to job in between the bark and the tree, and thus it was loosened all round, and would peel off quite easily. When off, a piece of vine was tied round each end to prevent it flattening out, and in the hollow dry leaves and small sticks were put and set fire to. While the fire was burning the bark was rolled about, and so it got equally heated all over. This, the blacks said, made it more pliable. When the fire had burnt out, but while the bark was still hot, it was loosened free of the vines tying it, and then both ends were bent up and tied in a bunch with string made for the purpose from "yurol" (Flagellaria indica). Through each of these folded up ends a wooden skewer was run and more string bound round kept all firm.

That part finished, to strengthen the sides, lengths of wattle (*Acacia*) or "nannam" vine (*Malaisia tortuosa*) were stretched along the top of the inside, and these were bound into place with more "yurol" string laced through holes made with a sharp-pointed stick. If the canoe was a small one, a piece of cane ("yurol") twisted like a rope was placed across the centre—the ends fixed to the sides: this prevented the canoe shrinking in with the heat of the sun. If a large one, then there were two of these crosspieces—one at either end.

As a freshly-made canoe got dry, it grew very strong and stiff. A large one would carry nine or ten people, while the smaller ones held about five. A canoe was called "kundul" after the bark it was made from. All bark went by that name, with the exception of that of the tea-tree, which was called "ngudur." In a small canoe a blackfellow stood up in the middle and propelled the boat along by paddling first on one side and then on the other with a long round stick, nine feet or so in length. In a large canoe two people had to do the same—one at either end, and it was surprising how quickly they could go along, also how well they could steer their course with these poles. Both ends of a canoe were the same, and for fresh or salt water they were made in the same way. The strongest and largest ones were used for catching turtle, and the smaller ones for crossing short distances. People in the boat not paddling always sat low down in the bottom out of the way.

As I have already mentioned, blacks in a canoe always carried a lighted firestick resting on some dirt or clay in the bottom. Also they had a shell they called "niugam"

(*Melo diadema*), to bail out with if any leak should start, and a ball of whitish clay to putty up the hole. (See Dr Roth's Bulletin, No. 7, page 14.)

Supposing they had no canoe and yet wished to cross a creek or river in travelling, the aborigines made small rafts with dead, dry sticks bound together with bark string. These rafts were covered with sheets of tea-tree bark, young children and other belongings placed on them, and then the men and women going into the water, swam alongside, pushing the raft. Before swimming in any large river, the blacks always threw in a stick which would float, to see, they said, if there were any sharks about—the shark would come to the stick, and in swimming any distance they always used as a help a small log, about four or five feet long, which would float. On this log they rested the left hand, and so pushed it along, while the other hand was used in swimming; it was supposed they did not get so fatigued then. A dilly would be carried on the head.

HUTS.—Huts were of two kinds, one a good deal larger than the other, and less easily made. They were all generally called "ngudur" after the tea-tree bark which covered them. To make the smaller or usual kind, the men obtained a long, thin sapling which would bend and crack in the middle without breaking through. Both ends of this were stuck into the ground, and then a forked stick was placed to support it on one side, and against the other a number of sticks were slanted and tied if necessary to keep them in place. Their ends were also stuck in the ground. Next sheets of tea-tree bark were fixed against this stick-wall, and a sheet bent over on top surmounted the lot. All round the hut where the bark stood, a drain was dug, and the earth thrown up against the base kept the bark in position. Extra supports were placed over all, if wind were blowing. As already stated, the doorway had nothing to do with the direction in which the wind came, but pointed to whence the occupants had come. When it was windy, breakwinds of bushes were always used, and these protected the fire at the entrance as well as the people inside. These huts would hold about four or five people.

Huts were never made very high; a man could not stand upright in them. However, the second kind were much wider, and held about ten people. This time the foundation was formed of four long saplings bent over (not cracked) in the shape of hoops—with both ends stuck firmly in the ground. These hoops were crossed one over the other at equal distances; and so the openings in between were all alike, and were filled up with sticks stuck in the ground at one end and tied to the hoops at the top, with the exception of one, which was left for a doorway. Then the whole was covered with bark, kept in place by heavy sticks leant against it. As in the former kind, a large sheet was put on the very top, and this hung over the doorway, and left only a tiny opening. A small fire was kept going in the centre of these huts (not at the entrance), and they were considered warmer than the others. One mostly saw them on the coastline, the inland tribes always used the others.

Tea-tree bark was often carried by women in travelling, if the travellers knew that they would be unable to get any for their huts at their journey's end. Sometimes other bark was used in place of the tea-tree, for instance that of the "diura" or stringy bark, and so in that way a hut was sometimes called "diura." Tea-tree was not so easily got inland as on the coast. Now and again grass would have to be resorted to, and, if the weather was fine, just a breakwind of bushes would be used for the night.

Huts were moved on to fresh ground every now and then, even if the owners were not travelling. Fleas got troublesome otherwise. The same materials, foundation and all, were used in this case again and again.

BOOMERANGS.—A boomerang was called "braggan," and, as I have said, there were two kinds—one used as a toy, and the other for fighting. They were made from the root or spur of a scrub tree. The spur grew in a half-circle, so all that had to be done was to cut this off at both ends, thin it down with a stone tomahawk, and afterwards scrape it with a shell to make it smooth. One side was made more rounded than the other. The toy boomerang would circle round, and return to the sender's feet when thrown, and this was the one which was sent in among birds to frighten them. The fighting one was heavier, rounder at both sides, and had less of a bend than the other. As well as for fighting, it was used to kill kangaroo and big game. When thrown it would go in a straight course first, then gradually swerve to the right or left. The owner would know by practice just in which way his boomerang would travel, and he could make it go to the left or to the right as he liked. Boomerangs were thrown on to the ground as well as up in the air, and when they struck the earth they always turned off in another direction. The fighting one was never thrown as high as the other. Blackfellows often practised throwing these weapons at young tree saplings—seeing if they could hit them. Father, when fifteen or sixteen years of age, could throw a boomerang with any native—or a spear or waddy. All these instruments he could make, and the natives greatly valued any so made, and would show them to other tribes at the time of a corrobboree. Sometimes they would give one or two away as a rarity to a great chief of another tribe, explaining who had made them. Boomerangs were notched at the end, held as a handle.

SPEARS.—One kind of spear, called "kannai," was made from saplings which grew on the edge of the scrub. These saplings were cut when from six to nine feet long, and they were scraped with a shell free from bark. Then another shell—a fresh-water mussel—or, in the case of coast tribes, a yugari (Donax), was used as a spokeshave. A small hole was made in the centre of the shell, and it was held in the palm of the hand, and so with this the sapling was sharpened into a point. (Referred to in Dr Roth's Bulletin, No. 7, page 21, Fig. 109.) The point was then held in the fire to harden. Afterwards grass and leaves were put on a fire to cause smoke, and the spear was blackened therein all over. Finally, however, about a foot away from the tip the point was scraped white again, and when thrown this white would gleam and show up against the black; a spear was more easily dodged on that account. This spear was used for fighting and for killing game. Sometimes, instead of sharpening the point, three or four prongs of wood were fastened there, and then the weapon was used for spearing fish.   The prongs were made about seven inches long.

Another spear, the "pi-lar," was made from the ironbark which grows on flats—the "tandur" (*Eucalyptus crebra*). This spear was about ten feet long. A tree would be picked which was straight in the grain, and the required length cut out. A man climbing the tree would cut up as far as he wanted, then across and down again, making the cut about an inch and a-half deep, and the piece to be cut out an inch and a-half wide. This would then be split out, and the spear made from it by first thinning down with a stone tomahawk, then scraping with a shell, and so on, just as the other was done. This spear, however, was left all black. It was used at close quarters, as it was too long and heavy to throw far. Sometimes these spears were notched almost through at the point, and then thrown at a special enemy with the hope that they would hit and break off, leaving the end stuck in the wound. Again, the sharp barb from the butt of a stingaree's tail might be used for the point of a spear. It was fastened on with bees' wax and string. Spears were thrown with the hand only; no wommera was used.

If a spear was not the correct shape when being made, it could be straightened by heat and then bent properly over the head. The Ipswich, or "Warpai" tribe, made spears from rosewood ("bunuro"), and these were sometimes exchanged for others; the Brisbane tribe valued them greatly. Before a fight, quantities of spears were made ready.

WADDIES.—Scrub saplings were used to make waddies, or else the ironbark mentioned for spear-making ("tandur") was utilised. They were of several kinds, and were always made black. One, the "tabri" (the one of general use), used for both fighting and hunting, was about two feet long, and though pointed at both ends, the same end was always used as a handle, which, to prevent the weapon slipping, was notched. The "tabri" was not of the same thickness all through, but tapered from three-quarters of

an inch at the handle end, before the point, to two and
a-half inches at the other. The points were short.

The "mur," used for fighting only, was about the same
length. It tapered slightly from the handle, and at the end
there was just a large knob. Sometimes these knobs were
carved, and the handles were notched. Waddies were also
slightly ornamented at times with white clay and red
"kutchi."

Lastly, a waddy made from a root, grown somewhat in
the shape of a pick with one downward point, was called
"bakkan," and a man hit his enemy on the back of the neck
or head with this. These were made flat like a boomerang,
not round like other waddies.

YAM-STICKS.—These were called "kalgur," and were
women's weapons. However, the "gentler sex" used them
as well for digging for yams and other roots. They were
about six feet long, and were much like a spear, only a
good deal thicker. One end tapered, and the other was
very sharp.

SHIELDS.—There were two kinds of shields, but both were
called "kuntan," after the timber they were made from—
corkwood or "Bat-tree" (*Erythrine sp.*). This tree grows
generally on the edge of scrubs, but is also found on a ridge
near a swamp. A tree would be from four to six feet long
in the barrel before the first branch. One was picked
which was about thirteen or fourteen inches through, and
cut down, then cut into lengths sixteen or seventeen inches
long. These lengths were split up and roughly shaped
with stone tomahawks. Then the wood was left to dry. In
about a week's time or more it would be quite light and dry,
and soft to work, and the handle was made, which was just
a solid piece of wood hollowed out in the centre of the shield.
First two holes were marked out with charcoal on either
side of the piece to be left for a handle; then these lines
were cut in with a sharp piece of flint stone, and afterwards
the holes were hollowed out in this way: A sharp stick was
used to job within the marked lines till the wood became
quite soft and pulpy, then live coals were placed there and
blown upon till they burnt the soft wood. The hole was

picked out again, more coals used, and so on till both sides
were hollowed, and met under the handle, and the excava-
tion was wide enough to allow three fingers to pass through
and hold the handle. The handle of a shield was always held
so—by the first three fingers of the left hand. To smooth
down the rough edges, a shell or sharp flint stone was used.

The shields used to fend off spears in a large fight were
broader, and not so round and heavy as the ones for a close
hand-to-hand fight with waddies. The latter were about
six or seven inches thick, to stand the blows from the
waddies. "Kunmarin" was the name for a shield further
north up the coast.

All shields were covered with a coating of native bees'
wax. This wax was always carried, and when wanted it
was held to the fire till quite soft, and in the case of shields
was rubbed all over on the outside till it stuck. When firm
and hard, white clay and red paint were put on over the
wax, in the case of shields for spears, but the heavier ones
had nothing beyond the wax. The clay was just wet with
the mouth, and rubbed on the shield at both ends about six
inches towards the middle; then the centre was rubbed with
red "kutchi," and fine lines of white clay were drawn over
this again, making a sort of pattern. The under surface of
shields (the handle side) was sometimes whitened with clay.

TOMAHAWKS.—It was not every man who had a stone
tomahawk to leave behind him; they were hard to make,
and, therefore, were not plentiful. When hunting, the men
went in groups with one of their number owning a tomahawk, which was useful on occasion—for instance, if a bees'
nest were found. A tomahawk, or "waggarr," was made
from a hard stone or boulder, generally found in freshwater
rivers. The piece was chipped out first with another stone,
then a point was ground down gradually at any odd
moments while in camp. This took a long time to do, and
no native had the patience to keep at it till finished, so a
tomahawk was a good while on the way. The grinding was
done on a sandstone or rock, wetted now and then. When
finished, a handle of wood was affixed, which was just a
length of strong vine bent over in the middle and there fixed

firmly to the stone by means of bees' wax. The two ends of the handle were tied together with string. Besides their other uses, tomahawks, without handles, were sometimes utilised in place of stones, to break up the bones of animals just eaten; the natives were especially fond of marrow as food.

KNIVES.—Stone knives were made from reddish-coloured flint stone. There was no grinding for knives, but they were simply split from the stone, so one can understand how they often did not split to taste, but were perhaps blunt and no good. Sometimes a man would be lucky and get one at the first trial, but at other times he might split ever so many first. Only fighting men carried these knives, which were used in fights or for cutting up animals; women used sharp shells. A knife or "tang-ur" was always ornamented at the butt end with opossum fur stuck on with bees' wax or "mappi" ("moppi"). Sometimes the fur was bound round with string and then smeared with the wax.

VESSELS.—The natives made various vessels in which to carry water and honey. One called the "niugam" was made from the bark covering of excrescences that sometimes appear on gum trees. When the sap was up in the spring time a native would climb to one of these knobs, and cut all round with a stone tomahawk, then with a sharp stick he would loosen the bark, which, after being beaten gently all over, would peel off easily. A handle of string was all that was required, and this vessel was used for holding honey. "Niugam" was also the name (as stated) for the large sea shell Melo diadema, and in later years for the white man's pots.

Another vessel called a "pikki," was fashioned from the sheath of the palm flower (*Archontophœnix Cunninghamii*). This palm the blacks originally called "pikki," but of late years it has been known as "pikkibean." Both ends were tied up, and had a small skewer run through them, then a long stick passing down the centre lengthwise formed a handle. The skewers and handle were kept in place by string.

From the "Bat-tree" (*Erythrine sp.*)—or, as the natives

called it, "kuntan"—another vessel was made, and it also
was called "pikki." If the tree felled was a large one, the
section cut out was split down the centre with a wooden
wedge (see Dr Roth's Bulletin, No. 7, page 18), and two
vessels were thus made from this, whereas if the tree was
smaller, a length was perhaps just thick enough for one
vessel without the splitting. These lengths were about
eighteen inches long, and they were first cut with a stone
tomahawk, then with a hard shell, into shape. Both ends
were rounded off into a point. The wood was then put aside
to dry, and afterwards the hollow of the vessel was made
with the help of a sharp stick and hot cinders, as in the case
of the holes in a shield. When finished the vessel curved
downwards somewhat in the centre, and so the ends stuck
up, and through these latter a hole was made for the string
handle.

These vessels were sometimes really splendid, and were
very useful for honey or water. The outside was rubbed
smooth with a stone, then cut or carved, and afterwards
bees' wax was put on over all. Timber from the stinging-
tree or "braggain" (*Laportea sp.*) was used as well as that
of the "Bat-tree" for these vessels, its inner wood being nice
and soft, and easily picked out. For the same reason (on
account of its softness) this latter timber was of no use for
shields, etc.

Yet another vessel was made from tea-tree bark, and
was used by natives on the coast for carrying cobra. A
sheet of bark was taken, the ends folded up, and tied so,
with a skewer run through them, then a long stick was put
lengthwise down the middle and formed a handle—in fact,
this "pikki" was made in the same way as the one from the
sheath of the palm flower.

DILLY BAGS.—Unlike a number of words that we white
people have picked up believing them to be aboriginal,
"dilli" is the genuine name for the baskets or bags the
blacks used. This name belonged to the Turrbal tribe;
others were different, as, for instance, the Stradbroke Island
people called a dilly "kulai."

One dilli was made from the small rush found in fresh-water swamps. These rushes grow about three feet high, and when pulled up the bottom end is white, then there is a red length, and the top is green. To prepare them for the dillies, the natives drew the lengths through hot ashes till quite soft, then they twisted them up on their thighs into round string. A loop of string the size of the dilli wanted, was got ready, then a gin sat down and put her legs through the loop to hold it firm, while she worked the dilli on the loop.

Very pretty dillies were made from these coloured rushes, which, however, were not always found on the mainland, though they grew plentifully on the islands. The Stradbroke and Moreton Island gins were especially clever at dilli making. Rush ones were very nice for fish, etc.

The inland women made dillies from a coarse, strong grass (which they called "dilli") found in the forests. (*Xerotes longifolio.*) It is broad and tough, and grows in bunches here and there. The gins pulled this up, split it with their thumb nails to a certain thickness, then softened it with hot ashes, but did not twist it. These dillies were made with the help of a loop held on the big toe.

Other dillies were made from bark-string, such as that of the "ngoa-nga" (Moreton Bay fig-tree), the "braggain" (*Laportea sp.*), the "nannam" vine (*Malaisia tortuosa*), and the "cotton bush" or "talwalpin" (*Hibiscus tiliaceus*), found on the beach at Wynnum or elsewhere. It was the root-bark of the two former which was used. When wanted for string, bark was generally soaked in water during preparation, and afterwards the outer part was peeled away, and the inner rolled into string.

Dillies were made in all sizes. Large bark-string ones were used for soaking certain roots and nuts in water. In travelling the women carried the large dillies, which contained sometimes food, sometimes bones of deceased relatives, and other belongings. A man always owned a small dilli, which he carried under his left arm, with the handle slung over his shoulder. This contained a piece of white clay, red paint, a lump of fat, a honey-rag, and a hair comb. The latter was a small bone from a kangaroo's leg, like a skewer; it was sharpened at one end by rubbing on sand-stone, and was used to comb out a man's hair. If the man was a "turrwan," he also carried his crystal, or "kundri," in the dilli.

Some dillies the blacks made in the same pattern as their fishing nets, and then two small round pieces of wood tied together were used as a netting needle. All nets were made so.

STRING.—Besides string that could be used for basket work, the natives made some from wattle ("kagarkal") bark. This did not need soaking, and was just the inner bark of the stem or branches. It was no good for dilli-making, but was used for binding up the dead, for tying on fishing net handles, and for fixing up huts, etc. Then there was other string, such as the kangaroo-tail sinew, used by women for sewing opossum rugs, and the human and opossum hair twine. The two latter were made from hair twisted and rolled on the thighs, and was splendid string, the human hair being specially valued for great men's belts.

CHAPTER XIV

Games—"Murun Murun"—"Purru Purru"—"Murri Murri"—"Birbun Birbun"—Skipping—"Cat's Cradle"—"Marutchi"—Turtle Hunting as a Game—Swimming and Diving—Mimics—"Tambil Tambil."

GAMES.—As a boy my father has often joined in with the games of the blacks. One of them called "Murun Murun," was played a great deal in the early days of Brisbane on the road to and from camp. As they came along their pathway into Brisbane the natives played this; then again as they returned in the evening. It was carried out so:—The men and boys picked sides, and each player had a small waddie, made for the purpose, which he hit on the ground to make it bounce. The object was to see who could make the instrument bounce furthest—there was a knack about it. The menfolk were very fond of this game; women never played with waddies or spears.

Another game was "Purru Purru." It was played with a ball made from kangaroo skin stuffed with grass, and sewn up. "Purru" meant ball. As in the first game, sides were picked, but the women joined in. The ball was thrown up in the air, and caught here and there, each side trying to keep it to themselves or to catch it from the opposite one.

"Murri Murri" was yet another game, and boys generally played it, though sometimes men joined in. The players picked a clear space, and stood in two lines, each holding a couple of small, sharp spears in their hands. In the open space between the lines a man stood. In his hand he held a piece of bark (generally gum), cut into a circular shape and some eighteen inches across. This, when the game started, he would throw on the ground, causing it to bowl along like a hoop about eight or nine yards from both lots of boys. As it passed they all threw their spears at it, trying to see who was best at hitting it. "Murri" was the native name for kangaroo, and this was really playing at spearing one of those animals.

The toy boomerang has been already mentioned—the natives spent hours with it.

Another instrument ("Birbun-Birbun") made from two lengths of wood tied together in the middle crosswise, was thrown and returned in the same manner. The lengths were about one and a-half inches wide, and eighteen inches long (or they were smaller), and one side of both was more rounded than the other. In throwing, one end of the cross was held. Often sides were taken for this and for boomerang throwing, to see who was cleverest at getting the return. This game is met with at present in the Cairns and Cardwell districts (Dr Roth's Bulletin, No. 4).

Yet another toy (which does not appear to have been hitherto drawn attention to or described) played with like the boomerang, was just a small piece of bark, obtained from the top branches of the fig-leaf box. The bark was taken six or seven inches long and an inch and a-half wide, then was rounded at both ends, and put into hot ashes. While hot it was bent into almost a half-circle, and kept so till, when cold and hard, it had taken on that shape. The bark mentioned is the only kind suitable for these toys, and they could only be made at one time in the year, when the sap was up, and allowed the bark to peel off easily. Father as a boy has made numbers of them, and, of course, has often thrown them and had lots of fun in the game. For sides could be taken for this also. These toys were thrown with the first finger and thumb, and circled and returned as a boomerang.

It may not be generally known that skipping with a vine was an amusement with the Brisbane blacks before ever they saw the white man's skipping-rope used. But so it was, and the vine was circled round and round just as we do a rope, and also, like us, either one person or two could skip at a time. Men or women went in for the amusement, and it was a great thing to skip on the hard sea beach when near the water. Whatever kind of vine was handiest at the time was used—either those of the scrub or a creeper which grew on the seashore. And the blacks skipped away, keeping things going for a long time, amidst great interest and amusement from the onlookers. Some natives were splendid skippers, notably "Governor Banjo" of whom I will speak later. It seemed almost impossible to trip this man out, and my father says one could notice how his eyes watched every movement of the hands of those who turned the vine—for, of course, they did their best to get him off his guard. An extra-determined attempt at this caused roars of laughter always, for Banjo was sure to be ready.

Another amusement which seems European, yet which was common to the blacks in their primitive state, is that known to us as "cat's cradle." An aboriginal held the string on his hands, while another took it off, and so on till they worked it into all sorts of shapes and forms. To the natives these shapes could be made to represent a turtle, a kangaroo, or, indeed, almost any animal or thing. They were very clever at it. The amusement was called "Warru Warru," and with the white man's appearance, his fences got the same name, because of the resemblance of posts and rails to the shape of the string when held in one way across the hands.

In hot weather the natives had lots of fun in the water, and would stay there for hours. It was remarkable that they always jumped in feet foremost, and the women all had a peculiar habit of bending up both legs and holding with their hands to each ankle before they "plopped" in. Many games were played in the water. "Marutchi," or "black swan," caused great fun. One man (the swan) would jump in, and when he had gone some thirty yards from the bank, several watchers would give chase. When they got within catching distance he would dive under, and they followed. If the bird were caught, he was held and tapped lightly on the head, and so died, and was taken ashore. However, he often escaped, because the captors laughed so much that they could not hold him, at the antics he went on with. He would cry out like a swan, and clap

his arms up and down frantically as though they were
wings. Father says it was great fun to watch this game,
and when one bird was disposed of another was ready, and
so on, for perhaps hours. He himself played the swan
sometimes, but, being a white one, was easily seen among
the dark forms, and so was captured quickly.

In something the same sort of way turtle-hunting was
played at. Shallow water (about eight or nine feet deep) in
creek or river, with a white sandy bottom, was chosen for
this sport, so that the players could see down through it.
Three or four people getting into a canoe would paddle
about, and presently a man who had in the meantime quietly
slipped into the water, would come up blowing as a turtle
does not far from the boat. Immediately he popped down
again, but the boat gave chase in his direction, one man
standing up ready to jump in on the next appearance, which
would not be long in coming. The "turtle" would hardly
show himself this second time when he would be gone
again, but the man on the alert would jump in and dive
after the prey, and then another would help bring him to
the surface, and lift him into the boat, when he was taken
ashore. During all the time laughing and joking went on,
indeed the blacks in those days were as "happy as princes."

Often when playing in the water the blacks would dive
down, and stay under to see who had the best wind, and
could remain longest beneath the surface, or they would
try their swimming powers in a race. And they were fond
of getting hold of white stones or bones in order to dive for
these. Throwing them in some yards apart, where the
water was about ten feet deep, the object was to see who
could find the most and bring them to the surface again.
Father has spent hours thus in diving with the blacks;
indeed, splendid as they must have been in the water, I
hardly think their white companion was behind hand at all,
judging from his after years.

Aboriginal children learnt to swim at a very early age.
Small "kiddies" (really babies) were thrown into the water,
and they seemed to take to it at once; swimming came
naturally to them evidently. Their elders stood round

bent on rescue if necessary, and they laughed heartily at the way the child, to prevent himself sinking, would paddle with his hands and feet. My father's brothers taught him to swim in this same way by throwing him into the water.

As I have mentioned before, the blacks were very clever as "mimics." They would amuse each other in that way for long hours together. Generally it would be when they were all lying lazily in the shade after a good meal or swim that some lively members would start with their antics. They perhaps imitated two fighters, or a man hunting, or a bird, or a kangaroo, etc.; indeed, everything they could think of; and they never failed to cause a laugh. At those times, too, they sometimes played with balls of mud in this way: Mud was rolled up into balls, and then two men, apparently solely to amuse the others, got hold of these, and dancing, with their bodies half-stooped all the time, they pelted each other. First one man in the dance turned and held out his cheek for a mud ball, then, receiving it, he threw one back, and held out the other cheek, and so on till they both would be smothered all over with mud.

Though their faces were grave they must have enjoyed the fun (fun with a question after it), and the onlookers, of course, were convulsed with laughter.

Often the young boys had sham fights, with the men joining them. Sides were taken as in the real thing, and everything was carried out after the same style, but the weapons were harmless enough. Tambil meant "blunt"— hence the name of the sport, "Tambil Tambil." The spears used were fashioned from small oak saplings about five feet long and half-an-inch thick, or from strong reeds (*Gahnia aspera*) growing in the swamps or waterholes. All of them, however, were chewed in the mouth at one end into a sort of brush, so that when they hit they did not hurt. The shields were made from a piece of gum bark about eighteen inches long and seven or eight inches wide; two small holes were made in the centre on the under side, and a piece of split wattle branch was bent and put through these holes to form a handle. Sham fights taught the boys how to manage when their turn came to take part in a real one.

My father has fought with the little darkies many a time in a "Tambil Tambil." Once during one held in the hollow below Beerwah on Gregory Terrace, a boy throwing a small sharp spear, which he should not have used in play, hit the white boy with it on the cheek immediately below his left eye. Though the wound was not a severe one and soon healed, a slight scar remains to this day. At the time the little blackfellow got such a scare at what he had done that he cleared out, and did not show himself again for two years. Afterwards, however, when they were both men, my father had a good deal to do with him; his name was "Dulu-marni' (creek-caught), and he was one of the twenty-five to be mentioned later, who bore P as a brand.

As well as the boys, girls were taught to fight and use the "kalgur," so that they could protect themselves later on. The blacks had their way of teaching children even as we have. And they seemed to derive fun from the task. For instance, it was a source of amusement showing the lads how to climb. They picked a leaning tree first, and would instruct the youngster how to hold an end of the climbing vine with his big toe, etc. And then they had games in which they practised throwing spears or waddies at small saplings, seeing who was best at it. All this helped the boys to learn.

Aboriginal children delighted in imitating their elders in every way, and played much as white children do. And they were mischievous, of course. One rather cruel habit they had was to catch a March fly, and sticking a piece of grass through its body, watch with delight how it flew off with its burden. If the March flies were as plentiful and as troublesome as mosquitoes are to-day, one could not wonder at the delight even multiplied one thousandfold. But, alas! one could not treat mosquitoes so.

CHAPTER XV

THE blacks were quick at running, and girls and boys would
sometimes run races together. They also had splendid
walking powers, and would travel long distances in a day
without tiring. Big journeys were seldom necessary, however, except in the case of messengers from one tribe to
another. These latter my father has known to walk from
Brisbane to Caboolture in a day. Of course, the blacks
nowadays lack energy, but in those times it was very
different. They had no sicknesses to speak of, some few
died of consumption, but with the exception of smallpox
there was nothing much else.

Pock marks, as mentioned already, were very bad on some
of the old blacks. Headaches they had, but no toothache
before the whites' arrival, their teeth being beautifully
strong and fit to tear anything almost. In those days,
too, the blacks were very good at bearing pain, some of their
wounds being frightful. They liked the heat better than
they did the cold, and never got sunstroke. Cold weather
was rather disliked, but firesticks were always carried, and
then where they rested nice warm humpies were made.
Some of the blacks were very strong, and they must have
had tremendous power in the neck, for a great weight was
always carried on the head, and, though perhaps miles were
traversed, it did not seem to affect them. In the infant
days of Brisbane father has seen a blackfellow many a
time carry a two hundred pound bag of flour on his head
some distance, from a boat ashore, etc. And a native often
bent or broke sticks across his head in the same way as a
white man will use his knee. It was noticeable that the knee

was seldom or never used for this purpose, but it was done either on the head or with the help of the foot.

By putting an ear to the ground the native could hear sounds a long way off, and he had good smelling powers. Many odours in the scrubs were recognised immediately. For instance, a native walking along would all at once loudly sniff the air, crying at the same time "kappolla! kappolla!" his name for the scrub opossum, which has a strong odour. However, as far as my father's experience went, it is all nonsense that the natives could smell a track, as some declare; they tracked by means of their keen eyesight, as I have already explained; and the fires of those advancing, but yet a long way off, were not smelt, but men, climbing tall trees, would look out for any sign of smoke; hence their knowledge of the approach.

The blacks had fertile imaginations, and in telling stories or "yarns" they stretched a great deal to make themselves look big. They always kept promises amongst themselves, and never stole from one another, though it was counted no harm to take from strangers if they could. However, there were good and bad among them just as there are with white people; though they certainly outshone us in the way they shared with one another. No native would ever be allowed to starve in those days. Old, helpless people were especially well looked after. If any one was sick, too, a great thing was a change of food. For instance, the inland blacks might go to the coast for a fish diet, and vice versa—this being apart from the dugong cure so believed in. Then in the bon-yi season the feasts of nuts were thought much of as a change. These nuts were evidently fattening, for my father says the blacks always returned from a feast extra fat and sleek-looking.

The aborigines did not look on each other as greedy when they ate a lot, but would laugh and joke over that sort of thing. Father remembers well an incident when he was a boy, in connection with a blackfellow especially noted for his eating powers. His big brother John thought he would try this man, just to see how far he could or would go. So he provided him with a loaf of bread and a leg of mutton.

Generally the blacks ate so much, then put anything over into a dilli for future use, but this man did not stop till it was all gone! After that he was dubbed "Greedy Mickey" always.

Weeping with the blacks was a sign of joy as well as sorrow. When visitors came into a camp they sat down and both sides would look at one another, then before a word was said, a crying match started as a sort of welcome. They were noisy creatures sometimes, and the singing and beating of hands indulged in under certain circumstances could be heard a long way off.

The aborigines, as a whole, were cowards in many ways; for instance, they were afraid of the dark. Also some men were very cruel in the way they beat the women-folk in their power. Children were well-treated, though. In a fight both men and women were brave enough, and would not give in readily.

Each tribe had its own boundary, which was well known, and none went to hunt, etc., on another's property without an invitation, unless they knew they would be welcome, and sent special messengers to announce their arrival. The Turrbal or Brisbane tribe owned the country as far north as North Pine, south to the Logan, and inland to Moggill Creek. This tribe all spoke the same language, but, of course, was divided up into different lots, who belonged some to North Pine, some to Brisbane, and so on. These lots had their own little boundaries. Though the land belonged to the whole tribe, the head men often spoke of it as theirs. The tribe in general owned the animals and birds on the ground, also roots and nests, but certain men and women owned different fruit or flower-trees and shrubs. For instance, a man could own a bon-yi (*Araucaria Bidwilli*) tree, and a woman a minti (*Banksia amula*), dulandella (*Persoonia sp.*), midyim (*Myrtus tenuifolia*), or dakkabin (*Xanthorrhœa aborea*) tree. Then a man sometimes owned a portion of the river which was a good fishing spot, and no one else could fish there without his permission. In this way a part of the North Pine River, near the present railway bridge, was owned by "Dalaipi," the head man of the North

Pine tribe. To primitive man it is clear that "property" was not "robbery."

When an aboriginal died his personal belongings, such as nets and weapons, were divided amongst his sons; and a woman's dillies and yamsticks were given to her daughters. The eldest children had the first choice, but if there were no children, the other relatives got the belongings. Sometimes a man's sons would be too young to get his tomahawk or knife, etc.; then perhaps his brothers got them. His wife, if alive, generally divided these belongings.

I have spoken of the belief the blacks had that the night-hawk had some connection with the origin of all women, while a small bat held similar relationship to all the men. These hawks and bats might perhaps correspond with the so-called sex-totems in other parts of Australia. Besides this, there were intimate relationships between the family and certain animals—possibly on lines similar to those fol-lowed in the "clan-totems" described from other districts. For instance, one old North Pine blackfellow is still alive, and his family, he says, was connected with the carpet snake. This man is of interest, as being the last of his tribe —the old Brisbane or Turrbal tribe, of which North Pine formed a part. He is of the same age as my father. The latter met him first in Brisbane when they were both chil-dren, and they used to play and fight together. The white boy saw the other—at Barrambin (Bowen Hills)—put through the "Kurbingai" ceremony and so made a "kippa," but he does not know if he ever went through the greater or "bul" ceremony. Afterwards when the blackboy grew to manhood, he was taken into the mounted black police, with whom he remained a long time. He has been all over the North of Queensland in that capacity.

This solitary member of a once numerous tribe is now at Dunwich, supposed to be dying. "Sam" they call him there, but his own real name is "Putingga." The meaning of the latter is lost now—he does not even remember it himself. His name as a "kippa," or young man, was "Yeridmou," which meant the mouth of a native bees' nest, with the bees continually going in and out. Sam is greatly rejoiced nowadays if he sees my father, and he feels himself a most important personage because he knew him so long ago. Asked once at Dunwich what his age was, he replied, "Ask Mr Petrie." The questioner, who related the incident afterwards, did not personally know father then, who was indeed miles away.

The writer saw "Putingga" at Dunwich once, and he was greatly indignant, or rather his tone of voice seemed to say he was, because she could not pronounce some of his words in the real way as father did. Many aboriginal words are simple enough, but others are dreadful, and no one on earth, according to those Dunwich blacks, is like Mr Petrie. They laughed at his daughter and wanted to know why she could not talk like him—no one else can, they say. The admiration they expressed, and their joy at seeing him, was really amusing. Being his daughter, the writer came in for a share of attention, and was simply laden with bouquets of wild flowers when she left them. There were two old gins there, the last of the Moreton Island or Chunchiburri tribe —blind Kitty ("Bournbobian") and Juno ("Junnumbin")— who had not seen their white friend for some fifty years, and they knew him immediately; blind Kitty by the voice. They wailed and cried round him in quite a pathetic manner. The blacks had excellent memories, as this will show.

CHAPTER XVI

Folk Lore—The Cockatoo's Nest—A Strange Fish—A Love Story
—The Old-woman Ghost—The Clever Mother Spider—A Brave
Little Brother—The Snake's Journey—The Marutchi and Bugawan
—The Bittern's Idea of a Joke—A Faithful Bride—The Dog and the
Kangaroo—The Cause of the Bar in South Passage.

It may surprise some people to learn that the aborigines
had their "fairy tales" just as we have, and these they used
to repeat one to the other even as we do. The name they
gave a tale was "mog-wi-dan." "Mogwi" meant ghost in
the Turrbal language (though it was "makuran" further
north), therefore I suppose the tales were really "ghost
yarns." Here are some of them taken, however, of late
years from the blacks (and related as told); for my father
did not pay much attention to their stories in the old
times :—

The Cockatoo's Nest

Once upon a time there lived happily together on an
island three young aborigines, a brother and two sisters.
This island was not very far from the mainland, and the
three often used to gaze across at the long stretch of land,
and think of journeying forth from their island home to see
what it was like over there. They felt sure they would find
lots of nice things to eat. So one day, by means of a canoe,
they really did cross over, and began without loss of time
to seek for 'possums, native bears, and so forth. In this
search round about they at length espied a hollow limb,
which looked uncommonly like a place where a nest would
be, and so, going into the scrub near by, they cut a vine for
climbing. Coming back to the tree, the young fellow climbed
up, while his sisters waited beneath. When he had cut
open the limb, he found to his joy a cockatoo's nest with
young birds in it, and these latter he proceeded to throw

down one by one to his sisters, the fall to the ground killing the poor little things.

Now it so chanced that as the young blackfellow picked up the last little bird from the nest, a feather detached itself from its tail, and floating away on the air at length settled fair on the chest of an old man asleep in a hut some distance away. This old man was really a sort of ghost who owned the place, and the feather disturbed his rest, and woke him up. Divining at once what was happening, he arose, and, getting hold of a spear and a tomahawk, sallied forth to the tree, where he arrived before the young fellow had started to climb down. Seeing the birds dead, the old man was very angry, and said, "What business you take my birds? Who told you to come here?" And he commanded the tree to spread out and out, and grow tall and taller, so that the young fellow could not get down, and, taking the dead birds, he put them in a big round dilly, and carried them to his hut.

Although the old man did not wait, the tree did his bidding, becoming immediately very wide and tall, and the young fellow tried his best to get down, but could not. So at last he started to sing and sing to the other trees all round about to come to him, which they did, and one falling right across where he stood, he was able to get to the ground that way. Somehow, though, in coming down he got hurt, and the gins had to make a fire to get hot ashes in order to cover him up in these. He lay covered up so for about half-an-hour, at the end of which time he was all right again.

Of course these three felt very indignant at the old man's behaviour, and they thirsted for revenge. So calling all the birds of the air to them, they sought their assistance. These birds went in front, while the three cut their way through the thick vine scrub to the old man's hut, and ever as they went, to drown the noise of the cutting, the birds sang loudly, the wonga pigeon especially making a tremendous row with his waugh! waugh! waugh! When they had got nearly to the hut, the old man, who had been trying to make up for his disturbed sleep, heard the noise of the birds, and called crossly to them, "Here, what do you make such

a noise for? I want to sleep!" But even as he spoke
he was dozing, and presently went off right, suspecting
nothing, and when the blacks reached the doorway, looking
in, they saw him quite soundly sleeping. So the three
clutched their weapons tightly, the man his spear, and the
women their yamsticks, and advancing into the hut, they
all together viciously jobbed down at the old man, and
lo and behold he was dead! His body was dragged forth
then and burned, and after the hut was robbed of the
young cockatoos and all objects worthy of value, it also was
burnt, and the three blacks found their way back to the
canoe, and departed home to their island, laden with the
spoil.

A STRANGE FISH

On Bribie Island once two young gins were wandering
round, and ended by losing themselves. When they found
that they were really lost, they were somewhere about the
middle of the island, at a place where lots of grass trees
grew. This place is still to be seen. Wasting no time in
idly crying over "spilt milk" these gins—two sisters—began
to look round for suitable camping ground, and coming to
some saltwater lagoons, they built their hut on a dry part
near by. Then leaving everything snug, they went to see
if there were any fish in the lagoons that they could spear.
They looked and looked, but could find nothing except one
great big round peculiar fish, which was the shape of the
moon. So with their yamsticks they speared this fish, and
capturing it carried it to the camp, where they made a big
fire, and got plenty of nice red-hot ashes. Opening out
these ashes they put in the fish, and then covered it up like a
damper, and left it there to cook, while they both went off
to seek some "bangwal" to eat with it.

Returning, to their dismay, this pair found the fish had
gone—the heat had brought it back to life again! There
were its tracks plainly showing—the gins could see the
ashes it had dropped all along as it went. So they followed
these tracks, and presently espied the fish against a big
bloodwood tree—half way up the trunk. One of the gins,
therefore, went back for the yamsticks they had left behind
in their hurry, while the other stayed to watch, and on the

former's return, they both tried to spear the fish, and pelted sticks at it, and did their very best, but to no purpose; it kept going gradually up and up. This made the gins feel very disgusted, and sad, too, because they had lost their feed, and one said to the other, "Sister, one of us should have stopped and watched that fish, then it would not have got away." The thought of the meal they had lost was too much for them, and after a little they broke down and wailed and sobbed with the pain of it! However, they waited for the rest of the day, looking now and then helplessly at the tree.

Towards dusk, what was the gins' astonishment on looking up once more, to see the fish actually travelling westwards in the sky. They stood and gazed open-mouthed some few minutes, then giving up all idea of ever again capturing such a strange fish as that, they left, and went back to the camp.

Next morning these sisters went out on to the main beach to gather yugaries there. The elder sister, by the way, had a little son with her—just a baby—and this child they left on the beach when the yugaries were gathered, covered with a 'possum rug, while they went to get more "bangwal," meaning not to be long away. However, during their absence the tide came up, and the child was washed over by the waves and covered with sand, and on the women's return they only found him by one little foot sticking out. Of course, they were in a great way at this, and, digging the little dead thing out, they carefully buried him beyond the water's reach. Then feeling restless, they travelled on and away along the main beach till they came opposite to Caloundra, where they swam the channel. Here on the mainland they found some fine caves, and camped in one of these for the night—this very same cave is still in existence.

Next day, travelling on again, the gins camped in another cave, and so they journeyed along the beach, till at length they came to Mooloolah Heads. Again they swam and so got to the Maroochy beach, and when they had come opposite the island "Mudjimba"—some people call it "Old Woman's Island"—they saw a great long "bon-yi" log (gigantic it must have been) stretching away from where they stood to the island. Thinking at once that it would be nice to find what the island was like, the gins crossed over on this log, when, lo and behold, the moment they stepped ashore it vanished and was gone. They knew that they were stuck there then, and said one to the other, "How do you like this place? We had better make up our minds to live here, because we can't swim ashore." Her sister answered, "What will we get to eat?" "Oh, whatever we can find, 'winnam' (breadfruit), and fish and crabs." Looking up she saw the moon. "Oh, look, look, sister, there's the fish we killed!" This made the other feel sad, and every night through the long, long time that followed, whenever there was a moon, these two thought it their fish, and sometimes they laughed and said it looked funny seeing only half a fish! And they are there on that island yet; and always in the middle of the day smoke can be seen rising from their fires, though they themselves are invisible.

A LOVE STORY

A little mouse or "kuril" (kureel) had a big round humpy, and in it she sat day by day making dillies. She was left all alone there for a long time, for her friends and relations had all gone off to a "bon-yi" feast. Now, it so happened that there was a young fellow among her acquaintances who liked her very much, and as he travelled along with all the others he began to miss his little friend. At first he had thought that she was somewhere among the crowd, but finding this was not so, he at length turned back all by himself to seek her. He was armed with a tomahawk, a spear and shield, and waddy, and was able to get 'possums and honey, etc., on the journey back. The way was long, and it took him some little time, but he came bravely laden with all sorts of dainties for his lady love.

Imagine the latter sitting in her hut, weaving dillies. She had made quite a number, when all at once everything seemed to go wrong. The string kept breaking, and breaking, and breaking, and she simply could not do a stitch correctly. She began to feel flustered, and wondered what on earth was the matter, and yet all the time she knew quite well that "some one" was coming nearer and nearer. At length, about four or five o'clock in the afternoon, the young man arrived, and found his little girl sitting with lowered head over her work. His shadow fell and darkened the doorway, and looking up, she saw him there, and, silly child, she fainted! "What is the matter?" he asked. But she did not answer for a long time, and then, "What you come for?" "I come for you." "What for?" And he replied, "To marry you. Your father and mother promised you to me long ago. I suppose you hungry?" "Yes," she murmured; and he gave her some food, tenderly, let us hope. Then the young fellow said, "We better travel tomorrow and join the rest of them." So next morning she went off with him, leaving all her dillies and belongings. They were about a week travelling until they came to their friends, by whom they were welcomed, and the young girl was satisfied to learn from her people that it was even as her sweetheart had said—they had been chosen for each other when quite young.

The Old-woman Ghost

A married couple once were left all alone to camp by themselves, the rest of the tribe having gone travelling to a fight. Now these two used to go out every day seeking food, and they were especially in the habit of going to the scrub for grubs in the dead trees there. One night the man lay dreaming, and as he dreamt he fancied they were again in the scrub, and while in the middle of getting out a grub his tomahawk slipped and cut his wife very badly on the chest. Waking in the morning, he informed his wife he had had a bad dream, and when she asked what it was, told her, and added she had better stay at home that day. But no, she said she would go, and, getting her own way, she went. While in the scrub she kept running to pick up grubs which fell from the rotten wood as he chopped, and, thinking of his dream, he warned her: "Keep away, keep away, the tomahawk may slip and cut you." However, she foolishly persisted in coming near, and at last what the man feared really happened—the tomahawk slipped and cut her a frightful gash across the chest. So he bound her up very carefully, and, carrying her home, put her to bed. Three days and nights he nursed her, and she was so ill that he thought she was going to die, and began to think he had better let her people know. He suggested this to her, and she said, "Yes, you go and bring them—I be all right here." So, as he had a good way to go, the husband made a nice, snug hut before leaving, and filled it with all sorts of things —food, wood, and water, all ready to her hand.

The poor thing was not to be left in peace, however, for when the husband had gone, and she was all alone, the old woman, half-devil sort of ghost of the place, thinking she smelt something, came along and called from the outside of the hut, "Barbang!" Now "Barbang" meant "grandmother," and so the woman inside answered, "If you are my grand-mother, come in." The old woman went in, and said she, "What is the matter with you?" The other showed her wound. "I'll suck it and make it better," said the hag. So she sucked and sucked, and began to tear and bite at the flesh as well, and the sick woman lying bearing this, knew then who it was she had to deal with, and if she wasn't careful she would be eaten up altogether. Politely she thanked her visitor, saying she felt easier, and asked where the old woman was camped. "Oh, not far. I have a little daughter there." "Well, you go and bring her, and come and stop with me and keep me company. Don't be long." At this the old woman went off, thinking she'd come back provided with weapons, and, sneaking in, would "do the deed." The moment she had gone, however, the sick woman got up, the thoughts of what might happen giving her strength; and, getting a hollow log, placed it where she had been lying on the floor, and, covering it up with 'possum rugs, made it look like herself. Then she told the log to moan and moan as if in pain, and, hurriedly leaving the hut, went to try and follow her husband.

By and bye, the old hag turned up again. As she drew near the hut she heard the moans of pain, and her mouth watered, and she smacked her lips, thinking, "My word, I'll have a good feed!" The log called out, "Come along, grandmother. Why have you been so long?" And the grandmother came along, and entering the hut, quickly went up to the heap of rugs, and plunging downwards with her yamstick, stooped, and started to bite and worry with her teeth. She found her mistake then, and set up an awful cry of rage and disgust, moaning at the good feed she'd lost. "Oh, how stupid of me to go away; why didn't I wait and watch her?" And she was so wild and blood-thirsty, that, after she had looked for tracks and couldn't find them—for the sick woman had jumped along in the grass on purpose—she went home, and killed and ate her own daughter. Whether the wounded one eventually reached her husband, or failed by the way, history omits to tell us.

THE CLEVER MOTHER SPIDER

A big spider had her nest in the ground, with its neatly-finished trap door. She had a number of children, this old spider, and sometimes would shut them all safely in, while she herself sat outside singing in the sunshine. At other times she allowed them out hunting, and then the youngsters would roam all round about everywhere, enjoy-ing themselves mightily and coming home laden with 'possums and other food, when they would have a good feast, and afterwards be ordered to bed and shut up for the night.

Now, there were some strange men who wanted to get hold of these spiders, and the old woman knowing this laid her plans accordingly. When she thought they were coming, she got all her brood inside and shut the door. It was such a dear, neat little door that one could hardly see it when shut up. Then the mother set to, and made fires all round about in a circle, so that the strangers coming would think they (the spiders), were sitting round these fires. The clever old thing sang then to herself, so happy was she that her children were safe, and climbing up and up by means of a web, she sat overhead, and when the strange men came, pricked her body and sent down blood on to them, and they were thus poisoned and died. Even so did this clever old spider get rid of her enemies.

A Brave Little Brother

A mother and father once had occasion to go a long way off, and leave behind them till their return their two children —a young girl and her little brother. These two, during their parents' absence, went into the scrub to look for yam roots; the sister dug for them, while the boy, who was only a little chap, played on a log and danced and sang. He sang so merrily that the sister became afraid, and asked him to "sing softly," for fear a strange blackfellow would come along, and, killing him, take her away. He promised, "All right, sister; don't you be afraid." And he sang very gently and softly for quite a long time, till forgetting, his song got the better of him again, and he sang loudly once more.

A second time the sister remonstrated, and again the boy was quietened, only, however, to forget, as before. This time his song did attract a strange man, who came and caught hold of the girl's arm and started dragging her away. The poor little boy said pitifully to him, "Oh, don't drag her like that!" But the man took no notice of the child, and went on dragging. So, as he was stooping down to do this, the little fellow went behind and struck with all his might at the back of the man's neck with a "bakkan" (instrument sharp-pointed like a pick), and killed him. "You see," said the boy, who was jubilant then, "I'm not frightened of blackfellows; I can fight them!" And his sister answered, "Oh, but two or three may come, and then you will be killed." So the boy said he would be quiet, and he was for some time, but in the end forgot again.

In the meantime, the spirit of the dead man went and told his mates that there was a girl and little boy in the scrub, the girl digging for yams, and the boy singing and playing on a log, and the little chap must be an awful little thing, for he had killed him. So two or three went together, and took a dog with them, and coming to the scrub, started to "sule" the animal on to the boy. The poor little chap got frightened, and begged, "Oh, don't send on the dog! Don't! Don't!" But fancy showing mercy to a venomous little thing who had killed their mate! The child was hunted and killed, and the sister was carried off.

THE SNAKE'S JOURNEY

A very long time ago a carpet snake and a black snake started out in a canoe, in time of flood, from the mouth of the Pine River. Marvellous as it may seem, their canoe was just a shell of the Moreton Bay chestnut ("mai")— probably a gigantic one! The black snake was ill, so the carpet snake had to do all the work in managing the boat, also he kept a sharp lookout on a native dog who swam and swam after them trying to catch them. The way was long, and the current was strong, and they were tossed this way and that, but ever just behind came the dog, swimming and swimming all the time, though he couldn't manage to catch up. What a queer sight it must have been, if only some one could have seen it! The two snakes in their tiny canoe; and the dog paddling close behind, despairingly, frantically, as though for very life, in the strong deep water. At length the current took them to Moreton Island, where they landed, the snakes first, who left the canoe and went up on to dry land; then the dog, who was so greatly exhausted with his swimming, that he just lay down on the beach and expired.

Snakes are not supposed to be able to smile, but these two did, when, on coming back to seek their canoe, they saw the carcass of the dog! However, their boat was washed away, and they had therefore no means of getting home again. Where they had landed was what is now known as an end of Moreton Island, near South Passage. In those days there was no passage, but one long island, so the snakes bethought them to travel along this island, and see what they could do that way. Coming at last, after a weary time, opposite Southport, they swam across to the mainland, so determined were they to get back again to their own home, that they journeyed from there overland to the Pine River.

THE "MARUTCHI" AND THE "BUGAWAN"

Once upon a time, a black swan ("marutchi") and a fish-hawk ("bugawan"), who were cousins, were playing together on the beach, when their companions all went off without their knowledge, travelling to get "bon-yi" nuts, etc. The hawk was painted red with a white neck, and the swan black with a red nose. When these two found they had missed the others, they knew it was no use going after them that night, but it would be better to wait till the morning. So when morning came, "What shall we do? I can't fly," said the swan. (It was moulting season.) And the hawk replied, "Well, it's not easy for me to walk." "Never mind," said the swan, "you will just have to walk and keep me company." So they walked, following in the track of their friends all the way.

For a long, long time they went on and on—it must have been for a couple of months—and every night they camped where their friends had camped, without seeming to come nearer to them. At last they came to a mob of strangers fighting with their own people, so pausing before showing themselves, they painted and "did up," even as blackfellows do, and then went forward amongst the fighters. They were armed with boomerangs, spears, and shields, and they fell to and fiercely fought the strangers. Before their advent the enemy were getting the better of it, but no sooner did these two appear on the scene, than the tide turned, and instead of their friends gradually losing ground, the enemy were beaten further and further back on all sides to their mountains and ridges, and rivers, and scrubs. It was all quite the work of these two new comers—this victory—and their friends thought them just wonderful, and ever afterwards looked upon them as "great men."

THE BITTERN'S IDEA OF A JOKE

One of those birds with a long beak, which sits and watches for fish—in fact a bittern—once set a dugong net at "Dumba" (part of Stradbroke Island). Next morning, to his delight, when he went to look at the net, he found he had been successful, and had caught a dugong. So he set to work, and fastened it to his canoe.

Now he had a lot of companions, this bittern, and he knew very well that they would all look forward keenly to a feast, therefore he made up his mind to have some fun with them first. So he got them all to get into their canoes, and leading the way, set off, towing the dugong behind him. They kept along the shore for a long, long way, and at length came to Russell Island, and landing there made a camp. Of course, every one looked forward to seeing the dugong cooked. But no, it was left in the water, and next morning they all were obliged to follow the owner in another journey to another landing place. This time it was Coochimudlo. Seeing that the dugong was still left in the water they all asked where it was to be cooked? "Oh," was the reply, "I don't know yet, we will go further on." So on and on they went from Coochimudlo to Peel Island, and from there to Green Island, then afterwards to St. Helena, and at each place they camped, and were disappointed again and again, for the dugong remained in the water. However, at St. Helena, the owner, looking all round him, said, "Well, chaps, Mud Island is the last island—we will cut up the dugong there, and have a feed." They were all exceedingly glad to hear this, for they were hungry, and had had about enough of travelling about in such an absurd fashion. So landing at Mud Island, the dugong was rolled up on shore, and a big fire was made, and he was roasted and cut up, and divided out to all—young and old—who had followed.

Whilst the enjoyment of eating was in full swing, what should happen but that the old woman ghost of the island should sniff the air, and she said to herself, "There must be something nice near at hand, I'll go and see." So arriving on the scene, she greeted them all with, "Hullo, my grandchildren, I'm living here, and am hungry, give me some food." They gave her something, and the old thing, making a pretence of going off for a dilly, went really to lay plans for the capture of all the flesh. But they suspected this, so the moment her back was turned, hastily got into their canoes, and made off with it all. Coming back, she found they had gone, and, looking seawards, saw them in their canoes. In her rage, she ran right out into the water, and hitting at the waves made them rise up and capsize the lot. Each separate piece of flesh then turned into a dugong, and the water round about was filled with them, also with the bodies of those who had waited so long for their feast. Some of the latter were drowned and some escaped, and so endeth the story of the bittern and his joke.

*   *   *   *

In some of these "fairy tales" mention is made of burial in the ground. Now, as I have before stated, the Turrbal tribe, when they did not eat their dead, always placed them up on trees. It was different, however, with the island tribes, who dug graves in the ground, most probably because the sandy soil was easily managed, whereas to the others it would mean a hard piece of work always. Graves were not made in the shape we make them, but always round. A body was not allowed to touch the sand, but first sheets of tea-tree bark were put in the hole, and the corpse, wrapped in more bark, placed on these. Then sticks were stuck in the earth round about the body, and these supported a sort of bark roof over it, on to which the sand was then shoved in. Some islanders had the idea that to mourn by the graveside of a relative cured their ills. Tales were, of course, repeated from one tribe to another.

A Faithful Bride

Three brothers once lived on Peel Island who all admired and wished to marry the same young girl—a daughter of a great chief. So they went in turn to her, taking an offering of food, to see if she would have them. But she evidently was saucy, and would have nothing to do with the first two who went, and the remaining brother was sick and thin, and anything but nice to look upon. When his turn came to go, his brothers kicked him and jeered at him, saying, "She won't have you!" However, he went for healing to the graveside of their mother, who had lately died, and when he came away he was quite well and strong and nice-looking, and, presenting himself before the young girl, she married him. So that his brothers should not know this, he hid her under the water, and day by day took food to her there.

At last the brothers began to notice something, and they more than once suspected the truth—that he had married

the young girl. So, by-and-bye, they offered to help him
build a hut for her, and to this he agreed. When the hut
was finished they used to coax their brother out with them
day by day, and did all in their power to cause him to meet
his death. Of course, they tried to hide this intention, but
he saw through it all very well, and told his wife, saying
that if a little bird came into her hut at any time, and
dropped from its beak a drop of blood, she would know
that he had been killed.

One day the three went fishing, and somehow the married man got his hands caught fast in a shell, and leaving
him there alone to perish, the brothers went home, thinking,
of course, that now one of them could marry the young
girl. In the meantime, though, the little bird had gone
to the hut, and so, knowing what had happened, the wife
killed herself before anyone could turn up. Finding this
state of affairs, the brothers went off to where they had
left the poor unfortunate, thinking that if he were still alive
possibly the wife's life might be restored. But he was gone
—had turned into a fish and drifted seawards.

And so the poor young wife's married life ended thus
early, and she turned into "winnam" (breadfruit) flowers.
And the husband did not remain a fish, but became a
rainbow, and always after this, to the end of time, the
pair of them were able to gaze one upon the other to their
heart's content, which must have been very satisfying.

The Dog and the Kangaroo

An old man who lived with his tribe on a little island
possessed a dog which he was exceedingly fond of. One
day this dog, wandering round, perceived a kangaroo over
on another island, and swimming across began to chase it.
Of course, the kangaroo made off, and the dog followed.
Now, the old man missed his dog, and picking out his
tracks, got into a canoe and crossed over after him. And
this is what he saw:—His dog was chasing a kangaroo, and
every now and then the animal would tire and lie down
to rest, and the dog, being tired as well, also laid down,
and the two would look at one another. The old man

thought that in these intervals he could catch up to the pair, but whenever the kangaroo saw the man approach, he made off again, and the dog followed, in spite of many calls and entreaties from his master.

This sort of thing went on till many, many miles had been traversed, and the old man often stood stockstill and scratched his head, wondering what had come to his dog. He did not blame his favourite, however, but all the time heaped curses upon the kangaroo, saying it was certainly his fault. At length the kangaroo and dog both got into the water, one after the other, and started to swim to yet another island. Landing, they were both so exhausted that they died. The old man could not see this, however. When he saw them swimming he stood helplessly watching and crying, and at length turned back again, and seeking his canoe, went home to his island, wailing all the way, for had he not but one dog, and that one surely lost to him now?

Time passed, and one day some strange men from the distant island, visiting friends, told the old man that they had seen the dead bodies of the dog and the kangaroo.

THE CAUSE OF THE BAR IN SOUTH PASSAGE

The following is not a "fairy tale," for the aborigines really thought and declared it was true :—

A young fellow from "Wiji-wiji-pi" (Swan Bay) was once travelling along the outside beach of Stradbroke Island when he came to a hut and a campfire. Now, he wanted a firestick, so took just one from the fire, and went on again. There happened to be an old woman in the hut who owned the fire, and she saw him do this, and was so angry that she followed in the blackfellow's tracks, right along the beach, on and on till they came to Point Lookout, and then round to Amity. Here on the beach at Amity there were canoes, and the young fellow, seeing this, hastily launched one and got into it, and pulled across to Moreton Island. The old woman did likewise, and then on and on again they went, as formerly on the outside beach, till at last they came to "Gunemba" (Cape Moreton), where a large number of blacks were camped.

In from the beach kippas were going through with their ceremony, and the young fellow ran in amongst these, thinking to hide himself. But the old woman was too smart for that, and she followed and picked him out from amongst the lot, and, shoving him into a huge dilly, so carried him back again away round to the canoes. Laying him down on the beach, she went to launch a canoe, and while her back was turned the prisoner contrived to get loosened somewhat, and taking a couple of bone skewers (used for combing hair) from his back hair, he was ready with these to poke the woman's eyes out as she stooped to lift him up again. After that, of course, she was helpless, and so the young fellow got free of the bag, and lifting and carrying his enemy, placed her in the launched canoe, and left her to drift away. She drifted out to the high bank in South Passage, and stuck there.

This old woman's bones, washed by the water, gradually heaped up and up on the bank, and formed what we now know as the Bar there. Wonderful, no doubt, this may seem to us, but to the aborigines it was all quite true!

*　　*　　*　　*

Sometimes short tales formed themes for the substance of a corrobboree, though these latter were generally founded on fact. As, for instance, the following:—

A young fellow went forth to fight with all his tribe, leaving his wife and child at home. Meeting the enemy, he got speared, and was killed, and his comrades buried him where he fell. On their return to camp the wife was told of what had happened, and putting her child on her back, she at once went to seek the grave. Finding it, she placed the child on the ground, and digging up the earth came to the body. Here she then lay, singing to herself in a lamenting fashion, while the child went in and out of the grave, up and down, playing all the time while the mother mourned.

In the corrobboree the wail this woman sang was repeated many times, and her action at the grave described.

*　　*　　*　　*

A water-lizard or "magil" (moggill) was lying on a log

in the water, and he was extremely comfortable, warming himself in the sun. A blackfellow came along and frightened the lizard, who slid off into the water, then as he swam away turned round and said, "You shouldn't disturb me; I was comfortable in the sun."

With regard to reptiles, animals, or birds, etc., the natives were wonderfully quick and accurate in noticing every little detail and peculiarity of habit, much more so than many white people. For instance, they could tell just how a "magil" would lie on a log in the water sunning himself, and they knew evidently that the warm sun was pleasant to him. They knew, also, just how he would slide off into the water when any disturbance came along. Exactly how a bird would sit watching for fish, almost the expression on its face as it pointed its beak (if it is allowable to speak of "facial expression" with regard to a bird), seemed to come to them instinctively. This gift of observing detail was natural to them, and they possessed it all unconsciously. It must have been very useful to them in those old days. White people with this same gift—people who see things with "seeing eyes"—love nature very, very much more than those who look and see nothing.

Of course, tales drawn from the imagination were recognised as such. No blackfellow really thought that animals went to a "bon-yi" feast, or that birds would go hunting kangaroos, as in the following:—

A magpie was once out after kangaroo, and, seeing some, he hunted them towards his son; the butcher-bird, calling out that they were coming. The butcher-bird, who was in readiness, called his sweet note in reply, and then he killed two and carried them home to his mother, camped on the edge of the scrub. This son then took to his wings, and went off hunting again, going far, far away from his parents, to whom he never came back.

CHAPTER XVII

Duramboi—His Return to Brisbane—Amusing the Squatters—His Subsequent Great Objection to Interviews—Mr Oscar Friström's Painting—Duramboi Making Money—Marks on His Body—Rev. W. Ridley—A Trip to Enoggera for Information—Explorer Leichhardt—An Incident at York's Hollow—An Inquiry Held.

I HAVE spoken of the way in which different aboriginal tribes were related one to the other by marriage. When a man had a wife given him from a neighbouring tribe, he stayed with that tribe for some time, hunting with them, etc., as though he were one of themselves, before he took his wife to his own people. When he did take her to his own tribe, he introduced her to his friends, and if his mother or sisters were alive they would look after and be very kind to her. Subsequently his friends invited some of her friends to live and hunt with them for awhile. This sort of thing was done from tribe to tribe. My father has known them all connected in that way—the Ipswich and Brisbane, the Brisbane and the Pine, the Pine and Bribie Island, and the Bribie Island and Maroochy blacks, etc.

Often in this way aborigines would stay for some time with tribes other than their own, just as white people travel to visit their friends. So it was that father encountered some of the very old blackfellows of early times, hailing from different parts, and he had long yarns with them on various subjects. Once at a "bon-yi" feast on the Blackall he came across two or three men who belonged to the tribe the white man, "Duramboi," had lived with those fourteen or fifteen years. These men said they were very sorry when "Duramboi" left them; they cried a lot, for they missed him very much. They all looked up to him. He was a great man to hunt for game, was always lucky in spearing kangaroo, and was a good hand at spear and boom-

erang throwing. He could also climb splendidly, using a
vine as they did, and was so smart in capturing 'possums
or honey. Then he was a great fighter.

When father was a boy of about eleven years old, he
was sitting one day on his father's verandah on the Bight,
listening to several squatters who were yarning there.
Presently one of these latter jumped up in excitement,
calling, "Here comes Petrie and his crew!" and sure enough
a boat was in sight coming round Kangaroo Point. Off
the squatters all ran down to the river bank, followed by
the boy, and they went to the spot where the steamers now
leave for Humpybong—there was no wharf then, of course.

This was the arrival of Andrew Petrie from his trip to
Wide Bay in 1842, when he brought back with him Davis
("Duramboi") and Bracefield ("Wandi"). When the boat
got in close to shore, "Duramboi," who was in the bow,
took hold of the boathook to fend her off, and to hold her
steady while the others got ashore. A little thing made an
impression on the boy's mind. As "Duramboi" stood there,
he licked the palm of his hand so that the boathook would
not slip, in exactly the same way as the natives licked their
hands preparatory to throwing a waddy or boomerang.

That same night of the landing, some of the squatters
got "Duramboi" and "Wandi" to sing aboriginal songs, and
tell them about the blacks. The two men sat down tailor-
fashion as the natives do, and one had a couple of waddies
and the other had boomerangs, and with these they beat
time to their songs. The squatters kept them going for
nearly half the night.

"That would have been the time," says my father, "if
some one had taken Davis in hand, to write the history
of his life among the blacks, it could have been got easily
from him then, before he got back into 'white' ways. Afterwards he and 'Wandi' would say nothing about their
former life. It was a great pity some one did not do it,
for such would have been worth reading. However, in
those days men were more for fun and devilment than for
writing peoples' lives.

"To show you how stubborn Davis was later on, I said

to him some time after his return, 'Davis, you ought to get some one to write your life among the blacks—you could make a lot of money.

" 'I don't want to make money. I get enough now to keep me. If anyone wants to know about the blacks, let them go and live with them as I did. I'll tell you a thing that happened the other day. A swell who lives in this town brought another swell with him to me, and said, "Mr Davis, allow me to introduce Mr So-and-so to you, from Sydney; he has come all the way to see you, and to get some information about the blacks." Do you know what I said to him? I said, "Do you see that door there? Well, the sooner you get out of my shop the better, and if you want any information about the blacks, take your clothes off and go and live with them as I did." And off they went with their tails between their legs, and I saw nothing more of them. No one will get anything from me about the blacks.' "

This was quite true, according to my father, and you might just as well have tried to pump the river dry as get anything from Davis in those days. He would never allow anyone to take his photo (there were no snapshots then), and I am informed that the well-known painting of him by Mr Oscar Friström, of Brisbane, was painted not without a great deal of trouble, after the man had died. I am indebted to that artist for my illustration, and to him belongs the honour of bringing into existence, the original from which all others have been taken.

Duramboi was a blacksmith by trade, and after Mr Andrew Petrie brought him back with "Wandi," the pair were not put with the other prisoners, but each got a "ticket of leave." Therefore they were free to work for others or for themselves, so long as they did not leave the country. "Wandi" was signed over to Dr Simpson at Goodna (called Red Bank in those days), and he was killed some time afterwards through a limb of a tree falling on him. Davis was started with a blacksmith's shop at Kangaroo Point, and he got on well, and made money. After some time he married, and later bought a piece of ground on the north side in George Street, next to Gray's boot shop, and there he put up a blacksmith's shop and started afresh. He prospered, and made a lot of money, so bought property in Burnet Lane, where he and his wife went to live. After this he built a small brick store alongside his smithy, and went in for selling crockery, giving up the other business.

So things went on till Mrs Davis took ill and died. The old man lived in single blessedness for some time, then, as is the way of man, although his married life had not been smooth, he "longed to be married again," with the result that he wedded a widow with one daughter, and this wife outlived him.

I have already spoken of the ornamental marks Davis had on his body. He had also spear and other marks gained through fighting. "Tom" saw all of these—Davis showed them to him when he was first brought back from the bush. "A few months after his return, though," father says, "I don't think he would have shown his marks even to the King."

In the early days the Rev. W. Ridley came to Brisbane to learn what he could about the Queensland aborigines, and he sought out my father, who was quite a lad at the time, to get information from him. He seemed very clever, and as fast as the boy could speak the language he was able to write it down. He took a part of the Bible and read out verse after verse, and the lad followed in the black's tongue. Afterwards reading out the aboriginal version for his young companion's approval, it was almost as though a black-fellow spoke.

This was after the return of Davis to civilization, and Mr Ridley wished an interview with this man of unusual experience, and asked father to manage it for him. He was about to journey to the Dawson River to see the blacks there, and wanted some words of the language that Davis knew. So father went to "Duramboi," and asked him to come to Mr Ridley, but the man flatly refused, saying, "If he wants to know about the blacks let him take his clothes off, and go among them and live with them, as I did." Father tried to coax and get round him, but he would not move.   However, nothing daunted, the young fellow went again next day, and at last "Duramboi" gave in, and said he would go, "as your father and mother were so kind to me; but he (meaning Mr Ridley) will do no good with the blacks." So the pair of them went to the reverend gentleman, and the latter started to read a verse of the Bible to Davis, who, however, would not follow, but said he would give names of animals and things like that, which he did, Mr Ridley taking them down.

On Mr Ridley's return from his trip he told father that nearly all the blacks he came across understood what he (father) had told him, but on the contrary, he only met two who understood the words from Davis.   This was because he had gone too far inland, for of course Davis thoroughly knew the language and all else about the tribe he had lived with.

At this time there was very little communication between Sydney and Moreton Bay—as Brisbane was then called. Only about once a month or two a vessel would arrive with stores for the settlement.   Some few days after Mr Ridley's return from the Dawson, and on the night before, a boat was to leave for Sydney, that gentleman, accompanied by a Rev. Mr Hausmann, turned up at my grandfather's house at about eight o'clock, with the object of getting father to go with them out to a blacks' camp.   Mr Ridley said he had heard there was a great gathering of natives at "Buyuba," or as the whites called it, "Three Miles Scrub" (now know as Enoggera Crossing), and as he was obliged to leave for Sydney next morning he would like to talk to the blacks that night.   Father said it was too late to look up a horse to accompany them (they both had horses), and his father (Andrew Petrie) thought so too.   However, Mr Ridley in the end persuaded the Scotchman to allow his son to go.   "He is a young lad, and it is only three miles to walk, it won't hurt him," he said.   So off they went, the boy tramping alongside as they rode.

When the scrub on the creek at the crossing was reached it was very dark, and they could see nothing, though the

blacks were heard talking in the distance. The road ran
through the scrub, and when the two riders got about half-
way through they dismounted, and the boy thought to
himself, "At last they are going to give me a spell on horse-
back." But no, down on their knees they went, and he
watched them as they prayed. When they had finished,
they warned the boy not to call out, as that would frighten
the blacks and make them run away, but "Tom" thought
he knew one better, and said the best way would be for him
to cooey, as they would know who it was then, otherwise
none would remain to be interviewed—they would all make
off, thinking some one was after them. His companions
agreed to this, and they both mounted again.

It tickles one's sense of humour to imagine the feeling
of half amusement and disgust with which the boy saw
them do this. No doubt his young legs had not been idle
all day, and he would like to have rested them. Boys, I
am sure, often think their elders do not consider their
feelings sufficiently, though this boy did not complain of
the incident. Still, they have feelings, of course, and one
would not lose by remembering it; rather the opposite, for
a right-minded boy would never take advantage of kindly
consideration. Most likely "Tom" would have refused if
he had been asked to ride more than just a little way. However, no doubt, Mr Ridley's mind was much preoccupied
and he did not, of course, think of such a thing as a
youngster's tired legs.

When this party of three had got through to the other
side of the scrub, father cooeyed (at that time he could
cooey as well as any blackfellow), and the natives knew his
call and answered, and some of them came forward to meet
their visitors. Arriving at the camp, the boy told them
what his white friends had come for, and they all clustered
round, men and women, and, squatting down, prepared to
listen. Mr Ridley brought out his notebook, and, opening
it, proceeded to read out something of what father had
previously given him; then he talked to them for about half-
an-hour, and sang a hymn he had made from the aboriginal
words. During all this the blacks looked at one another,

and the knowing ones pointed at the white boy, and made signs as though to say, "We know who told him all this." At length they began to tire, being kept at it too long, and one by one got up and walked away till at last almost all had gone off to their different huts. So the white men bade them good-night, and returned to Brisbane, and the boy was not sorry when the end of his walk came, as it was late. "I was glad to get to my bed," he tells me.

Next day some of the young blackfellows turned up at the Petrie's home, and they said to father they knew who had told that man all his rubbish, and picking up a piece of paper started mimicking Mr Ridley. Then they asked, "Where that fellow stop?" "Oh, he has gone away in a big ship to Sydney." "When he come back?" and so on. That night at Enoggera, there were some two hundred blacks in camp, and Mr Ridley and Mr Hausmann seemed pleased they had seen so many all together, and were able to speak to them.

Another gentleman, long since dead, whom my father remembers meeting when a boy, was the explorer, Leichhardt. He also visited my grandfather Petrie, and got "Tom" one day to accompany him through the bush and help collect plants and seeds.

Here I may mention an incident already spoken of by Mr Knight in his work, "In the Early Days." In 1849, when father was a boy of about seventeen, a man named Humby was brickmaking in York's Hollow, just about where the show-ring of the Exhibition now is. One night, between ten and eleven o'clock, this man came to the Petrie's house in a great state of fear, and said that a blackboy employed by Grandfather had told him that the blacks had run a bullock into the swamp at a place the natives called "Barrambin" (where Mr P. M. Campbell's house now stands), and that they had hamstrung it and intended to roast and eat it. Father's eldest brother, John, who was a young man then (some dozen years older than "Tom"), came and woke him up and told him Humby's story. Father said he didn't believe a word of it, the blacks wouldn't touch anything belonging to the Petries. "Never

mind," said John, "you must come and see if it is the case.
Humby has gone to inform the police, and we must get
out there before they arrive."

So they went off, accompanied by two men in Grandfather's employment—John Brydon and William Ballentine
—and reaching the camp at Bowen Hills, father who was
the only one who could speak the native's tongue, told
the blacks the story of the bullock. They said it was all
lies, that the blackboy had invented the story out of revenge
because an old gin had beaten him. Finding the boy, who
turned out to be one of his playmates called "Wamgul,"
father asked whatever made him tell such a story. The
boy owned to his fault, saying that the gin had beaten him
so soundly that he declared he would go and tell Humby,
the brickmaker, a story about a bullock being killed,
and then she would get punished along with the rest.
Hearing that this was how it stood, John Petrie asked his
young brother to get two natives to accompany them to the
swamp that the bullock was supposed to have been driven
into, but hardly had they got down the hill on the way
there, when bang! bang! sounded behind them at the camp
they had just quitted. Turning, they all started to run back
again up the hill, meeting as they ran the poor darkies
rushing frantically pell-mell down to jump into the creek,
bullets whistling overhead. John Petrie called out "stop
firing," and then he sought Lieutenant Cameron, who was
in charge, and explained to him that it was all stories about
the bullock. So the lieutenant called his men together and
gave the order, "Right about face, quick march!" and off
they went to Brisbane.

It seems that when Humby went for the police, Chief
Constable Fitzpatrick was in bed, and did not think it
worth while getting up, so he got a man under him to tell
Dr Ballow (a magistrate) about the affair. The latter in
his turn was not sure how he should act, so he asked
Lieutenant Cameron of the military, to take it over. The
lieutenant divided his men into two, and it was the half
who were not under his immediate supervision who so
thoughtlessly and cruelly fired on the blacks.

The next day Grandfather sent his son out to the camp to see if anything serious had happened. On the way the boy met a number of natives coming in, three of them wounded—one had been shot on the thigh, another on the arm, and the third had a flesh wound on his forehead, where a ball had grazed. They all said to father, "What for the diamonds (soldiers) shoot us? We did nothing." Their friend explained how it had all happened, and they were quite satisfied and told him to go to camp and he would find "Wamgul" lying there wounded, unable to rise; and also if he went to the swamp, he would see for himself that no bullock had been there. "Tom" went, and found "Wamgul" in great pain, and then going to the swamp, he saw that the natives were quite correct. So when he got home again, he told his father and his brother John, of the wounded men and the boy, and that there were no traces of the bullock. "Wamgul" was then brought into the hospital, and it was not very long before he recovered. About three years afterwards this boy joined the black police, and was sent up country. He remained in the force till his death.

An inquiry was held on this affair, and father was sent for to interpret for the blacks. Only two soldiers were found guilty, as bullets were missing from their pouches, while the others had theirs full. These two were sentenced to six months' imprisonment, and Chief Constable Fitzpatrick lost his billet through appreciating his bed somewhat too highly.

CHAPTER XVIII

A Message to Wivenhoe Station after Mr Uhr's Murder—Another Message to Whiteside Station—Alone in the Bush—A Coffin Ready Waiting—The Murder at Whiteside Station—Piloting "Diamonds" Through the Bush—A Reason for the Murder—An Adventure Down the Bay—No Water; and Nothing to Eat but Oysters—A Drink out of an Old Boot—The Power of Tobacco—"A Mad Trip."

IN about 1846, when my father was a young boy of fourteen or fifteen years, he was sent with a letter to Wivenhoe Station, on the Brisbane River, just after the murder by the blacks of Mr Uhr there. A blackfellow accompanied him, to show him the road to the station. After leaving Brisbane, the first night was spent at Moggill Creek, and the next day the two, after travelling a good many miles, came to a large scrub on the river, where a number of blacks were making a great noise hunting paddymelons. The black man cooeyed, and the others hearing him, came to the travellers, and finding where they were going, and who father was, they were very nice, and invited the pair to stay with them that night, which they did. The white boy lay half the night listening to the blacks exchanging news with the visitor, laughing and joking away quite happily.

Next day they resumed their journey, and on reaching the station father delivered the letter, and was taken inside and refreshed. They stayed the night there, and the following day the boy was given another letter to take back to Brisbane for Richard Jones, who lived where Sir Samuel Griffith now lives at New Farm, and who, if my father remembers correctly, was a relative of the murdered Mr Uhr. On the return journey another night was spent with the blacks, who welcomed them heartily, and sped them on their way to Brisbane, where they arrived safely.

On yet another occasion "Tom" was trusted with a

letter, but this time he went alone, and his destination was Whiteside Station. The letter carried the news that old Captain Griffin had arrived in Brisbane, and needed horses to take him out to the station, where his wife and grown-up family were already settled. It was late in the afternoon when the boy started, and darkness overtook him ere the scrub at the present Cash's Crossing was reached. He proceeded to go through the scrub, however, but it was so dark, that giving the horse his head, he retraced his steps back to the edge again, lest he should lose himself, and decided to wait till moonrise.

This is the one memory my father has of feeling a little afraid in the bush. He lay down with his horse's bridle fixed firmly to his arm, and in that position slept (?) off and on for some hours, being aroused every now and then by a pull at his arm, as the horse started at some noise. It must have been rather an uncanny feeling lying there alone in the darkness—alone, and yet not alone, if one counts the innumerable 'possums and other creatures with their weird noises.

Poor old Captain Griffin met his death through, one hot day, quenching his thirst from what he thought was a cask containing water. However, the fluid proved to be a wash for sheep with footrot. His widow was a lady, who, years before her death, had her own coffin prepared ready. It reposed somewhere up in the loft awaiting its day of use-fulness. My father has seen it many a time. It is said that she showed the curiosity to visitors.

Another time the blacks had attacked two shepherds at the Upper North Pine at Whiteside Station, and killing one, left the other for dead. The latter had his nose broken and his face otherwise disfigured with a waddie, but he lived. Word was sent to Brisbane about this murder, with the request that some one would be sent out to try and catch the murderers. Therefore about a dozen soldiers were told off for the duty, and instructed to go to the station and see what they could do. My father was sent for, and asked if he would accompany the red-coats, as they did not know their way through the bush.

Very early one morning the party started, and when they had got about half way the soldiers began to tire. It was a very hot day, and their heavy red coats and muskets made them grow damp and feel uncomfortably warm. So down they sat for a rest, saying prayers on behalf of the blacks, and some flung off their coats to get cool, and others turned to father and said, "How far have we got to go yet?" and when he told them they growled again.

After half-an-hour's rest they wearily continued their way, but every little while paused and asked again how far it was, blessing the road and the "black devils" until at length, when almost in sight of the station, they sat down again, declaring they would not move a foot further! "The station is just over the ridge, there," said father, but they only swore and said they didn't care; they'd stay where they were. After a little, however, five or six volunteered to go with their young guide, and when they reached the station the stockman was sent to bring the others.

Next day the soldiers were taken to where the murder had been committed, in order to catch the blacks, but it was of no use, as the latter by then were all down in Bribie Island, and the soldiers might just as well have tried to fly as catch them. Father returned to Brisbane without the "diamonds" for company this time, who, though they stayed a few days longer, did not accomplish their object.

Some years after the murder of this shepherd, the natives told my father why they had killed him. Once, they said, they went to his hut and looked in. No one was about, but they saw some flour, and feeling hungry went off with some, and made a damper of it. When cooked they commenced to eat, but found it "barn" (bitter); then some got sick, and three of the number "very much jump about," and died. The rest of the damper was thrown away, and the blacks swore that they would have revenge for their friends. They also said that while they were hunting for 'possums and sugarbags on this run, two or three of them were shot, and a white man riding, came unexpectedly upon one poor fellow, and caught and tied him to a tree and flogged him with a stockwhip, telling him on his release that if he caught him again on the ground he would shoot him.

Can one wonder that the blacks committed murder? Father remembers a yarn he had about fifty years ago with several very old blackfellows at one of the "bon-yi" feasts he attended. These men told him that a great many blacks and gins and pickaninnies were poisoned at Kilcoy Station —they were there at the time. The white fellows gave them a lot of flour, and it was taken to camp and made into dampers and eaten. Shortly after some of those who had eaten of it took fits, and ran to the water, and died there; others died on the way, and some got very sick, but recovered. The old men showed how each poor poisoned wretch had jumped about before he died.

Another time in the early days, during my father's boyhood, a Mr Hill, a contractor in Brisbane, asked Mr Petrie, senior, if he would allow "Tom," his son, to go with him to the Logan River, as he wished to take possession of a raft of cedar timber he had brought there. He said he would be very grateful for the lad's company, as he knew then he would be all right should they encounter any natives. My grandfather demurred at first, but afterwards gave in, and father had just to go and be content. Mr Hill also wanted a blackfellow, so the boy picked one of the name of "Wonggin-pi" ("Wonggin" is the tail part of a kippa's head dress). He had no trouble in getting this blackfellow—a dozen wished to go when they heard of the trip, and that father was going.

Mr Hill procured a boat about the size of a ferry boat, and got a sail for it, then put on board a three-gallon keg of water, also a kettle and rations to last about a fortnight. The party started in the early morning from Petrie's Bight —a crew of four—Mr Hill, his man (Old Tom), "Wonggin-pi" (the blackfellow), and last, though not least, my father. They had a nice gentle breeze from the north-east, and got along first rate, reaching Coochimudlo that night, where on the mainland they found two men and two or three blacks with the raft waiting to deliver it to Mr Hill. It was high water at the time, so the latter could not, of course, measure the timber, but in the morning the raft was high and dry, so it was then measured and taken over, and the men were given an order for their money in Brisbane. The raft was not very large, and the timber was all hand-sawn into square flitches, the bottom tier being held fast by chains, and a number of logs lay on top. The party made fast the raft to the bank, and stayed where they were that day, taking a look round about. It was a time of drought, and everything looked wretched and dry, and they had very hard work finding water—almost all the waterholes were empty. However, they got enough to fill their keg and kettle.

Mr Hill now decided to leave the raft where it was, go to where the sawyers were cutting the timber in the scrub up the Logan or Albert River (it is not remembered which), and pick it up on their return. So they made a start, the men and blacks who had brought the raft accompanying them in their own boat. Arriving at the place, the sawyers showed Mr Hill all the fine timber round about, and the party stayed there in the scrub a few days.

On the return journey, when the river had been traversed down to its mouth, they came across a bank of fine oysters, about two hundred yards from a small island. Thinking it would be nice to take some with them, they decided to fill a couple of bags, and in order to do so stuck a stick in the mud to tie the boat to, and intending to be but a short time away, left the sail up. Filling one bag, they carried it to the boat, and telling the darkie to get in and bail out, went to fill the second. Suddenly, while in the midst of this, a strong gust of wind blew up, and away went the boat, darkie and all. The tide was fast coming in on the bank, and the boat was fast drifting away, with the blackfellow helplessly putting an oar out first on one side, then on the other, which, of course, pulled the boat round, and every moment things got worse.

In the meantime, father was calling with all his might to the blackfellow to pull the sail down, and at last the distracted fellow heard and did so, but after that again he paddled with one oar as formerly, and, of course, went on drifting further and further away. He did not seem to hear, though the boy called his loudest to use both oars, and at last was so far away that father thought he would never get back. By this time, the water was up to the waists of the three on the bank, and it was rising quickly, and small sharks were swimming round them—they could not know but what at any moment a large one might appear!

Under these agreeable circumstances father was for swimming to the island, but it turned out Old Tom and Mr Hill could not swim, and they said to him, "For God's sake do not leave us." Father thought he could swim with one at a time, if they would just lean their hands on his back, but before he started to carry out this proposal he had another look towards the boat, and discovered that at last the blackfellow was pulling with both oars, and coming in the right direction. So they waited. Nearer and nearer came the boat, till she reached the three, not a bit too soon, for the water was up to their armpits.

"We were thankful to get into the boat," my father says, "and the poor old darkie was regularly fagged out. We put up the sail, and started on our journey again, but had not gone far when a strong north-east wind sprang up, and the sea got very nasty, so we ran for shelter to a small island, and pulled the boat up on the beach to save her being knocked about, and also to be certain that she would not be blown away from us again. Well, we were stuck there four days! At the end of the second we had no rations or water left—nothing but oysters, and the more we ate of these the dryer we got. Poor Old Tom kept saying he would not care if only there was a bit of tobacco to chew.

"On the fourth day the sea grew calm, so we launched the boat, and started once more on our way to the raft. It was a very hot day, so we decided to land on the mainland, and look for water. When we got ashore the darkie and I went off with the keg, hoping to fill it, and we also carried a tomahawk and a sharp stick. We travelled miles, but every hole we came to was dry, and though we dug in the swamps with the stick and tomahawk, and scraped the earth

out carefully with our hands—no water. At last we gave
up, and returned to the boat quite tired out, reporting our
want of success. Old Tom said, 'Oh, if only I could get
some tobacco, I would not care about water;' but Mr Hill
looked 'down on his luck,' and said nothing. I think, though,
he would have given his raft of timber willingly if he could
have got a drink, and the darkie was in a great way; he
kept rinsing his mouth with the salt water. My mouth
also was in a bad state—it was frightfully dry. The only
thing we could do was to eat oysters, and the more we did
that the more we wanted water. It was so hot that we
rigged up the sail of the boat for shelter, and when night
came on all lay down in a heap under it, and tried to go to
sleep; but none could. The thirst seemed to affect the
blackfellow most.

"About eight o'clock it commenced to thunder, and the
lightning came. We saw that a storm threatened, so prepared by putting our pint pots and kettle under the points
of the sail to catch the water. Old Tom had his boots off,
so the darkie, unseen by the owner, took one of them, and
placed it also under the sail. Then at last the rain came
down, and the pint pots got full, and didn't we all have a
good drink!

"The boot also got full, and the darkie, putting it up to his
mouth, soon emptied it, and put it back again for more!
The rain didn't last long, but we managed to get enough to
drink, and to fill the kettle.

"We started again then on our journey, and reached the
raft, which we found all right; so two got on to it, and with
long poles pushed it along, while those in the boat towed
it. We kept close to the shore, so that we could touch the
bottom, and we took it in turns on the raft and in the boat,
and worked with the tide. We got along all right till we
came to the bay on the south side of Cleveland Point, when
our water came to an end again, and the tide was on the
turn, so we had to drop anchor and wait. The tide wouldn't
suit till late in the afternoon, so the darkie and I started off
again in search of water, leaving the others to watch the
raft.

"When we got out of the boat we sank up to our knees in mud, first one leg, and then the other, and had to struggle on so with rests in between, for it was hard work, till we reached firm land. Then we trudged along, and, as before, every hole we came to was dry. At last in following a gully we came to one with water, which, however, didn't look extra clean; but as soon as the darkie saw it he dropped the keg, and, running to it, down he lay flat, and putting his mouth to the water drank till I began to think he would never stop. Then my turn came; and, afterwards, getting a supply, we carried it back to the boat. When in sight of the latter, the darkie started jumping about in delight, and called out we had plenty of water. Old Tom, when he'd taken his drink, said if only he had a piece of tobacco to chew he wouldn't call the Queen his cousin!

"After eating some oysters, I went with the blackfellow on to a bank covered by a few feet of water, and there we tried with a boathook to spear some stingarees, and small shovel-nosed sharks which swam about in plenty. They however, were too quick for us, so we had to give up all idea of that sort of meal and return to the boat.

"We now made a start for Brisbane, the darkie and myself on the raft, and the others in the boat, and we got round Cleveland Point, and went along towards Wynnum. It was getting late in the evening then, and we on the raft felt fagged out, so just lay down and went off to sleep. Waking some time in the night, we at first thought we had lost the boat, but afterwards found it had swung round and come in close to the raft, and the two occupants, who were also worn out, were fast asleep. As far as we could see, we were somewhere between St. Helena and Wynnum, and the flood-tide seemed to be taking us towards the Brisbane River; so we thought we would also get into the boat, lie down with the others, and let the boat and raft go where they liked. It was not long before we were asleep again, and when all woke in the morning we were high and dry on a mud bank in the Boat Passage. As luck had it, the tide had taken us in the right direction.

"About nine o'clock the Custom House boat came in

sight, coming to look for us—they thought we had all been drowned or killed by the blacks. They could not get nearer than one hundred yards because of the low tide, but Old Tom did not wait—he jumped out into the mud, and though he sank nearly to his waist, went on leg by leg till at length he reached them. The first thing he asked for was 'tobacco' —not something to eat, though he must have been very hungry—and when he got a fig he put half in his mouth and chewed away with great gusto. As soon as the tide rose they brought the rest of us food, which we 'tucked' into, and soon felt all right again. The blackfellow commenced to mimic Old Tom going through the mud for his tobacco, and he lay down and rolled about laughing at the way the old man had chewed it up. He had no laugh in him while he was hungry!"

When the tide was high enough the raft was floated, and the Custom House boat took it in hand as far as Lytton, and eventually the party of four arrived in Brisbane, after what my father now terms a mad trip. "It was madness," he says, "to venture out in such a small boat so badly prepared. We thought also we would only be away a fortnight."

CHAPTER XIX

A Search for Gold—An Adventure with the Blacks—"Bumble Dick" and the Ducks—The Petrie's Garden—Old Ned the Gardener— "Tom's" Attempt to Shoot Birds—Aboriginal Fights in the Vicinity of Brisbane—The White Boy a Witness—"Kippa"-making at Samford—Women Fighting Over a Young Man—"It Takes a Lot to Kill a Blackfellow"—A Big Fight at York's Hollow—A Body Eaten.

BECAUSE my father knew the blacks so well, he was often asked to accompany people on different expeditions into the bush. On his return from the Turon diggings in 1851, a merchant of Brisbane came to him, and said that gold had been found at Delaney's Creek, or, as the blacks called it, "Nuram Nuram"—"wart" (spelt "Neurum Neurum" on the map), and would he go with him and have a look at the place, for though it had been left it might be some good. The boy agreed, so the merchant procured a pair of horses, a mule to carry the rations and blankets, and a gun and ammunition. When all was ready they started from the town, leading the pack mule, and the first night got as far as the Upper Caboolture, to the old deserted station where Mr Gregor and Mrs Shannon had been murdered, and camped in an old hut there. This hut was not far from the graves of the murdered. Next morning the merchant did not feel well, so they rested where they were for the day, father strolling round and examining the graves.

The evening of the day following Durundur was reached, and after hobbling the horses father went to a blacks' camp near by in order to get a couple of natives to show them a short cut across the ranges to Neurum Neurum Creek. He succeeded in persuading two to accompany them—one an old fellow called "Dai-alin," and the other a young man, and they were to meet next morning. "Dai-alin" was some-what lame—had one leg shorter than the other.

When morning came they started off, with the natives leading, and travelled several miles without interruption. Then climbing up the spur of a mountain, and going down the other side, they came into a very thick scrub, where about one hundred blacks were hunting for paddymelons, making a great row. The two blacks who were with the white men sang out to the others, who immediately clustered round and asked questions. Some of the young fellows grew very bold, and the merchant suggested to father to get the gun ready, for by this time he was very much afraid; but the boy said to leave it to him, it would be all right, and he commenced to talk to and chaff them in their own tongue. Soon they were all laughing, and made no objection when the party started to push on, which they did with a will, reaching their destination that night, and camping there on the bank of a creek.

Next morning after breakfast father started to prospect for gold. There was an old cradle or two there on the bank, and a couple of crowbars, which had been left by those working some time before, and the holes that had been sunk were all filled in by a flood. He tried several places in the creek and got the colour, but no more, so, as it was getting late in the afternoon, decided to wait till next day.

Hanging about over this sort of thing evidently did not suit the blacks' taste, for next morning the young fellow bolted, and the old man wished to go too, and take the rations with him. The merchant at this, thinking there was mischief brewing, said, "We must get out of this," and their horses being handy, they accordingly packed the mule, father meanwhile making old "Dai-alin" hold the creature, telling him that if he offered to run away he would shoot him; but, on the other hand, if he piloted them safely over the mountain to Mount Brisbane Station, he would give him flour, tea, sugar, and other good things. So off they went again, but hadn't gone far when natives appeared on every side, and as they didn't look at all friendly father called to them in their own tongue that he would fire if they came any nearer. There were a lot of wild young fellows in the mob, and these set fire to the grass all round about, but did nothing else, so the party got through all right, losing sight of their black friends eventually, to the merchant's great relief.

Keeping on till they got over the mountain with "Dia-alin" still in front, they at length came in sight of Mount Brisbane Station. Here father told the black man he could go, and on receiving the tobacco and other promised things, the darkie did so, quite pleased with his possessions. His white companions went on to the station, where they stayed the night, and next day made through the bush in a direct line for Brisbane, where they arrived quite safe and sound, none the worse for their little adventure. In those days my father could find his way anywhere through the bush to where he wished to go, so long as the sun was shining, and he knew in what direction the place lay, or if he had been once before. One could never lose him in the bush, but, of course, over the mountains the blacks had tracks cut, and it saved time to be shown these.

Years before this, in fact, during the time of the convicts, there was a poor harmless half-cripple aboriginal, called "Bumble Dick," who belonged to the Brisbane tribe, and who hung about the settlement. He'd had half his foot burnt off when a child. This "Bumble Dick" went once to some sawyers working at Petrie's Bight, and told them that if they would lend him a gun, he would get them "plenty ducks." So they lent an old musket and powder and shot, and off Dick started, quite pleased with himself, taking his wife with him. He went to the Serpentine Swamp near Nudgee, for in those days there were lots of ducks there, and was delighted when he saw some swimming out from among the reeds. He started to load his gun, putting in plenty of powder and shot. Then catching sight of more ducks, and thinking that the more he put in his gun the more ducks he would shoot, he used up nearly all the powder and shot, then he put the gun up to his shoulder and pulled the trigger.

The gun went off—yes, but instead of killing a single bird it burst, and knocked poor Dick down with a cut on his forehead, also smashed up his left hand. The thumb and

the last two fingers were blown right off, and the remaining
ones came off at the second joint. It was lucky for "Bumble
Dick" that his wife was with him, for he was stunned for
some time. When he came to, his wife was crying over
him, and she put dirt on his hand and tied it up; then
they started back to the camp at Brisbane, taking with them
the broken gun.

Next day Dick's wife returned the gun to the owners,
and told them of what had happened to poor Dick, saying,
"Bael gettem duck." Two days after that, again, father
went out to see "Bumble Dick."

"I found poor Dick sitting in his hut in a fearful state,
the cut in his forehead full of wood ashes, and ashes on
his smashed-up hand, which smelt unpleasantly. The poor
fellow was in pain. I said to him, 'What for you put so
much powder and shot in gun?' He replied that the more
he put in the more ducks he expected to kill, and he did not
think the gun would break. 'How many ducks did you
shoot?' 'Bael me know; me shot self, no go see how many
ducks. Bael more me takem gun, that fellow very saucy.'

"Dick was a long time recovering, but eventually he
got all right again. If you said to him, 'Dick, you takem
gun, and shoot me some ducks,' he would reply, 'Bael; that
fellow too much saucy.' You could not get poor Dick to
take hold of a gun ever again; indeed, he would hardly
look at one. And no wonder. Even now I can see the
terrible state his hand was in, and just how his fingers
were torn off."

This misadventure of "Bumble Dick's" reminds my father
of one of his own, when he was a very small boy. When the
Petries first came to Brisbane they lived, as I have said, in
a building on the site of the present Post and Telegraph
Office until their own house on Petrie's Bight should be
built. This building had formerly been used as a factory
for the women prisoners, until they were moved to Eagle
Farm. It was a large building, and was surrounded by a
wall about sixteen or eighteen feet high, and some couple
of feet thick. One large gate in this wall faced what is now
Queen Street. Along the river bank, from Creek Street

to past where Messrs Thomas Brown and Son's ware-house is now, stretched the Petrie's garden, and here they had growing peach trees, figs, mulberries, and lots of differ-ent fruits and vegetables. The blacks used to come and steal the sweet potatoes, so my grandfather Petrie had a hole cut in this side of the wall so that a watch could be kept. The blacks used to swim from Kangaroo Point over to the gardens. In swimming, as before stated, a native used a small log as a help, and carried his dilly on his head.

It was generally on a Sunday, when no one was working in the garden, that the blacks came across for the potatoes. One Sunday six of them were busy at their little game when they were seen through the hole in the wall, and Grand-father and two of his sons—John and Walter—went quietly down to try and catch them red-handed. However, the blacks, seeing them approach, made off, and, taking to the water, started to swim to Kangaroo Point. In the mean-time the pilot boat hove in sight, coming round Kangaroo Point on its way from Amity Point station, and she gave chase, sticking all the time to one blackfellow. The man in the bow of the boat stood up with the boat-hook in his hand, ready to hook the darkie. Whenever they got near him the blackfellow dived down under the water like a duck, and then came up again in quite a different place to what was expected. The boat would have to be turned then, and a fresh start made; and so this went on till the swimmer was almost across the river and fairly beaten, when the man with the boat-hook succeeded in hooking him and then dragging the unfortunate wretch into the boat. He was tied with a rope and taken to the lockup. Next day he was tried and sentenced to a flogging.

My father used to get into scrapes in this garden as well as the blacks. His father's gardener, old Ned, a one-time prisoner (the natives called him "Dikkalabin"), was "an awful man to swear, and a cross old man. Many a time he used to hunt me," says father, "and swear at me, when he would catch me taking fruit or watermelons. He always kept a horse-pistol loaded with slugs, with which to shoot the blacks when he caught them stealing."

One day father watched Ned going to the far end of the garden, and then stole into his hut, and, taking his pistol, went to have a shot at some birds on a peach tree. There were a great number of birds, and so the boy made sure of getting some. He held the pistol close up to his face, in order to look along the barre:, and then pulled the trigger. The pistol did not burst, like "Bumble Dick's" gun, but it kicked frightfully, and the result was a cut lip, a bruised forehead, and a blackened eye for the boy. He was also knocked down, and when he saw the blood thought he was going to die, so started crying. Old Ned, hearing the report and the crying, ran up to the lad, cursing and swearing, and saying, "You will die now." Then he took the boy to his mother, who washed the wounds and put raw beef to the black eye, then put her son up in the kitchen loft. If his father had seen him in that state, the boy would have been severely punished, for my grandfather was a strict old gentleman. Many a "hammering" father got for smoking as a boy; which, however, failed to cure the habit. In this case the youngster was kept out of the way for several days until his wounds were better. When his father did at length come across his small son, he gave him a good talking to, saying he had a great mind to thrash him for using the pistol, and "Tom" promised he would not do it again.

In these days, fierce fights often took place among the aboriginals in the vicinity of Brisbane, and the white boy, who was here and there and everywhere among the blacks, of course, witnessed them. Once there was a great gathering from all parts of the country, the different tribes rolling up to witness a grand new corrobboree that the Ipswich tribe had brought. After the corrobboree a fearful fight came off, some Northern tribes—the Bribie, Mooloolah, Maroochy, Noosa, Durundur, Kilcoy, and Barambah blacks—ranging themselves against the Brisbane, Ipswich, Rosewood, Wivenhoe, Logan and Stradbroke Island tribes. Altogether there were some seven hundred blacks, and they were camped in this wise: The Brisbane, Stradbroke Island, and all from the Logan up to Brisbane had their camp at Green Hills (overlooking

Roma Street Station, where the Reception House is now), the Ipswich, Rosewood, and Wivenhoe tribes were on Petrie Terrace, where the barracks are, and the Northern tribes camped on the site of the present Normanby Hotel.

Previous to the corrobboree, kippas had gone through their ceremony out at the Samford ring, and these young men were now taken to where the women were all dancing and singing on the flat in front of the present Roma Street Station. They were made to walk in pairs, six men, all decorated and painted up for the occasion, preceding them, and six more bringing up the rear. They started with a war whoop from the top of the hill, where the road turns to go up Red Hill, down to where the gins were dancing and singing, and waving about their yamsticks with bunches of bushes tied to the ends. These gins, seeing the boys approach, were delighted to know that they were safe after having been "swallowed by the kundri men," and sticking their yamsticks in the ground awaited their arrival.

Always in these ceremonies the same sort of thing was gone through, and as they have been already described, we will leave them to come to where the old warriors were fighting. The Brisbane side chased the others as far as Red Hill, and then, two of the Northern blacks being wounded, one with a spear through the calf of the leg, and the other with a similar weapon through his thigh, a halt was called. This was done by the friends of the wounded yelling "tor," which meant hit or wounded. A halt in the proceedings was always brought about so. The Brisbane tribe then retreated, and were chased back as far as the road that now leads to Milton on the river bank, when three of their side got wounded—one with a boomerang in the chest, another with a waddie on the head, and yet another man got a spear through his foot. The man with the wound in the head was very bad, the waddie cut the skin right through to the skull; and yet next day he was walking about again.

After these happenings both sides decided on a rest for a while, and so they squatted down about one hundred yards apart. An interval passed, and then two men from one side got up and rushed in a threatening manner across to the others, who retaliated, and so things went on in the usual way of a fight. As the spears and waddies flew here and there the white boy was amazed to see how they were dodged. Looking on, he felt it was impossible for a man to escape being hit, and yet most of the weapons passed between legs or over heads, or were turned aside on a shield.

When some time had been spent in a general sort of fight, an Ipswich blackfellow challenged a Bribie Island black to fight with knives and waddies, accusing him of being the cause of the death of a friend, and calling him all sorts of names, also uttering dreadful threats. The two met, and started viciously hitting at one another, till the Ipswich black split the other's shield; then weapons were thrown aside, and a hand-to-hand fight with stone knives ensued. The cuts were frightful, and father was relieved when at length the pair were separated by those looking on. It was found that the Ipswich black had less wounds than the other, so the former had to stand and allow his enemy's friends to cut him to make things more equal. This, as I have already stated, was always done. It was the aboriginal's idea of justice.

A big fight always lasted several days, and time was allowed in between for the search for food. So in this case, when things had gone thus far, the different tribes separated, hunting all round about. Some, such as the Ipswich, Mount Brisbane and Wivenhoe tribes, hunted in the scrub which used to stand near where the Toowong railway station is now. The blacks called that part "Baneraba" (Bunaraba); Toowong was their name for the bend or pocket of the river on the left hand side travelling from Brisbane, just before crossing Indooroopilly Bridge. The Logan, Stradbroke, and some Moreton Island blacks went over to what we call West End. There used to be a large scrub there on the bend of the river in the early days, and the blacks called the place "Kurilpa" (Kureelpa), which meant "a place for rats." Some crossed the river in canoes, and others swam across. Then some Northern tribes hunted at "Buyuba" (Enoggera Crossing), and others at the Hamilton scrub.

The Brisbane tribe themselves kept to Bowen Hills, Spring Hill, New Farm, etc.

When father went out to the blacks next day to see how the fight was progressing he found every one in the midst of a great feast of all sorts of animals. After they were satisfied, however, they painted and decorated themselves again, and then much the same sort of thing went on. Women fought as well as men, and on this second day father noticed two gins of the same tribe—one a young girl of eighteen years, and the other over thirty—who seemed to have a quarrel to settle. They fought about a young man. One said he belonged to her, and the other said no, he belonged to her; and the jealous pair fought and squabbled very savagely, using not only their tongues, but also their hands and weapons. The younger one seemed to be getting the better of it, when the other suddenly made a prod with her yamstick, and sticking the sharp point into her enemy's body, killed her immediately.

The dead girl's brother at this ran and felled the conqueror to the ground by a blow on the head with a waddie. The blow was so severe that the skull bone showed out, and the woman lay as one dead. Her body was carried to her hut then, as was also that of the other gin, and a great wailing and crying and hacking of flesh began. Amidst all this noise of the mourning it was hardly possible to hear oneself speak, and the white boy, growing a little frightened, went home.

Next day, when father again went to see how things were, he found to his astonishment the wounded gin sitting up; he had expected to find her dead. The wound on her forehead was filled in with fine charcoal. The body of the dead gin had been skinned and eaten.

A good many were wounded before this fight ended, the Brisbane side getting the better of it eventually. Afterwards, when all the tribes journeyed homewards in different directions, they took with them their wounded, carrying them on their shoulders, a leg on either side of the neck.

My father has been present at numbers of aboriginal fights, and he says "it takes a lot to kill a blackfellow."

One thing surprised him greatly. During a big fight at "Dumben" (now called Pinkenba), a blackfellow, in stooping down to pick up a weapon, got struck with a spear, which went in just above the collar-bone, and after going right down through the body came to light again. It seemed impossible that the man should live. And yet he did recover, although he fell away to a mere skeleton first.

Another big "tulan," or fight, father remembers at York's Hollow (the exhibition). He and his brother Walter were standing looking on, when a fighting boomerang thrown from the crowd circled round, and travelling in the direction of the brothers, struck Walter Petrie on the cheek, causing a deep flesh wound. The gins and blacks of the Brisbane tribe commenced to cry about this, and said that the weapon had come from the Bribie blacks' side, and that they were no good, but wild fellows. The brothers went home, and the cut was sewn up. It did not take long to heal afterwards.

At that fight there must have been about eight hundred blacks gathered from all parts, and there were about twenty wounded. One very fine blackfellow lost his life. His name was "Tunbur" (maggot). In the fight he got hit on the ankle with a waddie, and next day died from lockjaw. They carried the remains, and crossed the creek where the Enoggera railway bridge is now, and further on made a fire and skinned the body and ate it. My father knew "Tunbur" well; he was one of the blacks who accompanied grandfather Petrie on his trip in search of a sample of "bon-yi" wood.

"Tunbur" was a splendidly-made blackfellow; he stood over six feet in height, and was very strong. When father heard he had been killed he rode out to the camp at Bowen Hills to see him, but found only a few old gins and men, who said the others had gone across the creek to eat "Tunbur." So as "Tom" was curious to see this performance, he rode on to the Enoggera crossing, but was again disappointed, as it was all over, and only a couple of old women left to clean the bones and put them safely in a dilly. The remains of the fire were still to be seen, and some little distance further a small mound of newly-dug earth with three sticks placed round, nicely tied with grass.   This the gins said was where the waste parts were buried.   Another stick about a yard away was stuck in the ground and also tied with grass rope, and a bunch of grass surmounted the top, which pointed south.   The ground was nicely cleared round this stick, and a footmark printed there, also pointing south.   This told any strange blacks who should chance to come along in which direction the friends of the dead had gone, and a dozen trees notched all round about with little notches marked the place where a body had been eaten.

CHAPTER XX

Early Aboriginal Murderers—"Millbong Jemmy" and His Misdeeds —Flogged by Gilegan the Flogger—David Petty—Jemmy's Capture and Death—"Dead Man's Pocket"—An Old Prisoner's Story—Found in a Wretched State—Weather-bound with the Murderers on Bribie Island—Their Explanation—"Dundalli" the Murderer—Hanged in the Present Queen Street—A Horrible Sight—Dundalli's Brother's Death.

A NUMBER of white people were murdered by the aborigines when my father was a boy, and some of the incidents I have already told you of. He knew all the black murderers of those early days well, and had many a yarn with them. One of them was well-known as "Millbong Jemmy." Now this man's native name was really "Yilbung"—pronounced in English, "Yilbong." He first put in an appearance at the missionary station at Nundah. (Nundah means "chain of waterholes.") Jemmy was taken in hand with some others to be converted. He got on very well for a good while; could say the Lord's Prayer, and the missionaries thought him a model. He had only one eye, this "Millbong Jemmy," having had the other burnt when a child, but he used it well, and always kept it open and on the lookout. His name—"Yilbung"—meant "one-eye."

One night, having noticed where the missionaries kept the flour and tea and sugar, Jemmy made arrangements with some of his mates to be ready at a certain time to help him carry some of these rations. When the missionaries were all asleep, he helped himself to a good supply, and also to the loan of one of their nightgowns, then made off to the bush to his mates, not waiting to say good-bye. In the morning when the missionaries got up, they found that their rations had disappeared, also Jemmy and the night-gown. There was a great to do about this, and going into town the missionaries reported they had been robbed by the blacks.

"Millbong Jemmy" made his way down to Amity Point on Stradbroke Island, and got the blacks there to mark his body, so that he would·be taken for one of them. The Stradbroke people had different markings to all other tribes. Theirs were larger and more raised, and were cut in with sharp shells across the body from one side to the other, about one inch apart, and reaching right down to below the waist.

Jemmy stayed till his cuts were healed, then he left Stradbroke and came back to Brisbane, thinking the whites would not know him again. However, it was not long before he got himself into mischief. One day he stuck up old Marten, the miller, at the old windmill, and took a bag of corn méal. He robbed the mill several times after this, and they failed to catch him always, so a policeman was told off to hide in the place, and watch for Jemmy when he came for his bag of meal or corn. He wasn't particular which it was, but always took the first he came to.

For a day or two the policeman watched, but no Jemmy came, till at last one mizzling sort of day he appeared. Marten, the miller, called to him, "Come on, Jemmy, here is a bag you can have." In went the darkie, thinking all was right, but as soon as he got hold of the bag, the constable pounced on him, and Marten helped to try and get him down. They hit him on the head, but Jemmy picked up an old rusty knife and stabbed the constable in the chest. As luck would have it, however, the latter had on a thick pea-jacket, and the knife only bent and did no harm. Then the constable beat the blackfellow on the shins with a baton, and that soon brought Jemmy to his knees on the ground, and they were able to put on a tight pair of handcuffs, and tie him up with a rope.

Word was sent for the soldiers to come, and ten or twelve marched up to the Windmill. Father, boy-like, seeing the redcoats marching, followed them to see what was on. Arriving at the Windmill, the soldiers were all formed up in line at each side of the doorway, and "Millbong Jemmy" was brought out well tied up and handcuffed—a constable on either side, holding him. To my father it seems as though it were but yesterday when he saw the soldiers and the constables march off with their prisoner from the Windmill—the present Observatory—and wend their way down the hill. Jemmy was lodged in the cells that used to stand where the Town Hall is now, and next day he was tried and condemned to twenty-five or fifty lashes. After the lashes he was to exist on bread and water for twenty-four hours.

The old archway where the prisoners were always flogged stood a little further up Queen Street than that part which Messrs Chapman and Co. now occupy. "Millbong Jemmy" was tied to the triangles there, and Gilegan, the flogger, punished him, but was only able to make brown marks on his dark skin. During the flogging it is said Jemmy called to his mother and friends to save him. Afterwards he was taken back to the cells to do his twenty-four hours, and was then set free, and given a shirt and pair of trousers, marked with the Government brand—broad arrow. His wrists were much cut with the tight handcuffs.

"Millbong Jemmy" after his release took a stroll up to the soldiers' barracks—where now the present Treasury Buildings stands. He walked in and looked about him with his one eye. The soldiers or "diamonds" chaffed him, saying, "Hello, Jemmy, you good fellow now, no more steal?" And Jemmy was emphatic in his agreement. All the same, he kept his weather eye open, and, seeing a little box with tobacco in it, watched his opportunity, and when the soldiers' backs were turned, helped himself to a pound, then cleared out and made his way to the Petrie's garden on the bank of the river. There he came across the old gardener, Ned, and gave him the tobacco in exchange for a dilly of sweet potatoes.

The next my father heard of "Millbong Jemmy" was that he had been stealing at Eagle Farm, then again at "Yawagara"—Breakfast Creek. Later, sawyers working in the scrub near the present Toowong railway station—"Baneraba"—spoke of his thieving, and other Government sawyers at Canoe Creek (Oxley) made the same complaint. He was a notorious thief. He was the only blackfellow my father knew who was not afraid to travel at night, and all alone, and would be heard of one day at one place, and then perhaps again the next day twenty miles away. He was blamed for the murder of Mr Gregor and Mrs Shannon, the sawyers at North Pine, and several other murders. Father often met "Millbong Jemmy" in the bush at Bowen Hills, and had a yarn with him, and gave him a piece of tobacco. To the white boy he seemed kindly enough. He never would own that he had killed anyone, but admitted he had often stolen, saying he did not see any harm in taking flour when hungry, and that as the white men had taken away his country, he thought they should give something for it.

About this time Davie Petty, who owned a cutter, was in the habit of using it for going down the Bay for oyster shells for making lime, and also for carrying firewood with which to burn the shells. One day he and his man were getting wood just at the mouth of Norman Creek, when the blacks came upon them, and the white men, thinking it better to be off, ran to the cutter. The man got on board first, and Mr Petty handed him the tools, then the gun— muzzle foremost. As the latter was pulled down the cock caught in Petty's shirt cuff, and the weapon went off, shooting the man through the body. The owner of the cutter then got her out into the stream, and, dropping anchor, put the wounded man into the boat and pulled up to the wharf at the Colonial Stores.

This all happened about four or five o'clock in the afternoon. Father remembers seeing them put the man on an old door and carry him so to the hospital, the poor fellow saying, "Little did I think, when loading my gun, that it was to shoot myself." The white boy followed the procession and in the hospital got up on to the window-sill and watched the doctor as he dressed the wound and took out the slugs. All the time he heard the poor man repeat again and again, "Little did I think, when loading my gun, that it was to shoot myself." When the doctor had finished, and was putting in some stitches, the man expired.

"Millbong Jemmy" was blamed for being one of those who frightened David Petty and his man. Eventually ten pounds a head was offered for the capture of some of these aboriginal murderers. A short time after the above event (1846), Jemmy made his way to the scrub at "Tugulawa" (Bulimba), to where some sawyers were at work. One of these sawyers afterwards told my father the following:—

Seeing Jemmy coming, and knowing that a reward was offered for his capture, they called to him, "Come on, Jemmy, and have a pot of tea and something to eat," and as soon as he was fairly seated and eating, they suddenly caught hold of him, and tried to tie him. But he struggled and fought manfully, almost getting free, and managed to pick up his waddy and strike one of them. Then they got him to the ground, and one of them seizing a gun shot him through the head. After that he was bound and put on the bullock dray, and taken to the settlement, dying, however, on the road up. Before his arrival word spread of his capture, and that he was being brought in, and father and a number of others started off down to the Government wharf (Colonial Stores) to see the much-talked of Jemmy. They waited till the dray appeared on the bank of the river at South Brisbane, and saw the driver back up as close as possible, then take the body by the leg, and pulling it off, let it fall like a log to the ground. A boat's crew of More-ton Island blacks were waiting at the old ferry to put the body in a boat and bring it across to the north side, and these men did not seem by their long and solemn faces to relish their job. The body was taken to the hospital—the site of the present Supreme Court.

The last my father heard of "Millbong Jemmy," the "great thief and murderer," as he was called, was that his head had been cut off and boiled free of flesh, so that a cast could be taken of it.

There is a place on the Caboolture River known as the "Dead Man's Pocket." It got its name this way. Three natives of twenty-five (to be referred to later on), who all in after years possessed my father's brand on their arm, were responsible for the death at this place of one white man, and at the same time the attempted murder of another. The survivor, who was left for dead, was one Peter Glyn, an old prisoner, and father saw this man afterwards when he had come out of hospital. The story he told ran thus: A party of white men left Brisbane in a boat to go to the Caboolture River to look for cedar timber. At the mouth of the river they picked up three Bribie Island blacks, thinking they would be of use in guiding them to the timber that grew in the scrubs. Leaving the others, two of the white men went off with the natives, while the rest stayed to take care of the boat. A big strong blackfellow—Dr Ballow, the whites called him—walked first through the scrub, and, following him, came Peter Glyn, then two more natives, then the other white man, Peter Grant. Both the men carried guns, the first one having a double-barrelled one.

Travelling along in this fashion for some distance through the lonely scrub, Peter Grant perhaps turned over in his mind all the tales he had heard of the blacks, for he grew afraid. Calling out to Glyn, he warned him to beware of the natives—they intended to hit him. Glyn turned round and answered: "If you are frightened, it is no use you coming. You had better return to the boat, and I will go alone." However, they continued as they were for some time. Then once again Grant's feelings got the better of him, and he called out as before. Turning suddenly in response, Glyn's gun struck the black in front as he turned, and the weapon went off, the charge of shot grazing along the fellow's back, causing a flesh wound. Maddened by this, the blackfellow tried to wrest the gun from Glyn, who sang out to Grant to shoot the beggar, and he would then quickly do for the other two. However, Grant seemed unable to move, and stood still like a statue while his life was taken, and all the time Glyn's hands were beaten unmercifully in order to loosen his hold on the gun. They continued to hit him on the hands and the head till he lost consciousness.

Coming to himself, Glyn saw Grant lying dead beside him, with a log across his body, and he tried to rise and walk. But his hands were so much bruised and swollen that the poor wretch could not use them, even to fix his trousers, which had fallen down somewhat and acted as a

regular hobble to his legs. So there was nothing left for
him but to crawl as best he might, and it seemed to him
that he went this way many miles, his misery increasing
with the hours. For the unfortunate could not even cast
off the clothing which hobbled him. He was in this
wretched state when found. He lived through this only
to meet a not very noble death in the end, some years
afterwards. Through being somewhat the worse for drink,
he fell from a fishing boat into the river (near Messrs
Thomas Brown and Sons' present warehouse), and was
drowned.

About a week or two after this murder, father went to
Bribie Island to look for a boat which had been washed
away by a flood. He started from Petrie's Bight, accompanied by his young brother George, two blackfellows, and
a half-caste boy, called Neddy. At Bribie Island no blacks
were to be seen, but fresh tracks appeared everywhere.
Father sent off one of the old men accompanying him to
follow the tracks, and tell all he came across not to be
afraid, that friends were there. In a very short space
about thirty turned up, some with fishing nets, and they
were just delighted when they saw father. Going into the
water they got their nets full, and then the shining treasures
were emptied out at his feet. So the visitors all had a good
meal of nice fresh fish.

On telling the natives what he had come for, father was
informed that there was a boat lying on the outside beach,
and that in the morning they would go with him, and bring
her round into the passage. Then nothing would please
them but that they must move their camp to near that of
the visitors. In the morning three volunteers were ready
to render assistance, and father did not know till some time
afterwards that they were the very men concerned in the
Caboolture murder. And he was without firearms! When
they got round the beach to where the boat lay high and
dry, it was found to be the one sought for, not much damaged; only a few planks split in the bottom. As luck
happened, there was not much of a sea that day, so the
three blacks after launching the boat walked in the water

beside her, keeping clear of the surf, and pulling her ashore to get rid of the water now and again, as she leaked a lot. And so on till smooth water was reached in the passage.

When the boat was hauled up on to the beach and turned upside down, the damaged bottom was examined, and the blacks suggested a whitish clay as a remedy for the cracks— they used it for their canoes. So father went across with some natives to the mainland (Toorbul Point) to obtain some, leaving his brother and the others on the island with the blacks. They were all right on his return, and the clay was a success. When dug from the ground it was soft and pliable, but after the blacks had worked at it with their hands, it became quite hard, and could only be removed from the boat in the end with a hammer and chisel.

That night a regular gale blew from the south-east, and there was no hope of returning to Brisbane. It kept up, and at the end of three days the Petrie brothers' supply of rations, which was gradually diminishing, ran out, and they had nothing left. The blacks, finding this, were very good; they brought plenty of crabs, oysters, fish, and a fern root they used to eat ("bangwal"), also the small fruit we call "geebung." (The correct native name for the latter is "dulandella.") Thinking of everything, the kind-hearted creatures even offered tobacco!

After living for ten days on this sort of diet, the younger Petrie, and also the half-caste, grew quite sick of the food, and could not eat much; in fact, they did not feel at all right. My father, however, enjoyed things thoroughly. He thought, though, that under the circumstances it would be better to send his brother across to the mainland, and let him walk to Brisbane with Neddy and two or three blacks. They could then also give the information there that father was all right. So with some extra blackfellows to bring back the boat, the party started off, but had not gone far when another boat hove in sight sailing down to the island. Seeing this the party returned, and father had the boat hauled up on to the beach, and then he and his brother and Neddy hid behind it, leaving no one to be seen but the blacks. He watched from behind and saw the boat come sailing along, and when it got to within fifty yards of the shore, the sail was pulled down, and a man in the bow of the boat stood up with a fig of tobacco in his left hand. This he held up, trying to induce the natives to swim out for it. Father noticed he kept his right hand in his coat pocket, and, seeing this, and that the party were afraid to land, showed himself with the others.

There were but two occupants in the boat, these being my grandfather's men sent to look for the lost ones. When they landed they said there was a report in circulation that the little band had all been murdered by the blacks on Bribie Island, and, "if we had not seen you when we came along, we intended shooting some natives in revenge." They meant to coax out men into the water for tobacco, and then shoot them with their loaded revolvers.

That night for tea there was meat and bread, etc., and so everybody brisked up, and things were lively. The blacks were got to show off some of their games, and they were very merry too. Next day the wind changed, and the return to Brisbane was prepared for. Father asked the three blacks who had helped with the boat to journey with them to his home at Petrie's Bight, and he would get the blacksmith there to make a tomahawk each for them. They agreed, and the whole party started off, with the recovered boat in tow. The wind was fair, and they landed before dark at Breakfast Creek. The three natives were told to come in the morning for their presents, which they did, and while standing near the blacksmith's shop waiting, a Mr Williams appeared in the yard. As soon as the blacks saw him they took to their heels, and ran as fast as they could into the bush. This Mr Williams was one of the party who went to Caboolture for cedar timber, and he recognized the three natives as those who had accompanied his companions into the scrub, murdering one of them.

The next day father went out to the aboriginal camp at Bowen Hills, and took with him the presents he had promised the three natives. Arrived there these three came up to him, and when he had presented each with a tomahawk, he asked why they had run off the day before?

"Because," they answered, "the man who came into the yard was one who was in the boat at Caboolture when we killed the men there, and we thought he might catch us." They then told how it had all happened. They said they had no thoughts whatever of murder, until the white man got frightened and the gun went off, then, thinking they would be shot if nothing were done, they did not hesitate to act promptly.

Another aboriginal murderer, known of as "Dundalli"— the native name for the wonga-wonga pigeon—hailed from Bribie Island. Like "Millbong Jemmy," he was said to have had a hand in the murder of Mr Gregor and Mrs Shannon, and the sawyers at North Pine; also Gray, on Bribie Island, and others. Father remembers when he was captured. A brickmaker named Massie engaged this man, and the darkie was cutting down a tree for him when surprised. The scene was somewhere in the present Wickham Street, Valley, between the site of the Byrnes statue and the Brunswick Street corner. The police had hidden near by, and a blackfellow (Wumbungur) of the Brisbane tribe was sent on to catch "Dundalli." The pair had a struggle, then the police appeared on the scene, and after a great deal of trouble secured him.

"Dundalli" was tried and sentenced to death, and the day he was hanged (5th January, 1855), my father was there in the crowd. The hanging took place where now the Post Office stands, and the Windmill (Observatory) Hill was simply lined with blacks, some coming from Bribie ("Ngunda" tribe), and others of the Brisbane tribe. When "Dundalli" got up on to the gallows he looked all round, and, seeing father, appealed to him in his own tongue. Then he noticed the blacks up on the hill at the Windmill, and called to them (still in his own tongue), telling them that "Wumbungur" was the cause of his being taken, and so they must kill him. The cap was put over his head then, and the bolt was drawn, but owing to Green, the executioner, misjudging the length of rope according to the drop, the unfortunate man's feet came down upon the coffin beneath. Then as he bounded up into the air the

coffin was taken away, and the executioner, catching him
by the legs, bent and tied them upwards, and so hung to
him till he died It was indeed a horrible sight, and one
that father devoutly hoped he would never see again.

"Dundalli" had a brother, "Ommuli" (which meant the
breast), who was also a great murderer, and was connected
with his brother in some of the same misdeeds. He was
one of those for whom a reward was offered. A man called
Isam, a native of the Isle of France, undertook to catch him.
This man was a prisoner in the early times, but had got
a ticket-of-leave. He lived with the blacks at Amity Point
("Pul-an," the natives called Amity), and he had a boat,
and used to catch fish and salt them for sale. He also
caught turtle and dugong. Once a week he left his home
at Amity and went to Brisbane to sell whatever he had,
returning with rations.

One night this man, with four or five of the Amity Point
blacks and two or three constables, started off to where the
natives had a camp—a little above the present Wickham
Terrace Presbyterian Church—in quest of "Ommuli." At
that time, of course, it was all wild bush round about. Isam
took with him half-a-pint of rum and a tinpot to treat "Ommuli" to a drink, and one of the natives had a rope with a
noose at the end. Coming near to the camp, the constables
and most of the blacks waited hidden while Isam and two
others went forward. They found "Ommuli" in his hut,
and Isam sat down alongside him and commenced to talk
to him, and brought out the rum, while all the time the
native with the rope hidden in his shirt stood ready watching. Seeing his opportunity at last as the pair talked away
together, this man threw the rope over the unsuspecting
blackfellow's head, and then, getting it down over his arm,
drew it tight, and with the assistance of the blacks, who
rushed out at this moment from their hiding place, dragged
"Ommuli" along the ground.

An awful row began then; the blacks of the camp threw
spears and waddies at the others with their victim, and a
constable got speared through the arm. Still Isam and the
Amity blacks would not give up "Ommuli," and they

dragged him right down the hill, passing over the ground where the church is now, and on to cross over the creek that used to run up Creek Street. Pausing on the site of the present Gresham Hotel, they had a look at their victim, and found that his arm had come free of the noose, and the rope was tight round his neck. Of course, it goes without saying—the man was dead. So they took the body to the hospital, and that was the last of the unfortunate "Ommuli."

CHAPTER XXI

The Black Man's Deterioration—Worthy Characters—"Dalaipi"—
Recommending North Pine as a Place to Settle—The Birth of
"Murrumba"—A Portion of Whiteside Station—Mrs Griffen—The
First White Man's Humpy at North Pine—Dalaipi's Good Qualities
—A Chat with Him—His Death—With Mr Pettigrew in Early
Maryboro'—A Very Old Land-mark at North Pine—Proof of the
Durability of Blood-wood Timber—The Word "Humpybong."

MOST people speak and think of the aborigines as a lazy,
dirty, useless, unreliable lot.   But, as I have tried to show,
it is unfair to pass judgment upon them because of what
they appear to be now.   They were not always so, and the
white man is accountable for their deterioration.   He
taught them to drink and to smoke, and to feel that it was
not worth calling up sufficient energy to make a canoe, a
vessel for water, or even a hut to sleep in.   As the natives
got more and more into the ways of the white man, they
would often lie huddled up in the rain, rather than trouble
to make a hut to cover them.   And so they went down
and down, travelling on the path which led to laziness,
disease, and degradation.   Poor souls!   They did not teach
their children to do as they had done, and the children never
really knew what the old life had been.   How different a
native was in those old times!   He was full of manly vigour
and energy, his life was a joy to him, and the search for his
food one long pastime.   It is useless to think that we can
ever blot out the injury we have done by mission schools
and unnatural teaching.

To show that there were besides murderers really worthy
characters among the aborigines, it may interest some
readers to hear of "Dalaipi," a fine old blackfellow my father
knew.   When the latter was a small boy he used to play
with this man's son—a little chap called "Dal-ngang"—and

"Dalaipi" himself was then nearly sixty years of age. Later, when father had been married some months, and had decided, upon the advice of Mr Tiffin, the Government Architect, to take up land for cattle, he sought out "Dalaipi," and asked him if he knew of any country suitable for what he wanted. This old blackfellow was the head man of the North Pine tribe, and often came into Brisbane. He replied that there was plenty good "tar" (ground) at "Mandin" (fishing net)—the North Pine River railway bridge crossing. When father agreed to go and look at it, "Dalaipi" was greatly pleased at the idea of him settling there, and said, "You take my son, 'Dal-ngang,' with you, he will show you over my country, for he can ride, and any you pick on I will give you. I would go, but cannot ride—would tumble off. When you make up your mind to settle, I will go with you, and protect you and your cattle, or any one belonging to you."

So my father, a young man of about twenty-eight, journeyed forth with "Dal-ngang" to look at the place which was really to become his future home, though he did not know it. There he was to live for the rest of his lifetime, and form the now well-known homestead, "Murrumba." This name, by the way, is the blackfellows' word for "good."

The two horsemen—the black man and the white—camped for the first night just where the latter's milking-shed now stands, and father was greatly taken with the country, which, in those days, looked so nice and green and open, and was covered with beautiful kangaroo grass, a couple of feet high. The young fellow thought to himself what a pity it was he could not take it up; he knew it to be a portion of the Whiteside run. "Dal-ngang" said to him, "You take this fellow ground, belong to my father?" and he was not at all reconciled to the fact when told that it already belonged to Mrs Griffen (Captain Griffen's widow).

After looking at North Pine, father and "Dal-ngang" went on to the mouth of the Pine River, and then round to Humpybong and Deception Bay. From there they went to Caboolture, and always as they travelled they examined

the country for miles round about. At the end of four days
they found themselves on the "Old Northern Road," homeward bound, my father with his mind made up to obtain
a map of the country, so that he could see which portions
were still open to choose from. However, arriving at the
North Pine upper crossing (Sideling Creek), they met a
bullock dray loaded with cedar, making down the river
towards the salt water, whence the timber was to be rafted
to Brisbane, and who should be riding alongside the team
that his man was driving but John Griffen, with a horse
pistol on either side of the pommel of the saddle, and a
carbine hanging at his side. As soon as he saw father he
called to him, "Hullo, Petrie, where the devil are you
going?" "I am looking for a nice piece of country on
which to put some cattle. Can you put me on to anything?" "Yes, go down towards the mouth of the Pine."
"But that belongs to your mother." "The old lady will be
only too pleased to give it to you. We can't keep a beast
down there for the blacks, they run them into the swamps
and spear them, then have great feasts. If any of us go down
in that direction, we have always to be on our guard—that
is the reason I am armed like this (touching his weapons).
You never know when those black wretches may appear
and tackle you. You had better go back to the station,
Petrie, and see mother. I know you will get the land all
right."

My father, after some conversation, turned and went to
Mrs Griffen's station, where the old lady met him heartily,
and asked him in for the night. When he told her what he
had come for, she said she would be only too pleased to let
him have that portion of her run; it was of no use to them;
it was unsafe for any one to go down there, and they could
do nothing with the cattle on account of the blacks. "Yes,
you can have it certainly, but," she added, "would it be wise
for a young man like you to settle in such a place—would
it be safe?" Fancy "Tom Petrie" being afraid of the
natives! "Mrs Griffen," he answered, "if you are willing
that I should take over the land, I shall not be afraid to
settle there, as I can speak to the blacks in their own

tongue, and know their ways, and will be all right." "Very well," she said, "I will go to town with you to-morrow, and make arrangements that you get the land."

So it came about that the lawyer transferred ten sections over to my father, and the latter had ten square miles in his name. His boundary was from Sideling Creek down the coast right round to Humpybong.

And now to return to "Dalaipi." When everything had been finally settled, my father started from Brisbane in a boat to go to North Pine with rations, taking with him "Dalaipi," "Dal-ngang," and four other blacks. When they got to the mouth of Brisbane River, a fair wind was blowing towards St. Helena, and the natives suggested that the party should run across to the island and camp there for the night—they looked forward to a feast of dugong. To this my father agreed. At that time St. Helena was nearly all scrub, and some white men were living there who caught dugong and boiled them down for the oil for Dr Hobbs. As luck had it, when the boat landed a large creature had just been caught, so the darkies had a great feast, and father also enjoyed some of the meat. Next day, on their departure, the men of the island gave them a quantity of flesh, so the blacks were in great glee, as dugong was a favoured dish, and this meant a supply for several days. The wind, again favourable, took the party to the Pine, up which they travelled as far as Yebri Creek, and camped there.

Next day my father looked about for a suitable place in which to build a humpy, and picked upon almost the spot where his barn stands now near the N.C. Railway line. With the help of the blacks he cleared a couple of acres, and then teaching them to split slabs, and posts, and rails, he got a hut and stockyard built.

Whenever he had occasion after this to go for a few days to Brisbane, he found on his return that everything was all right, just as already related. The man who took charge of the humpy was "Dalaipi," and the two young blacks mentioned, who watched the cattle, were lads of about seventeen, one being "Dal-ngang," and the other, "Dippari," a brother of "Dick Ben." ("Dick Ben" was one of those concerned in the murder of Mr Gregor and Mrs Shannon.) These two young fellows were very useful; their master taught them to do all sorts of things about his place, and they were bright and quick at learning, and could do their work as well as any white man. Later on, when he had a house built to which his wife could come, these boys took turn about in travelling to Brisbane with a pack-horse every week, taking in little fresh things from the country to Mr Petrie, senior, and returning with supplies for the station. And nothing ever went wrong.

" 'Dalaipi' was," my father says, "a faithful and good old black to me. He was a great old fisherman, and used to keep us supplied with fish, crabs, and oysters, and in the season when turkey eggs were found in the scrub on the Pine brought these as an offering. He was the only black-fellow I knew who neither smoked nor drank."

"Dalaipi" was not an extra tall blackfellow, but was good and very reverent looking, and carried himself with an air as though he were some one of importance, as, indeed he was, for his word was law among the tribe, and he was looked up to by every one. He and his son, "Dal-ngang," were very gentle and courteous, and never seemed to join in with a rough joke. "Dalaipi's" wife also was a tall splendid-looking woman, with the carriage of a queen. She it was who used to follow my mother on her walks abroad for fear harm should come to the white lady. When the latter had gone far enough, or with her child had approached some sacred burial place, the gin would quicken her pace and say, "Come back now, missus," in a beseeching sort of voice, which my mother is afraid she did not always pay heed to.

My father has had many a yarn with poor old "Dalaipi" on the subject of the murders committed by the blacks, and this man told his white friend much the same as the murderers did themselves. "Before the whitefellow came," "Dalaipi" said, "we wore no dress, but knew no shame, and were all free and happy; there was plenty to eat, and it was a pleasure to hunt for food. Then when the white man came among us, we were hunted from our ground, shot, poisoned, and had our daughters, sisters, and wives taken from us. Could you blame us if we killed the white man? If we had done likewise to them, would they not have murdered us?"

"But," my father said, "the blackfellows killed poor whites who never did them any harm."

"That is nothing. If a man of one tribe killed someone of a second tribe, the first person in the former that the others came across was killed for revenge. That is our law. And, besides, look what a lot of blacks who did no harm were shot by the native police! And what a number were poisoned at Kilcoy! Another thing the white man did was to teach us to drink, smoke, swear, and steal."

"They did not teach you to steal."

"Yes, they did. They stole our ground where we used to get food, and when we got hungry and took a bit of flour or killed a bullock to eat, they shot us or poisoned us. All they give us now for our land is a blanket once a year."

"But 'Dalaipi,' did not the white men settle the missionaries at Nundah to make you better, and teach you not to kill, steal, or tell lies? Did they not show you how to work for them, and so earn a living?"

"Yes, the missionaries were settled at Nundah, and what did we learn from them? The young blacks got to know too much of the whites' ways and habits—too much of what was right and wrong. Before any white people came here, we never stole anything from one another, but divided everything we had, and were always happy."

"But what about when you beat the poor gins and often killed them for a mere trifle? And sometimes you sneak upon an unsuspecting blackfellow in another tribe, and kill him."

"It is our law that a gin should be killed when she steps over anything belonging to us—or for other things. And if a man dies, or gets killed by fighting with one of his own tribe, we don't blame the man who seemed to kill him, but find out the real murderer by chopping the dead man's bones together, which always crack at the right time. You have seen that done many a time, and you know."

"Yes, thats all right, 'Dalaipi.'"

"The missionary and white fellow tell us that if a black-fellow kill a white man they catch him and kill him by putting a rope round his neck; and if a white man kill another white fellow, they do just the same. That is your law. Well, the blackfellow is different. We do not blame the man we see killing the other, but go by the cracking of the dead man's bones. And when we get a chance we do not put a rope round the murderer's neck, but kill him with a waddy, a spear, or a tomahawk. That is the difference, and we do not see any harm in killing that way. It was our law before the white fellow came among us to teach us all sorts of things. Why did not the white man stop in his own country, and not come here to hunt us about like a lot of kangaroo? If they had kept to their own land, we would not have killed them."

"No, that is true, 'Dalaipi;' but, you see, the white man likes to go and find new country, and bring bullocks and horses, and grow potatoes and corn; then you get plenty to eat."

"No fear, they won't give us anything; they are too greedy. They put corn and potatoes in our ground that they took from us at Eagle Farm a long time ago, to tempt us when we were hungry. There were several shot there stealing corn. You mind 'Dalantchin,' who was lame in one leg? Well, he was shot in the hip with a ball while taking corn; that was what made him lame."

"Well, you know that was not right. He was stealing it."

"I don't see that. The white fellow stole the ground, and I don't see any harm in taking a few cobs of corn or a dillyful of potatoes when one is hungry. We should not be shot like birds for it."

" 'Dalaipi,' you see it one way, and the whites another, that's certain."

"You say the white fellow don't tell lies. I know plenty who did. They would get the blacks to bring them fish, young parrots, and all sorts of things; then, in place of giving them what was promised, they took the things, and, with 'Be off, you black devil!' gave them a hit on the side of the head. What do you call that but stealing? That is the way a good many whites were killed. Let us see a white man to-day and speak to him, and then even though we do not see him again for a long, long time, we know him, and remember what he did."

"Now, 'Dalaipi,' I see I cannot make you see the right from the wrong. Tell me how it is you never drink grog nor smoke?"

"When the blackfellow took to drinking rum—that you call it—they would go mad, and beat one another with waddies, and cut themselves with knives; sometimes they would kill their friends in a quarrel. I knew if I took it I would go mad, too, so I would never touch it. They used to try me to take it, but I never would. I tried the tobacco, but it made me very sick, and I never would try it again."

" 'Dalaipi,' how is it that the blacks never tried to kill me?"

"Because your mother and all your people were kind to us, and would always give us something to eat, and you were a small little boy growing up with the black boys, who used to go about your father's house. In those early days we were not allowed to go near the 'croppies' (the native name for prisoners), but could always see you. You learned our tongue, our ways and secrets, and you never broke our laws nor ill-treated us, but were always kind. We would do anything for you, and looked on you as one of ourselves. If all the whites were like you there would not have been so many killed."

In spite of conversations like this, "Dalaipi" was not a man of many words. He would never speak much unless questioned. His English was broken, of course. He and his never became aggressive, nor troublesome in the way of asking for tobacco, etc., as some did.

As I have said, "Dalaipi" was the head man of the North Pine tribe, which numbered about two hundred, and he was supposed to own the kippa ring there. He was looked on as the great rain-maker for his part of the country. At one time it was rather dry, and the waterholes were getting low, so my father said to him, "You make the rain come and fill the holes again, 'Dalaipi.'" He answered, "Byamby me makeim come." About two days after this it got very cloudy, and "Dalaipi" turned up and said, "Me go now and makeim rain come up." So taking his tomahawk with him, he went down to the river just above where the ballast pit is now, where there was a point of rock and a deep hole. Here the end of the rainbow with its spirit "taggan" was supposed to go down into the water. "Dalaipi" jumped in with his tomahawk, and went under, coming up again with a small cut on his head, which was bleeding. On his way back to the house his master met him, and asked how he had come by the cut. "Oh, I been feeling about for 'taggan,' and hit my head longa 'mudlo' (stone)."

That day a shower fell, which soon cleared off, however, so my father asked, "How is it you didn't make more rain, 'Dalaipi'? that not enough." The old fellow replied: "Oh, I only cuttem 'taggan' half through; byamby me go down and make plenty more come." So after this his master did not tease him again.

At that time during summer thousands of flying foxes camped in the scrub on the Pine, and the blacks used to catch great numbers, almost living entirely on them now and then. Always in winter they disappeared, so one day my father asked "Dalaipi" where the foxes went in winter. "They go down," he said, "under the water, in that hole where the 'taggan' stops, where me makeim rain. They stop there till the hot weather comes back, then they come up again and go longa 'kabban' (scrub)." He firmly believed this, and so did all the others.

Poor old "Dalaipi" wished once to go for a change to "Tugulawa" (Bulimba) to be with some of his friends for a week or so. He came to his master and said, "You let me go, me not be long away; I been telling the other black-fellows to mind you till I come back." But the poor old man never came back, he took a cold and died there. When the news reached the Pine of his death, there was great lamenting, and cutting of heads. He was well known all over the country. When my father went, as a boy, to the "bon-yi" feast (on the blackall) with the blacks, he was introduced as belonging to "Dalaipi's" tribe. On another occasion he went with Mr Pettigrew to Maryborough, to look round the country and notice the timber. (Mr Pettigrew wished to start a sawmill, and he knew if my father accompanied him he would be saved trouble with the blacks.) Two young blacks they took with them. "Dal-ngang" and "Kerwalli" (meaning "spilt"); the latter was afterwards known as old King Sandy, and he died at Wynnum in 1900.

In those days Maryborough consisted of only a few houses. Mr Pettigrew and his companion walking along a road there, came in sight of two gins coming towards them, and my father remarked, "When they get within speaking distance I will have a bit of fun." So he called to them, "Yin, wanna yan man?" (Where are you going?) They jumped at this in great excitement, saying one to the other that here was a white man who could speak their tongue, so father had a yarn with them. That night he, with Mr Pettigrew, slept on board the steamer, and next morning the wharf was black with natives come to see the white man who could talk to them. Again he was introduced as belonging to "Dalaipi's" tribe, by the two blacks accompanying them, and "Dal-ngang" being "Dalaipi's" son was also made much of. The whole crowd volunteered to go with the white men and show them timber, but only one man and his wife were taken.

The party went up the Susan River, and to Fraser Island, and Tin Can Bay, and they saw plenty of timber. Mr Pettigrew afterwards started a sawmill at Maryborough.

My father says he was never afraid that the blacks would do him harm, but, in those early days, felt he would far sooner trust them than most of the whites. "Duramboi," the man who lived so long with the blacks, said, when he heard my father was going out to settle in the bush, "You are a foolish young man to go; as soon as you get some rations out the blacks will kill you for them. I know their ways, as I ought—having lived with them so long." "Oh well," was the answer, "if that happens, I won't be the first

white man they've killed." Small comfort, one would think.
He adds now, though, "In place of killing me they were
very kind, and I am alive yet."

*   *   *   *   *

In the year 1824, before Brisbane town had been founded,
and in the days when Humpybong was Queensland's penal
settlement, a party of men journeyed up the then unnamed
and obscure North Pine River, and entering Yebri
Creek (below the homestead, "Murrumba"), landed, and
proceeded to make a camp. Having come from the only
part of Queensland inhabited by white men—the penal
settlement at Humpybong—they were, most probably,
soldiers in charge of a gang of prisoners, and were evidently
in search of timber.

On the south side of Yebri Creek, near a portion of it
my father has since had spanned by a bridge, and in what
is now known as his "Lower Paddock"—which latter is
bounded on one side by the North Coast Railway line—lay
at that time a limb blown from a bloodwood tree. This
limb must have been dead and dry, and so have lain on the
ground for some time, for the prisoners started to cut it up
for firewood, some with a crosscut saw, and one with an
axe. Hardly had they begun operations, however, when
natives who had noticed their approach, and who probably
looked upon everything in the vicinity as their especial
property, stole upon the intruders, and succeeded in making
off with an axe. Instead of waiting to reason out the case,
the white men fired upon the blacks, shooting one unfortunate dead; then made off to the boat, and started down the
creek on their return to Humpybong.

"Whoso sheddeth man's blood, by man shall his blood
be shed." The natives, determining upon revenge, watched
their opportunity, and, subsequently, killed two of the
prisoners at Humpybong.

Almost forty-five years ago, when my father first settled
at North Pine, it was the honest old "Dalaipi" who showed
his young master this fallen limb with its markings (a chip
taken out by an axe, also a cut from a saw some two inches
deep), and he it was also who related the story of its strong

link with the past. Ten years ago, my father showed the limb to Mr William Pettigrew whose name is well known in Brisbane, and whose knowledge of timber makes interesting some remarks he writes in a late communication *re* that bloodwood limb.

The marks of the axe and the crosscut saw were quite distinct when Mr Pettigrew saw the limb and heard the story, and he now sends along a copy of some notes jotted down at the time:—

"29th December, 1893.—T. Petrie has a fence up thirty years. Posts of this (bloodwood) sound. Another fence up twenty-five years, sound. Rails, iron bark, replaced twice. Had been eaten by white ants.

"A branch of a tree lying at Petrie's was cut in 1824 or '25 by a party in a boat, when a black stole an axe, and was shot dead; whites cleared out."

Mr Pettigrew adds that he saw the tree (standing) from which the branch had fallen, and he further remarks that the limb was evidently lying on the ground at the time the scars were made. "That limb," he says, "had lain on the ground for sixty-eight years (in 1893). What would be the age of the tree in 1824 or '25, when the limb was blown off? People in West Australia have been boasting of some of their durable timbers, but I think the bloodwood will beat any they have got."

At the present time (October, 1904), this interesting bloodwood limb is still in existence, and its wood is perfectly sound. Some few years ago, however, bush fires charred and disfigured the surface of it, and there are now no distinguishing marks, save its unaltered position, it being too heavy to move. The parent tree also lies prone near by, having been burnt down, probably at the time the limb was disfigured. The tree, when the branch was blown from it, must have been a good size, judging from the limb, which is no baby one. And, as I have said, the branch, when the prisoners started to cut into it, was then dead wood, so who knows what length of time prior to 1824 it lay on the ground?

The fences Mr Pettigrew mentions are yet in existence,

the posts still being sound. Some few of the latter have recently been taken up, and are as solid as the day they were put in, nearly forty-five years ago.

The Brisbane blacks called the bloodwood tree, or *Eucalyptus corymbosa*, "buna." And the tree mentioned grew on clay subsoil—my father has a dam not far from where it stood.

In concluding this subject, I may say that the word "Yebri" was the natives' name for a portion of the creek under discussion, and meant "put, or lay it down." My father gave this name to the authorities, and it has been generally accepted. With regard to the word "Humpy-bong," we are told that that was the name given to the deserted place at Redcliffe by the blacks. They called it "Umpi Bong," meaning "dead houses." Now "bong" was their word for dead, but "ngudur" (after tea-tree bark) stood generally for a hut or house on the coast, hence, I am led to believe, as humpy is of Australian origin, that it is one of those words coined by the Australian white man and adopted by the blacks.

CHAPTER XXII

A Trip in 1862 to Mooloolah and Maroochy—Tom Petrie the First White Man on Buderim Mountain—Also on Petrie's Creek—A Specially Faithful Black—Tom Petrie and his "Big Arm"—Twenty-five Blacks Branded—King Sandy one of them—The Blacks Dislike to the Darkness—Crossing Maroochy Bar Under Difficulties—Wanangga "Willing" his Skin Away—Doomed—A Blackfellow's Grave Near "Murrumba."

IN 1862 my father started from the North Pine River in a ship's longboat with about ten blacks (a few having their wives with them), to go to Mooloolah and Maroochy, to look for cedar timber. Calling at Bribie Island on their way, more blacks were picked up, four being murderers of white men. One of these was "Billy Dingy," of whom I have spoken, and the other three were the natives who had attacked the two men at Caboolture, killing one and leaving the other for dead.

Crossing to the mainland, some of the party walked along the beach, while the rest of the natives occupied the boat with my father; they thus journeyed to Mooloolah. Arriving there, they camped for the night, and next morning made for Buderim Mountain, and, having climbed it, the blacks informed father that he was the first white man who had ever set foot on the mountain. He had a good look round through the scrub, escorted by the blacks, and saw forests of fine timber, then had the satisfaction of being the first to cut a cedar tree there. However, he saw that it would not be possible to get timber from the locality to the water without the assistance of a bullock team, as the Mooloolah River is some distance from the mountain, so he decided to leave it till a more convenient time. The party then started back to the boat at the river's mouth, and remained there all night, leaving next day for Maroochy. Maroochy Bar is a difficult one at times to cross, but they got in all right, shipping a little water. After landing and refreshing themselves, they went up the river for some miles, turning at last up a creek on the left, which is now known as Petrie's Creek, as my father was the first white visitor there.

Continuing on their way some distance, they came upon a large gathering of blacks, and this was the gathering I have spoken about, when some natives from the interior were so amazed at the sight of a boat. Among the blacks (twenty-five) who accompanied my father to cut cedar was a man from the Pine called "Wanangga," which meant in English "Left it." He was also called Jimmy. He was a specially faithful black, and was father's right-hand man in everything. He had great talks with the natives assembled, telling them all sorts of wonderful things about the white man, whom, he said, was a "turrwan." In his dealings with the blacks, my father was always looked up to as a "turrwan," or great man. As I have stated, he first got the honour when a boy. So "Wanangga" only told these strangers what he himself believed. He spoke of the white man's power of killing, etc., and declared that he had taken many a stone from a blackfellow's body, and so made the sick one well. They believed everything, did these simple-minded people, and he was allowed to sleep in peace that night in the boat with "Wanangga," while the rest of the party camped ashore. Next morning, he was interested in the corrobborees, etc., which, by the way, were very differ-ent to what one sees nowadays, when the blacks perform for the amusement of onlookers, for they will do anything now just to please the white man.

When my father went off that day with his party of blacks to cut cedar, he left "Wanangga" to keep an eye on the boat, and to cook some salt beef and make a damper, so that all would be ready on his return. This blackfellow always did the cooking. A damper, I may mention for the information of those who have not lived in the bush, is made from flour mixed with water and a little salt, into the shape of a round cake, which is then put into hot ashes, well covered up, and left till cooked. If made properly, it is quite eatable, even nice, but it is difficult for inexperienced people to make it properly. My father used to bake very good ones for us when we were children, just to show what he had often to eat in those early times. Nowadays soda is used, and simplifies matters.

Going into the scrub, where there were lots of cedar trees, my father had some cut down near the bank of the creek, so that they could easily be rolled into the water. Then, returning early in the evening to camp, he found that the strange blacks there were about to move off two or three miles down the creek to hold another corrobboree. They wanted his men to accompany them, and these latter wished to do so, too, asking if all hands could not just go and take the boat. Father replied that they could go, but he and "Wanangga" would remain where they were with the boat, as it was too far to come back to work in the morning. This the men declared would not be safe—it would not do; the strange blacks would be sure to kill the two camping alone, and they did not want that. He answered they would be all right, he was not afraid to stay with "Wanangga," and he told them to go, and come back in the morning. Still they said they did not like it, and they persisted in their objections, though evidently wishing to go themselves.

At last in desperation my father got up, and said he would show he wasn't afraid, and off he went into camp among them all, where he picked up a waddie and shield, and declared in the blacks' language that he would fight everyone of them, one at a time if only they came to him face to face, and not behind his back. They looked at him, and some laughed, and one man remarked, "I would not like a hit from him, he has got too big an arm." After that no more was said, and "Wanangga" and his master had their way, the rest returning again in the morning quite ready for their work.

These twenty-five blacks, with their white leader, moved further up the creek that day, and made a permanent camp, where they stayed about a fortnight cutting cedar. The blacks made their huts in a half-circle round the front of father's so that they might be a protection to him. On

Sundays they would hunt or rested, and yarned away the time, as they weren't required to work.

One Sunday the blacks got talking of getting branded as the cedar logs were, with a Ⓟ, so that it would be known to whom they belonged. Their white friend heard the remarks passed—one thought it would be too sore to be branded like a bullock, and another reckoned it best to get the Ⓟ cut on their arms, and in the end this idea was carried. So going up to their master they said to him, "We want you to cut a mark like that on the logs, on our arms; so that when we go to Brisbane, every one will know we belong to you." Father said no, that he would just mark the brand, and they could do the cutting themselves; but this did not please them, and he had perforce to fall in with their suggestions.

He started to draw the brand on the arm of one fellow with a small sharp-pointed stick like a pencil, and this left a white mark on the dark skin. They then gave him a prepared piece of glass, and he commenced to cut with this, but as the blood came, he felt turned, and his hand shook. However, they asked him to cut deeper, so after one was finished, he didn't care any more, but went ahead and did the whole twenty-five of them. They were delighted, and as proud as possible; and went off and got some of the outer bark-chips from a bloodwood sapling, which they burned in the fire, and then rubbing the burnt part up in their hands, it became a fine powder called "kurrum," which they rubbed into the brand. (This is how charcoal was prepared for wounds.) In a week their arms were healed, and the brand had risen up, showing a splendid Ⓟ.

The last of these twenty-five blacks (King Sandy) died at Wynnum ("Winnam," meaning bread-fruit) in May, 1900. A little before his death the writer got him to show her his arm, and the mark was still there, and he proud of it even then.

Father frequently visited the locality again in quest of cedar timber. Mr Pettigrew's steamer conveyed the timber to Brisbane. The blacks worked splendidly. They did all the work in making the roadway and getting the logs into the water. Sometimes while rolling a log along they would just roar with laughter. As my father chaffed them now and again, they were quite happy at work, and worked like tigers. He says they could never be persuaded to do any good by bouncing, but were almost like a lot of children—they needed to be coaxed and considered. They would get very hot at times, and then a jump into the river refreshed them, and on they went again.

One night my father remembers having a laugh. He was resting while the blacks were "jabbering" away among themselves, when he began to feel mischievous, so flicked an oak cone into their midst. There was silence instantly, and they listened intently. Of course, the white man "laid low" until their suspicions were quietened, then repeated his trick. They were positive this time something was wrong, and jumped up, catching hold of him and wakening him as they thought, saying there were strange blacks— enemies—at hand. After that some of them sat up all night watching, for they are very suspicious in that way. In the morning, he told them what he had done, and they good-naturedly burst out laughing.

In travelling to and fro father always left some of the natives at Bribie Island on the homeward trip, till he returned to pick them up again, for they were afraid to go to Brisbane or the Pine because of having been connected with several murders. The blacks he took right on, he always allowed to go to Brisbane for a day or two, giving each some few shillings to spend there, and also a suit of clothes. They used to make more coins by exhibiting their brands—some one would give them a penny, and others perhaps a sixpence—and so they went back to their master quite delighted and proud of themselves. To please the natives left on the island he took back presents to them.

As an instance of how the blacks disliked being disturbed at night, my father tells me that when up on Petrie's Creek, getting cedar timber with his twenty-five natives, one day he told them that that night he would call them when the tide was full, in order to move a raft which had got stuck on a bank. When the time came it was very cold; he called,

but in vain; they were all deaf apparently, and lay still like
logs. So after a time he gave up trying to make deaf creatures hear, and, saying he would go off alone and do it himself, got hold of a firestick, and off he walked. He hadn't
gone far, however, when, looking back, he saw dark forms
coming, all armed with firesticks. When they found he
really would go alone, they went to his help, putting aside
their dislike of the dark and the cold. They were awfully
good to my father always, and stuck like leeches to him.

On another occasion, while still on Petrie's Creek, having
been there for some time, he had run out of provisions, and
the blacks, thinking he would suffer through living just on
fish and what they could bring him, urged him to leave and
get some of his own food. However, he had a raft he wished
to get down the river first, and nothing they said moved
him. Seeing he was determined to do as he said, they
turned to and worked their hardest, working, too, with
that generous and ungrudging spirit one does not always
come across.

On yet another occasion, when about to return to the
Pine, the mouth of the Maroochy River was reached, but
the sea was so rough and the breakers were running so
high that it was impossible to cross the bar; so the party
were forced to wait over a week till the sea went down.
Meanwhile they lived on fish and oysters, as the rations
had run out, but that was no hardship to my father. He
enjoyed his meals as much as any of them. The natives
always carried three or four hand-nets for catching fish,
as well as their weapons.

After the sea had abated somewhat, my father, who had
waited long enough, started to cross the bar, but the first
breaker struck the boat, and turned her broadside on, half-
filling her with water, and breaking the rudder. However,
they managed to right her before the next breaker struck,
and getting back to smooth water, retired to the shore to
bail out and fix up. While in danger some of the blacks
called out for their mother, and some began spitting at the
waves, for it was a superstition of theirs that to spit on
waves when the water was rough would still the sea.

Father rigged up a steer oar, and again they started, the natives calling out to turn back, when the breakers faced them, but their leader said to stick to it, and they would get through all right, and he kept the boat's head straight to the waves. Then, as a breaker struck, the native at the bow oar was thrown nearly on top of the white man, who sang out to him to take the stroke oar, and all hands to pull with all their might.

When all danger was passed and smooth water gained, the blacks simply yelled with laughter, mimicking each other in the frightened way they had called out, also my father how he stood with the steer oar in his hand, and the spray dashing up in his face. In writing of corrobborees, I mentioned that the blacks once composed one about my father, and this was the incident then alluded to.

After bailing out the water the party put up the sail, and with a fair wind steered for Caloundra Heads, which they reached safely, and crossed that bar all right, camping for the night in Bribie Passage. Father says they had a grand supper of oysters, crabs, and fish, which made up for everything, for he had nothing to do but eat while they roasted and brought the food to him. Next day they left for home.

A few days after this return from Maroochy and Mooloolah, my father's faithful blackfellow, Jimmy ("Wanangga") complained of his throat being very bad. He had spoken of it some time before, and his master had doctored him, thinking though, that there was nothing more serious than a cold. However, this day the man called his master into the outside kitchen, where he always slept before the fire, evidently having something on his mind he wished to speak of. Father went to him. "Well, Jimmy," he said, "what is the matter?"

"I want you to get another blackfellow to go with you and look after you, as I won't be able to do so any more. My throat is worse, and I shall die in three days." (This all in his own tongue.)

"Nonsense, Jimmy," was the reply, "does not my medicine do your throat good?"

"No, master," answered the poor soul. "You ask me several times if I could not get you a blackfellow's skin; well, when I die in three days, you get the blacks to skin me, and you keep my skin; if you don't want it, don't let them eat me, but make a hole and bury me; then when my sister comes, show her my grave, and she can get my bones to carry about."

Father said he would do as was requested. "But," he said, "you are not going to die yet, you will be all right before we start again."

However, the third day in the evening Jimmy asked if he could go to the camp; he would like to sleep there, he said, with his companions that night. Father answered, of course he could, never dreaming that the poor fellow's death was really near, and expecting to see him again in the morning. The camp was some three hundred yards from the Petrie's garden, and when the master visited it the first thing next morning he was greatly surprised to find that "Wanangga" had died two hours earlier. There the others were all crying over his body, so father got them to dig a grave in a quiet place, and "Wanangga" was laid to rest. His body was rolled up in tea-tree bark, tied round with wattle bark string, the feet being left exposed, and so, crying all the time, they carried him to the grave. There they put a sheet of bark in the bottom of the hole, and another on top of the body—to keep the earth off, they said —and the grave was filled in.

As I have shown, the natives about here never buried their dead in the ground, but if not eaten would place them up on trees. So this burial of "Wanangga" was unusual. The other blacks wished to eat him, as he was in good order, but my father would not hear of this; he told them the poor fellow had wished to be buried, and buried he must be. So there he lay, till his sister came to dig up his bones.

Often, my father says, a blackfellow died in this fashion; the idea would possess him that he was "doomed," and then nothing could save him—he made no effort, but would just sulk and die.

"Wanangga" was a faithful blackfellow, and a very useful one; he could split and fence as well as any white man, and could turn his hand to almost anything. He was the especial one who always stuck to my father when no white man would go near him, being all so afraid of the blacks. So poor Jimmy was missed when they journeyed back to Maroochy, but his name was never mentioned among the others. It was "dimmanggali"—that is, "sacred to the dead." The blacks never ever refer to the dead, in their wild state. You could hardly do anything worse, in the old days, than to mention a dead man's name—they would be more likely to kill you for that than for anything. If, as on rare occasions (for they had a great variety to choose from), another person bore the same name as the dead man, it was changed at once to "dimmanggali." In later years, when the white people's names began to be used, a black-fellow called "Tom" died, and so my father was dubbed "dimmanggali."

About four months after Jimmy's death his sister came to inquire where his resting place was. She had three or four old gins with her, and they opened up the grave and took out the bones, separating them from each other. Then, making a great fire, they burnt everything with the exception of those bones which were always kept and cleaned. These they put into a dillybag and carried to within fifty yards of where the other blacks were camped, waiting, and sitting down on the ground, the others all gathered round in a circle, and the ceremony already described took place. The sister then put the bones carefully back into the dilly, and they all started off to the camp, crying as they went along. They said to their white friend, "You see now who caused his death, and you shoot him when you come across him." For months the sister carried these bones about wherever she went, and they were cried over every night and morning. In the end, she put them in a hollow tree, hanging out of sight in the dilly on a forked stick, and there they were left for good. My father never heard whether the particular blackfellow who was blamed for killing "Wanangga" was done to death or not, but he knew of many cases where an unfortunate was murdered when he probably knew nothing whatever of the death he was blamed for.

Any one walking below the "Murrumba" orchard even now could, if they cared to be sentimental, drop a tear of sympathy on the exact spot where "Wanangga's" body once lay. However, the hole is gradually filling up. As a child, the writer used to wonder why a blackfellow had just a big, open hole for a grave, not realising that it had been opened up for the sake of the bones.

Two old blackfellows, great friends and both characters in
their way ("Puram" and "Karal"), who belonged to the
country up round the Maroochy River, my father knew very
well. "Puram" was considered the great rain-maker for
that part of the country he came from (the Maroochy district). He had but one eye, having lost the other by rolling
into the fire when a baby, and he also had lost half a foot
through a tiger-shark, while fishing. In spite of his de-
formity, he was very active, and my father has often seen
him climb a "bon-yi" tree with a vine, going up it as well
as any of the others. "Puram" often accompanied my father
on his trips for cedar to Petrie's Creek, though not one of
the "brand brigade."

At one time, when my father had gone to the Pine to
settle, and "Puram" was there, it seemed setting in for wet
weather, so the old man, of course, proceeded to bring the
rain. He commenced by spitting up into the air, and making
signs; then he pulled the "kundri" stone from his mouth,
chanting words which had this meaning, "Come down, rain,
and make the 'bon-yi' trees grow, so that we shall get
plenty nuts, and make the yams to grow big, that we
may eat them." It did happen to rain for about four days
after this; in fact, too much came, so father asked "Puram"
to make it stop. "Oh, byamby," he said. So the cunning
old chap waited till he saw a break in the sky, then started
throwing firesticks up into the air, to dry up the rain, he
said, and then making a great row in his throat, he showed

his "kundri" stone to the others, who stood round, with admiration on their faces   Then the old chap walked up to his master, and said, "Now, you see, me bin makim altogether dry with fire—no more come."   It cleared up, and fine weather came, and the others really believed that it was all "Puram's" doing.   They thought he could bring rain, or send it away as he liked.   And he himself evidently believed in his own powers.

There was a cattle station at Nindery Mountain, on the Maroochy River, and some time after my father gave up going to that district for cedar the blacks told him that poor old "Puram" had been shot by one of the station hands there.   It seemed that he and another blackfellow were in a canoe on the Maroochy River harmlessly getting cobra— "kambo" the blacks there called it—when a shot was fired, and "Puram" fell dead.   The other blackfellow got away, and told the tale.

"Puram's" mate, "Karal," seemed to be a good age even, when my father remembers him first. He was half silly, and very comical in his ways.   He could not speak a word of English properly, and therefore caused many a bit of fun and a good laugh.   Father was the first to take him into Brisbane.   This was on the journey from Bribie to Brisbane after the trip there in search of a lost boat, and after the murder at Caboolture at Dead Man's Pocket.   My father remembers his father standing at the back door when he came up with "Karal," and introduced him as coming from Nindery.   Grandfather, who was blind at that time, felt the blackfellow all over with his stick, and then said, "I christen you Governor Banjur, of Nindery."   "Banjur" was a class name of the Turrbal tribe.   It meant a man above a working man—a great man, in fact, though not so great as "Turrwan."   This name fell into "Banjo," and so the man was known till his death.

Governor Banjo used to stay with the Petries, sometimes sleeping in the kitchen before the fire.   They got him a brass plate made, with "Governor Banjo of Nindery" cut into it, and this he wore hung round his neck by a chain, and mighty proud he was of it, too.

My father and his brothers and sister used to try and teach Banjo to say fresh words, but he never could get his tongue round them. Many a laugh these young people had over this, for he was a good-natured sort of a fellow, and always made the required attempt. One day "Tom" got hold of a Jack-in-the-box, and taking it to Banjo said, "Here, Governor, you open this fellow." The poor soul took the box, and touching the spring the lid, of course, flew open, and a little soldier jumped up. Banjo dropped the box like a hot potato, and with a yell ran off into the bush without even waiting to look round, so scared was he. They did not see him again till next day, when he came up to father shaking his fist at him, and then putting his hands together, said, "My word, Jack Nittery—hanker—policeman"—meaning that my father's big brother, John, would get a policeman to handcuff "Tom" for frightening him. Then he held up his brass plate as much as to say he was too big a man to be insulted, and walked off with a great air. He carried himself in a very upright manner, this old blackfellow, and walked along very smartly.

Another time father gave his sister a little red toy man to put in the cupboard beside the plate Banjo used for his dinner. The poor chap, opening the cupboard door, saw the red man, and made off as hard as ever he could go, in a great fright. They got him to come back again, however, afterwards. "My word!" was a great expression with Banjo, and "hanker" he always used for handcuffs. The latter had gained a firm hold on his mind, because one day the soldiers had pounced upon him in mistake for another blackfellow, and handcuffing him, led him off to the lock-up. Passing the Petries' house on the Bight, the poor old man cried out for help—"Jack Nittery, come on—poor fellow Governor Banjo!" "Jack Nittery" (Petrie) did come on, and got him off, explaining he was just a harmless old creature—it was a mistake.

Banjo never forgot the handcuffs, and whenever anyone displeased him he always threatened—"policeman—hanker." But though he seemed to be in a great "scot" for a few minutes, it was all over immediately, a more harmless creature one could find nowhere. He was also most kind-hearted, and had very often to be watched when given his meals, for he would just take a mouthful, and then carry the rest out to the other blacks and gins about the place. He always kept very thin, and probably this was the reason, for no matter if he went hungry himself, he would give food to others he thought wanted it.

In spite of his simple nature, Banjo was a grand worker. He often accompanied my father, when the latter went as a boy to the scrubs to find the different timbers, and cut roads to the river, as an outlet for it. There used to be a very dense scrub at Toowong just where the road turns to go up to the cemetery, and also all along the river to Milton. A lot of pines and yellow-wood timber grew there. Banjo and two or three other blacks were useful in finding out this timber, and helping to cut the roads, and afterwards men came with bullock teams to do the rest.

My father, as a young fellow, went to several goldfields discovered at the time, which caused excitement. On his return from Bendigo, he showed the blacks pieces of quartz stone containing specks of gold, and asked them to have a look about the Blackall Ranges when there next, and tell him if they found anything similar. This was long before the finding of Gympie. One day old Governor, who had been away at the Blackall, came in great excitement, and said, "My word! me bin find big fellow stone, longa yinnell (creek or gully)—plenty sit down." So father said not to tell any one; that if it was all right he would give him money and plenty of tobacco. The old fellow seemed pleased, and the two got horses and some rations and started out without telling anyone where they were going. Poor old Governor had never been on a horse in his life before, and it was some trouble to get him on, but at last he got fixed up, and off the pair went, quite pleased with themselves.

"I gave Governor a switch with which to make his old horse keep up with mine," father says, "and when he would be a little behind, I would call to him, 'Now, hit your horse, and make him keep up.' So Governor would give the horse

a hit on the flank, and when the animal commenced to trot
he would let go the reins and hold on to the mane like
'grim death,' bumping up and down about a foot from the
saddle, calling all the time for me to stop the horse, that
he would sooner walk the whole way. Whenever the animal
got up to its companion, it stopped of its own accord, but
it was not so easy for me to stop laughing; sometimes I
would nearly tumble off my horse at the picture the old
man made, and then he would jerk out to me, 'My word
—Brisbane—policeman—hanker—Mese Nittery.' Meaning
that when he got back to Brisbane, he would tell Mr Petrie
to get a policeman to put handcuffs on me for laughing at
him. Then I would make it all right with the old chap."

Banjo, the first night they camped, felt very much
bruised, and the next morning was very stiff, but after the
second day he got on better. He used to put each stirrup-
iron in between his big and second toes, and hold it so in
the same way the natives held a vine when climbing.

In this fashion the two at length came to a little dry creek
off the South branch of the Maroochy, and here Banjo had
nicely covered up with bushes a fine reef of quartz full of
iron pyrites, something the colour of gold.

"You see, the old man did not invent anything; if it had
been gold I would have been all right," says father.

When the travellers returned to Brisbane the blacks, who
were just as fond of getting fun from Banjo as anyone else,
asked the old man how he managed to get on to the horse
and how he rode it. Governor, to show them, got a long
stick, and with a switch in his right hand, held an end of
the stick with the other, and then with a jump threw his
right leg over and made off, galloping along, up and down,
beating the imaginary horse, the blacks and gins rolling on
the ground with laughter. As he galloped back to them
he would stop and say, "My word, Governor no gamin."

The natives used to get Banjo to do all sorts of queer
things to amuse them, and they used to enjoy seeing him
try and read a book or newspaper. More often than not
he held whatever it was upside down, and then would quote
with quite a grave face, "Itishin, Governor, plour, 'bacco,

tea, sugar, planket, shirt, waiscoin, trouser, pipperoun (half-a-crown). Chook here (look here). My word, no gammon Governor."

At times Governor Banjo's good nature was taken advantage of by an outsider, but generally it was all pure fun, for no one, of course, cared to really hurt the poor old man. He was a source of amusement to all. The head of the Petrie family would quietly laugh to himself when he heard his only daughter at her tricks with Banjo; and his employees, during the dinner hour, had many a bit of fun with him. The Petrie household at this time boasted a little pet monkey, and this creature once or twice got up on to Banjo's head, and the poor man was in an agony of fear lest his face should be torn. There he stood as still as a mouse, while the monkey ran its hands over his hair. Poor Banjo! He dare not make a movement lest something dreadful should happen.

This monkey evidently interested Governor Banjo. One day he took a strange fancy. Going to Miss Petrie he made her understand that he wished to be tied up as the monkey was. So she, nothing loath, when a piece of fun was in view, entered into the spirit of the thing, and tying a rope round Banjo's waist, fastened him to the leg of a kitchen table. There she placed a jar of water at his side, and just as he went down on all fours to creep about the floor, mightily pleased and proud of himself, a man coming along with a message looked in at the doorway to deliver it. He got quite a start, so quickly did Banjo jump round and open his mouth, as he had seen Miss Monkey do. The man's surprise changed to mirth then, and—"Well, Miss Petrie," he said, when he could speak, "I never have met any one like you for tricks. I wonder whatever you will be thinking of next!"

Some years after all this, when both my father and his sister were married, and grandfather was dead, Governor Banjo, as active as ever, divided his time out staying at each place in turn. He was a good hand at chopping wood, and made himself useful to Mrs Robert Ferguson (Miss Petrie), John Petrie at the old place, and "Tom" out at

North Pine. With the latter he took "Dalaipi's" place, when that good old man had died. Although old, Banjo was very active in his movements, and it was wonderful how quickly he could climb a tree with a vine. He always went to the "bon-yi" feasts, and on his return would generally present father with a dilly of nuts.

Poor old Banjo! Surely he was missed when he died. Methinks there must have been a big gap in the world of fun. He lent himself so readily to anything at all that was proposed. He would patiently be dressed up and decorated in the most ridiculous fashion, and then his proud, grave face was the irresistible point. One wet day Mrs Ferguson says she remembers well. She thought she would dress up Banjo, and send him on a message. So she got the old chap to come along, and she whitewashed his face, put white cotton gloves on his hands, white socks and old slippers on his feet, a tall hat decorated fantastically on his head, and so on, till Banjo was indeed a sight to behold. Then she gave him a note, which he carefully put into his waistcoat pocket, and sent him off with an old umbrella torn right down at every rib. This he held over his head, just as though it were a protection, and proudly he walked away, with the air of one who thought he looked quite grand and nice. As he went, the road was wet, and the old slippers stuck fast in the mud, so Banjo just kicked his feet free and went on again in his one-time white socks.

Arriving at his destination Governor Banjo was met with shouts of laughter, which, however, did not lessen his pride. He sought out Mrs Ferguson's brother, and daintily putting his thumb and forefinger into his waistcoat pocket, drew forth the note, which he presented in great style, and with quite a serious face. One can imagine the fun and laughter he caused. When he got back to his mistress he was sopping wet, but still carried the skeleton umbrella, held upright above his head.

At another time Mrs Ferguson was watering her flowers, when all at once she wondered where Banjo was. Holding the hose in her hand, she went on round towards the back to some fruit trees there, when she espied Banjo curled up asleep in an outhouse. The sight was too tempting, and Banjo was awakened by a spurt of water suddenly drenching his face. Up he got and made towards his tormentor, who, in spite of her laughter, still kept the water playing on his face right between the eyes. "I can almost see the poor old creature now," she says, "with his little monkey face, and the little bit of short hair which the water made stand on end." When Banjo could collect his wits sufficiently to get away, he ran to the Rev. James Love's house near by, calling loudly, "Marsa, Marsa, come on— Missus cranky!" And then he bethought him of the handcuffs and "Jack Nittery." Going to the latter he gasped out, "My word, Bom's (Bob's) missus cranky," and to emphasize the fact, put up his fingers, and pointing like a hose, made a noise as of water pouring against his face. Of course, no one knew what he meant, but they guessed it was only some fun. That night, when back again at Mrs Ferguson's, he had regained his usual good temper, and evidently felt towards his mistress as though she was all that was good.

Governor Banjo, being a man of importance, had two wives, one about his own age and the other quite a young thing. He also had a son of some seventeen years. He was very kind to them all, and would go without food himself at any time to satisfy them. The son was in the end taken into the mounted black police, and sent up country, and poor old Banjo was in a great way at this. He often talked of his boy to my father, and wanted to know when he would come back. Soon after this his "old woman" died, and then the young wife ran away, so the poor old soul was left alone. He evidently liked his old wife best, and wasn't at all pleased when anyone laughed, and called her "a greedy old thing." The young wife seemed to make him jealous. When he had no one left he stayed at North Pine for a long time, and used often to tell his master lots of yarns about himself.

Once, Banjo said, he and another blackfellow were nearly poisoned at Nindery cattle station, on the Maroochy. A white fellow there gave them a bit of flour which they took down the river, and made into a damper, then cooked and ate it. Before eating much, however, fits came on, and knowing at once what was wrong, they ran to the river and drank a lot of salt water, which made them very sick, but cured them. "My word!" said Banjo, "that fellow saucy, he no good—byamby me hanker—policeman—lock up." "I could not but burst out laughing," says my father, "at the poor old man when he showed me the way he and his mate jumped when in the fit, and the way they were sick— although, no doubt, it was very wrong of me. But I could not help it, he went on in such a comical way."

Banjo used to take it into his head to go off to Maroochy for a change, then come back again, and afterwards, per- haps, go to Brisbane, and so on. It is the black's nature to roam about. In their native state they would never stay in one place for more than a few months at a time. They said if they did the game would become scarce, also the yams and roots, and there would be no honey; so they moved, if only a few miles, and these things would all grow again by the time they came back. In the end old Governor took ill and died at Maroochy. When dying he asked his nephew to be sure and take his brass plate and give it to his friend at North Pine for him. The nephew did so, but my father, of course, told him to keep and wear it himself.

CHAPTER XXIV

Prince Alfred's Visit to Brisbane in 1868—A Novel Welcome to the Duke—A Black Regiment—The Man in Plain Clothes—The Darkies' Fun and Enjoyment—Roads Tom Petrie has Marked—First Picnic Party to Humpybong—Chimney round which a Premier Played—Value of Tom Petrie's "Marked Tree Lines"—First Reserve for Aborigines in Queensland (Bribie Island)—The Interest It Caused—Father McNab—Keen Sense of Humour—Abraham's Death at Bribie—Piper, the Murderer—Death by Poison.

NOWADAYS it is a common enough sight to see natives marshalled together and taking part in a procession, but when the late Duke of Edinburgh (then Prince Alfred) came to visit Brisbane in 1868 such a thing had never been seen before in Queensland. Father, who had then been living at North Pine for some nine years, went in to Brisbane to see the Duke's arrival, and Mr Tiffin, the Government Architect, coming to him the evening before the great event, asked if he could manage somehow to gather a number of blacks together as a sort of novel welcome to the Duke. It wanted then but an hour to sundown, so there was not much time; but, as luck would have it, a native passed on his way to camp soon afterwards, and my father speaking to him, asked if he would tell the rest of the blacks to come in early and bring their spears, waddies, shields, boomerangs, etc., also some "kutchi" and white clay, with which to decorate themselves.

In the morning the natives turned up—about sixty of them—and it was a piece of work to get them all painted and fixed up to represent the different tribes. When that was done, "I told them," says father, "what to do and how to march and follow me, and I had just got them ready when the procession came in sight near the Post Office, coming along Queen Street. So I hurried the darkies off in a trot to meet it. I had already told off one blackfellow to go to the arch near the Post Office, telling him that a man there would show him how to get up, and which way to stand and hold his boomerang, and I impressed upon him that he must stand steady and make no movement until the whole procession had passed through under the arch.

"As I hurried my regiment along through the crowd, in order to reach the landing place near the Gardens in time, the ladies cried out about their dresses, saying they would be spoilt and dirtied with the paint of the darkies; but my followers took no notice of this, rushing on excitedly after me. We arrived just in time to allow me to place them properly. Two I put on the arch erected there—one on each side—each with a boomerang in his hand, held as though ready to throw; and the others I placed on either side of the landing-stage. They looked very well, with their weapons and shields poised warlike fashion, and some had parrot's feathers up and down in strips on their bodies, and others had swansdown; some were painted, one exact half white, and the other black; others the same but red and white; some were all black with white spots, and others had white stripes, etc. As the Duke stepped ashore I saw him look first to one side at the blacks, and then to the other, as he walked through them, then up at the archway, and he was gone. The darkies asked which was the Duke, and when I told them the man in plain clothes they were surprised, and said he was the same as another white man. They thought the one with the cocked hat and the bright things on his shoulders and glittering buttons was the Duke.

"After this I pushed my men through the crowd, and, getting to the front, marched them alongside the first division. As we went along I got them to give a regular war whoop every now and then, and it was amusing to see how the people on the sideways and the balconies gave a jump every time at the sound. Then I got them to sing their war song. As we passed under the arch in Queen Street, the darkie there stood still as a statue. He told me afterwards that he was afraid to look down on the crowd lest he should tumble amongst them.

"When we arrived at the entrance gate to Government House, I stationed my regiment thirty on each side, standing at ease. The Duke's carriage and the rest passed through, and when all was over and the vehicles and societies had turned back to parade down the streets again, I kept my lot behind, then marched down George and Queen Streets, the blacks giving their war cry and song as they went. The people were pleased at this, and those on the balconies kept throwing down oranges and biscuits, which the darkies caught in great glee.

For their part in the proceedings that day the blacks were each given half-a-crown, and then they had to end up with three cheers for the Queen. They enjoyed it all so much that they said to me in their own tongue that they would like to march every day, and wanted to know if they'd come again to-morrow. I said no, that was all I wanted with them just then, so off they went merrily to spend their half-crowns, not waiting even to wash off their paint. An every-day march would have been all very well for them, but poor me—I got nothing for my trouble."

My father deserves some recognition for all he has done for his country gratuitously. For instance, he has opened up lots of roads. The present one from Brisbane to Humpybong was marked by him right from Bald Hills to the sea. When he came first to North Pine there were no roads, of course, but just a timber track from Bald Hills to Brisbane. For his own convenience, he therefore marked a road from the Pine to reach this, which is the present one in use to Bald Hills. At one time he had two or three tracks cut through the scrub at South Pine.

Before his arrival anyone travelling from the direction of "Murrumba" had to go up to Sideling Creek to get on to the Old Northern Road to Brisbane. Then the first picnic party who ever went to Humpybong—Sir James Garrick and some other gentlemen—came to him and got him to pilot them through the bush to the coast. Later on he marked a tree line when the father of the late Hon. T. J. Byrnes inquired about land for cattle. Father took him down to the Lagoons on the way to Humpybong, and there the Irishman afterwards took up country and settled. He also took him to Humpybong, and showed him the old brick kiln made in the time of the convicts' settlement there. The bricks were good, and Patrick Byrnes made use of some of them for his chimney—a chimney round which afterwards the future Premier played. Still later again my father marked the present road to Humpybong, when it was made shorter by the bridge across Hayes's Inlet.

In those days a company started growing cotton at Caboolture. They came to father and asked if he could find them a shorter way to their plantation than the track which went away round by Sideling Creek. So he marked the present road to Morayfield. Then from there he marked the road for Captain Whish to his property. Also he showed Captain Townsend the land that gentleman took up on the Caboolture, and marked his road, which is the present Caboolture road crossing the bridge.

The road to Narangba was marked by him, also the one from South Pine to Cash's Crossing, and from the lagoons on the old Northern Road to Terror's Creek on the Upper Pine. The latter has since been altered.

When Davis (or "Duramboi") was asked to mark a road to Gympie, he sought my father's assistance for the first part of the way, saying he would know where he was all right when he got to the Glass House Mountains, as he had been there before when living with the blacks. So father took him to the other side of Caboolture and put him and party on his ("Tom" Petrie's) marked tree line to Petrie's Creek, on the Maroochy River. Then when the line to Gympie was marked, he went with Cobb and Co. to help them pick out stopping places for the changing of horses. The road was just frightful at that time; we in these days could not recognize it for the same.

When quite a youngster, my father marked a road for the squatters from Cleveland Point to the Eight Mile Plains, so that they could bring their wool down to the store at Cleveland.

Also when a boy he piloted the first picnic party through the bush to where Sandgate is now, though he did not mark the road to that place.

Surveyors have often come for a talk with my father, and they always used his marked lines. When the present railway line to Gympie was being surveyed, he went with the surveyors to show them the different ways to Caboolture. And he accompanied his friend, Mr George Phillips, C.E., to Gympie, traversing the different trial lines. Also he showed the surveyors the proposed line to Humpybong.

In 1877, during the Douglas Ministry, the first reserve for aborigines was formed. Deciding that there should be such a reserve, the late Hon. J. Douglas and several Ministers of the Crown journeyed by steamer to Bribie Island, in order to pick a suitable spot there. They were accompanied by my father, who, because of his intimate knowledge of the blacks, was asked by the Government to supervise the workings of the reserve, and encourage the natives to settle there. Arriving in Bribie Passage, anchor was dropped opposite the White Patch, and the whole party went ashore, including several blackfellows who had been brought down in the steamer. These and others who were on the island were got together, and the Premier spoke and explained what the Government meant to do for them, saying that my father would overlook everything. The latter gentleman interpreted what the Premier said, and the darkies were very pleased at the idea, cheering the party when they were leaving, and waving to the steamer till it was out of sight.

The blacks on this reserve were supplied, under my father's management, with a boat, a fishing net, harpoons for dugong, and other necessaries, and they had to work in exchange for their rations, catching fish and curing them, and making dugong, shark, and stingaree oils. These and sometimes a turtle, were all sold in Brisbane in exchange for the rations, which afterwards were doled out to the blacks by an old man, who, with his wife, was engaged to live on the island. Father went about once a month to see that all was well. When he first mustered the blacks there were about fifty, some of these being very old women.

In winter time the blacks caught great hauls of sea mullet, and at other times there were other fish, etc., and everything went well, and the settlement bid fair to become self-supporting, when in 1879 the Palmer Government did away with the whole thing. My father asked what was to become of the old men and women? "Oh, let them go and work like anyone else," was the reply. "What is to happen to the boat and fishing net?" "Oh, let them have those." So the news had to be told to the blacks, who were all very miserable about it, and the old gins cried and asked how they were going to get anything to eat. Their friend told them to cheer up, that he was sure the others would not see them want. "No, but they will take us back to Brisbane, and when there they will get drunk, and beat us. We would like to stay here, where we are happy—there is no drinking of grog here, nor fighting." "I cannot help it," father had to tell them; "I have got orders from the Government to break up the settlement, and so it has to be."

Several gentlemen in Brisbane at that time, among them a Church of England Bishop, were very much interested in favour of this settlement for blacks, and they were much against the ending of the concern. However, it had to be. It was a pity, as it was quite true what the gins had said, and many deaths occurred in drunken fights. Numbers of those blacks might have been alive to-day. My father asked the Government, during the life of the settlement, for authority to keep the blacks from the city, where they could get drink, but this was not granted. His powers for good were limited as he had no fixed salary, and no free passes. Some of the Brisbane tribe would not go to the island, as they could get drink in Brisbane, making the excuse that they would not be happy away from their native part.

During the time of this settlement, a Scotch priest named Father McNab came to North Pine to my father, and stayed a few days, getting information about the blacks' ways and language, saying he wished to go to Bribie Island, and see what he could do in the way of teaching religion there. So during my father's presence at the island he arrived one day with a man, and they pitched their tent near by the blacks' camp. Next morning, gathering the natives together, he talked to them, and showed them pictures, explaining what they meant. The listeners appeared attentive at first, but it soon became apparent that the work was useless. One morning (the priest told my father afterwards), while he was holding prayers, a black named "Prince Willie" came to join in with his pipe in his mouth. The priest remonstrated, telling Willie it was wicked to smoke at prayers. "Father McNab," said the man, "I smoke when I like." And so things went on for a good while, till the priest, finding he could do no good, gave up the attempt altogether.

In the meantime, though, during one of his visits to the island, while the priest was absent in Brisbane, my father came upon "Prince Willie" with all the blacks and gins gathered round him, acting Father McNab's part. There he was with an old book, from which he pretended to read, jabbering away like a parrot, and he had water at his side in which he dipped his hand, and then sprinkled the blacks he was about to name. He made these latter cross themselves, and then others he married with a ring. The white man had to laugh till his sides were sore at the way the absurd fellow went on, although he felt he should not, and there were the rest of the blacks simply rolling on the ground with laughter. A native's sense of humour is very keen. "I tried to be serious," father says, "and told them that it was very wrong for them to mock a minister, as his wish was to make them better; but one might just as well have tried to make a stone speak as try to convert those blacks."

During the years of my father's management at Bribie Island, there were only two or three deaths there. One, he remembers, was that of a very old gin, and another that of Abraham, the coxswain of the fishing boat. The latter took dropsy, and his legs swelled to a great size. The poor fellow, when father was leaving the island one day, asked him to bring back a watermelon the next time; he fancied it would make him better. But when the next time came he was dead. His people skinned him, but said they did not eat him. Their friend had his doubts about this latter fact. They skinned him because he was the son of one of the great men of the island, and they wished to give his relatives the skin. They came and said they wanted to go over to the north point of Humpybong, because some Durundur blacks were camped there, and the friends of the dead one were among them. So my father took them over, and went to the camp with them.

On the way three of the Durundur blacks and some gins came to meet the old woman who carried the skin, and when she showed the dilly they all commenced to wail and cry and cut their heads, the men with tomahawks and the women with their yamsticks. Blood flowed freely; the sight was a terrible one, and the sound of the crying was awful. The other blacks then rushed and took the weapons from these mourners, who gradually became quiet enough to talk over the death, and the supposed cause of it. They blamed a blackfellow called Piper by the whites, and they swore they would kill this man at the first opportunity. Then the dilly was opened, and a small one inside containing four pieces of skin was given to an old woman of the Durundur tribe, a relative of the deceased. Gathering up their belongings, then, they all went on to camp, crying again as they went.

After this my father left these blacks, who, however, stayed on where they were for awhile, and about a week later Piper himself happened to turn up. He came with a few Maroochy blacks, and camped alongside the Bribie lot. So it was arranged that one night a man of Bribie called "Dangalin" (or Pilot by the whites) should sneak up in the darkness to Piper and kill him. This was tried, but as it turned out Piper was not asleep, and the blow missed its aim, and therefore as Pilot retreated he in his turn was struck at, and received an awful tomahawk cut at the back of the knee. Father saw this cut two days afterwards, and it seemed to him that the leg was almost severed—the man could not move then. However, he recovered in the end, though he was always lame. At the time father said to him, "How is it you made such a mess of things?" The reply was that the man was too quick, and the moment he

struck he ran away, and was not captured, though some
chased. However, they would have him yet.

Piper got back to Maroochy among his friends, and
stayed there a long time, until he thought the feeling against
him had been forgotten. He was the blackfellow who had
murdered a botanist at Mooloolah. On this account he had
been an outlaw ("tallabilla" the natives called it) for a
good many years, then he was captured, and tried and ac-
quitted; because of the long interval between the trial and
murder the latter could not be brought home to him properly. Some time after the Bribie affair he came into
Brisbane with a number of others to attend a corrobboree,
and camped at Kedron Brook with some Durundur blacks,
thinking he would be safest with them. But one of these
blacks, called Sambo, a friend of the dead Abraham, had
been on the watch, and actually had been carrying about
poison for Piper, thinking he was too smart for another
death. This poison was what the white men used for native
dogs, and doubtless had been got at some station. So
Sambo obtained a little rum, and mixing in the poison,
offered Piper a drink. The unsuspecting blackfellow had a
good drink, then handed the bottle to another man, with
the result that they both died. Sambo did not intend the
second death, of course. An inquiry was held in Brisbane
on this poisoning affair, and my father interpreted for the
blacks. However, Sambo could be found nowhere, and
the matter had to drop. Such was the end of Piper, the
murderer, and such was often the way in which a blackfellow would be hunted to his death by his fellow blacks
for a deed of which he was perfectly innocent, though he
may have been guilty enough in other ways.

PART II

CHAPTER I

THE following extract from the "Brisbane Courier," dated 22nd February, 1872, may be of interest to some readers as an introduction to what I have to say of my father's father—his explorations, discoveries, etc. :—

DEATH OF MR ANDREW PETRIE

"The death of the oldest free resident in our community and colony is an event not to be allowed to happen without notice; and the aged, revered, and useful citizen who has just left our world for a better was no ordinary man. The name of Andrew Petrie is indissolubly connected, not only with the early history of Brisbane, but of the colony. Although for some years past incapacitated by a painful malady from active interference in the more prominent duties of life, he never relaxed his interest in all that was going on around him in the colony. For thirty-four years and more he had watched its growth and advancement from the ignoble position of a mere outlying penal settlement of New South Wales to the dignified and important status of an independent province. From 1837 to the time of his death, he watched its progress with a solicitude which never flagged, rejoicing in its prosperity, and sorrowing in its adversity. Though long deprived of bodily sight, his mental vision could, nearly to the very last, realise all that had been effected in the way of advancement in the city,

which has grown up on the comparative waste on which
he first landed.

"Mr Petrie was a native of Fifeshire, in Scotland, and
was born in June, 1798. In early youth he removed to
Edinburgh, where he was connected with an eminent building firm, and served four years in an architect's establishment in that city. He embarked in business on his own
account, and was induced to emigrate to New South Wales
in 1831, on the representations of Dr Lang. Arriving in
Sydney in that year, in the ship *Stirling Castle*, he was
employed in superintending the erection of the doctor's
well-known buildings in Jamison Street, and subsequently
entered into business for himself. While thus engaged
his ability and probity brought him into notice, and at the
solicitation of Mr Commissary Laidley, he entered the
service of the Government as a clerk of works in the Ord-
nance Department. Shortly afterwards the late Colonel
Barney arrived in Sydney with a detachment of the Royal
Engineers, and to this officer the control of the department
with which Mr Petrie was connected was transferred, and
the deceased gentleman retained his position. In the same
capacity he was employed until his removal to Brisbane in
1837. The buildings which had then been erected in the city,
and were in course of construction, had been designed
and superintended by a junior military officer, and were,
naturally enough, not models either of architectural skill or
of substantial workmanship. Mr Petrie was accordingly
sent up as a practical superintendent or engineer of works,
and he arrived with his family (Mr John Petrie, the eldest,
being then a mere boy) in August, 1837, in the *James Watt*,
the first steamer which ever entered what are now 'Queensland waters.' His duties were to direct and supervise the
labours of the better class of prisoners—mechanics and
others—who were employed in an enclosure situated where
St John's School now stands. The windmill had been
erected, but the machinery could not be made to work,
although the sapient military officer had the bush cut down
all around to allow the wind to reach the sails, and Mr
Petrie's first labour was to take down the machinery and
set it up again in a proper manner. On his arrival the

only quarters available for himself and family were to be found in the female factory (now the Police office), which had been rendered vacant by the removal of the female prisoners to Eagle Farm. There Mr Petrie resided until the house in which he lived and died was built, and as an instance of his foresight, he insisted on its being erected in a line with the court-house, 'as there might some day be a street running that way.' The locality was then 'simply in the bush.'

"In 1838, while out on an excursion with Major Cotton, the Commandant, Mr Petrie and his companions were lost for three days, and found their way back to the settlement at last by taking bearings from the hill on the south side of the river, now known as Mount Petrie. In 1840, accompanied by his son John, two or three convicts, and two blackboys, the deceased gentleman made an exploring trip into what is now known as the Bunya Bunya country, and the party were in extreme peril of their lives, but they succeeded in bringing back to Brisbane some specimens of the fruit. He was, in fact, the first to discover the bunya bunya tree, although its botanical name, *Araucaria Bidwilli*, does not give him the credit. In 1842, in company with Mr Henry Stuart Russell, the Hon. Mr Wriothesley, and others, Mr Petrie explored the Mary River, which had not before been entered by a boat; and it was while on this expedition that he discovered and brought back to civilization the well-known 'Durham Boy,' who had been living in a kind of semi-captivity with the blacks for fourteen years. While on one of these exploratory journeys, and once subsequently, Mr Petrie ascended to the summit of the almost inaccessible Beerwah, the highest of the Glasshouse Mountains, from whence he took bearings for the assistance of the surveyors who were then commencing a trigonometrical survey. On the latter occasion, Mr Petrie and his companions struck across the country to Kilcoy, which had then been formed as a station for about three days by Sir Evan Mackenzie. On his way back to Brisbane, Mr Petrie met and camped with Mr David Archer, who was out looking for country, on the site of the present Durundur Station.

"Soon after the settlement was thrown open in 1842, the
Governor, Sir George Gipps, visited the settlement in company with Colonel Barney, and the latter endeavoured to
persuade Mr Petrie to return to Sydney, as his office was
abolished, but that gentleman preferred remaining here,
and trying his chances in what he foresaw would be a
flourishing colony. In 1848, while on a trip to the Downs,
he suffered severely from an ophthalmic attack, the treatment for which resulted in the loss of his eyesight; and in
the same year another calamity befell him in the loss of
his son, Walter, who was drowned in the creek which
crosses Queen Street. (Singularly enough, Mr John Petrie
lost a son of the same name, in the same creek, some years
afterwards.)   Although thus deprived of one of Nature's
most valued senses, the deceased gentleman continued for
years to assist in the superintendence of buildings and other
works, and many residents will remember, even of late
years, his daily visits to works in progress.

"During the last few years, however, Mr Petrie's
activity of mind had to succumb to infirmity of body, and
he was seldom able to leave his own premises. Up to two
years ago, blind as he was, he rang the workman's bell
with his own hands every morning, and was made acquainted with the details of the business of which he had
been the founder.

"Mr Petrie was not a man to obtrude himself upon
public notice, but although he never actively interfered in
political and other movements, he could express his views
decidedly and vigorously in private. As a father, he was
kind and indulgent; as an employer, he was respected,
though strict and watchful; and as a friend and companion,
he was genial and hearty—nothing pleasing him better than
"a chat about old times." Surrounded by all the surviving
members of his family, and by a goodly number of grandchildren, he passed peacefully away on the afternoon of
20th February, on that last journey in search of final rest
which all humanity must one day undertake.

*   *   *   *   *

"The funeral of the late Mr Andrew Petrie, which took
place yesterday afternoon, was one of the largest which has

been seen in Brisbane for many years past. The greatest respect was shown for the deceased by all classes in the community. The flags of all the vessels in the river were half-mast high, a number of mercantile establishments were entirely closed, while others partially relinquished business in the afternoon. The cortege moved from the late residence of the deceased, at Petrie's Bight, at about four o'clock, and the procession extended over half-a-mile in length. After the hearse came four mourning coaches, then nearly sixty followers on foot, forty-five carriages, and upwards of fifty horsemen. Amongst those present were Sir James Cockle, Chief Justice, Sir Maurice O'Connell, the Hon. the Colonial Secretary, the Hon. the Colonial Treasurer, several members of the legislature, the Mayor and aldermen, and many other gentlemen holding important positions in the colony. The funeral service was read by the Rev. E. Griffith and the Rev. C. Ogg."

*   *   *   *   *

In portioning out and directing what work the better class of prisoners had to do, my grandfather travelled about a good deal. He watched to see that the buildings put up were done correctly, and he visited different places, such as Ipswich (Limestone then), Dunwich, Logan River, Amity Point (for the pilot station), etc. He went to Ipswich to see how the Government sheep and cattle under the management of Mr George Thorn were doing, also to inspect the limekiln worked by the prisoners there. To take him about he had a whale boat manned by a crew of prisoners. "Tom" recollects well one trip his father made to Limestone with this boat. On this occasion, as an outing for them, grandfather took his wife and two or three kiddies —my father included. The child of those days has memories of how they carried a tent with them in the boat, and how, stopping when they came to the first batch of Government sawyers at work on the river, he was carried ashore by one of the boat's crew; then afterwards the men fixed up the tent for his father. Next day they went on again up the river to Limestone, where they stayed a couple of days at Mr Thorn's house, while the head of the expedition made his inspections. At that time Limestone (Ipswich) consisted of Mr Thorn's house and the yards for the cattle and sheep, also the limekiln and the stockade for the prisoners. On the return journey to Brisbane, Mr Petrie called in at all the places where men were at work on the river.

Not only on the Brisbane, but on the Albert and Logan Rivers, the Government prisoners worked sawing cedar. Then they burnt mangrove trees for ash for soap-making at the mouth of the Brisbane. Mr Petrie inspected these places with his whale-boat, as he also now and then visited Dunwich to see that the prisoners there were all right, and also that the cedar timber was loaded on the vessels for Sydney. At other times he took a survey of the Bay and the soundings of the different parts of the water there.

On the return from one of these trips of inspection to Dunwich "Tom" remembers his father bringing a black-fellow back with him to the hospital with a fearful wound. The man's name was "Parpunyi." He had been fighting with another blackfellow, who had become possessed of a razor. In the fight the razor made a fearful gash from the small of "Parpunyi's" back round to the flank, letting some of the inner parts out. Mr Petrie heard of the event soon after it happened, and he went and had the man's wound attended to and sewn up, and then took him in the boat to Brisbane, where in the hospital he very soon re-covered. It is wonderful how the blacks' flesh would heal so quickly.

Another time an incident of the same sort happened in Queen Street, opposite where the Bank of New South Wales now stands. Two blacks were fighting there, and as at Dunwich, one of them—"Murrki"—had a razor in his hand, and the other man—"Kebi"—was wounded in much the same way as "Parpunyi." In this case, however, there was no hospital, but the man pushed the protruding parts in, and holding them so with both hands, walked off to camp, which was near the present Roma Street station. There he had to lie on his back, and the blacks put very fine charcoal and ashes in the wound, and that was all the doctoring he got. He had to keep on his back for a long time, but in the end recovered all right, though the wound left a very large scar. My father, who went to see the black several times during his enforced quietude, says that a white man so doctored would not have lived. The man told the boy that the wound did not pain him much then.

CHAPTER II

WE in these days can hardly imagine Brisbane without horses in drays and carts and traps of all sorts, but at first when my father was a little chap there were none. One comical conveyance he remembers well. It was an old spring cart with a cover on it, drawn by a black and white poley bullock, yoked in shafts as a horse would be, and driven by a prisoner called Tom Brooks. This turnout belonged to the Government, and was used to convey the prisoners' dirty clothes to the women convicts at Eagle Farm each week to be washed. Two or three times when Mr Petrie went out to inspect these quarters at Eagle Farm he took his wife and children, making a picnic of the trip. They all drove in this grand buggy drawn by "Tinker, the bullock." On these occasions old Tom Brooks, the driver, would walk alongside and lead the bullock, but when carting the clothes he sat in the buggy and drove as though the animal were a horse. Sometimes "Tom's" brother John, being a bigger boy, would accompany old Brooks, when he went with the clothes, and considered it a great honour to drive "Tinker." On the picnic occasions, the party always stopped on the road to boil the kettle (there were no billies in those days), and to give "Tinker" a rest. The halting place was past Breakfast Creek, on the river bank where the ice-works were afterwards built. There was a spring there, and it was a nice place to rest. This road, which is the present Hamilton Road, had formerly been made by the women prisoners. Looking at the cutting now it seems impossible to realise this. Of course, it has been extended since.

A Dr Simpson had charge of these prisoners at Eagle Farm (about the years 1840-41). In his cottage he had a little room off the kitchen containing a sofa, table, and some chairs. Here he was in the habit of retiring for an after-dinner smoke and rest. On one occasion, when young "Tom" had accompanied his father and mother to Eagle Farm, he happened to go into the doctor's kitchen, and saw there the man cook with a large Indian pipe. The youngster watched the man and saw him place the bowl on a little shelf on the side of the wall next the doctor's room, then noticed him put the stem, which was two or three feet long, through a little hole in the wall. This made the boy very inquisitive as to what would happen next, and he watched more intently. The cook then filled the big pipe with tobacco and put a red hot coal on this, and "Tom" dodging round the doorway, saw the doctor, from where he lay on the sofa in the next room, take hold of the stem, and, putting the end in his mouth, calmly start to puff. This was intensely interesting ot course, and "Tom" thought it very funny the way the doctor enjoyed his after-dinner smoke.

Dr Simpson also smoked cigars at that time, and in after years he evidently gave up the long pipe, for he was known never to use anything but a cigar. Some notes *re* this gentleman kindly sent along by a reliable correspondent, may be of interest:—

"When Dr Simpson was a young man he was in the army in Ireland—whether as a surgeon, or as a private or otherwise, I do not remember. He studied as a doctor in Edinburgh, but was an Englishman. He was employed by two ladies of the Royal Family of Russia to travel with them from St Petersburg through Europe to Rome, etc., and back. He studied homeopathy, or rather that system of curing diseases, under Hahnemann (a German), the originator of that system, and was remarkably successful in effecting cures. He was employed as doctor

for the children by the Duchess of Devonshire. He wrote
the first book in the English language on homeopathy,
and the doctors were so offended at it that they perse-
cuted him out of the country. He informed the Duchess
of Devonshire of his resolution, and she was sorry to
lose his services, and told him if she could assist him in
any way she would do it. He came to Sydney and then
got permission from the Government to come to Brisbane,
then a convict colony. Making it a free settlement was
talked of, and officers, police magistrate, and commissioner
of Crown lands would be required. He then used the
influence of the Duchess of Devonshire, and that put him
wherever he wished. He took the Commissioner for Crown
Lands, but had to act for some time as police magistrate.

Dr Simpson had the reputation of being very clever
at curing illnesses in those early days of Brisbane. My
father remembers him well, also his friend, W. H. Wise-
man. A writer in a South Brisbane paper recently speaking of the convict days, says:—"It is only just to say there
were bright reliefs to this dark outlining. 'Old hands'
named with gratitude Dr Simpson, the medical officer,
afterwards a resident of Goodna, and the chaplains of the
penal times as their best friends. Commandant Cotton was
considered their best governor. Mr Andrew Petrie, senior,
foreman of works, had won all their hearts. They never
tired praising these good men. Let the present time fully
honour their memories as lights shining in a dark place."

The better class of prisoners were not hobbled as the
chain gang were, but they worked in a place called the
lumber yard, which stood where the Longreach Hotel is
now. This was a walled enclosure containing different
buildings where the prisoners worked at trades of every
description. They made their own clothes, caps, and boots,
and kept the chain gang supplied with these also; then they
made the nails and iron bolts, etc., required for buildings;
they tanned leather, and made all the soap and candles
needed for the settlement. Also there were blacksmiths,
carpenters, cabinet makers, coopers, wheelwrights, barbers,

etc. The brick wall surrounding this place was high, with one opening—a gate facing Queen Street. Close to this gate on the outside there was a sentry-box, where the soldier who kept the gate could retire if it came on to rain. This soldier had to march up and down in front of the gate to prevent any escape, and after so many hours he was relieved by another man, and so on through the day till about six o'clock, when half-a-dozen or eight red coats arrived with their sergeant. Then the overseer (a head prisoner) would muster the men, and placing them in rows, would call out their names to see if any were missing; after which they were all marched out of the gate and down to the barracks which stood a few yards above Messrs Chapman & Company's establishment. The overseer, or gaoler, then searched each man before locking him up, in order to ascertain that he had no tobacco or anything on his person.

"Tom" often went with his father to the lumber yard when a boy. He can remember events of those days better than he can happenings of twelve months ago. The prisoners had a cook amongst them, who cooked each man's food for him. Twice a week tea, and sugar, and meat, were doled out. Meat was divided in the following fashion: It was cut up into equal junks, as many small pieces as there were men, and placed on a bench ready. Then one prisoner was blindfolded and put in a corner, while another stood by the meat, the rest waiting in a row. The man near the meat touched a piece with his finger, calling "Who for this?" and the blindfolded prisoner made answer with one of the waiting men's names, the owner of which then went forward and took his piece. So it went on till all was finished. This was done that there might be no grumbling about more bone in one piece than another, and all seemed satisfied with the arrangement.

Besides this tea and sugar and meat twice a week, the prisoners daily were fed on rough corn meal porridge. This was served out in kids (small wooden tubs, like cheese vats, but shallow, which held about two quarts of the mixture, flavoured with salt, but, of course, eaten without milk. The chain gang got nothing but this hominy three times a day.

My father says some of them looked fatter and stronger than those with the extras.

Though Grandfather Petrie had nothing to do with how the chain gang were treated, his young son "Tom," as might be supposed, often came into contact with them. He has seen about three hundred of these men marched from the barracks down to where Messrs Campbell and Sons' warehouse now stands. They worked from here towards the Government gardens, chipping corn and hilling it, and soldiers kept guard to see that no one ran away. As soon as the men arrived on the ground, they all pulled off their shirts before starting to work. Father has heard them say this was in order to keep these upper garments clean. They worked away with only their trousers and caps and boots on, and their bodies were all tanned with the sun. "You would see," says father, "the poor fellows' backs marked with the lash, some not quite healed from the last flogging." They had each so many yards to get through before time to "knock off" came. Some would finish beforehand, and these would be allowed to sit down, and rest, but now-and-again one could not get through in time, and he was therefore flogged.

A pine tree stood on the bank of the river, one hundred yards up from where the steam ferry now lands its passengers, and to this tree these prisoners were tied to be flogged.

Though my father has many a time seen men flogged in Queen Street, he does not remember the scene at this pine tree. But often the little chap sat and listened to the prisoners as they rested and told stories of how they had been treated in Logan's time. They pointed out to the boy the tree where the floggings took place for unfinished work, or for an answer to an overseer. The overseers were picked prisoners, and they were generally cruel men who would report everything to the Commandant, in order to gain favour. They had freedom to go about without a guard watching them, and they were kept apart from the others, as they ran a risk of being murdered for their cruelty. Father has often heard the prisoners say it was awful the way they were treated in Logan's time, and they thought it a blessing when his end came, for they had then better times. The blacks, they remarked, got the credit of the murder, but they themselves knew who did it, and it was all right for he deserved his death.

The chain gang was generally divided up into lots who worked at New Farm, Kangaroo Point, South Brisbane, from Turbot Street along the river towards Roma Street station, and from the present steam ferry at Creek Street along the river to the Government gardens. Mostly the work they did was to hoe the ground and plant and hill corn. Father has often seen the convicts cultivating the ground about Brisbane, and it was all done by hoe—no plough. "I have seen," he says, "the poor fellows march with chains on their legs to their work at New Farm and back again." On each cultivated part when the corn was in cob, a prisoner was put to keep away the crows and cockatoos. He was dubbed the "crow-minder," and he had what was called a clapper to make a noise to frighten these birds. This clapper was made of three pieces of board, two about seven inches long and four inches wide, and the third some six inches longer, which was shaped like a butter pat with a handle. The two shorter pieces were fastened one on either side of the long one by a piece of cord or string put through the holes made in the boards, and when this affair was held in the hand and shaken about it made a great noise. The man was supposed to walk up and down through the corn shaking this, for the benefit, or rather otherwise, of the crows who came inquiring.

These "crow-minders" were prisoners under short sentence, and they were not chained like the others. The man who watched the land running along the river from Creek Street was called "Andy," and he had a hut built up in the fork of a gum tree on the bank of the river, down a little way from the pine tree already mentioned. This gum tree had steps made of pieces of iron, driven in like sawyers' dogs, and it was called "the crow-minder's tree." "Andy" used to climb up to his hut and watch that the blacks did not swim across from Kangaroo Point, or come in a canoe to steal the corn or sweet potatoes. The blacks were very daring in those days. "Andy" had an old flint pistol which he fired off to give the alarm when the darkies appeared. The hut was a protection from them, and when up in it he could keep any number off. The "crow-minder" at New Farm had a similar tree and hut; it stood on the river bank near where the residence of Sir Samuel Griffith now stands.

Father has often gone about among the corn with "Andy" while the clapping was going on. The boy was told in those days that once in Logan's time, when Kangaroo Point was under a crop of corn, the blacks were very troublesome; nothing seemed to prevent them from stealing. So one was shot and skinned, then stuffed and put up among the corn to frighten the rest. It turned out a good cure, the corn wasn't troubled afterwards. Whether this was true or not, my father does not know, but he was told it as a fact many a time.

CHAPTER III

"ANDY" had an instrument he called a fiddle, made (in the shape of a grater) from a piece of tin, with holes punched in it with the end of a file, and nailed on to a piece of flooring board. This he used to grate down cobs of corn for meal to cook and eat on the sly. If he were caught at this he would be flogged, he said. He had a small bag in which he carried this meal. In those days the creek which ran down Creek Street, existed of course, and a bridge spanning it opposite Messrs Campbell and Sons' warehouse, entered with its northern end the Petrie's garden. Under this part of the bridge there was a nice flat bank, which always kept dry as the tide did not reach it, and here Andy used to cook his maizemeal and the other eatables he got hold of. "Tom," with his brothers Andrew and Walter, used to take him tea and sugar and flour on the quiet, and one boy kept guard while the cooking was going on, so that Andy would not be taken unawares and flogged. In this out-of-the-way place the prisoner made round things which passed as doughboys, and when the peaches were ripe the youngsters brought him some from their father's garden, which he stewed and cooked up. (This garden, which I have before mentioned, often contained lots of fruit. Mr Knight speaks of it in his book as "a large area of cultivation, with groves of luxuriant orange, lemon, lime, and guava trees.") The boys thought Andy's cooking far better than what they got at home, and when they watched him and then joined in the eating part, everything tasted most delightfully sweet and delicious. "Stolen waters are sweet," I suppose.

Many a time "Tom's" mother gave her boys tea and sugar, and meat and bread for the prisoners, unknown to anyone else. It was against the rules, of course. And through her intercession, the prisoners afterwards used to say, they were saved many a punishment. Grandfather himself, though kind, was strict, but yet during all his reign, according to his son "Tom," he never had one man flogged. "He used to threaten them whenever he caught them doing anything wrong," my father says, "then after a little, would think no more about it. He always carried a walking stick, and when going into any of the workshops in the lumber yard never forgot to make a noise on the floor with this stick. The prisoners hearing, knew who was coming, and had time to put anything aside and be on their best behaviour. They used to make little tubs and other things on the sly for the soldiers, and these were smuggled out by means of the sentry, and in exchange tobacco was smuggled in. The prisoners were not allowed to smoke, so if they got hold of a pipe and tobacco, they hid them in their workshops, and waited a chance, or some of them preferred chewing the tobacco."

The plant known as the tobacco plant came up and grew like a weed on all the cultivated ground in those days. Whether the seed was originally set or not, my father does not know. It grew in the Petrie's garden, and old Ned the gardener used to make tobacco from the leaves. He proceeded in this way: After drying the plant well, he took all the big stalks from the leaves and boiled them in a pot for a certain time, with some water and black sugar (in those days sugar was black and no mistake). When this mixture was cold he soaked the leaves in it for a while, then taking them out, folded them into a square, flat cake, and wrapping a cloth (also wet in the juice) around this cake, he put it between two flat, heavy stones and left it to become pressed. The prisoners in the lumber yard also made tobacco in this way. Father says, "I have many a time taken the leaf to them on the sly from our garden, and have seen them make the tobacco, sometimes pressing the cake in a vice instead of between stones."

Sometimes the chain gang got hold of a piece of tobacco made like this, but very seldom. They got it through the crow minder, who would bury a piece for them in the field where their work lay with the corn. He hid it in a certain place, and marked the spot that it might be easily found. At night, when they were all shut up together, he would tell them about this, and next day when they went to work they had no trouble in finding it. The bother was to smoke it, for the only chance was the dinner hour, when the overseers were away for an hour or so. There would very likely be only one pipe among a dozen of them, so one man filled and lit the precious object and had a few draws, then passed it on to another man, and so on till all had had a turn. It went from one to another till finished just as the blacks' "honeyrag" did in camp. The soldiers looked on and said nothing so long as the overseers were away. Father has often sat with the convicts while they indulged in this sort of smoke, and seeing their enjoyment, was what first made him learn the habit when quite a tiny chap. He used even to make tobacco in their way for his own use.

Captain Logan met his death in 1830, and my grandfather arrived in Brisbane in 1837, so the latter's son, "Tom," did not witness the worst of the convicts' sufferings. However, the sights he saw were bad enough. Many a time he has seen members of the chain gang flogged in Queen Street in the old archway at the prisoners' barracks. They got from fifty to two hundred lashes at a time. They were stripped naked, and tied to the triangle by hands and feet, so that they could not move. Some were flogged for a very small offence, and on the backs of others were unhealed marks of a previous flogging. The rest of the prisoners were arranged round in order to get the benefit of the sight, and a doctor stood by in case the unfortunate fainted. Then the punishment began, and as each stroke fell the chief constable counted aloud the number. Out of all those he has seen flogged, father does not remember even one man fainting, though sometimes the blood flew out at every lash.

Some poor wretches cried aloud in their agony for mercy, or to their mothers and friends to save them, others cursed and swore at the flogger and all the officials, and others again remained perfectly still and quiet. At times the lash went too far round the side of the victim's body, and as it hurt more then, he swore and called to the flogger to "hit fair on the back."

In Logan's time a man called "Old Bumble" was the flogger. He was an inhuman wretch from all accounts, and was hated by the prisoners. The man who succeeded him was Gilligan, the flogger, and my father remembers this man once being flogged himself. Gilligan was the Commandant's gardener, and lived apart from the other prisoners in a little hut near his work, where he cooked his own meals of hominy, and the vegetables he was allowed from the garden. The Commandant's quarters were situated where the new Lands Office is being built now, and his garden extended down along the river bank. It was a nice one, well laid out and well kept, and contained vegetables of all sorts, also fruit trees and flowers galore.

Once Gilligan was caught doing something very wrong in the eyes of the law, and he was tried, found guilty, and sentenced to one hundred lashes. The day for his punishment was fixed, but it was found difficult to get a prisoner to volunteer to flog him. However, at last a black man named Punch (from the Isle of France) came forward. Father remembers the incident well, and can almost now see Gilligan brought forth from the cells and stripped and tied to the triangles. Then a number of other prisoners were marched up and placed in line to look on, and the chief constable (Fitzpatrick) stood close by to count the strokes aloud, while another constable jotted them down with a pencil on a piece of paper. The doctor was also there. When the word was given, Punch, who was left-handed, was ready with his shirt off and the "cat" in his left hand. He flourished it round his head and came down so severely that blood showed the first time, and got worse afterwards, and Gilligan cried out for the mercy which was not shown. Indeed, the prisoners stood round grinning with delight to see the man who had so often flogged them getting it himself. Punch hit nearly always on the same place, which grew raw, and his unfortunate victim was covered with blood from shoulder to heel at the finish.

Some five months after this Punch got into trouble and was sentenced to fifty lashes. Now was Gilligan's revenge! Father remembers how Punch's black skin shone when he was stripped and tied up, and how Gilligan rolled up his sleeves and spat on his handle of the "cat" so that it would not slip. But the hit he gave only made a brown mark on the man's dark skin, and even at the end very little blood came; his skin was too thick for Gilligan. The latter's shirt was ringing wet with perspiration, and one could see he tried his best to give it hard to Punch, who, however, stood all like a brick, and made no sound nor movement, though his back was well marked. The prisoners standing by understood, and they seemed to enjoy the "fun."

Some time after this, Punch ran away, and got into the bush, and the poor fellow's body was found floating on the Bremer by John Petrie on his way to Limestone. It was supposed he took cramps while swimming across the river.

In those days there was a prisoner among the others who made baskets for the Government called "Bribie, the basket maker." He was not chained, and was allowed to go about in a boat to get cane from the scrubs for his work. He only had a short sentence, and it was not worth his while to run away. Indeed, if any of these prisoners with liberty to go and come, attempted to escape or misbehaved, they were put back into the chain gang, and it was known too well what that meant. Some who worked in batches (like the sawyers) had an overseer (also a prisoner) always with them, and he reported behaviour. It was from this man Bribie, my father thinks, that Bribie Island got its name. He cannot remember distinctly on this point, but has some vague recollection of a connection between the man and the island—whether he was blown ashore there, or what, he does not know.

At the mouth of the creek which formerly ran up Creek Street, just where the steam ferry landing is now, a place

was built by the prisoners for the catching of fish and crabs.
Two beams were put side by side across from bank to bank
at highwater mark, and they were flat on top, so that one
could walk on them. Between these beams slabs were
supported, which extended down into the mud. They were
close together, but in the middle an opening was left about
six feet wide, which was bound by two piles standing some
nine feet above the beams. These piles were joined across
the top with a piece of timber, and this had a ring bolt in
the centre for a block and tackle, by which a light frame-
work made of wood was worked up and down. To this
frame work was attached a large basket (Bribie's handi-
work) made so that the fish and crabs which entered were
caught, and it had a square hole (with a cover) on top by
which they could be taken out.

When the water was high, and just on the turn, the
basket was lowered, then when the tide had gone down,
it was hoisted up level with the beams. Fish were plentiful
in the river then, there being nothing much to disturb them,
and sometimes the basket contained a great supply. Old
shank bones, with a little meat attached, were thrown into
the creek to encourage the fish to come in, and the basket
trap was only worked two or three times a week, so that
the fish did not grow afraid, having several days of undisturbed comings and goings. A prisoner had charge of the
working of this trap, and he took the fish caught to the
Commandant, Mr Andrew Petrie, and all the other officials
in turn.

Just at the corner of Elizabeth and Albert Streets, where
a public house now stands, there used to be a large building
erected for holding and thrashing the maize grown by the
prisoners. This barn was built with walls of tea-tree logs
notched into one another, the roof was thatched with blady
grass, and it had a wooden floor. Bags were nailed all
round the walls to prevent grain flying through the openings when the corn was thrashed. The thrashing was done
by six men at a time working in pairs, each man with a
flail, and they kept very good time, swinging their instruments round their heads and coming down one after the

other on the cobs—hit for hit. Other prisoners shovelled
the corn up, and sifting it in sieves, put it into bags ready
for cartage to the windmill, where it was ground into meal.
Alongside this barn a short-sentence prisoner lived in a hut;
he was a sort of clerk, and kept books which showed the
quantity of grain coming and going.

The corn in cobs was taken from the fields to the barn
in what was called a hand-cart. These carts were something after the style of a small dray with low wheels, and
a pole instead of shafts. Each pole had two bars across, one
at the end and another three feet from it, and four prisoners
dragged the cart, two on either side of the pole holding
to the bars. The bars reached about to the men's waists,
who as they walked, thus pulled the cart. Other two prisoners helped by shoving, and a red-coat walked along
behind with a gun on his shoulder—the bayonet shining
brightly in the sun. Thus the poor fellows, chained as
they were, had to drag the empty carts down to the river
bank where the corn grew, then after loading up they
dragged them back to the barn. When full the carts held
nearly as much as a dray would, and generally four of them
were kept busy—two going and two coming—when the
corn was ripe. As they passed, one would hear the click,
click of the chains on the prisoners' legs. Sometimes these
hand-carts were utilised for carrying the grain from the
barn to the windmill, but mostly bullock drays were used
for that purpose.

CHAPTER IV

THE Windmill (the present Observatory, much altered, of course) is said to have been erected in 1829. It was built for the purpose of grinding the maize grown by the prisoners into meal, but there was something very wrong with the machinery evidently, for the wind would not move the "fans" round in a decent fashion. For years everything thought of was tried to alter this defect; even the ground round about was cleared of its heavy timber, so that the wind would have fair play, but all to no purpose. However, the maize was ground in spite of all, for the mill was turned into a treadmill, and by way of punishment the prisoners' legs had to do the work the wind refused to perform.

Mr Knight in his book says: "The year 1837 marked two important events in the early history of Brisbane— the arrival of the Petries, and of the first steamer which ploughed the waters of Moreton Bay." Mr Andrew Petrie, who before his departure from Sydney was attached to the Royal Engineers there, examined the windmill on his arrival, at once discovered the fault of the machinery, and had it put to rights. So after that the mill could do its own work, but still the "treads" were used as a punishment for the badly-behaved prisoners, and at these times the corn was ground by double power. It was no light punishment, as many a prisoner could tell to his cost, especially a heavily-ironed man—poor wretch.

My father remembers a time in those days when the vessel which came from Sydney with supplies for the settlement was a long time overdue, and it was thought she must be wrecked. Tea and sugar and flour and a number of other things were scarce, on account of her non-arrival. Here it may be mentioned that the tea then was all green tea, and very coarse, like bits of stick—indeed it was christened "posts and rails." The sugar the prisoners called "coal tar," for it was almost black like tar. "I do not know," father says, "what the people of to-day would say if they had to live on such stuff; they would think their last hour had come. But we all lived and kept in good health." One thing which was "grand," according to him, however, was boiled pumpkin and sweet potatoes, mashed and mixed together, and then baked in the oven in the shape of a sugar-loaf, alongside a piece of roast-beef. Another idea was sweet potatoes mixed with cornmeal and made into cakes. Then they used to roast the Indian corn in a pan and grind it to make coffee, sweetened with the "coal tar."

To return to the overdue vessel. In order to gain a good supply of meal to make up for the other things, Grandfather Petrie got the better class of prisoners to volunteer to work the treadmill, as it was calm weather (no wind to speak of), and the mill was slow in its work. The prisoners did not object, as it meant plenty to eat for themselves as well as for the rest of the settlement. The boy "Tom" marched alongside with the convicts up to the mill, and when there he saw them go in turns to the wheel, so many on at a time. It was a very hot day, and the first lot took off their shirts, and then went up some five steps to get on to the wheel, which was like a water-wheel, and was thirty or forty feet long, and the treads being about nine inches wide. An iron bolt at one end held it steady till the prisoners were on, then when that was withdrawn the weight of the men started it moving, and they simply had to step up or be hit on the shins; they had a rail to hold on by, of course. A shaft ran through from the wheel into the windmill, where it connected with the cogwheels there—the works were something like those of a chaffcutter. To look at the convicts stepping, one would think they were going upstairs. They had to tread so many minutes, and when one man got off at the far end, another one took his place at the starting point. The man just off would have a rest till his turn came round again. Some took to it so well that they could just hold on with the left hand as they stepped, and with the right scribble on the boards drawings of ships, animals, and men —others seemed to tire altogether. However, on this occasion, it was not a punishment, and most of them were very jolly over it, chaffing one another, and calling, "Hullo, Bill, or Jack, what have you done to be put on the treadmill?" And so they went on till plenty of meal was ground to keep things going, and a couple of days later the expected vessel turned up. She had been windbound in some bay on the coast.

Father also saw the unfortunate chained men on the treadmill working out their punishment. You would hear the "click, click" of their irons as they kept step with the wheel, and those with the heavier irons seemed to have "a great job" to keep up. Some poor wretches only just managed to pull through till they got off at the far end, then they sat down till their turn came to go on again. They all had to do so many hours, according to their sentence; an overseer kept the time, and a couple of soldiers guarded them. When they had put in their time they were marched back to barracks.

The leg irons for the chain gang were made in the lumber yard by a blacksmith prisoner there. A supply was kept always on hand, some light and some heavy, and when a prisoner was sentenced to wear them for a certain time he was taken to this blacksmith's shop to be fitted up; then when his sentence had expired he was sent there to have them taken off again. Father has many a time watched both performances. The rings which went round the man's ankle were made in two half circles the size of the leg, the ends flattened having holes punched in them for rivets. One end was riveted loosely, so that it would act as a hinge, then the man standing near a small anvil put out his foot, and the blacksmith fitted the iron on and riveted the other end. He then tightened the loose one. When both legs were fixed up, a piece of leather, made round, like the top of a boot, was put in between the iron and the man's leg, so that the skin would not be so readily chafed. When the irons were taken off, the rivets were cut through with a cold-chisel.

The lighter irons had links about the size of a plough chain, the others being much heavier. The chains were some two feet long between the legs, and in the middle of each was a small ring with a string through it, which, being connected to the prisoner's belt, kept the irons from dragging on the ground during motion. Prisoners wearing chains had a peculiar way of walking, and you would see the poor fellows just released after six months or so, going along as though they still wore them. Heavily-chained men always dragged their feet along in a weary fashion— life to them could not have been much joy. Ordinary trousers would not go over a man's irons, so the chain gang all wore these garments opened right down the outside seams, and buttoned there with big black buttons.

At that time "Tom" was the youngest son of the Petrie family, and there being of course no school to go to, his father used to take him two or three days in the week to the lumber yard to his office, there to get lessons from his clerk. This clerk was a prisoner, and he was called "Peg-leg Kelly," because he had a wooden leg, but grandfather himself said, he was a very good scholar. He kept books for the lumber yard, and could tell from them what the prisoners made and everything that was done in the yard; also all the prisoners' names, why they were sent out, and the length of their sentence, etc. Father says, "I have often heard my father say that some of the poor fellows got fifteen or sixteen years for stealing turnips, others were sentenced for life because they had stolen sheep, or for forgery. Nowadays, for the same offence or worse, they pay a fine or earn a few months in gaol, where they are kept like gentlemen with everything they want, and very often the moment time is up something is done to get back again. If they were treated as the prisoners in the early days, they would not be so anxious to get in again, but would turn honest, even as the convicts did. Those poor fellows when they once got free could be trusted with almost anything.

Very little in the way of lessons my father says he learnt in those days. So soon as his father left the office and went from the lumber yard to inspect the outside works, "Tom" was off out among the prisoners watching them as they made nails, and all the other various articles, without a thought to his lessons. "Poor Kelly," he says, "would never tell on me. Although I used to get many a thrashing from father for not knowing my lessons, and Kelly got many a scolding for not getting me along better, he would never 'split' on me. I used to take him now and again a bit of tobacco and a little tea and sugar, or a piece of bread, all unknown to father, and sometimes I gave the other prisoners some, so that I was a great favourite among them, and no matter what I did they never let it out. I have often thought since that if I had taken poor father's advice, and stuck to my lessons, it would have been better for me to-day. But I only thought of playing in those days, and though I had, of course, no opportunity to become what my father was, the few poor chances which came in my way were passed unrecognised. Just at this time myself and brothers (John, Andrew, and Walter) were the only boys in the settlement, with the one exception of the barrack sergeant's son. (Of course, later on there were lots of youngsters.) This boy (Billy Jones) was not allowed in among the prisoners, and we were really not supposed to be there unless we went with our father. My brothers, like myself, were in great favour with the convicts, as they used also to bring food and tobacco to them. The prisoners would do anything for us."

A convict called "Joe Goosey," an odd job man, was much disliked by the others, because he told tales about them. He could never grow any sign of whiskers, and for this reason and because he wore small silver rings in his ears, he was jeered at, and called "The Lady." The convicts could not stand a "tell-tale" at any price, and poor "Joe

Goosey," a soft sort of a fellow, had anything but a pleasant life among them. But even he had no complaints to make of the Petrie youngsters.

The building where the prisoners slept (the barracks) was divided up into wards for the different classes—the chain gang occupied one, and so on. The beds the poor fellows had to lie on were merely movable boards six feet long and two feet wide, and these were supported by ledges one higher than the other, so as to cause a slant from the head downwards to the feet. Also at the higher end a piece of timber rounded off and nailed there served as a pillow. Add to this a double blanket, and we have the one-time convict's "feather bed."

In the centre part of the barracks was a room used as a church, and here service was held every Sunday. (This room was afterwards used as the Supreme Court.) The chain gang always clanked upstairs to the gallery, while the mechanics sat below. The barracks, as I have said, were situated a little above Messrs Chapman and Co.'s warehouse, and further down (from the Bridge) on the right-hand side, at the corner of Queen and Albert Streets, the stockyard once stood, used by the prisoners for yoking up the working bullocks. Then, on the bank of the river, opposite the present Ice Works, the Government saw-pits stood, and at Roma Street station, in the hollow there, the convicts made the bricks.

When my father was nine or ten years old, he saw the first execution by hanging in Brisbane—that of two aboriginals, who were found guilty of the murder of the surveyors, Staplyton and Tuck. The execution took place at the Windmill, which was fixed up for the occasion. After it was over a prisoner, taking young "Tom" by the hand, drew him along to have a look in the coffin. Stooping, he pulled the white cap from the face of the dead blackfellow, exposing the features. The eyes were staring, and the open mouth had the tongue protruding from it. The horror of the ghastly sight so frightened the child that it set him crying, and he could not get over it nor forget it for long afterwards. As a man he remembers it still.

While talking of these days I may mention the story
told of the planting of prepared rice. This was done in
Logan's time by Mr Peter Spicer, the superintendent of
convicts. My father has often heard his father laughing
and telling the tale as a joke to the early squatters. The
land prepared for the rice was a swamp, which extended
from Bulimba to Newstead, and doubtless there are those
who remember the drains on this land. After all the trouble,
because the rice did not come up, the land was declared
to be unsuitable for the growing of that crop!

CHAPTER V

It has, of course, been recorded how in 1838 Mr Andrew
Petrie got lost in the bush with the then new Commandant,
Major Cotton. They went out on a visit of inspection to
Limestone, accompanied by Dr Alexander (the medical
officer to the 28th Regiment), an orderly, and a convict
attendant. Travelling up by boat, they reached Limestone
(Ipswich) without event, and on the return trip Mr Petrie
suggested to the Commandant that they should journey
through the bush to Redbank to see the sheep station
formed there. This was done, and on the way some new
specimens of timber were discovered by my grandfather,
whose taste for exploring was therefore aroused, and he
again proposed a lengthening of the trip. This time it
was to Oxley Creek, where convict sawyers were at work.
All went well until, after leaving the latter place, the party
got "bushed" in the thick forest, in an attempt to come out
on the river, where they had instructed the boat to wait for
them. The boat did wait, and waited till her occupants
grew weary; then went on to the settlement to report the
new turn events had taken, and search parties were sent out.

In the meantime the "lost sheep" wandered about for a
couple of days and nights; then, on the third day, coming
to a mountain, Mr Petrie ascended it, hoping to be able
to see then where they were. He was successful, and they
managed after that to find their way to the river, coming
out near the present Lytton. Here my grandfather (he

could not swim) proceeded to make a raft of dry logs to
cross the river; but, while in the midst of this, one of the
search parties with a black tracker came up, and immediately after a boat belonging to the Government happened
to pass, which took the exhausted party back to the settlement. A good deal of excitement was caused over this event,
for it was thought that the travellers had met with Logan's
fate, guns being fired, and black trackers employed, for so
long, all without result.

The search party, which came up with the lost ones while
the raft was being made, told them how the black man
("Tal-lin-gal-lini") had followed their tracks. He seemed
to know grandfather's from the others, and once, coming
on a certain place, called "Look here! Mr Petrie been
stand and shoot bird!" and proceeded to show the way
that gentleman had fired off the gun, standing with it to his
left shoulder. Mr Petrie always held a gun so, but was
nevertheless a good shot. He thought it wonderful how
the black man had noticed, for it was quite true; he had
shot a swamp pheasant at the place described. "Tom"
often heard his father speak of this time afterwards, saying how strange it was that the tracker should know the
position in which he stood, and declaring that the swamp
pheasant was very sweet, but hardly a mouthful among
them all; they were tired and very hungry. The hill from
which Mr Petrie found his bearings as regards the Brisbane River was afterwards called Mount Petrie, a name it
still is known by. With reference to this, some years ago,
the *Brisbane Courier* contained the following :—

"Mr Thorn drew the attention of the Belmont Board at
Wednesday's meeting to the fact that there was a tree lying
on the summit of Mount Petrie, Mr Prout's property, which
bore a relic of the early days. The tree had a scarf cut
out, and in its place there was carved the name 'A. Petrie,
ᴀ838.' This was the father of Mr T. Petrie, of North Pine,
and the grandfather of the present member for Toombul.
Mr Thorn thought the relic ought to be in the Museum,
and for this purpose moved that Mr Prout be written
to, asking permission to cut and remove the portion of the

tree referred to. Mr Lees seconded the motion, which was unanimously agreed to."

A trigonometrical station was built on Mount Petrie, and Mr Andrew Petrie's tree was cut down to make room for the beacon. In 1896, when the board sought the tree, it had just been burnt by bush fires. The writer is indebted to Mr Lees for a rough sketch of the tree while standing.

In Mr Andrew Petrie's explorations he found many new specimens of timber. Says Dr Lang, on page 135 of his book, "Cooksland":—

"I shall enumerate a few of the more important species of the timber of Moreton Bay, with notanda, illustrative of the qualities, localities, and uses, for which I am indebted in great measure to Mr Andrew Petrie, the able and intelligent superintendent of Government Works at Moreton Bay, while that part of the territory was a penal settlement."

Dr Lang speaks first of the *Araucaria Cunninghami*, or the Moreton Bay pine. He ends his description by saying: "There are two varieties of this pine—that of the mountain, and that of the plains or alluvial flats on the banks of rivers. Of the former of these varieties, Mr Petrie, who first observed its superior qualities, states that it is little inferior to the Bunya Bunya pine. It is well adapted for masts and spars, and grows nearly as large as the bunya; no sap or knots to injure the spars."

Secondly, Dr Lang speaks of the *Araucaria Bidwilli*, or the Bunya Bunya pine, and he again quotes from his friend. He writes:—" 'This tree,' observes Mr Petrie, 'grows to an immense height and girth. I have measured some ordinary sized trees, one hundred and fifty feet high, and about four feet in diameter. They are as straight and round as a gun barrel. The timber grows in a spiral form, and would answer admirably for ship's masts of any size. This pine bears a great strain traversely, one of its superior qualities; also there is no sap wood nor knots in the barrel, the lateral branches being never above two or three inches in diameter, and growing from the outer rind of the tree. The fruit of this pine is a large cone or core, about nine by six inches, and covered with small cones, similar in appearance to a pineapple. It is these small nuts that the blacks eat; they travel two or three hundred miles to feed on the fruit. It is plentiful every three years. The timber grows in latitude twenty-five and twenty-six degrees, and about sixty miles in longitude. It is not known at present to grow anywhere else. It grows plentifully in this latitude. I was the first person who risked my life with others in procuring the first plants of this tree, and Mr Bidwill was some years after me.' "

Dr Lang next writes of the red cedar, and tells how in the prisoners' time, the Government had it all cut down to give employment to the convicts, and large quantities went to waste. Then he quotes yet again from Mr Petrie:—

" 'IRON BARK.—This tree grows plentifully in the forest, and is suitable for house or shipbuilding, and is a valuable timber.

" 'BLUE GUM.—This is another valuable hardwood timber, and is well adapted for all kinds of carpentry work.

" 'BOX.—This timber is very suitable for all agricultural implements, and for many other purposes.

" 'ROSE OR VIOLET WOOD.—This is a valuable timber, and is suitable for gig shafts, etc., being similar to our lance-wood at home. The aborigines make their spears of this wood, and they know the art of straightening them when crooked.

" 'SILK OAK.—This is a very beautiful tree, and the timber is well adapted for the sheathing of vessels, and many other useful purposes.

" 'FOREST OAK.—Known also by the name of beefwood; suitable for tool handles, bullock yolks, etc. It is used principally for firewood.

" 'TULIP WOOD.—This wood is suitable for fancy, cabinet, and turning work. It grows in the scrub. The tree appears like a cluster of Gothic columns.

" 'There are a great many other species of valuable timber in this district,' observes Mr Petrie, 'that I have not described, not having specimens to give you. Logwood and Fustic have been procured here. The timber trade will form one of the principal branches of commerce. I also send you a small sample of the native gums. Gums could be procured in this district in considerable quantities.' "

It is interesting to compare the first opinions formed of the timbers of Moreton Bay with those of the present day. Mr Petrie was correct in his prophesy that "the timber trade will form one of the principal branches of commerce." We will now follow him in his adventures whilst obtaining specimens of the Bunya Bunya pine. The exact date of his discovery of the tree is not remembered, but several years after he gave a Mr Bidwill specimens, and that gentleman forwarding them to England, got the credit of the discovery, for the tree was named after him—*Araucaria Bidwilli*.

During an excursion to Maroochy in those early years Mr Petrie succeeded in procuring what has been spoken of as "the first specimens of Bunya pine seen by those in the settlement." "From the plants he brought with him," says Mr Knight, "which were obtained at considerable risk, owing to the unfriendly attitude of the blacks, may be said to have sprung many of the fine specimens now to be seen about Brisbane and Sydney." On this excursion he was accompanied by his son John (so well known after-wards in Brisbane), two convicts, and two native blacks as guides—"Tunbur" and "Dundawaian." They also had with them a pack bullock, which carried the rations and blankets. Mr Petrie got specimens of different kinds of timber besides the Bunya, and years afterwards, when his son "Tom" travelled with the blacks to their feast of the Bunya season they showed the young fellow where his father had been (between Dulong and Razor Back), and the direction he took through the scrub.

On the return from this trip, Mr Petrie camped at the foot of Beerwah Mountain, for he was anxious to ascend it and take observations from the summit. (He always carried his instruments with him.) He tried to get a black-fellow to climb also, but in vain, for the man declared that should such a thing be done the spirit who lived at the top of the mountain would kill him. John Petrie, therefore,

accompanied his father, and they carried with them a bottle
of water, reaching the top after great difficulty. Mr Petrie
took bearings for the assistance of the surveyors, who were
then commencing a trigonometrical survey, and after a good
look round and a rest, he wrote his name, with date attached, on a slip of paper, and corking this up in the now
empty bottle, placed it safely under a rock, and descended
to the camp. (In after years John Petrie called his house
on Gregory Terrace "Beerwah.")

The next person who climbed Beerwah was Mr Burnett,
the Government Surveyor (after whom the Burnett River
was named), and he also put his name in the bottle. Several
others have been up since. The story of the bottle was told
my father by grandfather years after the event, when the
old gentleman was blind. The blacks had a strange idea
about that same blindness—they declared that the spirit
of the mountain had caused it in order that Mr Petrie
would be for ever afterwards unable to see his way up
again.

I have already quoted from a book written by Mr T.
Archer—"Recollections of a Rambling Life"—and now add
the following extract, which is of interest, here :—

"Before finally 'squatting' in this unpromising land, we
made some efforts to discover something better by making
excursions into the surrounding country. I set off on foot
one day on one of these search expeditions, accompanied
by Jimmy, and a native of the country named 'Jimmy
Beerwah,' who could speak a little 'dog English,' or blackfellow slang, having been occasionally at the German Mission, near Brisbane.   He led us ten or a dozen miles
eastward through thickly-timbered and very poor country,
when there appeared ahead of us a huge isolated sugar-loaf
mountain, presenting an apparently inaccessible wall of
bare rock. When we reached the foot of it I sat down on a
stone, thinking our adventures for that day were over, but
'Jimmy Beerwah' continued to advance, making use of some
crevices and projections to haul himself upwards, and
beckoning to us to follow. Not to disgrace my Norwegian
training as a cragsman, I did so, and the other Jimmy

brought up the rear, and never have I forgotten the magnificent view that met our gaze, when, after half-an-hour's scramble, we reached the top. Nearly the whole of the Moreton Bay district lay spread out beneath us, and about a dozen miles to the eastward of us was 'the sea, the sea, the open sea,' glittering in the sunlight, with Briby's Island, Moreton Island, and Moreton Bay to the south, and a hundred miles of coast, stretching away to the north. For two years I had not beheld this, my favourite element, and was delighted to see it once more; but Jimmy, who had never before seen a sheet of water bigger than Wingate's Lagoon, was transfixed with astonishment, and stood staring at it in mute admiration, though he was far too proud to give vent to his feelings by indulging in undignified gestures like his more unsophisticated and barbarous countrymen on their first introduction to a flock of sheep. I had begun the ascent of that mountain laying the flattering unction to my soul that I was the first white man to accomplish the feat, but when about half way up, I began to notice indications of whites having been before me, in sundry scratches on the rocks that could have been made only by the nailed soles of boots, and what was my disgust, on attaining the pinnacle, to discover a cairn of stones containing a bottle in which was a scrap of paper with the names of Andrew Petrie, and John Petrie (his son), and one or two others written on it in pencil; this was a mortifying discovery, but one that had to be borne with becoming resignation. The name of the mountain was Beerwah, and it was the highest and most westerly of a cluster of peaked hills, scattered irregularly between it and the sea, called the Glass House Mountains. Our guide, 'Jimmy Beerwah,' had probably that name bestowed on him by Mr Petrie, the Government Engineer at Brisbane, for guiding him and his party to the top of the mountain shortly before our arrival. 'Jimmy Beerwah,' no doubt, tried to explain this to us, but our ignorance of the Moreton Bay blacks' slang prevented us from understanding him."

The writer came across Mr Archer's book after describing Mount Beerwah's ascent by Mr Andrew Petrie. It will be seen that the latter climbed with his son without the assistance of a blackfellow, but perchance "Jimmy Beerwah" was the black who refused to climb on that occasion.

This "Jimmy Beerwah" was, my father says, a regular messenger man among the blacks. He carried messages from tribe to tribe by means of the usual notched stick. A messenger could travel anywhere with safety, going unharmed even amongst hostile tribes.

Another time my grandfather journeyed from Brisbane to where Caboolture is now, to obtain a block of timber from a Bunya pine. This time he had with him the same blackfellows, two or three convicts, and his son John. The first night they camped at North Pine, where the "kippa" ring was then, and, of course, round about was all wild forest—no roads to Caboolture, nor bush tracks even. Long afterwards, when my father went to live at the Pine, the aborigines showed him just where his father had camped— they said he had with him a bullock on which chains were put, "all same as 'croppies' (prisoners), so that fellow not run away."

The "kippa" ring at the Pine owned the curious native name of "Nindur-ngineddo," which means a "leech sitting down." The larger ring was made just where the present road is opposite the blacksmith's shop, and the roadway to the smaller one (where the travellers camped) ran up behind the shop to the top of the ridge, where in the paddock behind "Murrumba" even yet a part of the ring and roadway can be seen.

When Mr Petrie and his companions had reached the Caboolture River they had to go up it a little way in order to be able to cross with the pack-bullock—the pine they were in quest of stood on the north bank. Arriving at the tree, they started to cut out a piece, and the blacks showed they did not like this at all, complaining that they had piloted the party to see the tree, not to cut it. I have previously mentioned that the aborigines would not (in the very early days) even cut notches in a bunya pine, and on this occasion they almost cried in their distress, saying the tree would die of its wounds. Mr Andrew Petrie had to assure them it would not, and he promised supplies of tobacco. So the deed was done; and, after camping that night, the junk of wood was put on the pack-bullock next morning, and eventually Brisbane was safely reached. Mr Petrie had the block of timber cut up, and some of it polished to show the grain.

Doubtless there are farmers still on the Caboolture River who remember seeing that old bunya tree with the piece cut from it. It stood close to where the bridge now crosses the river.

Mr Henry Stuart Russell, author of "Genesis of Queensland," refers to the Bunya pine. He says:—

"The Bunnia-Bunnia (*Araucaria Bidwilli*), which expresses so much in aboriginal traditions, claims a few remarks before passing on from Wide Bay.

"Andrew Petrie, who held the post of Foreman of Works, January, 1836, under the Government, Brisbane, was the first white intelligent discoverer of this tree, some time, I think in 1838. Under the guidance of some blacks, he had visited a spot on which it grew, took a drawing of it, and brought in a sample of the timber, the finding of which, and his opinion as to its value, he at once reported. It got the name of *Pinus Petriana*; deservedly, I should have thought; but not, it seemed, in accordance with the manorial rights of red-tape."

Mr Russell then speaks of meeting (shortly after returning from Wide Bay in 1842) a Mr Bidwill, "an attache to the Botanical Society in London," in search of Bunya plants to send to England. He sent three, two of which Mr Russell afterwards saw growing there. The latter adds:—

"Being reported in this fashion, it became known, *de riguer*, as the *Araucaria Bidwilli* for all time; the true worker's—Petrie's—solid claim was outbid by the less title to fame. I can recollect cones of the Bunnia being sold at Covent Garden, London, for ten guineas each."

Yet another extract from Mr Archer's book:—

"They (the blacks) were quiet and peaceable and not nearly so numerous as at Durandur, except in the bunya season, when they mustered in large numbers from great distances; but then the bunya cones supplied them so amply with food that they were not tempted by hunger to supply themselves with animal food from our flocks. I need not describe to you the bunya tree, as you have all seen one growing in the Gracemere garden, where it thrives, though it is not a native of that district. The tree when in its native home is confined to a comparatively small space of country, beginning about Cunningham's Gap in the south and extending northward along the Main Range for about one hundred and fifty miles to the head of the Cooyar Creek, there a spur branches off from the Main Range eastward toward the coast, separating the waters of the Brisbane from those of the Mary River, and approaching the coast between the Glass House Mountains and the Moorochie River, its length being about another one hundred and fifty miles. Along this range and all its spurs the bunya flourishes, and supplies (or supplied) the blacks every third year with ample stores of food from its huge cones, larger than a man's head, and containing kernels as large as an almond. Its botanical name, the *Araucaria Bidwilli*, was given to it because Mr Bidwill is supposed to be the first white man who brought it into notice. But this is a mistake. The tree was first discovered by Mr Petrie, the Government Engineer, on his expedition mentioned above, when he ascended Mount Beerwah, and found the Mooroochie River. He, however, was not a scientific botanist, and only reported his discoveries in the colonies, whereas Mr Bidwill sent the cone to England, and thus got the credit of being the discoverer of the tree."

In Mr Andrew Petrie's diary of his trip to Wide Bay in 1842 (to be quoted later), speaking of that part of the world, he says:—"In this scrub I found a species of a pine, not known before. It is similar to the New Zealand Cowrie pine, and bears a cone. It forms a valuable timber, etc." This evidently is the pine *Agathis robusta*, known to the early blacks as "Dundardum" (Dundardoom). The white man has mispronounced it so—"Dundathu."

An article on Brisbane by an unsigned writer, appearing in the *Town and Country Journal* some time since, speaks of Mr Andrew Petrie's discoveries, then adds :— "He was, in fact, so indefatigable in developing the natural resources of the district, and labouring for its welfare, that any attempt to write the story of Brisbane would be absolutely incomplete without reference to the pioneer Andrew Petrie and his descendants." With regard to his coal discoveries, Mr J. J. Knight says :—"In several other ways did Mr Petrie demonstrate the capabilities of the district, not the least important being the discovery of coal at Tivoli while on a visit to Redbank station. So impressed was he with the importance of this find that he sent two sample casks to Sydney; it was tested, and pronounced highly satisfactory. At a later period, it may be mentioned, a tunnel was run into the hill, and a plentiful supply obtained for the penal establishment. It may also be remarked that Mr Petrie found, though some time after the discovery at Tivoli, the black diamond at Redbank and Moggill, and mines at these places were in subsequent years worked by the veteran John Williams. The value of such discoveries was not wholly apparent in those bygone days; it is now that the trade has grown to such dimensions, and forms so important a part in the commercial worth, that we can realise their importance to the full."

CHAPTER VI

In 1842, Mr Andrew Petrie discovered the Mary River. On this trip he was accompanied by Mr Henry Stuart Russell, the Hon. W. Wrottesley (third son of Lord Wrottesley), and Mr Jolliffe. Five prisoners of the Crown formed the boat's crew, and two aborigines belonging to Brisbane made up the party. They left in an old Government boat called a "gig," and were away about a month. The trip was a most eventful one, and I cannot do better than give an extract from an old diary which my grandfather kept in those days, and which reads as follows:—

"Wednesday, 4th May, 1842: Left Brisbane town at daybreak; pulled down to the first flat (Breakfast Creek); set sail; wind from the south-west; made the north end of Bribie's Island Passage at dusk; could not distinguish the passage. Lay at anchor and slept in the boat till daybreak.

"5th: Made sail for the River Marootchy Doro, or the Black Swan River; arrived there at two o'clock, but was afraid to enter, it being low water at the time, and a heavy surf on the bar. Made way for Madumbah Island, distant about two miles from the river, but could not affect a landing, on account of the surf. Set sail for Bracefield Cape, and arrived shortly after sunset in the bay or bight. There was a very heavy swell, which made it difficult landing. Before leaving the boat we were surprised to see twenty or thirty aborigines running along the beach, coming to meet us. I made signs to them to carry us ashore, and they immediately jumped into the water up to their arm-pits. I was the first who mounted their shoulders. They appeared bold and daring, and I immediately suspected that this must be the place where several shipwrecked seamen had been murdered by these black cannibals. Little did I think at the time that the one who carried me ashore was the principal murderer. The moment he put me off his shoulders he laid hold of my blanket, but I seized him and made him drop it. He then took hold of a bag of biscuit, and would have taken it away had I not taken strong measures to prevent him. There were no guns on shore, and those on board were not loaded, so I called for my rifle, and, loading it, kept them at bay, and at the same time made them carry our luggage on shore. We then gave them a few biscuits, and ordered them off to their camp, retaining the murderer and another, and kept regular watch all night, each of us taking an hour in turn. During supper I made enquiries after "Wandie" (the bush name of the runaway Bracefield), and was informed by the natives that he was only a short way off.

"6th: Early this morning I despatched our two blacks and one of the strange ones with a letter to Bracefield. He could not read, but one of the blacks mentioned my name to him when he gave him the letter, and he started instantly to join us, accompanied by three of his tribe—his adopted father and two of his friends. About eleven o'clock the black observed them coming about five miles off, and Mr Jolliffe and I, also Joseph Russell (one of our crew), and the blackfellow went along the beach to meet them. Bracefield, when we met him, had the same appearance as the wild blacks; I could only recognise him (as a European) from having known him before. When I spoke to him he could not answer me for some time; his heart was full, and tears flowed, and the language did not come readily to him. His first expression was to thank me for being the means of bringing him back to the society of white men again. He was anxious to hear about the settlement, and to know whether anything would be done to him; I assured him that no punishment would be inflicted on him, but rather things would turn to his advantage. On coming along to our camp, Bracefield said to me, 'I suppose, sir, you are not aware that the black you have got with you is the murderer of several white men.' The moment the man observed us talking about him he darted off into the bush in an instant, just as I was looking round at him. The men at the camp were very kind to Bracefield, got him washed, gave him clothing, and something to eat and drink, and he felt himself a different being. After dinner I took him up some adjoining hills, which I named after him and his friend, the blackfellow, who gave me the names of the different mountains. This bay or inlet has a river in the bight, which forms several large lakes, or sheets of water. A few miles inland from one of these lakes, Mrs Frazer (wife of Captain Frazer, of the *Stirling Castle*), was rescued from the blacks by Bracefield, and conveyed to the boats which were anchored at the same place where we encamped.

"7th: Set sail about eight a.m., wind south-east, for Wide Bay, taking Bracefield with us; landed about four o'clock; distance thirty miles; found it difficult to land owing to the heavy swell in the bight. After landing I found an excellent boat harbour; we stayed there for the night.

"8th (Sunday): Went up on the Cape and Russell Hill to take some bearings, but the morning being so hazy nothing was satisfactory; after returning, about eleven o'clock, we set sail over the bay with a south-east wind; about three p.m. were in the passage leading into what is called Wide Bay. Landed for the purpose of getting a blackfellow that knew the river; Bracefield despatched a black after him across Wrottesley Bay. He arrived about an hour before sundown. We sailed down the passage about six miles, and camped on Frazer's Island.

"9th: Started at sunrise, taking the direction from the strange blackfellow. A dense fog continued until eleven o'clock. We steered north-west, and the wind springing up from the north-east, we continued sailing and pulling about among the islands, looking out for the river, but without success.

"10th: Started early; circumnavigated Gammon Island, and landed nearly where we started from. Observing a blacks' fire on Frazer's Island, I proposed making for that point, intending to take bearings from the high land, from which I also thought I might see the river. While engaged in taking bearings, I descried the river accordingly. It is called the Wide Bay River. While I was on the hill, the rest of the party procured some fresh water, and tried all they could to persuade one of the natives to accompany us across to the river, but were not successful. They appeared afraid of us, more especially of Mr Wrottesley's red shirt. We left the island about three p.m., reached the mouth of the River Barney at sundown, and encamped on Jolliffe's Head. This point of land is of marine formation, being calciferous ironstone strata, is peculiarly laid up and intermixed; lies at about an angle of seventy degrees, forming a ridge of land covered with scrub, along the north side. In this scrub I found a species of pine not known before. It is similar to the New Zealand Cowrie pine, and bears a cone. It forms a valuable timber. The blacks make their nets of the inner bark of this tree.

"11th: Ascended the river about twenty miles; next day, about twenty-five miles higher; and the following day, about four miles—about fifty in all, where we found the navigation stopped with rocks and shingly beds. After we landed, I despatched Bracefield and our black "Ullappah" (or "Alloppa"), to see if they could find any natives, but they did not succeed, blacks were afraid. I went in among the scrubs and procured some specimens of timber. "Ullappah" speared a fine fresh water mullet, with flat mouth and red eyes, about two and a-half pounds weight. Shortly after, I took a stroll, but without my gun, and quite alone, not expecting to meet with any blacks; I had not gone above half-a-mile from the camp, when I heard the sound of natives, who appeared to be numerous. I immediately returned to the camp, and sent off Bracefield and the black to them. They were absent about an hour and a-half, and reported on their return that they were afraid to go near the blacks' camp—the darkies were so numerous. Bracefield was sure there were some hundreds of them;

he and the black were both very much frightened; he told me he would require two more men with firearms. Bracefield informed the man we were in quest of, Davis, or "Duramboi" (his bush name), was sure to be with the tribe, on which I offered to accompany him and assist him in procuring him. Bracefield said it would be much better for me to remain at the camp, as I should otherwise be running a great risk, and proposed that two of our party, Clark and Russell, both prisoners of the Crown (convicts), should go along with him, as if they succeeded in bringing him into our camp, something might be done for these men in the way of mitigating their punishment. I assented, arranging with them to go to their assistance if we should hear their guns fire, and they went off accordingly about half-past four p.m., and about sundown returned with Davis. Bracefield behaved manfully in this transaction. He directed Russell and Clark to remain at a distance, while he and the blackfellow should steal in upon the strange blacks. Soon after the two got in among them, the two white men were observed, and the strange blacks immediately snatching up their spears, were running off to murder them, when Davis and Bracefield prevented them, and, no doubt, saved the lives of the pair. By this time Bracefield had been recognised by a great number of the Wide Bay blacks, who knew him, and told him (as the reason of their murderous intentions towards the two white men) that the white fellows had poisoned a number of their tribe. But Bracefield explained to them that we knew nothing of it whatever, and that we were come to explore the river and the country, and would not interfere with the blacks, provided that they did not meddle with the white men. If they did, there were a great many white men and firearms, and they would be shot immediately. I had written a note to Davis informing him that nothing would be done to him if he came in to the settlement. He had, however, during this time darted off to Russell and Clark, and gave himself up to them without waiting for Bracefield and the black, and when they appeared, he told Bracefield that he (Bracefield) had come to take him for the purpose of getting his own sentence mitigated; in fact, insisted that he had, refusing to believe Bracefield's asseverations to the contrary, until the latter got into a passion and sang a war song at him. With that Davis bolted off towards us, our men being scarcely able to keep pace with him. I shall never forget his appearance when he arrived at our camp —a white man in the state of nudity, and actually a wild man of the woods, his eyes wild and unable to rest for a moment on any one object. He had quite the same manners and gestures that the wildest blacks have got. He could not speak his 'mither's' tongue, as he called it. He could not even pronounce English for some time, and when he did attempt it, all he could say was a few words, and these often misapplied, breaking off abruptly in the middle of a sentence with the black gibberish, which he spoke very fluently. During the whole of our conversation, his eyes and manner were completely wild, and he looked at us as if he had never seen a white man before. In fact, he told us he had nearly forgotten all about the society of white men, and had hardly thought about his friends and relations for these fourteen years past; and had I or some one else not brought him from among these savages, he never would have left them. One of the first questions he asked me was about the settlement at Moreton Bay, which I gave him to understand was now a free settlement, and a very different place altogether from what it was when he left it fourteen years ago. I only guessed at the period from some of the prisoners mentioning about the time he absconded, as he had no idea of it himself, and could not tell what time he had been in the bush. At the same time I assured him that no punishment would be inflicted on him for absconding.

"I then told Davis it was my intention to proceed to Baphal (Bopple), an adjoining mountain, but he strongly advised me not to attempt this, for if we divided our party, the men that we left at the boat would all be murdered before we returned, as there were some hundreds of blacks at their camp who could surround the party and kill them all. He told me we would require three or four men to keep watch during the night, for in all probability they would then attack us. At the same time he asked if I would allow him to go back and remain with the blacks for the night, and he would try and make it all right with them; he pledged his word he would return to us by daybreak. I told him by all means to go, and we would wait for him. He said the blacks were determined to attack us, as they would have revenge for the poisoning of their friends at some of the stations to the South. Davis then bade us good night, and left us. The greater number of our party, mostly all except myself, never thought he would come back, or, if he did, they thought it would be heading the blacks against us. This made our party very timid, and I therefore took what I thought the most prudent plan, which was to put everything in the boat and sleep on board, keeping a regular watch all night. The men and ourselves would have been so much fatigued, and knowing some of our party would not prove firm, and were not accustomed to firearms, we concluded it must be the best plan to camp in the boat. We were then in a position to defend ourselves, although hundreds had attacked us. We kept watch all night; some of us did not sleep much, we were all prepared for them. At daybreak I ordered three musket shots to be fired at intervals, to let Davis know that we were still in the same place, waiting his coming. About sunrise he joined us, accompanied by a black, who had possession of a watch belonging to a man, a shepherd of Mr (now Sir Evan) M'Kenzie's, who was murdered by the blacks at Kilcoy station some time before. I gave the blackfellow a tomahawk for the watch, according to promise. He appeared very much afraid of us.

"Bracefield and the black, 'Ullappah' had accompanied Davis to the native encampment, and when they reached it, seeing our black so plump and fat, the Wide Bay natives asked Bracefield and Davis if the white men would take the part of the black, and attack them if they were to kill and eat him. They both gave them to understand, in reply, that there were a great many white men and arms at the boat, and that in that case they would come and shoot them all. At this time Davis was at a loss to know how the white men had got there. He imagined they came overland. The moment our men appeared before their camp they immediately said these were the men that killed their people to the southward, and instantly manned their spears and waddies, and would have sallied forth on the white men had Davis not prevented them. By this time Bracefield had stripped himself of the clothes we had given him, and he went in among them, and was immediately recognised by a great many, who invited him to sup with them and remain for the night. Davis and he made them believe that they would both return to them, and before leaving the camp Davis made them an oration, informing them that it was not to molest them, but to explore the river and the country, and to search for him (Davis), that the white men had come, and that they knew nothing of the poisoning of their friends. They intended no harm if they (the blacks) would not molest them, but if they did, they would all be shot by the whites. He also made them understand that their spears were nothing compared to our guns, and made them believe that the guns were something terrible. This had the desired effect, for in the morning, at the first report of the musket we fired, not a murmur was heard, the mothers making their young ones lie quiet lest we should hear them; at the second report the greater part of them took to the scrub; and on hearing the third report, they nearly all fled in the greatest consternation. Thus terminated our manoeuvres with the natives.

"14th: Descended the river about twenty miles. During our encampment we were all very much entertained with Davis's description of the manner of life and customs of the blacks, also he gave the account of the manner the blacks murdered the two white men (Mr M'Kenzie's shepherds). They took a very ingenious mode, and one of the men must have suffered an awful death according to the description. Davis also described the way the blacks hunted the kangaroo and emu, which was very amusing. They make a play or game of this sport among themselves. Happening in the course of the evening to ask him if he could climb the trees with the wild vine, he started up instantly, threw off his clothes, and, procuring a vine, was at the top of one of the trees with it in a few minutes. His clothes were a great annoyance to him for some days.

"16th: Arrived at our former camp on Frazer's Island about 5 p.m. Conversed with a native of the island who knew Davis and Bracefield. We showed him how far our guns carried, which appeared to astonish him. There were six canoes with about twenty blacks, fishing out on a flat about three miles from us. Jolliffe fired off a musket; they saw the ball hopping over the water towards them; I believe it frightened them very much; after consulting a little they all took to their canoes, and made off from us. At this time Davis was conversing with the blacks on shore.

"17th: On continuing our journey, we were met by a great many natives, who were fishing at the mouth of the passage. I got Davis and Bracefield to inquire of them where the white men's bones were buried (those of Captain Frazer and Brown, of the *Stirling Castle*); they pointed round the point about two miles. Mr Wrottesley and I landed and went along the beach. While travelling along with them we ascertained the bones were those of black men. When we arrived at their camp we saw three miserable old gins; a blackfellow went into his humpy and brought out a dilly full of bones. We let him understand that it was the white fellow's bones we wanted; he told Davis they were a long way off on the main beach—about ten miles. We would have gone this far, but our time was up, and we had to return. Wrottesley bought a dilly from the natives for a fishhook, then we left them, and proceeded across the bay to Cape Brown; landed about 5 o'clock, got into that commodious boat harbour, remained there for the night.

"The blacks are very numerous on Frazer Island; there is a nut they find on it which they eat, and the fish are very plentiful. The formation and productions of the island are much the same as those of Moreton Island; the timber is a great deal superior, and also the soil; the cypress pine upon Frazer Island being quite splendid. The island is sixty miles long, by ten or twelve wide.

"18th: It blew very fresh from the south-west; lulled towards evening. About 4 o'clock p.m., ordered everything into the boat, and in a short time were out at sea. After rounding Cape Brown there was a very heavy swell setting in from the southward, and it kept on increasing so much that we could not bear up to windward. Jolliffe lost one of the guns overboard. Going nearly four points off our course, we continued on till about 9 o'clock, when I ordered about-ship; we were only about eight miles from Cape Brown. It was no use hammering about all night, and the breeze still increasing, we landed at our old camp about 11 o'clock. Next day set sail about 11 o'clock with a south-west wind. About three miles off Cape Brown the wind got more southerly. Continued about the same course and distance we did the night before. I thought it would be better to return, and it was fortunate we did, as the wind still increasing, and a very heavy sea on, we never could have reached Bracefield Head. We landed again in Honeysuckle Camp about 3 o'clock p.m.; ordered everything out of the boat to be cleaned and overhauled; hauled the boat up on the beach; the bilge water was smelling very badly. Mr Russell and some of the boat's crew got quite sick, so much so that the former threw up his breakfast, and some of his chat went with it. Only a few ejaculations escaped his lips, a repetition of a beastly boat, a beastly sail, etc., during all the night and following days.

"The Wide Bay River is navigable for a vessel drawing 9 ft of water for about forty miles up. The country on its banks is a good sheep country, and the farther you proceed to the westward the better the land. The blacks informed me there is a river about ten miles beyond the Wide Bay River, and another more to the north-westward, and a third larger than all the others still farther to the westward, and pointed a long way into the interior to where the water came from. This last river we thought must be the Boyne. They also informed us that there was a beautiful country about forty miles from the Bahpal Mountain, extending quite to the ocean, and abounding in emus and kangaroos. According to their account, this country is thinly wooded."

CHAPTER VII

The Alteration of Historical Names—Little Short of Criminal—
Wreck of the *Stirling Castle*—Band of Explorers—Sir George Gipps
—Trip Undertaken in a "Nondescript Boat"—Mr Russell's Details of
the Trip—A Novel Cure for Sunstroke—Gammon Island—Jolliffe's
Beard.

THIS whaleboat trip to Wide Bay, and Mr Andrew Petrie's
discovery of the river there, was recently referred to by
Sir Hugh Nelson at a conference of the Royal Geographical
Society, held at Maryborough. The river discovered was
known as the Wide Bay River for some years, but afterwards was christened the "Mary" in honour of Lady Fitz-
roy. Nowadays, following Mr Andrew Petrie's diary, one
fails to recognise all points of interest by the names given.
With regard to this, Mr Knight, in his description of the
trip, says:—"On the following day the party reached a
place named by Mr Petrie Bracefield Cape, but during later
years renamed Noosa. And it may here be remarked that
it was little short of criminal to substitute the present
names for those bestowed by this band of explorers." It
was near Noosa that Bracefield or Graham ("Wandi" the
blacks called him) was found, hence the name—Bracefield
Cape. He was a convict who had deserted in Logan's time,
and he it was who rescued Mrs Frazer (wife of Captain
Frazer, of the *Stirling Castle*) from the aboriginals. The
wreck of the *Stirling Castle* (the boat, by the way, in which
the Petries travelled from the old country some time previously) is ancient history now, and it will be remembered
that Mrs Frazer was obliged to live alone with the blacks
until the time when Bracefield took her down to within a
few miles of the settlement, and so was the means of her
release.

Mr Henry Stuart Russell, one of "this band of explorers,"

refers to the naming of the different places. In one part he says:—

"Of the coast of the mainland between Cape Moreton and Sandy Cape little had hitherto been known. No survey of it had under any close examination from seawards been made; none whatever from landwards. Petrie being in the service of the Government, and acting under Sir George Gipps's instructions, considered himself authorised to name mountains, headlands, or any remarkable spot not yet distinguished on a chart, as he thought fit, with the view of sending in his report, under which such designations would be printed on the Government maps. The low bluff which formed the southern and most eastern point of the sandy bay in which we were he called 'Bracefield's Head' (now Noosa Head), being most suggestive of the occurrence which had so much preoccupied us of late. From a higher ground further back we could see several noteworthy eminences which we had remarked from the boat when following the coastline. Of these Bracefield told the native names, which were written down on the spot."

It seems matter for regret that any of these names should have been tampered with, or that a true discoverer should in any way be overlooked. In those early times, however, many mistakes were made in different ways—of course it could hardly be otherwise. With regard to Brisbane town, it may not be amiss to mention an instance here. Governor Gipps, when the town was about to be laid out, was not pleased with the surveyor's plans—the roads were too wide, and too much land had been wasted in reserves for his taste; consequently "the whole design had to be altered," says Mr Knight. "This, it appears, was a common trick of Governor Gipps's" (still quoting Mr Knight), "for in every other case where he had anything to do with the laying out of a place he acted in exactly the same manner. His argument in favour of narrow streets was novel, if unsound— namely, that the buildings on either side of such thoroughfares would have the effect of keeping out the sun! Mr Andrew Petrie actually came to loggerheads with the Governor over the foolish proposition, and to mark his condemnation of the opinion of others, His Excellency ordered the width of all streets in Ipswich as well as in Brisbane to be reduced to sixty-six feet. Eventually the surveyors, after a good deal of trouble, were allowed to make the principal thoroughfares about eighty feet. Looking at Governor Gipps's grabbing propensities, it is a matter for wonder that the Queen's Park escaped being cut up into town lots."

But to hail back to Wide Bay and the trip undertaken in what Mr Russell terms a "nondescript boat." "Certainly," he says, "when in the water, with her full burden, her 'midship's rowlock was but a measured five inches above the water; for I tried the distance afterwards. But I found that we could step two lug-sails and carry a bumpkin, stuck out for a bit of after canvas—that was a comfort." Mr Jolliffe being a sailor, was bound (Mr Russell says) to laugh at the boat.

How these gentlemen came to join Mr Petrie on this trip happened in this wise. Mr Russell was on the lookout for a fresh run for sheep, and so also was Mr Jolliffe. Mr Russell had just determined to purchase a small craft or yawl, and start out, and was thinking over his plans, when Mr Jolliffe, bursting in upon him, informed him that Mr Petrie had heard of his intention.

"I've had a long yarn with Petrie about your going, and I will tell you what he says: You've heard of that Bunnia-Bunnia which the blacks here talk so much about; Petrie is the only white man who has looked for and found it; he has a bit of its wood, you know; it's called Petrie's pine, and mighty proud of his discovery he is. Well, the Governor gave him orders before he left to go to the river on which they say it grows most, and examine it thoroughly and report. A proclamation has been issued that no settlers are to encroach on its quarters, and no white man is to cut down any of it. Petrie says he must go at once; the place is on the banks of a river, a little north of the river called the 'Morouchidor.' Petrie says that queer-looking oyster boat isn't fit for any sea; he wants you to join him; and his work, your own, mine, too, perhaps, may be knocked off by one trip." "What boat can we have, though?" "Why, there is a five-oared kind of mongrel whale-boat, which was built by a prisoner here, in a fashion, which he will take. You know that there will be no more Commandants at Brisbane; he will take five ticket men to pull, a mast to stick up, and a bit of a sail when the wind serves; the boat is new and sound, whatever she looks like, the other thing's rotten.' ("Genesis of Queensland.")

And so this party set out, and, in spite of many difficulties and hardships, surmounted all drawbacks, and in due course arrived safely back at the settlement again with their interesting addition in the way of numbers.

Mr Russell is amusing in some of his details of this trip. On the party's start out he begins to ask Mr Petrie questions concerning the crew. When he finds that one man's name is Russell, like his own, he asks no more on that point. Later on, during the journey up, he loses his hat overboard, and on this account evidently gets a touch of the sun, for when the blacks carry the party ashore his head is splitting, and intolerable pains creep through his limbs. Writing of it, he says:—

"I suppose I was in some sort tortured by sunstroke; that night was a horrible seal upon my recollections thereof. One of the men was trying to make me a head-covering out of some canvas; but why should my limbs torment me? Well, no explanation of the cause could have cured me, and thus I miserably stared the stars out of countenance with the help of the dawning day. My friends were alarmed, but could do nothing. Our two blacks were in such a 'funk' that they kept me wakeful company throughout, though the whites watched in turn by pairs.

"With the sun's return came that of the natives. After much gesticulation to the party, an old man squatted on his hams on the hot sand, and with a queer crone began to scoop out a hole with his hands alongside me. I took little heed, until it had assumed, under his vigorous and odoriferous exertions almost the appearance of a shallow grave. As a man under his first 'flooring' by seasickness, so was I absolutely careless of what was going on around. Petrie and others gravely looking on, rifle in hand, reassured me on one head, yet I could realise nothing. I believe I must have been fast becoming unconscious. What happened I can tell, however, now. When all was ready, I learnt that two younger natives had lifted me into the grave, divested of every rag on my back. Our own blacks had assured Petrie that the old man could put me on my legs again; he was too anxious about me to repel their proffered service, as long as there was no unreasonable means resorted to. Some large leaves of a water plant had been brought and placed over my head to protect it, and that again was raised upon the roll of my clothes. Well, I remember the queer sensation of hot sand being shovelled by their wooden implements—'eelamans'—over me, up to the very chin. After that I knew nothing till I came to the sense of where I was. In fact, I seemed to wake up from a painful dream. I could move but my head. The leaves were lifted from my face, and the assemblage at first puzzled me. Arms had been packed in with the rest, and I was in a straight jacket of hot sand, pressed in a solid heap upon my carcass. But I felt no pain. The perspiration was still (for I was told it had been doing so for the last quarter of an hour) running in tiny rivulets from my head over my face into my eyes and ears. I was in a vapour furnace! Quickly I was unearthed, covered with blankets or anything that caught their eye, and fell fast asleep. When I woke—in about six hours—I was well! Weak but terribly thirsty. I could have hugged the whole tribe in my gratitude—but they were all gone! I could see that the minds of my compagnons de voyage were much relieved, especially that kind-hearted Scot, Andrew Petrie. Some efficient headgear had been manufactured for me in the meanwhile, to commemorate which the hummock at the point was named 'Russell's Cap.'"

And so Mr Russell goes on with the trip. He tells how they christened what is now Double Island Point "Brown's Cape," because Bracefield and the blacks assured them it was there that Brown, the mate of the *Stirling Castle*, had been killed and disposed of. Further on he describes a mist

into which they were entrapped—"so dense that, except
the water immediately about the sides of the boat, nothing
out of it could be distinguished." Getting free from this at
last, they fell into other difficulties, christened an island
"Gammon Island," because, after leaving it, and pulling and
sailing about in and out all over the place, they landed at
exactly the same spot, much to Mr Russell's disgust. He
suggested the name as suitable to "his good Scotch friend"
—Mr Petrie—"who jotted it down with the ghost of a
smile."

In Mr Petrie's diary he describes a point of land as
"Jolliffe's Head." With regard to this, Mr Russell says:—

"Jolliffe's long black beard had been an object of mirth,
and I must add, admiration, all the jaunt through, especially
to the blacks. This new river-head which we were leaving,
and perhaps should never see again, tufted with that thick,
glossy patch of dark pine brush, by some process associated
itself with it, and down on the rough outline, the base of a
future report, went under our official friend's hand, 'Jolliffe's
Beard,' for its baptismal name. I wonder whether it is
called so still? Maybe it bears some later comer's."

CHAPTER VIII

The Early-time Squatters—Saved by the Natives from Drowning Mr Henry Stuart Russell—"Tom" Punished for Smoking—"Ticket-of-Leave" Men—First Racecourse in Brisbane—Harkaway—Other Early Racecourses—Pranks the Squatters Played—Destiny of South Brisbane Changed—First Vessel Built in Moreton Bay—The Parson's Attempt to Drive Bullocks—A Billy-goat Ringing a Church Bell—The First Election—Changing Sign-boards—Sir Arthur Hodgson—Sir Joshua Peter Bell.

THE finding of the famous Duramboi and the story of his fourteen years' adventures among the aborigines has already been enlarged upon in many works. He said he was welcomed by the blacks as one of their number returned from the dead. When the white men were first seen by their dusky brethren they were all supposed to be ghosts or former black men come to life again. All the different tribes had a name for "ghost;" for instance, with the Turrbal, or Brisbane blacks, it was "mogwi;" with the Moreton Island tribe, "targan;" Noosa tribe, "maddar;" and with the Wide Bay natives, with whom "Duramboi" lived, the word was "makuran."

I have already written of the landing of "Duramboi" and "Wandi" in Brisbane, and mentioned the excitement of the early time squatters over the event. These squatters came often to the old home on the Bight—Mr Andrew Petrie's. That gentleman had a skillion put to his house, and here they slept, and they were always very jolly and full of fun. Mr John Campbell writing of these early visits of the squatters to Brisbane says, "There was no hotel in Brisbane then, but we were kindly and eagerly invited by the officers residing there to stop at their houses—in fact, vieing with each other who should receive us. For myself, I went to the late Mr Andrew Petrie's, and a friendship then commenced between us which only ended with his life."

My father used often to swim across from Petrie's Bight to Kangaroo Point with some of these squatters and two or three blacks. They went for the purpose of fishing there with lines. If they had good luck they would perhaps stay nearly all day. Often they caught lots of bream and flat-head, and the natives would then carry these in dillies fixed to their heads back to the other side. One of the squatters was a Mr Glover, and the blacks could not say his name, but called him "Blubber."

One day in swimming homewards "Tom" got into a shoal of blubbers, and they stung him so frightfully that he could not swim. He called for assistance to the natives, and they only just came up in time, for he was sinking. Getting hold of the boy, they put him on the back of one fellow, and swam with him to the shore, thus saving his life. Landing, the native who had carried the burden turned and said to Mr Glover, "My word! Mr Blubber, your brother very saucy fellow!"

Some of these blackfellows were very comical in their doings and sayings. There was another one of the name of "Billy Bing" ("Bing" meant father), and the squatters used to have great fun with him. He had a very large mouth, and would burst out laughing at them, then suddenly shut his mouth like a snuff box, and pull a long face. The squatters would nearly be ill laughing at this man, especially one gentleman, who would say, "For God's sake, take him out of my sight!" This was Mr Henry Stuart Russell, already referred to. Father remembers him well, and says, "He was a great man to laugh." He evidently had a keen sense of humour, and at times became quite powerless with laughter. He married a Miss Pinnock, niece of a Governor of Jamaica, and sister to Mr P. Pinnock, of Brisbane, the late Sheriff. Strange that in after years Mr Andrew Petrie's granddaughter ("Tom's" firstborn) should marry this same Mr Russell's nephew, the present Major Pinnock.

But to return. One day Mr Russell said to Billy, "Here Billy, come and have a glass of grog." And when he came, "Now, Billy, hold the glass so, and say, 'Here's good health, gentlemen.'" The squatters all stood round, and

Billy, who could not say "health," took the glass, and this was his toast: "Gentlemen, here you go hell!" Of course, this caused roars of laughter, indeed some of the squatters were so overcome that they rolled about on the grass. Always just the mere sight of Billy was enough to cause amusement.

Mr Andrew Petrie had a slaughter-house put up in those days, so that he could have a sheep or bullock killed for meat—a lot of meat was used when the squatters were about. One day, my father remembers sitting in the killing-house talking to the butcher, and as he sat the youngster enjoyed a pipe he had got hold of, when suddenly in the doorway appeared his father. Grandfather never smoked himself, and he strongly disapproved of the habit in his young son. Many a thrashing "Tom" got for this same habit, but, alas! it did not cure him. On this occasion he was caught and beaten soundly. His screams brought the butcher's wife, who put in a good word for the boy, who thus made off, still, however, holding firmly to his short pipe. So soon as ever he got into the bush he struck a light with his tinder-box, and had another smoke! In those days there were no matches, and every one carried flint and steel and tinder-box.

Feeling himself ill-used after this beating, "Tom" made up his mind to run away and go to the blacks. So next day he started out to Bowen Hills to their camp, and there, falling in with some of his blackboy playmates, they all occupied themselves in making a new humpy. Before dark he joined in a good meal of fish and crabs, and then when it was time to turn in, repaired with two or three blackboys to the hut they had made. "Tom" had a suspicion that some one might come after him, so he kept his boots on in case of emergency. He remembers he had a new hat, and this he stuck up in the roof of the hut, so that it wouldn't get broken. Then he got under a 'possum rug.

He had been there about an hour when suddenly he heard a great row—barking of dogs, and a running about and shouting of the blacks. All at once he felt his leg grabbed, and he was hauled out by his brother. He managed to get

his hat, and then, just as his father came up, got away and
ran off as fast as his legs could carry him all the way home.
Going upstairs to his room, he stood there ready to climb
out on to the roof should his father come up. However, he
heard the arrival and the inquiry if he had come home, and
then someone said he had better be left alone, so the boy
ventured to go to bed. He was up betimes in the morning,
and kept out of his father's way for a couple of days. My
grandfather soon got over his anger though, and always
forgave his son.

The squatters in those days nearly all had Government
"ticket-of-leave" men signed to them for a certain length
of time. If they had a quarrel with a man, there was no
taking him to court, but off would go their coats, and after
a round or two master and man would shake hands, good
friends again. They were mostly well-born, these squatters,
and they were also gentlemen who enjoyed a piece of fun and
mischief. Their bullock drays used to come down to Brisbane with wool, and these would be left on the south side,
because, of course, there was no bridge or any other way of
getting across. Beside these drays the squatters often left
a cask of rum with the head knocked in, and a pannikin
alongside, for any one who cared to help himself to a drink.
They would swim their horses across behind the ferry boats.

The very first racecourse in Brisbane was started by the
squatters on the ground now occupied by the present Post
Office, etc. I have before mentioned "The Old Woman's
Factory." This building was empty when the Petries arrived
in Brisbane, and there they lived till their own house on the
Bight was built, and afterwards it was used as a gaol and
court house. Well, the course was from the corner of the
old wall surrounding this building (just where the Telegraph Office now stands), down as far as Albert Street, and
it was about here that a three-railed fence and a ditch some
feet wide were jumped. Then the course continued round
towards the Gardens, the same ditch and fence being jumped
again lower down; then up round by the R.C. Cathedral,
and back to the corner of the wall. The ditch mentioned
was cut as a drain to carry the water (for the land was

swampy) into a small creek that ran into the river at the present Post Office wharf. The place all round was fenced in in cultivation paddocks, where the prisoners worked.

My father remembers well one race run on this course. Four horses started. When the foremost reached the first fence he tripped on the top ra'l (no hurdles then, of course), throwing his rider into the mud in the ditch. The young squatter got his nice leggings and all his fine jockey's rig-out in a beautiful mess. He, however, picked himself up, and catching his horse, mounted and was off again, although the others had jumped all right and were some distance ahead. The next jump was taken successfully, and the squatter overtook the three and passed them, winning eventually with a length to the good. There was great excitement and hurrahing at this. The horse's name was Harkaway, and he was a black animal with white feet. "The horses in those days were horses," says my father, "and could stand a three mile race with ease—they were no weeds. Most of the squatters carried the regular jockey's dress with them, and they were splendid riders."

When people commenced to settle a little and build, a man named Greenyead built a house at South Brisbane, at Kurilpa (pronounced in English Kureelpa)—what we now call West End. This man obtained a licence for a public house, and the squatters then started a racecourse there. The next one was at Cooper's Plains, and the next at New Farm.

Father remembers all sorts of pranks the young squatters used to play in those days. When they turned up at the old home on the Bight they slept on stretchers in the addition to the house, and when one of the number was found fast asleep by the others, he would be tied down and then quietly carried out into the bush one hundred yards away, and there left to the mercy of the mosquitoes. A watch would be kept till he called for help, then he was taken in again. The victim was generally one who did not care to join in the fun. He would know, however, that it was no use getting into a "scot," and he therefore took it all as a joke.

It was not often in those days that a steamer came to "Moreton Bay," as Brisbane was then called; so whenever one did come it caused quite a stir and excitement. The steamers always anchored at South Brisbane just below the present bridge. On the arrival of one, the squatters would go over to her at night and have some fun. Mr Russell would sometimes borrow a dress and bonnet from "Tom's" mother, and, dressing up, he would then go off arm-in-arm with another squatter, as man and wife, across to the steamer. When there, they would hoist all sorts of things to the masthead in place of the flag, and the skipper would laugh, too, and enjoy the fun. Generally the boat would be cleared of all "grog" before she left for Sydney again.

On the 15th May, 1847, the first vessel built in Moreton Bay was launched. She saw the light at Petrie's Bight, where the Howard Smith wharf is now, and was a two-masted vessel, with both ends pointed—no square stern. The launching ceremony caused quite an excitement, and amongst those who witnessed it were the military and a party of ladies. To Miss Petrie (Andrew Petrie's only daughter), a tall, dark, handsome girl of some fourteen summers, fell the honour of christening the vessel, and it is not surprising to know that her brother "Tom" (two years older, who was in everything), was one of those on board at the time. Miss Petrie stood on the shore with a bottle of champagne in her hand attached to the bow of the boat by a string, and as the vessel slid into the water she threw the bottle from her, christening the craft *Selina*. In the meantime, however, the sailors, thinking how lovely a drink of champagne would be afterwards on the quiet, had contrived a trick, and the bottle did not break, but this was noticed, and a crowd gathering round Miss Petrie, got her to go out in a boat and finish her work. The *Selina* slid into the water with such an impetus that she would have gone right across to Kangaroo Point had the anchor not been dropped to stop her. After she was rigged and finished up she started out for the Pine River, and having got a cargo there of cedar logs, left for Sydney, her builder, a Mr Cameron, being in charge. But the little vessel was doomed, in spite of the brightness of her birth, and the crew were never heard of again. For a long time the whole thing remained a mystery, then on the 20th October, 1848, she was found on the beach at Keppel Bay, water-logged, and with her mast cut out. The cargo was quite undisturbed, and it was thought that as the crew only had enough provisions to take them to Sydney they had set out and perished at sea through starvation or otherwise. "Poor Mr Cameron," my father says, "was a very nice man, and as far as I can remember, he had with him another shipwright and two sailors."

While on this subject, I may mention an incident whicn happened later on, and which changed the destiny of South Brisbane. A tree which grew near the spot mentioned, was used as an anchorage for the steamers—that is, they were tied to the trunk. A Scotchman, who owned the land, one day for some reason or other, objected to his tree being made use of any longer, and he cut the rope by which a Sydney steamer was tied. After that another place had to be found, and the steamers went down the river to the north side of the stream, so spoiling the chance South Brisbane had of first place. This tree was very large in the trunk, but some of the branches were lopped to make room for the balcony of a stone hotel near by.

The following is a yarn my father remembers the squatters telling one another; whether it was founded on fact or not he cannot say :—

A man was once driving a bullock-team either to or from Brisbane, laden heavily with wool or provisions. The roads, of course, were rough in those days, and, coming to a creek, the bullocks would not pull hard enough to get over it. So the man began to swear at them, using all the "swears" he knew. While he was in the midst of this a parson rode up, and, said he to the bullock driver, "My good man, you should not use those words; it is very wrong, and bad words won't make the bullocks pull any better." The driver threw down his whip. "You try and see if you can drive them, sir," he said. So the parson dismounted, and the bullock driver held his horse. Then began a series of pattings and coax-ings, and the bullocks doubtless were flattered at the pretty names they were called. They, however, swerved to this side and to that, but they would not pull. The parson tried a long time; and only at last when his patience must surely have given out, "Damn the bullocks!" he said, and flinging aside the whip he had gently stroked them with, mounted, and rode off. Always afterwards this particular bullock-driver felt he had absolute freedom to swear as he liked.

One night the squatters got hold of a billy-goat, and, tying him to the bell rope of the Church of England in William Street, "planted" to see the fun. "Billy" commenced to ring the bell furiously, then the police came along to see what was what, and nearly all the inhabitants of the place—there weren't so many—came running from all directions. As the goat moved about, to try and get free, the bell would ring, and the police were very active in running round the building to try and catch the party who rang it. It was dark, and the squatters had used a good long rope, so the goat was some distance off. At last, however, a policeman tripped over the rope and fell. He got hold of it then, and holding on, poor Billy came to him. As may be imagined, he was disgusted when he saw how he had been taken in, and there were the squatters bursting with laughter, but jeering with the crowd, just as though they knew no more than anyone else. The police asked if any one could tell them who had tied the goat to the bell-rope, but no one knew, of course.

During the first election ever held in Brisbane the squatters had a cask of ale rolled out on to the side of George Street, opposite Gray's bootshop, and they had the head knocked in and a pint-pot ready for the people to help themselves. There was a good crowd, and a piper playing his pipes for amusement, and everyone was jolly, helping themselves to the beer. Suddenly a squatter, going behind the piper, stuck a penknife in his pipes. Of course there was a sudden collapse, and a great to-do to know who had done the deed, the poor old piper threatening instant death. There was no more playing of the pipes that day. Later, when the people were all helping themselves to a pot of beer from the cask a

very little man, named Shepherd, a tailor, not content with
a potful, brought along a bucket in order to carry it away
full. As he was reaching in to fill this Mr Russell caught
him by the legs and tilted him head first into the cask.
When rescued he was wringing wet with beer—in fact, was
nearly drowned, and he went away with the empty bucket
amid great cheering.

When people commenced to open little shops in Brisbane
and put up signboards, the young squatters used to go at
night and change these boards from one shop to another.
This had a comical effect in the day time, and caused many
a laugh. Often things like that were done, but my father says
he does not remember the squatters ever doing anything
really wrong or unmanly. Indeed, he maintains at bottom
they were very kind-hearted, and he wishes there were more
of their stamp nowadays. People on the whole, he thinks,
were kinder and more honest then than they are now.
Everybody knew every soul in the small place, and a workman would leave his tools down alongside his work and
come back to find them all right.

Talking of squatters, there is a story told of one which
may not be out of place here, though the writer does not
guarantee it had is origin in those very early times, but
understands it related to later days. The story runs so:—
In his travels once a squatter came at night to an inn
which was full to overflowing, and could not therefore
obtain a bed. Finding he knew one of the gentlemen who
had a room there, and who had not yet turned up, he
"tipped" the housemaid to lend him a lady's dress and shoes
and other articles of wearing apparel. She wanted to know
why he wished for these, but, paying her handsomely for
the loan, he soon satisfied her that it was all right. Taking
them to his friend's room, he placed the articles about in
prominent positions, then went to bed. His friend, coming
in late, made for his room, and opening the door heard a
shrill, squeaking voice, which exclaimed in horror, "A man
in the room! A man in the room!" Of course, the retreat
was hurried and precipitous, and the lady's laughter was
smothered as she thought with delight of the joy of a well-
earned bed. Next morning the landlord got a fierce

"dressing down" from a gentleman who wished to know how he dared put a lady in the room he had paid for. The landlord was profuse in his apologies, but declared he had done no such thing. Then afterwards the story came out.

"I was extremely sorry to read of the death of Sir Arthur Hodgson," father said, when the news was cabled to Brisbane. "He was one of the good old sort. I knew him well. When he first came to Moreton Bay he came along to our home on the Bight with the other squatters. Many a time, when a little chap, I had a ride on his horse on the racecourse. He used to give me his horse to hold for him, and I would then get on the animal and ride him about till wanted. Sir Arthur was a real good-hearted gentleman, one of the right sort, full of fun. One doesn't meet too many of his kind in these days."

Another of these early time squatters or men of "the good old sort," was the late Sir Joshua Peter Bell—one of Queensland's best known men. He arrived in 1846, and was a big, fine-looking man. He was a great friend of the blacks, his nature being such that they always placed the greatest confidence in him. His name and that of Jimbour are strongly linked, and I am indebted to his son, the Hon. J. T. Bell, our Minister for Lands, for the illustration of "Warraba," taken at that station. This black, as a small boy, came to Jimbour with the first or second party of Europeans under the late Mr Henry Dennis about 1843. He came from the Namoi, in New South Wales, and was an exceptionally fine specimen of an aboriginal. In manner, dignity of bearing, and intelligence, he resembled a superior type of white man. He died in 1891.

Another well-known black on the northern end of Darling Downs was "Combo," who came over from the Big River, in New South Wales, sometime before 1850 with the late Mr O'Grady Haly, of Taabinga, on the Burnett. The party travelled up from New South Wales, via Logan and Nanango. "Combo," soon afterwards, went to work on Jimbour, and remained there until his death in 1903. His gin was a keen, shrewd woman, Mary Ann by name, and of their children, two became well known athletes. The eldest, George, a short, thick black, was the crack runner on Darling

Downs somewhere about 1875 or 1876, and defeated all local white runners at Ipswich. The other son, "Sambo," better known as Charlie Samuels, a long, lean boy, after vanquishing all comers at Dalby and on Darling Downs, was taken to Sydney by a Jimbour stockman, and there swept the board. This was at a time when pedestrianism and professional running was at its height. "Sambo" or Samuels defeated the English champion, Harry Hutchens twice, and thus earned the title of champion of the world. On the third occasion Hutchens defeated "Sambo," but the latter does not hesitate to say that he allowed the white man to win—saying, "the poor fellow hadn't enough money."

CHAPTER IX

"OLD COCKY"

To write of the time of these early squatters, etc., and not mention the "Petrie's Cockatoo" would indeed be an insult to the memory of that wonderful bird—a bird who lived for forty-five years. During those years his fame spread far and wide; indeed, "Petrie's Cocky" was a household word everywhere. As he grew older it was quite a recognised thing that his "life" would be worth recording, and such was meant to be done. It never was, however, and therefore much with regard to "Cocky's" clever ways has been lost.

People there are alive, yet, of course, who remember "Cocky," and to them the tales I have to tell of him will seem no exaggeration; others there surely will be, though, who, like Thomas of old, will doubt. To these I would say that there have been wonderful birds before in the world's history, and if they will consider it, this cocky grew up in an exceptionally good school, living as he did in those early days, and continually mixing with the prisoners—two or three hundred of them.

In a book written of the Australian pioneers by Mr Nehemiah Bartley, mention is made of this bird as "the ancestral cockatoo, rival of 'Grip, the raven,' and who lived for forty-five years with the Petries, and was only excelled by the seventy-year old 'sulphur crest' who domiciled with the Sydney Wentworths, patriarchs there like the Petries were here, a bird who lived till his bald chest made him fain in the wintry July to singe his featherless bosom by the hearth fire logs."

When the late John Petrie (the eldest son) was a boy, in fact not long after the arrival of the family in Brisbane, "Cocky," then a little fledgling, was presented to him by a prisoner named Skinner—a man who was a sort of overseer over other prisoners. The little bird thrived and flourished, and as he grew he learned to speak most distinctly—one could never mistake what he said—indeed, people sometimes would hardly believe that the voice was that of a bird. He picked up almost anything in the way of talking, and could also, of course, swear beautifully, as the prisoners did.

"Cocky" was a white cockatoo, and was a big, handsome, pretty bird. He walked along proudly, and called himself "Jack's Cocky"—sometimes "Jack's pretty Cocky." If caught at any mischief it was then "Jack's poor Cocky"; he evidently thought he could stave off punishment so.

An amusement "Cocky" had was to sit on the fence and call all the fowls round him. When they had gathered together he would cackle like a hen, then laugh as though jeering at them. He was a great bird to laugh, and generally ended his mirth with an awful screech. He could also whistle well, and would whistle for the dogs, and call "Here! here!" then bark and jeer at them. Cats also he teased. "Puss, puss! Poor puss, puss!" he would say in an insinuating sort of fashion, then would pinch their tails and mew. If he saw a blackfellow it was, "Baal you yacca, baal you tobacco!" The natives used to sing and dance for "Cocky," and the bird would try and mimic them, bobbing his yellow-crowned head up and down, and jumping in a sort of dance. Indeed, there was one blackfellows' song of which he knew a part. The darkies would be very amused, and laugh at him, then "Cocky," too, would laugh and say, "Baal you budgery." Like most birds, "Cocky" was very fond of being scratched, and he seemed as though he would keep a person scratching him all day if they were only willing. He would first remark, "Scratch 'Cocky,'" then when that was done, turning his old head round, and directing with his claw, it was, "Just here," then again in another place, "Just here," and lastly he held up his wing with the request to "Scratch 'Cocky's' blanket." His wing was always his blanket.

In those days a gentleman owned a garden on Kangaroo Point, opposite Petrie's Bight. A Highlander worked this garden, and sold the cabbages he grew there. When any one on the north side wished to buy vegetables, they went down to the river's bank and called, "Boat ahoy—cabbage!" and the man would answer, "Ay, Ay!" and pull over with a load. One day, John Petrie saw "Cocky" walking along extra proudly down towards the river, and he thought by the bird's strut as he put one foot out after the other, that some mischief was afloat—so watched. He saw "Cocky" climb up a wattle tree which grew on the bank, and settling himself there, call, "Boat ahoy—cabbage!" The old man on the opposite side made answer, "Ay, ay," and after a little, arrived with cabbages in his boat. Seeing no one, he turned about in a surprised sort of fashion, and presently discovered "Cocky," who then began to laugh and screech at him. The man fell into an awful rage at this, and swore at the bird, who, however, but laughed the more. In the end, John Petrie had to come forward from where he watched, to the rescue, and buy a few cabbages for the sake of peace.

In the same way many a time "Cocky" would bring the ferrymen from Kangaroo Point across to the north side all for nothing. This is a well known fact. He would fly to a tree on the bank of the river and call, "Over!" Father has seen the ferryman come across and go up the bank and look about to see who called, then finding no one, start to return, swearing to himself at being made a fool of. When he got a few boat lengths away from the shore, there would be another "Over!" and the ferryman, this time seeing the bird, would swear still more, and threaten to wring his impudent neck if he caught him. "Cocky," however, was too smart. He seemed to know well when anyone was in a "scot," and would fly away home after his jeer and laugh. He had a marvellous power with his voice. It is said to be perfectly true that one day he almost backed a horse and dray into the river—someone coming up just saved it in time. He could say "Whoa, back," etc., in the most natural manner possible.

"Cocky" had a very strong beak. People he didn't like had cause to think it a "terrible" beak, for these he pecked viciously at times. He could open oysters easily—would just break off the edge, then put in his beak and prize the shell open, afterwards eating the oyster. Also it was an easy matter for him to open those windows which shove upwards (worked on pulleys), unless they were extra stiff. He would work his beak in under the bottom of the window, then shove up the lower sash far enough to get his head in. People inside generally helped him then. One wretchedly cold day Grandfather Petrie happened to be in the sitting-room, when he saw "Cocky" come and try to open one of the windows there. It, however, happened to be stiff, so the bird gave up and went off round to a bedroom window. Succeeding there, he shoved in his head, saying, "Poor 'Cocky'—it's devilish cold!" A son of the house was in this room, and Grandfather, when he heard what the bird had said, laughed very heartily.

As I have said, there are a good many people still living who remember "Old Cocky" and his ways. Those who know him best say he was a strange bird, and seemed human in the way he understood things. My mother says the first time she saw him he rather embarrassed her by asking "Who are you?" in a tone of voice as though she had no business near him. If he came out with any expression he had learnt, it was sure to fit the occasion. One day a pilot from the Bay came to Andrew Petrie's house to talk over some business. Dinner was just about to be served, and he was taken in to have a meal with the family. He was a great drunkard, this pilot, and happened to be rather unsteady that day, so Mr Petrie remonstrated, and lectured him for his bad habit. "Cocky" generally, when there was a stranger in the room, perched himself as though to listen on the back of a chair the newcomer sat on, so here he was, of course, on the pilot's chair. He seemed to listen to the lecture with his head on one side, then, as the pilot promised to try and do better, "You ought to be ashamed of yourself!" he said. "So I ought, 'Cocky,' " said the man, turning round. "Ashamed of yourself" was a great expression with "Cocky." On this occasion all the family sat round the table; the only two who are now left—Mrs Ferguson and my father—remember the circumstance well.

Round towards the back of the house, near the office door, a half-cask of pipeclay stood, and "Cocky" loved to get into this cask and work away with his beak, imagining he was very busy, like the workmen, digging and throwing up the earth as they did. One morning John Petrie put him down near this cask, saying, "Go on, 'Cocky' to your work." The bird jumped up on to the edge of the cask, then down to the pipeclay, on top of a rat which had sheltered there. "Cocky" got an awful scare as the rat moved, and was up on to the edge of the cask again instantly, then turning and looking down on the rat, with his feathers ruffled and his topknot up, "What the devil are you doing there?" he said. One can imagine how John Petrie stood and laughed, and laughed again, helpless, while the offending rat made his escape.

Years afterwards there was another small cask which "Cocky" played in—this time an empty one, except for some little bits of sticks and rubbish which the bird loved to break up with his beak. The present Andrew Petrie (member for Toombul), grandson to the old gentleman, tells this story. He, a boy at the time, discovered, with some other youngsters, a cat with kittens in this cask, which was "Cocky's" special property. It was in the morning before the bird's usual time of working there. So the boys looked for some fun, and watched to see what would happen when "Cocky" came along. The bird climbed up the cask in the usual manner, and, gaining the top, he put his head over, preparatory to climbing in. The cat, of course, resented this, and spitting viciously, she threw up her paw and hit "Cocky" on the side of the head. The frightened bird waited for no more, but climbed down again instantly, muttering all the time, "Poor puss, puss! Poor puss, puss! Poor puss, puss!" The boys, of course, screamed with laughter, and "Cocky" the moment he was safely on the ground exclaimed, "Baal budgery! Hip, hip hurray!" One cannot describe the comical effect of a cheer from "Cocky"—he always threw up his topknot when he came to "Hurray!" He kept away from this cask for sometime afterwards—wouldn't go near it.

The Miss Petrie of those days had a king parrot who was a great pet, and was very clever—he could call each of the three dogs of the household by their right names. This bird lived for about nine years, then took cramps. Finding him unable to stand one day in his cage, his mistress took him out, saying, "Poor Joey—poor fellow!" and "Cocky" was walking about watching. Miss Petrie doctored her bird, then put him on her bed on a piece of flannel. "Cocky" followed, and catching the counterpane in his beak, climbed up on to the bed, then lifting Joey's covering looked at him and said, "Poor Joey—poor fellow!" Then he climbed down again and walked off.

"Cocky" picked up any word or expression he heard very quickly. He was always surprising people. On one occasion down by the side of the road in front of the house, two men lounged idly talking. "Cocky" noticing the pair strutted down to them and inquired "What ship?" Then he commenced to talk, "Jack's 'Cocky'—Jack's poor, pretty cockatoo, me boy," he said. The men got him to make friends, then bringing him up to the house told them there, "This bird wanted to know what ship we came in, and said he was Jack's pretty 'Cocky.'" "Cocky" listened to this with head on one side, then broke in with "Baal you yacca, baal you tobacco!"

"Cocky" could say all the names of the family. In the morning when Andrew Petrie walked along the veranda to call his son George, "Cocky," hearing the footfalls and the sound of the walking stick, never waited for the voice, but would be first in calling—"Jordy! Jordy!" rapping his beak on the floor in imitation of the sound of the stick. My grandfather had many a laugh at this.

A working man called Johnnie Bishop could imitate a drunken man very well. He often used to come to "Cocky"

and assume drunkenness for the sake of hearing the bird
string on a lot of swears at him, and say, "You ought to be
ashamed of yourself!" Poor "Cocky," he was often teased.
The wild young squatters used to laugh at him, and he
would chase them. When he chased anyone he always said,
"Sule 'im," and then would bark like a dog. One day these
squatters poured gin and water down the poor bird's throat,
and this evidently made him tight, for he could not stand.
Always afterwards he would run from a glass even of water,
and the squatters laughingly declared "he was a teetotaller
for ever!"

Whenever "Cocky" had done anything wrong, he always
wanted to "kiss," one knew so that he had been in mischief
and was afraid of being punished. He was a terrible bird
for destroying furniture, and often narrowly escaped being
killed for the damage he did in that as in other ways. Once
a large brick oven in the house was repaired. The workmen,
when they had finished, went off, leaving everything all
right, but the mortar, of course, was wet. "Cocky," when
their backs were turned, set to work, and, using his powerful beak, gradually loosened the key bricks, causing the
whole thing to fall in, and how the bird escaped is a marvel.
All the work had to be done over again. Another similar trick
at another time, he played upon the Petrie's washerwoman.
She had the clothes out drying, and, when her back was
turned, "Cocky," climbing along the line, pulled out every
peg thereon, causing the clean clothes to fall to the ground.
The washerwoman, who was a one-time convict, used some
rather choice language when she saw what had happened.

"Cocky" had a perch up under the kitchen veranda, where
it was boarded in, and here he made a little hole, where he
could put his head out; was very busy making this hole;
worked at it every night till finished. From here he could see
the ferry and anyone passing to it. It was a great thing then
for a person who wished to be funny to call "Hey!" then
when the other looked round, "That slewed you!" "Cocky"
picked this up, and would do it beautifully to passers by.
Some of them got quite angry with him. The moment he
got anyone to look, he would bob in his old head out of

sight. The present Andrew Petrie says he has often heard Dr Hobbs say "Cocky" "had" him many a time, by either a whistle or a call.

One day by some means or other, "Cocky" fell in the river, and would have been drowned but for his wings. He was discovered calling "Jack's poor 'Cocky'!" and at his rescue was terribly excited, repeatedly kissing and saying, "Kiss—poor 'Cocky'—Jack's poor 'Cocky.'"

"Cocky" hated to see people barefooted. The sight of bare feet irritated and made him savage, and he would chase the owner. He also hated the doctor with intense hatred, and "went" for him. At one time my father's brother Andrew was ill in bed, and "Cocky" took it upon himself to sit alongside the sufferer, of whom he was very fond because of being fed by him. He would sometimes even get under the blankets, and whenever anyone went near the bed "Cocky" got very cross, and swore at and chased the intruder. Then when Dr Hobbs came along he vented his rage on him. He would no sooner be put out at the door than he was round at the window, which if closed he prized open with his beak, and there he was in the room again and at the doctor. So he had to be shut up in a cage till the doctor left. During his imprisonment he continually called, "Baal budgery—Jack's pretty 'Cocky!'—kiss poor 'Cocky!'"

"Cocky" seemed to know when anyone was ill. All the time my grandmother was laid aside before her death, he spent part of each day at her bed head, watching to see that no one came near, and now and then saying, "Poor fellow!" When she died he was present, and afterwards seemed quite dull for a day or two—it was almost as though he knew something. He went on in the same way years afterwards when the old gentleman died. They could not keep him out of the room, and when the coffin was brought in, he flew fiercely at those who went to lift the body. The poor bird had to be shut up out of the way. He was found, however, afterwards, on the edge of the coffin, looking down into it, and was heard to remark, "Poor fellow!" before he got down and walked away.

Although "Cocky" was forty-five years old when he died, he might have lived even much longer but for an accident he had. One day he perched himself on a half-cask of pitch, and somehow fell into it. It was a hot day, and the pitch was soft, and in the struggle to get out the feathers on the bird's breast got stuck and pulled out. They never grew again. So in the summer he had to be put in a cage and covered with a net, as the mosquitoes tormented him very much, then in winter it was a piece of work to keep him warm. The unfortunate bird fell into the habit of continually picking his bare breast, which made it bleed. Though he lived this way for years, at last he looked so miserable that it was thought truer kindness to put an end to his misery, so a stranger was paid to do the deed. This, then, was the last of poor old "Cocky."

To the older members of the Petrie family yet living it is a sort of sacrilege in a way, to laugh at or doubt any of the tales told of "Cocky." But yet they realise that it must be difficult for people who did not know him to understand how a bird could come to such perfection. My father will talk of him, then say, "But people won't believe that—they will think it all bosh." And his nephew, Andrew Petrie, says, "Never have I seen such a bird since. I have come across many a clever bird on steamers and elsewhere, but never one has been able to touch 'old Cocky.' He was truly marvellous. He was a great bird to 'take off' people. Many a time, when I sang as a boy, 'Cocky' would mimic me, then laugh and jeer. Often the blacks brought in tiny young cockatoos for us, and 'Cocky' would go upstairs to where they were, and feed them just as a parent bird does, then he would make exactly the noise they did, and laugh over it. There was a little pet pig, too, he was very fond of; he often carried food to it. Once these two were found getting drunk together! A cask of beer was leaking, and piggy was sucking up the liquid, while 'Cocky' caught the drops with his beak. Poor 'Cocky'—I used to be amused at the way he would climb up father's chair, then pull his sleeve and say, 'Jack!' If no notice were taken, he kept at it till he got the answer, 'Well, what is it?' 'Give "Cocky" a piece of bread.' "

Governor Cairns, when he came to Queensland, had heard so much about "Cocky" that he asked to be taken to see him. Poor "Cocky" was then very disreputable looking with his bare breast, and young Andrew was rather ashamed to show him. However, he brought the bird forth and made him talk a little, saying to His Excellency that he was "Jack's poor, pretty cockatoo, me boy." But his best days were over then.

CHAPTER X

AFTER the settlement was thrown open in 1842, Mr Andrew
Petrie's office was of course abolished, and Colonel Barney
and others, recognising that gentleman's ability, endeavoured to persuade him to return to Sydney, and continue
under the Government there. However, taking an interest
in Queensland, he preferred remaining where he was to try
his luck in what he foresaw would become a flourishing
colony. Therefore, he started business on his own account,
contracting for Government and other buildings, and here
his engineering and architectural training stood him in
good stead.

In 1848, while on a trip to the Downs, Mr Petrie caught
sandy blight, which was prevalent at the time; his eyes
got very bad, and though everything was tried to cure them
nothing seemed to work. Being an active man, he became
impatient at the waste of time consequent, and though his
wife begged him to wait awhile and rest, he insisted upon
going to the doctors. Simple remedies and time, no doubt,
would have worked the cure—the doctors in those early
days were not as skilful as they are now. My father, then a
boy of about seventeen years, remembers leading his father
to the hospital, which stood where the Supreme Court is
now, and there they went in to the doctors to see what
could be suggested, my grandfather saying, "Whatever you
do, don't cut anything." "Oh, no!" was the reply, but the

boy saw one of them take up a small pair of tweezers, and catching hold of the skin or scum which had formed over the sight, he held it while the other cut through with another instrument. Then caustic was put in the eyes, and the doctors declared that though it would pain a little, everything would come right, and Mr Petrie would be able to see. All the way home, however, the poor gentleman was in great pain, and that whole night through he walked his room in agony, and one of his eyes burst. Father could never forget that awful time afterwards, and to this day he thinks his father's sight may have been saved under different treatment.

Some time after, when the pain had gone from his eyes, my grandfather was taken to Sydney to see if the doctors there could do any good; they told him that one eye was quite hopeless—the sight was gone altogether, but there might be some chance with the other. In the latter he always thought he could see a little glimmering, but nothing further ever came of it.

It is a pitiful thing when a strong active man loses his eyesight. When Mr Andrew Petrie realised that he would never see again, his agony and suffering must have been frightful, for he could not become reconciled just at first. It was a sad, sad time for his wife, who had to comfort him and witness his struggle, helpless to effect a cure. He was only fifty years of age at the time, and had always been used to leading others, so that the eternal darkness facing him must naturally have been almost more than he could bear. Could he have known, he was to live (a blind man) for twenty-four years—being nearly seventy-four at his death. However, in time, it was wonderful how he managed, people marvelled at his aptitude.

"He was always at work with his mind," my father says; "I have seen him when tenders were called for erecting a building or bridge, etc., getting my brother John to explain the plans and read the specifications to him; then he would take a slate and with the forefinger of the left hand on the top of the slate, he wrote across, moving down his finger each time he finished a line until both sides were filled. He never crossed the lines, and would state the quantity of timber required, the amount of nails, and everything else needful; or if it was something to be built of brick or stone, he was scarcely out in a brick, etc. Indeed he was very seldom out in his reckoning."

Father goes on to say that his father always rang the workmen's bell at eight o'clock, then again at one and two and six. "He gave all the men their orders for the day; he knew each by their step, and called them by their names. To one drayman he would say to take so many loads of loam to the scene of action, and to another so much sand, lime, or bricks; and then the carpenters, blacksmiths, and sawyers got their orders. Going to the carpenters' shop he would feel the work being done all over, and knew at once if it was correct—they could not deceive him. In the same way he went to the blacksmiths and stonemasons, and I have heard the men say they would sooner see anyone coming into the shop to examine their work than father. They said if anything was wrong or not finished off properly he would find it out by feeling, for he knew where a joint should be, or a nail driven, and was never imposed upon, but would have things done properly at all costs. He always carried a walking stick, and at times would use it when displeased, but in a moment or two his temper was gone, and asking for a piece of board, he drew on it with chalk the shape of the moulding or anything that they were making, explaining how it was to be done and all about it, telling them to be sure and work correctly."

Mr Andrew Petrie was led every day to all the buildings and other works under construction; he was never satisfied till he went the rounds to see what was required for the next day. His son John after a time had a pony broken in for him to save any walking, for he had a sore leg. Before leaving the old country his thigh was broken; while riding a young horse from his work in Edinburgh, the animal shied and ran him into a cab. The young fellow's leg got caught in the spokes of the wheel, and was broken, and also the shin and side of the leg above the ankle was very much skinned and bruised. The broken part (thigh) was set and recovered, but the bruise on the leg would heal up and then break out again, and years afterwards, when his sight was gone, it was very bad at times.

"One could almost see the bone of this leg," father remarks, "but my father would never lay up with it; though you could see that it pained him sometimes very much, he would never give in. He had a great spirit, as well as an active mind, and his memory was splendid. He often gave us (his sons) little things to do and remember, and though we perhaps forgot all about them, he never did, and would afterwards ask had we done such-and-such a thing? When I told him I'd forgotten, he would say the wretched tobacco smoke had taken all my brains away!

"A boy led the pony on which my father rode round to the different works in progress, and you would see him taken to a ladder leaning on a two-story building, up which he would climb just as though he could see. Getting to the top and on to a plank, he would poke about with his stick on the sides and all along the plank, then all over the building, feeling with it the different parts of the work; and all the men had to do was to tell him what portion of the building he was on, and he seemed to know where each piece of timber should be fixed, and where every joint should be. It was wonderful to see him going over a building—he had a grand head, much better than any of us, his sons. His leg never got well, though it healed up somewhat before his death. He was very independent with regard to this leg, and dressed, washed, and bandaged it himself night and morning, seldom allowing anyone else to touch it."

In the same year in which Mr Andrew Petrie lost his eyesight (1848) his son Walter was drowned in the one-time creek from which Creek Street now takes its name. In those early days Mr Petrie ran a couple of punts, one of which was employed in carrying stone (used for buildings) from the hard stone quarry at Kangaroo Point, also sand and shells from the bay for lime-making; the other journeyed to Ipswich with flour, etc., for Walter Gray's store, and brought back tallow and bales of wool. On one occasion the latter was loaded and ready to start, but lay

at anchor opposite Kangaroo Point, waiting for the tide,
which would not suit till eight o'clock; and Walter Petrie
(a boy of twenty-two) intended making the trip in charge
of the boat (as the head man was ill), and had gone down
the township before the hour of departure to visit some
friends and get some tobacco. When eight o'clock came
round, however, there was no sign of the young fellow.
and one of the crew (former prisoners) on board, wondering
what he should do, went ashore at last to ask instructions.
Mr Petrie started off at this to look for his son, saying to
"Tom" to come along, and they would find him. Father
remembers well leading his blind father to a number of
different places, and at last they came to a friend who said
the young fellow had been there some hours previously
leaving with the intention of going to the boat.

That night no trace was found. Next morning Mrs
Petrie, with one of those unexplained insights into the
unseen, said that her son would never be found alive, for
he was drowned down in the creek; and she pointed her
hand as she spoke. Her remark was, however, made light of,
the hearers little suspecting how true it was, the boy being
a splendid swimmer. In the meantime, a story had been
started, born quickly like a bubble, as empty tales are at
those times, that the young fellow had run away.

The boat waiting to start was sent off, and "Tom" took
his brother's place. Whether it was because of his mother's
remark he does not know, but all the time the boy had the
same strange feeling that Walter was drowned, and going
up the river everything he saw floating gave him a turn.
At that time R. J. Smith's boiling-down works had opened
on the Bremer, and after entering that river, the boat's party
came upon a dead body floating a little way ahead. "I
thought it was him," says my father, "and I nearly dropped;
but when we got up to it it was a dead sheep with the wool
all off floating in the water. Then when we got to Ipswich
I was told that my brother had been found drowned in the
creek at Brisbane on the same day as I had seen the sheep."

Strange, but true, is the following, which illustrates still
further the strong feeling which Mrs Petrie had with regard

to her son's disappearance. In those days a small scrub
grew on the north bank of the creek, just behind where the
Commercial Bank is now, at the corner of Queen and Creek
Streets. Before any trace was found of the missing lad two
men were sent by Mr Petrie to this scrub for vines for
binding up shingles (which were always bound so then, in
bundles, the vines being twisted into the shape of hoops),
and Mrs Petrie hearing the order (she had never been out
of the house all this time) called after them, "You will find
my poor boy down there in the creek," and then she persisted in watching the men, for from the doorway the creek
could be seen. Her daughter stayed by her side, seeking to
draw her away, but the poor lady was in such a dazed
condition, that she seemed unable to think of anything but
her lost son. She watched as the men reached the creek,
then noticing them pause and draw back—"They have
found him now," she said. The men returned and asked
for Mr Petrie. "Why do you ask that?" she said, "I know
what has brought you. You have found my boy." All the
time she was unable to weep, and they had to take her
away to another part of the house. Mr Petrie himself had
discredited the idea of drowning, saying Walter was too
good a swimmer, and now the shock seemed to come to him
twofold. Pitiful it must have been, to see the poor blind
gentleman going to his wife's side as he did when he heard
the truth, and the body having been in the water, he could
not even have the comfort of feeling his son for the last
time—the bonny boy who was a favourite with all.

It was found afterwards that the young fellow had gone
to cross the bridge (or rather apology for one) which
spanned the creek opposite to where Campbells' warehouse
is now, and the logs being wet (for it had been raining), he
slipped and fell. The bridge was originally composed of
three long logs put across the creek, then slabs on top, and
dirt covering all; but at this time the dirt had fallen off,
and also nearly all the slabs lay beneath in the mud. As
the young fellow crossed to take the short cut to the boat,
simply as such accidents happen, he slipped in the dark
(though he may have crossed safely a hundred other times),

and falling head foremost on to the slabs (it was low tide),
he was stunned and lay unconscious. Indeed from the
examination afterwards it was said his neck was broken.
However, he lay there all alone in the dark, while they
sought for him in other places, and the water which knew
him so well, and in which he had learnt to swim, rose
slowly and lapped against the stalwart young form as
though to rouse it. Then, gaining no answer, and growing
bolder, the tide lifted and carried the lad up the creek to
where he was afterwards found.

Of all Andrew Petrie's children, Walter was the only fair
one with blue eyes, and he was said to be exceedingly handsome. Grandfather himself was fair, but my grandmother,
who was a Cuthbertson, was dark, and a very big woman.
They thought it wisest not to let her see her dead son, but
she would not be comforted otherwise, and the sight proved
too much. "That is not my boy," she insisted, and then
the mother lost consciousness.

It was a very peculiar coincidence, but nine years afterwards, at the end of 1857, in the same creek, another
Walter, a little son of John Petrie, was drowned, the first
Walter being twenty-two years, while the second was a
baby of twenty-two months. The child's accident also
happened at a broken bridge, though it was further up the
stream—in fact, it stood in the present Queen Street, near
where Shaw's ironmongery shop used to be, now occupied
by Russell Wilkins. The boy wandered off from his nurse,
and, she being sent to seek him, came upon the little chap
drowned in the creek. The alarm was given, and the body
was recovered quickly, but life was extinct. In that part
the water was only five or six feet deep.

Walter Petrie, as I have said, was only twenty-two years
of age when he met his death, and he was an exceptionally
strong young fellow. His brother "Tom" says of him,
"I have seen Walter take two two-hundred pound bags of
flour, one under each arm, and walk by a plank on board
the punt with them. Also many a time in my presence has
he taken a blacksmith's sledge hammer by the handle,
and held it out at arm's length." He was a splendid swim-

mer, learning the art with his brothers not many yards from where he fell, and had the water been high when he attempted to cross the logs, all would have been well.

Before his death, Walter Petrie used, with his brother John, to row a great deal in the early boat races. The sport was very different then to what it is now. The boats were heavy and ungainly, and the races were consequently won by sheer strength. Boats after the style of a present-day ferry boat were used for one occupant, and both Walter and John won many of these single-handed races. Then together they pulled in the whaleboat events with equal success, their boat being called the *Lucy Long*. Whaleboats held five oarsmen always, and another man who stood up and used the steer oar, holding it in his left hand, while with his right he assisted the stroke. Such races would look odd in these days, of course, but my father says a whale-boat race was well worth watching. The men all kept good time, feathering their oars alike, and so on. The course taken was from the Colonial Stores (Queen's Wharf), down to the Garden Point, where a buoy was anchored, then round the buoy and back to the point on South Brisbane above the present Commercial shed, then called Womsley Point after a sawyer who used to cut timber there. Another buoy was anchored here, and the course continued round it, then back home to the wharf. When John Petrie was pulling in these races he acted as stroke.

By way of variety, what was called a dinghy race was indulged in. It was great fun. The dinghy only held one man, of course, and John Petrie was very often chosen because of his aptitude. He was allowed so many yards start, and the idea was that the bow man in the whaleboat follow-ing had to catch him within a certain length of time (about twelve minutes). When the whaleboat got close to the dinghy the later would spin round like a top, and the big boat lost ground in turning after it; and so they went on until, if the whaleboat got too near, the pursued man jumped overboard and dived beneath his opponent's boat. "Bow" followed after, diving also, but when John Petrie was in the race he was seldom caught before time was up, as he was a grand swimmer and diver in those days, and very few could catch him in the water. Of course, there was no bridge across the river then.

Being a good deal younger, my father, was out of these races, but he witnessed them, nevertheless. Another exciting event he remembers in this connection was a race between two lots of natives. Each crew occupied a whale-boat, and the prize was a bag of flour and some tea and sugar. It was a splendid race, and well pulled, the winners, who were Amity Point blacks, beating the others (Brisbane tribe) by a length. The successful crew were fine, big, strong men, and good pullers, having had more practice than their Brisbane brethren, as they mostly had belonged to the Pilot's boat's crew. That night in camp there was much feasting, the prize being greatly appreciated.

CHAPTER XI

Great Changes in One Lifetime—How Shells and Coral Were
Obtained for Lime-making—King Island or "Winnam"—Lime-burn-
ing on Petrie's Bight—Diving Work—Harris's Wharf—A Trick to
Obtain "Grog"—Reads Like Romance—Narrow Escape of a Diver.

As an instance of the great changes which have taken place
in Brisbane in even less than one lifetime, it is interesting
to follow my father's experiences of the way in which
shells and coral for lime-making were obtained when he
was a boy. As already mentioned, a punt did the carting
from the Bay, and as a protection to them from the blacks,
"Tom" was sent with the crew, for, being so well known
among the darkies, the lad was a safeguard to anyone in
his company.

The shells used were obtained from the sandy point on
the Humpybong side of the mouth of the Pine River, where
they were plentiful then in the required dry, dead state; and
this point the blacks called "Kulukan" (pelican), because
at low water the bank there was crowded with pelicans.
Four men besides my father manned the boat, and they
went with the ebb down the river, anchoring at the mouth
till the tide turned again and came up some two feet, thus
enabling the party to surmount the difficulty of sandbanks.
Planks were fixed along each side of the punt, so that the
men could walk from end to end, and each man had a long
light pole with which to shove the boat along. They kept
in as close to the shore as was possible, and so with the help
of the tide got slowly along past where Sandgate is now,
onwards to the mouth of the Pine, father steering.

Four baskets made by old Bribie, the basket-maker, also
two or three rakes to gather together the shells, formed
part of the punt's outward-going cargo, and two men would

fill the baskets whilst the remaining pair carried them into
the water, dipping them up and down to rid the shells of all
sand. The punt was left dry on the beach as the water
receded, but the tide coming up again would float her when
she was laden. Sometimes natives were present, and they
helped with the work, their payment being tobacco and
flour. Almost always the homeward start was made at
night, as it was calmer then, and as the tide rose the men
poled away along the shore till they got into the river, the
tide carrying them there. The outgoing journey was commenced at night, too, generally.

Coral for the lime-making was obtained in much the
same way from King Island or "Winnam" (breadfruit),
as the blacks called it then. The punt was taken through
the Boat Passage, and kept close to the land all the way,
being poled along the shore as before in the night hours,
then over to the island. These punts held big loads, but
later their place was taken by a cutter Mr Petrie had built
for the purpose, and for carrying oysters from the oyster
banks for the lime. Lime-burning was carried out at
Petrie's Bight, and there also the cutter was built.

When writing of the habits of the aborigines, I have mentioned how my father, as a youngster, used to spend hours
day after day in the water with the black boys, diving (as
amusement) for white bones and pebbles. This made him
very dexterous, and so whenever there was a difficult water
job in those days he was in great request. The first thing
he remembers tackling was a large steam boiler which had
sunk in a punt during the night at the wharf where Thomas
Brown and Sons' warehouse is now. The punt lay on a
slant, one end being some twenty feet beneath the water,
and the other six feet, and my father had to try and see
where a chain could be got under the boiler to rise it. He
went down the chain, which was fastened to another large
punt on the surface, and this is his description of the
experience :—

"The water was very clear, and I could see as well as if
out of it. Coming to the lower end, after going along holding to the boiler, I let go to come up, and although I could

see the light above, thought I would never reach the surface, and, when I did arrive there, was pretty well out of breath. After a rest, I started down again, taking with me a small line by which to pull the chain under the boiler. I succeeded in getting the line under, and came back along the chain, making sure that I would get up this time all right. The men in the punt above pulled on the line, and then I went down again, and pushed the chain under, and they pulled again, and were successful in getting it through. The chains were fastened to the punt above during low water, so, of course, as she rose with the tide, the punt beneath was lifted too."

Another water job was undertaken after a large flood which carried away what was then Harris's Wharf in the present Short Street, next to where Pettigrew's mill stood. The wharf was taken a good many yards into the river, and it had to be raised. So a punt was put alongside with shear legs attached to hoist the logs, and father went down time after time and put a chain round one by one, and he also prized them asunder with a crowbar. A man called Tom Collins, a bricklayer, assisted by sitting astride a log in the water, and he handed the crowbar and chain as they were wanted—thus saving a lot of swimming on the young fellow's part. The man himself could not swim, but, says my father, "he was a good worker, though very fond of his nip."

"At this time it was rather cold to be in the water every day, and the work went on for some months, so they used to give Collins a glass of grog each morning before work, and then again when he knocked off. One day, however, this little attention was neglected, and as it happened to be extra cold, Collins informed me that he would make them give him his usual. So, crawling along the log to the shore, he tumbled off into the mud, then picking himself up and putting his tongue out at me, scrambled up the bank and into the store. Up the stairs he went, shivering and shaking, the mud and water dripping from him, and when they saw him there—'For glory's sake go down out of this; see what a mess you are making!' But the dirty, wet object only shivered and shook the more, and making his teeth chatter, he gasped, 'I can't go till you give me a glass of grog.' To get him out of their sight was all they thought of, so he triumphantly returned to me wagging his tongue and carefully fondling a bottle of gin under his arm. 'I'll be all right now,' he said, 'and will be able to hold the bar fine and steady.'"

Collins, sitting there on the log in the water, dangling his legs, must have cut rather a comical figure, and people who came and paused to look on would call to ask what he was doing. "Oh, I am holding a lamp under the water, so that the chap below can see to prize some logs apart!" would be his reply. Poor Collins! his fondness for a nip ended his days; for, many years after he sat there on the log, he was found one day quite dead on the bank of the Bremer River, his head in the water; and it was supposed that, being drunk, he lay down to try and get a drink, failing miserably in the attempt to rise again.

If the water had been clear and warm during this work, things would have been much more pleasant, but father says it was full of floating dead fish (after the flood), and to come up and strike one with his face was anything but nice. At this time he wore a ring made on the Bendigo diggings from pure gold he had found there himself, and one day, while working in the water, a chain caught this ring and knocked it off his finger. He dived, but could not find it, being unable to see in the muddy water, so a day or two afterwards got a couple of blacks to come along and try. They were also unsuccessful, though trying a long time, so the ring was given up for lost. However, on the Saturday afternoon, when work was done, my father, feeling sad about the ring because of its associations, said to Collins, "I will try once more for that ring, the water is low, and I know just where it dropped." With that in he jumped, and the first thing he felt when touching bottom was the ring on a stone. The young fellow's delight can be imagined. This reads somewhat like romance, but 'tis all quite true, and one of my father's daughters now wears the ring, he having had it cut to fit her finger. To go further with its history, I may add the ring was lost a second time. For months it lay on a lawn, and when hope was given up, it caught one day on the prongs of a rake a gardener was weilding.

Yet another piece of water-work will I mention. This time the scene was the Bremer River, and the first Roman Catholic Church was being erected at Ipswich. A punt laden with shingles and freestone for the building sank one night when only about twenty yards from the bank—having sprung a leak. Father was sent up with two natives to do the diving, and he first of all went down to find out how the punt lay, so that he could fix the position of the floating punt above. Then poles were put down to enable the divers to judge where to come up safely, the water being muddy, and they took it in turns to get the shingles up (with the help of shear legs). This did not take much time, but the stones were more troublesome, they were heavy—some of them my father could not move when on land, but beneath the water could lift an end, and so get the sling fixed. "One day," he says, "one of the darkies in coming up got under the floating punt, and you could hear him bump! bump! on the bottom. We thought it was a case with him, but he bumped all along the bottom of the punt till he got to the end, then came up. We caught him, and pulled him out, and he was nearly done for, but soon recovered. However, nothing would induce the poor fellow to go into the water again, so the job had to be finished without him."

CHAPTER XII

Characters in the Way of "Old Hands"—Material for a Charles
Dickens—"Cranky Tom"—"Deaf Mickey"—Knocked Silly in Logan's
Time—"Wonder How Long I've Been Buried"—Scene in the Road
Which is Now Queen Street—A Peculiar Court Case—First Brisbane
Cemetery.

MR ANDREW PETRIE had several "old hands," who had
served their time and were free, working for him, in different ways. One, "Cranky Tom," was quite a character, and
would have served as material for a Charles Dickens. He
used to do odd jobs, such as cutting firewood, loading drays,
etc., and the poor man was not quite in possession of his
senses in all things. He would never sleep in a bed, but
would "camp" beside the kitchen fire, or, if a limekiln were
burning, there for a certainty would he be found, rolled up
in a blanket, surrounded by dogs. When asked, "Tom,
what were you sent out to this country for?" he invariably
answered, "For pulling the tail out of a donkey, and beating
him with the bloody end of it."

One day a dray loaded with timber entered the yard, and
the drayman called to "Cranky Tom" to chock the wheel.
The stupid man, instead of getting a stone or stick, ran and
used his foot as a stop, but it quickly came out again, and
its owner danced about crying, "Oh, my country, what I've
suffered for you!" The wheel had given him a nasty
squeeze, but did not go over the foot.

Another time, one Sunday morning, when Jimmy Porter,
one of the 'prentice boys, got up to light the fire, and put
the kettle on, he was surprised to find all the kitchen utensils gone, pots, pans, kettle, cups and saucers, plates, knives
—everything—even the long iron rake for the ashes! Before
the family could breakfast a messenger had to be sent
across for fresh things to the general store then kept at

Kangaroo Point by a man called Davidson. "Cranky Tom" was suspected of having hidden the utensils, but he could not be found anywhere about the place, so a policeman's help was sought. Father, boy-like, accompanied the "Bobby," and he remembered how they went past Petrie's Bight, and as far as to where the Union Hotel stands now in the Valley, and there they came upon "Cranky Tom," sitting on the roadside laughing, and looking quite pleased with himself, his trousers all soiled with pot-black. The policeman said to him, "Well, Tom, how did you get all that black stuff on your trousers?" "I don't know." "Why did you take all those things out from Mr Petrie's kitchen, Tom?" "I done it for a change." "Where did you put them?" "I don't know." After some more—"Well, I will have to take you to the lock-up," and the hand-cuffs were put on. Going along, the poor fellow began twisting the irons about on his wrists, then suddenly exploding with laughter he said, "Oh, my country, they don't fit!" The Police Magistrate could get nothing further from Tom than "I done it for a change," so in the end he was declared to be insane, and there being no asylum in Queensland, was sent to Sydney. The kitchen utensils' hiding place was discovered in this wise: The ferryman crossing the river came upon a couple of articles floating, so it was at once thought that the whole lot had been thrown into the water, and an old blackfellow, "Bentobin," a head Brisbane man, was got to pick up "Cranky Tom's" tracks, which he did very soon, and some of the things were recovered by him diving. They had been thrown in just where the steamer from Humpybong now lands her passengers.

Another man who worked at the same time as "Cranky Tom" was "Deaf Mickey," a small man, who was also half silly, like Tom. Whenever he got his wages on the Saturday he would go to the store, and buy a week's supply of rations, then repair to the old windmill (as it was then called, being in disuse), and camp there till his fare ran out. Every day between meals he walked some two hundred yards from the mill into the bush backwards and forwards speaking to himself, and "squaring up" to a gum tree, which stood at the end of his walk, putting up his fists as though to fight it, talking all the time. He made quite a plain beaten track to the tree, and "go when 'you liked," says my father, "you would see Mickey walking up and down and fighting with the gum tree."

Mickey had a quart pot and pint for his tea, and also a bag to hold his rations. When the latter were finished he would go back to his master and say, "Be the Lord I have been walking about this long time looking for work and can't get any; please will you give me a job?" Then he would work again for another week. He was not a bad worker, but could never be depended on for more than a fortnight at a time before he was off again to fight the trees. It was "as good as a play," my father says, to see Mickey and "Cranky Tom" crosscutting a log—many a time he watched the pair. The latter would call, "Mickey, pull the saw—you are not pulling it," and laugh at him. His companion would stare with not a smile on his face, then say, "I think you're cranky," and Tom would reply, "Oh, my country, I think you're gone in the head—you can't hear." Father would sometimes watch the two unseen, and sometimes from pure "devilment" would egg them on to one another.

Once Mickey was sent to Moreton Island to work at a building there. It was thought that being away from stores, he would keep on longer. However, at the end of a fortnight he took it into his head to walk to Sydney, and disappeared for that purpose. No one troubled over him, all feeling sure that he would turn up again when the rations he had taken were finished. It was said that in a week's time he came back, having evidently walked about the island, and going to his former employer, said, "Be the Lord I have been walking all over the country looking for work, and can't find any; please will you give me a job?" He was put to work, but the manager took the first opportunity of sending him back to Brisbane, fearing something might happen the man when he took it into his head to go off again. Poor Mickey's end was also the asylum. "I think," says my father, "that both 'Deaf Mickey' and 'Cranky Tom' had been knocked silly in Logan's time with the punishment they got in those days. They both seemed harmless poor chaps." There is much which is indeed pathetic in this world, mixed side by side with the comical.

Another of these "Old Hands" was a man called Daley, who was fond of "going on the spree." One night the Petrie boys found this man, very far gone, lying in the yard, so what did they do after some discussion but go to the carpenter's shop and get a coffin, and this they carried to Daley and put him in it. In the morning the young jokers got up early to see the fun, and going to where they had left the coffin, found the man sitting up in his gruesome bed talking to himself. They heard him say before they burst out laughing and roused his anger—"Oh, Henie, I wonder how long I've been buried." "Henie" was a favourite word with him, and the boys called him nothing else. Many a bit of fun they had with this man. At another time they nearly frightened him out of his senses by stuffing his old clothes with shavings, and hanging the figure to a beam in his doorway. Coming home half drunk, "Henie" thought, of course, some one had committed suicide, and he bolted. The boys had made the figure most natural looking, with boots and hat and all complete.

Strange things happened in those days. Old Bob, a sawyer (one-time convict or "old hand"), lived at Kangaroo Point with his wife—they had no children. The wife used to "go on the spree" now and then. One day she was the worse for drink near her home, and making a great noise, so two policemen secured her to take her to the lockup. A ferry punt was pulled across the river by a rope in those days, and the police got the woman into this punt to take her to the north side. When about to land, the man who held Mrs Bob let go to hold the rope, and the woman immediately jumped over into the water. However, she was dragged back again, and lay down in the punt a wet heap, saying, "If you want to take me to the lockup, you will have to carry me, for devil the foot will I walk." The instruments of the law were compelled to take her at her word, and carry her ashore, then, finding her still obstinate, one of them went up to Mr Andrew Petrie's for a wheelbarrow! Picture the scene! The old woman was lifted into the barrow, then one man held her while the other wheeled, and there she sat blessing the police and calling them all manner of nice names; and following up this procession, which wended its way up the road which is now Queen Street, came boys and men, laughing and having great fun—my father among them. Can one imagine such a procession now in Queen Street? The policemen took turns to hold and to wheel, and so they went on till they got about to where the Town Hall is now—to the lockup, and then the three, the victim and the victimised, disappeared from the eyes of the crowd, Mrs Bob being detained some twenty-four hours for being "jolly."

Some time after this event Bob made a bargain with Bill, another sawyer. He handed over his wife to Bill in exchange for a horse and dray. So Bill had some one to cook and wash for him, while Bob had a horse and dray. Prehistoric times, surely! All went well for some months, then Bill came to Bob, who was carting wood and water for sale, and told him he wanted his property back again. Bob refused flatly, saying it was a fair bargain, and the end of it was he was summoned to court. My father remembers the case well. The court was held in a room in the old Government building, a little above the old archway that stood then in Queen Street. After the evidence was taken on both sides, the Police Magistrate said that Bob had to give up the horse and dray, and take his wife back. "Yer worship," Bob said to him, "I don't think it's right that I should have to give up the horse and dray, as it was a fair, honest bargain." The magistrate replied, "Man, you are not allowed to sell your wife, and you must do as I say." So it was done. And, strange to relate, the pair seemed to live very happily together for years after this. A kinder and cleaner woman one could meet nowhere when away from drink, and no one who called at Bob's humpy was allowed to pass without a meal. She was a good cook and an excellent washerwoman, and could do up shirts with any one. However, the curse of drink on both sides told its tale, and when old age came the couple had to repair to Dunwich, where they died some years back, taking their story with them.

Before leaving these days, I should like to mention a peculiar habit the "old hands" sawyers, etc., had when boiling their tea in the bush. There were no "billies" then, but quart pots were used, and invariably two little sticks were placed crosswise across the pot. This was done to draw the tea, they said, and the men saw nothing strange in the habit.

*   *   *

Milton graveyard (where Grandfather Petrie was buried) seems a thing of the far past now, but there was a cemetery older still. It was on the opposite side of the street to where the coal shoots are now at Roma Street station. There the prisoners and soldiers were buried. Before that again North Quay had been used, but not sufficiently to be called a cemetery. When the place at Roma Street was disused four or five men were set to dig up the graves, and the bones were moved to Milton. One of these men (his companions related afterwards), a little stout Irishman, coming to a coffin lid, raised it, and exposure to the air caused an old gray cap on the skeleton to fall to pieces. Throwing up his hands, the frightened Pat exclaimed, as he recovered himself, "My good soul, keep your cap on; I'm a poor man like yourself." This Pat, it was said, used to take the coffin boards home to his cottage in the Valley, and with them he put up a fine skillion. The boards were cedar, and quite sound, although some had been underground for a number of years. And so the big place we now call the Valley had its beginning.

LIST OF PLACES, NAMES, PLANTS, AND TREES
With a Few Specimens of Aboriginal Vocabulary

(For the benefit of those unacquainted with the form of spelling used,
English spelling is given in brackets in cases of some difference.)

PLACE	NATIVE NAME	NATIVE MEANING
"Murrumba" (T. Petrie's Homestead)	Murrumba	Good.
North Pine Kippa Ring (near blacksmith's) ..	Nindur-ngineddo	Leech—sitting down.
Portion of North Pine River, near Railway Bridge ..	Mandin (Mundin)	Fishing net.
Small Island (T. Petrie's) below "Murrumba" ..	Gumpu (Goompu)	
Site of former lagoon in paddock near gatekeeper's, North Pine	Yimbun (Yimboon)	Bulrush
Creek below "Murrumba" ..	Yibri (Yebri)	Put or lay it down.
Spring below Inverpine, North Pine	Berrimpa	Present place.
Pocket in River above Inverpine	Bungil	Grass
Big hill near Petrie's Pocket	Mudlo-Mudlo	Stone—stone.
Cottage Hill, mouth of Pine (Petrie's Pocket)	Andurba (Undurba)	
Sandy Point, mouth of Pine, north side	Kulukan	Pelican.
Scott's Point, Humpybong ..	Banda-mardo (Bunda-mardo)	White clay—getting it.
Another Point, Humpybong	Warun (Waroon)	
Redcliffe (part of)	Kau-in-Kau-in	Blood—blood (red like blood)
Redcliffe (part of)	Yura	Spotted gum.
Caboolture	Kabul-tur	Place of carpet snakes.
Caboolture (Bribie dialect)	Wonga-dum (Wongadoom)	Same meaning.
Narangba	Narangba	Small place.
Stony Creek, Narangba ..	Bulba	
Neurum Neurum Creek ..	Nuram Nuram	Wart—wart.
Two small mountains above Delaney's	Bulburram Jerim	
Sideling Creek	Kurwongbah	
Mt Samson	Buran (Boorun)	Wind.
Samson Vale	Tukuwompa	
Rush Creek	Bargira	
Brown's Creek	Tugoui	
Samford	Kupidabin	From Kupi, an opossum.
D. L. Brown's land, Samford	Karandukamari	
Straight stretch of water, Enoggera near saleyards	Bu-yu-ba	Leg (shin).

PLACE	NATIVE NAME	NATIVE MEANING
Mt Coot-tha	Ku-ta	Dark native honey.
Moggill Creek	Maggil (Moggil)	Large water lizard.
Toowong (near Railway Station)	Baneraba (Bunaraba)	
Bend in River below Indooroopilly Bridge	Tu-wong	Black goat-sucker (bird).
Site of Railway Bridge, Indooroopilly	Mirbarpa	
Site of Regatta Hotel, Toowong	Jo-ai Jo-ai	
Indooroopilly should be ..	Yinduru-pilli	
Yeerongpilly	Yurong-pilli	Rain coming.
West End	Kurilpa(Kureelpa)	Place for rats.
Woolloongabba should be ..	Wulonkoppa	
Mt Cotton (near Mt Petrie)	Tungipin (Toongipin)	West wind.
Mt Gravatt	Kaggar-mabul (Kuggar-mabul)	Porcupine resort.
Norman Creek	Kulpurum (Koolpuroom)	
Hemmant (Wynnum dialect)	Kuwirmandadu (Koowermandado)	Place for curlew.
Mt Hant (Logan dialect) ..	Gir-an-guba	Opossum.
Queensport	Maurira	
Pinkenba	Dumben (Doomben)	
New Farm	Binkin-ba	Place of the land tortoise.
White's Hill	Bulimba (Boolimba)	
Bulimba	Tugulawa, known to Queensland Railway authorities as Toogoolawah	Shape of heart (indicating river bend at that spot).
Booroodabin	Burudabin	Place of oaks.
Wooloowin should be ..	Kuluwin	
Hill, Garrick's house, Bowen Bridge Road	Gilbumpa (Gilboompa)	
Exhibition and Hospital ..	Walan (Woolan)	Bream (fish).
Ashgrove	Kallindarbin	
Observatory	Wilwinpa	
Breakfast Creek	Ya-wa-gara	
Newstead	Karakaran-pinbilli	
Breakfast Creek, near Railway Bridge	Barrambin	
Boggy Creek, Eagle Farm .	Tumkaiburr	
Petrie's Bight	Tumamun	
Nundah	Nanda (Nunda)	Chain of water holes.

Place	Native Name	Native Meaning
Nundah (racecourse) ..	Gilwunpa	
Nundah (site of former German Mission)	Tumbul	
Sandgate	Warra	Open sheet of water, or river.
Nudgee	Murgin Murgin	
Tingalpa	Tingalpa	Place of fat.
Amity Point	Pul-an	
Swan Bay	Wiji-wiji-pi	
Canaipa	Kanaipa	
St Helena	No-gun	
Mud Island	Bangamba (Bungumba)	
Green Island	Mil-warpa	
Stradbroke Island, near South Passage	Dumba	
Cape Moreton	Gunemba	
Wynnum	Winnam	Breadfruit.
Dunwich	Gumpi	
Moreton Island	Mulganpin (Moolgunpin)	
Manly	Narlung	
Coochimudlo Island ..	Kutchi-Mudlo	Red stone.
Ipswich	Tulmur	
Goodna	Gudna	Dung.
Brisbane (Garden Point from the Bridge round to Creek Street, taking in the settlement)	Mi-an-jin (Me-an-jin)	
Gympie (Wide Bay dialect)	Gimpi	Stinging tree.
Pialba (Wide Bay dialect)	Pilba	Butcher bird.
Noosa Head	Wantima	Rising or climbing up.
Portion of Scrub at Maloolah	Jippi	Bird.

MAROOCHY DIALECT

Nambour	Nambour	Tea-tree bark.
Budderim Mountain ..	Badderam	Honey-suckle
Yandina	Yandinna	Small Place of water.
Toorbal Point ..	Ningi-Ningi	Oysters.

BRIBIE ISLAND PASSAGE

White Patch	Tarrang-giri	Leg.
Oyster Camp Reserve ..	Banya	
Long Island	Nu-lu	Small.
Glass Mountain Creek ..	Daki-bomon	Stone—standing up.
Coochin Creek	Kutchi	Red paint.

GLASS HOUSE MOUNTAINS

1. Birwa (Beerwah)—up in sky . .. .|Brisbane dialect.
2. Bir-barram (Beer-burrum)—parrot .. ..|Maroochy dialect.
3. Ngulun-Barung—neck crooked .. .. ..|Brisbane dialect.
   or
3. Kudna-war-un—neck crooked .. .. ..|Maroochy dialect.
4. Chibur-kakan (Chebur-kakan) — squirrel biting|Brisbane dialect.
5. Tunba-bula-bula—mountain two .. .. ..|Maroochy dialect.
6. Yinni—lawyer cane .. ..|Maroochy dialect.

TREE OR PLANT	NATIVE NAME	SCIENTIFIC NAME.
Bunya Pine	Bon-yi (Bon-yee)	*Araucaria Bidwillii.*
Pine similar to New Zealand Cowrie	Dundardum	*Agathis robusta.*
Cyprus Pine	Burogari	*Callitris columellaris.*
Moreton Bay Pine	Kumbartcho	*Araucaria Cunninghamii.*
Red Ironbark	Biggar	*Eucalyptus siderophloia.*
Ironbark (narrow leaved) ..	Tandur	*Eucalyptus crebra.*
Blue Gum	Mungar	*Eucalytpus tereticornis.*
Spotted Gum	Yura	*Eucalyptus Maculata.*
Stringybarks	Diura	*Eucalyptus Acmenioides.*
Bloodwood	Buna	*Eucalyptus corymbosa.*
Swamp Mahogany ..	Bulurtchu	*Tristania suaveolens.*
Fig Box	Tabbilpalla	*Tristania conferta.*
Cedar (red)	Mam-in	*Cedrela toona.*
Moreton Bay Chestnut ..	Mai	*Castanospermum Australe.*
Moreton Bay Ash	Kuran	*Eucalyptus tesselaris.*
She-Oak	Bill-ai	*Casuarina glauca.*
Forest Oak	Buruda	*C—— torulosa.*
Moreton Bay Fig	Ngoa-nga	*Ficus macrophylla.*
Small Fig	Nyuta	*Ficus platypoda, var. Petiolaris.*
Apple Tree	Bu-pu	*Angophora intermedia.*
Rosewood	Bunuro	*Acacia glaucescens.*
Dogwood	Denna	*Jacksonia scoparia.*
Corkwood or "Bat Tree" .	Kuntan	*Erythrine sp.*
Mangrove	Tintchi	*Bruguiera Rheedii.*
Large Honeysuckle	Bambara (Bumbara)	*Banksia latifolia.*
Small Honeysuckle	Minti	*Banksia amula.*
"Geebung"	Dulandella	*Persoonia.*
Breadfruit	Winnam	*Pandanus pedunculatus.*
Stinging-tree	Braggain	*Laportea sp.*
Grass-tree	Dakkabin	*Xanthorrhœa.*
Cabbage-tree Palm	Binkar	*Livistona Australis.*
Common Palm	Pikki	*Archontophœnix Cunninghamii.*
Wattle (black)	Kagarkal	*Acacia Cunninghamii.*
Scrub Vine	Nannam	*Malaisia tortuosa.*
Lawyer Cane	Taigam	*Calamus sp.*
Lawyer Cane (Bribie dialect)	Yinni	
Vine with yellow berries ..	Barra	*Cudrania Javanensis.*
Scrub vine used for climbing	Yurol (Yeroll Creek on Stradbroke evidently same name)	*Flagellaria indica.*
Coarse grass used for dilly making	Dilli	*Xerotes longifolia.*

Tree or Plant	Native Name	Scientific Name.
Swamp plant used for fish poison	Tang-gul	*Polygonum hydropiper.*
Cunjevoi	Bundal	*Alocasia macrorrhiza.*
Large bean in scrub	Yugam	*Canavalia obtusifolia.*
Swamp Fern	Bangwal (Bungwal)	*Blechnum serrulatum.*
Bullrush	Yimbun	*Typha angustifolia.*
Wild Yam	Tarm	*Dioscorea transversa.*
Ground Orchids	Chingum	{ *Caladenia carnea.* { *Caladenia alba.*
White green-spotted berry..	Midyim	*Myrtus tenuifolia.*

White's Name	Native Name	Meaning.
"Sara Moreton"	Diniba	
"Catchpenny"	Gwai-a	
Other black women	{ Ta-ruchi { Bingi-Bingi { Munan { Turpin	
"Bob Clift"	Gangginda	
"Millbong Jemmy"	Yil-bung	One eye
"Dundalli"	Dundalli	Wonga pigeon.
"King Sandy"	Ker-walli	Spilt.
"Sam" at Dunwich ..	Yeridmou	Mouth of native bees' nest.
"Kobban Tom" . ..	Mindi-Mindi or Kuttigri	
"Daiarli"	Dai-arli	Taylor fish.
"Jimmy"	Wananggr	Left it.
Other men	{ Kuta { Ommuli { Tunbur { Dulu-marni	Native honey. The breast. Maggot. Creek caught.

Turrwan	.. Great man.	Baggur	.. Wood.
Kippa	.. Young man.	Bunggil	.. Grass.
Mallara	.. Grown man.	Banyo	.. Ridge.
Jundal	.. Woman.	Bippo	.. Mountain.
Puddang	.. Mother.	Mundo	.. Ridge (Wide Bay dialect).
Nam-ul	.. Baby.		
Narring	.. Son.	Tunba	.. Mountain (Wide Bay dialect).
Bing	.. Father.		
Yinnell	.. Creek or gully.	Yaggaar	.. No.
Warril	.. Creek (Ipswich dialect).	Ya-wai	.. Yes.
		Bi-gi	.. Sun.

Killen	..	Moon.	Kirri	..	North.
Mirrigin	..	Stars.	Yun-gur	..	South.
Kurumba	..	Big.	Wian	..	West.
Berpi	..	Little.	Burgin	..	East.
Kal-lang-ur	.	Good (Maroochy dialect).	An-an	..	Grey eagle hawk.
			Tu-wai	..	Black eagle hawk.
Kanggungun (Kang-goon-goon)	..	Laughing jackass.	Budar	..	Eagle hawk (Wide Bay dialect).
Tunggi	..	Native companion.	Tallabilla	..	Outlaw.
Kundurkan	..	Ditto (Stradbroke Island dialect).	Nallan-kalli	.	Liar.
			Mirbong	..	Net for kangaroo.
Wargan	..	Crow.	Muntong	..	Net for paddy-melons.
Konggong	..	Egg.			
To-wan	..	Fish.	Bula	..	Two.
Kinnen	..	Mosquito.	Bula-Bula	..	Four.
Dibbin	..	Common house fly.	Darlobolpal	.	Camping place.
Tchidna	..	Track of foot.	Tabbil-yanmunna.		Running water.
Muru	..	Nose.			
Murra	..	Hand.	Inta tabbil balka-i	..	You water, fetch it.
Mil	..	Eye.			
Pidna	..	Ear.	Mianjin ngatta yarrana	..	Brisbane, I'm going.
Tambur	..	Mouth.			
Tiar (tear)	..	Teeth.			
Mag-ul	..	Head.	Inta wanna yarrana	..	You, where going?
Wadli	..	Bad.			
Mugara	..	Thunder.	Yin wanna yan man	..	Same meaning (Wide Bay dialect).
Kan-nang-ur		Thirsty.			
Millen	..	Plenty.			
Tu-gun	..	Sea waves.